LAW AND DEVELOPMENT:

Gen   on

First published in Great Britain 2003 by
Cavendish Publishing Limited, The Glass House,
Wharton Street, London WC1X 9PX, United Kingdom
Telephone: + 44 (0)20 7278 8000   Facsimile: + 44 (0)20 7278 8080
Email: info@cavendishpublishing.com
Website: www.cavendishpublishing.com

Published in the United States by Cavendish Publishing
c/o International Specialized Book Services,
5824 NE Hassalo Street, Portland,
Oregon 97213-3644, USA

Published in Australia by Cavendish Publishing (Australia) Pty Ltd
3/303 Barrenjoey Road, Newport, NSW 2106, Australia

British Library Cataloguing in Publication Data
Data available

Library of Congress Cataloguing in Publication Data
Data available

ISBN 1-85941-798-1

1 3 5 7 9 10 8 6 4 2

Printed and bound in Great Britain

PREFACE

In June 2001, Peter Slinn convened the third in a series of conferences on law and development to be held at Cumberland Lodge, Windsor Great Park, UK. Forty-five participants, who embraced a broad spectrum of opinion from the developing and developed world, attended. As this was the final time that Peter would act as Convenor, it was the wish of all present to mark the occasion by dedicating this book to him.

It has been our pleasant task to oversee its editing. The book itself contains revised papers from many of the participants to the 2001 conference together with contributions from other friends and colleagues who were unable to attend but who did not wish to miss the opportunity of celebrating Peter's contribution to the field of law and development. Indeed, one of our problems as editors has been to limit the number of contributions so as to keep the book to a manageable length. Jim Paul, one of only a handful of people who have been with Peter at all the conferences, has also kindly provided us with a fascinating foreword, highlighting the background to and themes of the Cumberland Lodge conferences, and placing Peter's own contribution in perspective.

Selected papers from the two earlier Cumberland Lodge conferences were published in the 1984 and 1992/3 issues of *Third World Legal Studies*. As the Guest Editor for these issues, Peter provided a lucid, compelling and (to use one of his favourite words) masterly overview of the range of issues discussed at the conferences. With some trepidation we have sought to follow in his footsteps by providing our own Introduction to the papers along the theme that so clearly emanated from the 2001 conference discussion: 'Complexity'.

Participants left Cumberland Lodge in June 2001 intent on ensuring that the Law and Development Conference series lives on. As Peter Slinn himself has put it: 'Clearly there is some real point to the decennial periodisation in view of the profound changes in the structure of international society...'. As the contributions to this book demonstrate, a regular review of this complex area is certainly needed, albeit more regularly than the period envisaged by Peter.

Looking back at the names of the participants to the first two Cumberland Lodge conferences, we were struck by the fact that they represented a veritable *Who's Who* of legal scholars and practitioners in the field of law and development. Sadly some, perhaps most notably Tony Allott, are no longer with us. However, this book demonstrates that there is now a new generation of scholars in the field of law and development, thus ensuring that there is no diminution in the interest and importance of this fascinating topic.

As the majority of participants at the three conferences were academic lawyers, it is not surprising that an abiding sub-theme has been the role of the legal academic community in the area of law and development. At the First Conference, for instance, Paul Brietzke argued that the role encompassed 'devising badly needed theories of the right to development' and this role was again touched on at the Second Conference. The involvement of the Commonwealth Legal Education Association (CLEA) in the Third Conference emphasised the importance of ensuring that law students and legal practitioners of the 21st century are provided with the necessary tools with which to tackle law and development issues.

It was therefore significant that the Third Conference included a session on 'Teaching Law and Development' and explored ways of developing a 'model curriculum' and materials for use in Commonwealth law schools. The differing views expressed as to what such a curriculum might contain merely went to emphasise the uncertain scope of the area and its 'complexity'. Yet the need to encourage law teachers to incorporate law and development

Law and development: Facing complexity in the 21st century

issues into their teaching was recognised and this remains an important goal for 21st century law schools. Hopefully this book will serve as a useful tool for assisting them to do so.

To fulfil this aim, we are anxious to ensure that the book reaches as wide an audience as possible in both developing and developed countries. We are therefore extremely grateful to Cavendish Publishing Ltd for their assistance in keeping production costs to a minimum and to the CLEA for undertaking to ensure the book's wide distribution.

As for Peter Slinn's contribution to the conference series, we are happy to echo the words of Sam Gyandoh in his Introduction to the 1992 issue of *Third World Legal Studies*:

> I believe I speak for all of us who were present at Cumberland Lodge when I convey our collective debt of profound gratitude to Peter Slinn for being such a splendid host and accomplished Conference organiser. We cannot ever forget his seemingly infinite capacity for combining high intellectual acuity and rigorous academic discipline with generous and easy-going hospitality, dispensed in an inviting and utterly charming environment of gracious living, untouched by any affectation or bombast.

John Hatchard and Amanda Perry-Kessaris

London

January 2003

CONTENTS

FOREWORD: LAW AND DEVELOPMENT AND PETER SLINN

James C N Paul[*]

It is fitting that this volume is dedicated to Peter Slinn. He has contributed in many ways to our understandings of the various roles of different realms of law in the diverse tasks of development, not only as a scholar of consequence,[1] but as a convenor of productive international seminars and conferences and as an editor of important volumes—including the Law Reports of the Commonwealth—which all reflect the evolution of this amorphous subject.[2]

The three Cumberland Lodge conferences, which Peter initiated in 1983, 1990 and 2001 provide a rich source of materials reflecting the intellectual history of law and development.[3] I participated in all of these conferences, and I would like to review their history here, and link themes of it to Peter's recent scholarly work, which focuses on the crucial task of building on a comprehensive International Law of Development. I hope this effort will demonstrate the debt which many of us owe to him.

The first section of what follows examines the origins and early, confusing history of law and development, notably in the USA. This subject may be unfamiliar, although hopefully revealing, to some readers of this volume. In any event it provides an historical context for what follows, and it reminds us that one's view of the tasks and functions ascribed to law in development depends very much on one's concept of development. The point seems obvious, yet its implications are often overlooked by those who write academic essays in very general terms about law and development.

The second section reviews the Cumberland Lodge conferences and Peter's efforts to use these events to promote interest in the roles of international law and the tasks of harmonising domestic regimes of law with international norms.

The 1990s witnessed what may become a sea change, in the discourse and policies of international development agencies (IDAs) such as the World Bank and UNDP. They also saw a new more sophisticated academic interest in law in development, coupled with—and affected by—the growth of many kinds of legal activism concerned with various development issues. The conclusion to this forward links this recent history to Peter's views on development and developing international law.

LAW AND DEVELOPMENT: 1960-1980

Law and development, as a subject of scholarly interest, probably first grew out of the experiences of US academics in Africa during the early 1960s. I was involved in some of this activity, first as one of a small group of US law professors who collaborated to create the SAILER project, generously funded by the Ford Foundation; and then as a consultant for the Peace Corps, charged with negotiating arrangements for the placement of highly qualified law trained volunteers in all sorts of legal or quasi-legal positions in these African countries where

---

[*] William J Brennan Professor of Law (Emeritus), Rutgers, The State University of New Jersey.
[1] See attached Bibliography for some of Peter's contributions to the 'Law and Development' literature.
[2] Havens, 1972; Seers, 1969.
[3] The published papers of Cumberland Lodge 1, 1983, and Cumberland Lodge 2, 1990, are published in the 1984, 1992 and 1993 volumes of *Third World Legal Studies* (TWLS 1984, 1992, 1993).

legal talent was a scarce commodity; and then, from 1962, as founding Dean of Ethiopia's first University Law School.[4]

All told, probably more than 150 American lawyers participated in various assignments—many in law schools—during the decade 1961-1971.[5] While various motivations have since been imputed to us—some rather sinister[6]—I think that most of us were infused with the long-gone idealistic zeitgeist of the Kennedy era and we believed that the experience of working in a legal field in Africa would be intellectually rewarding and that there was much challenging law work to be done in many countries. Further, many of us also believed—as did our supporters in the Ford Foundation[7]—that a long-term project of building some kind of workable, context-related, 'rule of law' was one important condition for the realisation of some kind of essentially 'people-centred' development.[8]

Despite this limited, pragmatic outlook, some scholars in the US began to dilate on broader, more ambitious themes. In the early 1960s, perhaps under the influence of the gospel of 'legal realism',[9] some prominent American law professors (notably Wolfgang Friedman) wrote influential pieces on the potential—rather grandiose—'role of the lawyer in developing countries'.[10] These exhortations no doubt helped to motivate efforts funded by the International Legal Center in New York (ILC, which took over SAILER) to organise regional conferences on the reform of legal education in Africa, Asia, and Latin America—on strategies to make it, and its 'outputs', more 'development-oriented'.[11] Much of this 'first-generation' (role of law, lawyer and law school) literature drew, implicitly or explicitly, from 'modernisation theory' then in vogue. The modernisation—that is, westernisation—of law was seen to be an essential part of a broader process of induced change to establish—or expand—'modern' economies, institutions of governance and social systems in 'traditional' countries.[12]

In the 1970s, Robert Seidman published a provocative paper, which offered a model to show how properly crafted laws could be used to help guide and govern development in poor countries.[13] Other US legal academics who were steeped in social science training, notably David Trubek and Marc Galanter, saw the study of law and development—'LD' as it came to be called—as a challenge to initiate ambitious interdisciplinary research on the relationships between law and society in Third World countries.[14] The US Agency for International Development (AID) was somehow persuaded to award a massive grant to the Yale Law School to promote understanding of the domain of LD. While little empirical research was actually launched, the AID grant did bring visiting scholars from many parts of the world to

---

[4] See Paul, 1987; and Johnstone, 1972. See 'Twenty Years After', 1986, containing reflections on this history including a paper by Frank Sutton, of the Ford Foundation, on the Foundation's reasons for supporting legal education in Africa; and the reflections of many 'Sailerites' who went to Africa during the period 1962-1975 on why they went, what they did, and the impact of their experiences on their professional careers.

[5] Paul, 1987.

[6] See Friedman, 1969; cf Gardner, 1980.

[7] 'Twenty Years After', 1986.

[8] Ibid. See also Harvey, 1966, for a scholarly, nuanced view on law and 'modernisation'.

[9] Dias and Paul, 1981.

[10] Friedman, 1963. See also Franck, 1972; Gower, 1968; and ICJ, 1961.

[11] Dias and Paul, 1981.

[12] Galanter, 1966. Cf Harvey, 1966.

[13] Seidman, 1972.

[14] See, for example, Trubek, 1972.

New Haven, and the programme produced some interesting working papers.[15] But perhaps the ultimate outcome of the Yale programme was disillusion with LD, and incubation of the erstwhile Critical Legal Studies movement in American legal education.[16]

In 1973 the ILC tried to salvage LD by convening an ostensibly 'international' committee—dominated by some rather opinionated US academics with limited overseas experience—which was asked to map the domain of study, charting a course for future LD research. A curious, rather unedifying report was finally produced.[17] There seemed to be no consensus on what was to be studied,[18] but whatever that 'it' was, the majority of the Committee was adamant that the research should be 'basic' not 'applied'; and it should be informed by (unspecified) social science theories and methods. Concerns that law facilities, particularly those in the Third World, were neither interested nor equipped to engage in such ambitious, problematic projects were brushed aside. Even more puzzling was the scant attention paid to the meaning of development. The Committee assumed a rather general, quite flabby definition of the term and ignored important current controversies. 'Dependency' theory was then in some vogue, for when the report was in process in 1974 there was the much publicised movement in the UN to create a new body of international law establishing a New International Economic Order (NIEO). At the same time the World Bank (under Robert McNamara) was increasing its staff and the volume of its lending five-fold, to organise a massive campaign to alleviate poverty by 'meeting basic needs', and the Bank's portfolio had expanded to include urban housing, education, health, and population projects—activities which might well have invited LD interest, notably because they were unregulated by, and thus virtually unaccountable to, any law.[19] Yet the Committee paid little attention to the actual business of development. Indeed, the ILC report seemed to sink without a trace. So, a few years thereafter, did the ILC and much of the interest in North America in LD, the role of the lawyer and of legal education.[20]

The propagation of modernisation theories, of Promethean roles for lawyers and of LD research grounded in Weberian and other grand sociological theories, proved to be attractive targets for both sceptics and radical critics—who emerged in force during the latter 1970s. Sceptics could point to various case studies of legal transplants which showed how hard it was to import western laws, 'legal culture' and legal institutions into 'non-western' settings.[21] Research on the vast varieties of legal professions found in different African, Asian, and Latin American countries showed how problematic was the role of the lawyer in development if one examined carefully what most lawyers—both private and public—actually did to earn their living, and how removed these roles were from the business of development. Indeed these studies also cast some doubt on whether it was useful to hypothesise the existence of *a* legal profession, in many countries.[22] Studies of 'legal pluralism' in African countries portrayed the enduring presence and power of various forms of non-state law, and the force of tradition—for example in determining systems of land tenure, gender roles, social structures and power

---

15 Paul, 1987. Some of the Yale papers and reports of meetings are published in the ILC Newsletters (1968-1975).

16 Trubek and Galanter, 1974.

17 ILC, 1974.

18 See, for example, Havens, 1972, for an interesting analysis of the research agendas of different paradigms or approaches to development—from 'Marxist' to pure 'growth-centred' objectives.

19 Ayers, 1984.

20 Merryman, 1977.

21 Geraghty; 1969; Singer, 1970; Daniels and Woodman, 1976; and Bryde, 1976 and 1978.

22 Dias *et al*, 1981.

in rural communities. They also showed the hostility of most poor people to 'state law', which was seen as a body of alien rules and institutions used by the government to tax, exploit and repress poor people.[23]

Socialist critics—and there were many of these in the 1970s—emphasised the use of 'the state' and of 'ideology' to transform economies and societies. In this perspective law, especially law drawn from capitalist societies, was often suspect; at best, the role of law was simply to be the handmaiden of socialist policy as determined by those leading the great transition. These critics saw 'modernisation' as a project, thinly disguised as pseudo-social theory, to transplant capitalist systems.[24] Doctrinaire Marxists dismissed law as 'superstructure'; the real challenge of development was 'revolutionary action' to change 'relations of production' and the social foundations of society.[25] Nor was this an easy task even in avowedly socialist states. For example, in the late 1970s Issa Shivji (of the University of Dar es Salaam Law Faculty) wrote some provocative pieces portraying his view of the 'class struggle', then unfolding in Tanzania, between the new, socialist 'bureaucratic bourgeoisie' who now controlled the economy and the rural and urban poor whose condition seemed to remain as before.[26] The notion of a bureaucratic bourgeoisie—and the problematic character of governance in Africa—also became a more explicit focus of concern of other, non-Marxist, LD scholars.[27] Gunnar Myrdal's celebrated depiction of the 'soft state', whether socialist or otherwise, in Asia and Africa—the state incapable or unwilling to confront poverty and inequality—suggested that LD should be grounded in a new political economy context.[28]

Many radical critics of LD also turned to dependency theories, and some became active advocates for the recently proposed NIEO.[29] But the firm opposition of most 'First World' governments coupled with the increasingly despotic character of many Third World states— notably the military regimes in Africa—cast some doubt on both the validity and viability of the NIEO as a vehicle to promote meaningful development.

In the late 1970s, some of the remaining LD scholars became interested in a growing movement to promote an alternative to state-managed, growth-oriented development.[30] 'Alternative development' emphasised endogenous, self-reliant participatory, collective efforts by the rural and urban poor to promote their development, as they conceived it. These efforts were used to promote community civic education, create local self-managed group economic enterprises of various sorts, and to resist state managed development projects which threatened community harms—such as displacement, discrimination, and/or degradation of habitats.[31] Further, at a time of increasing legal activism on behalf of the poor and other 'public interest' causes in some First World countries, there emerged a complementary interest in strategies to develop 'legal resources' for the poor in Third World countries—that is, to develop group capabilities to use law both as a means to 'de-legitimise' governmental measures deemed harmful to communities, and to legitimise local efforts to demand 'pro-

---

[23] Woodman, 1989.

[24] Ghai, 1976.

[25] Shivji, 1975 and 1986; and Gutto, 1984.

[26] Shivji, 1975.

[27] Seidman, 1992.

[28] Ibid. Myrdal, 1968 and 1977.

[29] Leys, 1975.

[30] Spurred by the Dag Hammarskjöld Foundation Report, 1975, and then the funding of the International Foundation for Development Alternatives in Geneva. See ICLD, 1979. World Council of Churches, 1976.

[31] See ICLD, 1979; and 'TWLS 1982'.

poor', participatory policies and programmes.[32] But when Peter Slinn convened Cumberland Lodge 1 in 1983, many LD scholars still tended to dismiss 'alternative development' as a strategy of marginal importance.[33]

Indeed, by 1980, 'law and development' seemed in some disarray, if not disrepute. Different streams of LD writing had been animated by quite different perceptions and ideologies of both development and the relevance and roles of different realms of law—non-state, state, and international—in addressing different development tasks. Much of the existing literature was quite theoretical or ideological, and cast in very general terms. There was a dearth of case studies showing how land figured, or failed to figure, in the structuring of particular development projects. While much lip service had been given to the importance of interdisciplinary research, little had been generated.[34] In the mid-1970s the ILC had funded some regional workshops concerned with devising socio-legal research projects related to development. But these efforts demonstrated both the remarkable resistance of lawyers to the pursuit of expensive, time-consuming social science methods, and (in the view of some of us) they also demonstrated the disarray of the social sciences when it came to understanding the problems of development.[35] An attempt to mount socio-legal research to aid understanding of the role, or the limited impact, of law in the structuring and management of public corporations in Africa—a rather important subject then—seemed to get bogged down in confusion about the appropriate research design.[36]

Other criticisms of LD could be offered on the eve of Cumberland Lodge 1. One point seemed increasingly important though seriously neglected: if one eschewed ideological notions of 'development' and simply looked at the actual activities carried on by IDAs—for example, the World Bank—and governments in the name of 'development', there was, in fact, a remarkable *absence of law* governing these measures: That is, an absence of legal standards stipulating the policy assumptions and specific objectives of different kinds of project (for example, standards to mediate conflicts between growth versus poverty-reduction outcomes); an absence of law governing the processes of decision-making at all stages of a 'project cycle', from its design through its management and evaluation (for example, law enabling participation); an absence of law providing for the imposition of accountability for failed projects and for corruption and malfeasance; and an absence of law providing remedies for the serious harms which many projects seemed to inflict on people and habitats.[37]

THE CUMBERLAND LODGE CONFERENCES

Each of the Cumberland Lodge conferences, while co-sponsored by several other organisations, was carefully planned by Peter. Each brought together an appropriate diversity of participants (notably from Africa, Asia, the UK, and North America), in a beautiful bucolic setting where there was also a memorable mix of hospitality with a very full, substantive agenda.

---

[32] IFDA, 1979; ICLD, 1979; International Commission of Jurists, 1982; and 'TWLS 1985'.
[33] Brietzke, 1984.
[34] ICLD, 1978.
[35] ILC, 1968-75.
[36] Ghai, 1977.
[37] 'TWLS 1982' contains case studies illustrating this point. Paul, 1988.

The papers of Cumberland Lodge 1 (1983) and 2 (1990) were carefully edited by Peter and published as annual volumes of *Third World Legal Studies* (TWLS), which is a valuable source of many other symposiums on LD subjects even though this publication has never achieved a wide circulation.[38] Several concerns were common to the Cumberland Lodge conferences: (1) the legal implications of changing concepts of development; (2) the legal implications of 'development' and 'globalisation' unregulated by law; and (3) the need to develop international law in response to the above.

Cumberland Lodge 1 was convened 'to review the critical relationship between human rights and development... having regard to... the notion of a "human right development."'[39]

International Human Rights Law (IHRL) was becoming a presence in the early 1980s following the coming into force of the International Covenants in 1976 and the UN Women's Convention (CEDAW) in 1979. These instruments were slowly gaining more attention by scholars, activists, and the international community. Further, in 1983 the General Assembly was preparing a draft 'Declaration' designed to create a *human* 'Right to Development' (the UN DRD) which was intended to become part of the corpus of international law.

Moreover the relevance of IHRL should have been obvious: promotion of 'participation', equality, 'workplace', education, health, 'subsistence', and 'remediation' rights could certainly be seen as interdependent ends and means of development. Further, the Universal Declaration, both International Covenants, CEDAW, and the UN DRD all speak to the processes of the development. The rights established by these instruments are to be realised not simply through conventional 'rule of law' institutions such as courts, but in and through development measures—for example, by incorporating rights of participation into all phases of programmes and projects.

Despite the obvious challenges posed by IHRL, Cumberland Lodge 1 suffered from several constraints, which limited its output. The conference reflected the curious paradox that (as of 1983) legal scholars interested in development—the very people who should be steeped in IHRL—had long ignored the relevance of IHRL and displayed a myopia which can only be explained when we appreciate the anachronistic, intellectual baggage which had burdened LD in the 1970s. A second constraint on our deliberations was the confusion created by the 'abysmally drafted' (Peter's words)[40] UN DRD. On the one hand the Declaration was a *development policy statement*, setting out an aspirational agenda of steps to be undertaken by the international community, and one of these was the establishment of an NIEO. On the other hand, the DRD plainly was intended to be read as a *human rights instrument*, in effect calling for the integration of *all* universal human rights into development policy-making and implementation at all levels.[41] Regrettably many participants were lured into a discussion of the DRD as a fresh attempt to incorporate the NIEO into international law—even though that subject seemed (in the 1980s) to have little relevance to *human* rights, and no prospect of rebirth.

A few Cumberland Lodge 1 contributions, however, are of more than historical interest. In a stimulating paper Tony Allott—whose death in 2002 we continue to lament—deplored the conventional notion of development as a purely economic concept, which celebrated 'growth' as the sole objective and used 'growth-oriented statistics' as development benchmarks. 'I see development as the enhancement of life and of life's possibilities for the ordinary individual,'

---

[38] See 'TWLS' volumes cited in bibliography.
[39] 'TWLS 1984,' Slinn's 'Introduction'.
[40] 'TWLS 1992,' Slinn's 'Introduction'.
[41] United Nations Commission on Human Rights, 1979; Paul, 1992; *cf* Kibwana, 1993.

Tony wrote, going on to argue that 'economic'—that is, growth-centred—development should be seen as a means to promote this more holistic view of development.[42]

Allott's paper carried important human rights implications, and it was nicely complemented by Alain Pellet's elegant elaboration of the view that the UN DRD not only called for the promotion of universal rights as ends and means of development, but also it established the right of all people, acting individually or collectively, to pursue and demand a kind of human development that facilitated 'self-realisation'.[43]

While noting that most participants were essentially 'pessimistic about the future role of law and lawyers' in development, Peter rendered an optimistic conclusion, suggesting that, despite the confusion and contention provoked by the DRD and NIEO, international law was now firmly established on the UN's agenda, and it might yet become a more 'positive' force in establishing a consensual framework of principles to guide 'international co-operation'.[44] That observation was vindicated when he convened a second conference seven years later.

Cumberland Lodge 2 in 1990 came at a time when, as Peter noted, 'profound changes' had affected the international scene. These included: (1) the evaporation of cold war concerns and socialist dogmas as forces affecting development; (2) a growing international consensus on the universal duty of all states to promote and protect universal rights; (3) a recognition of the need to incorporate environmental objectives into the conceptualisation and practice of development; and (4) the explosive appearance of all sorts of NGOs as active actors in the many theatres of 'development'.[45]

These interrelated trends helped to sharpen awareness of two other themes. First, the *absence of law* governing the business of development, notably as practised by the World Bank—the *lawlessness* of development—had clearly produced many development wrongs. The much publicised *Brundtland Report* on 'development and the environment' had excoriated the Bank's failure to assess the impact of its projects, and it explicitly called for creation of an 'international environmental law', grounded in the concept of 'sustainability', to regulate IDA and governmental development activities.[46] The ill-fated, Bank-financed project to dam the Narmada Valley in India had produced massive, unredressed human displacement, as well as other social and environmental harms. The Bhopal tragedy had shown how difficult it was for the thousands of disempowered victims of this event to gain adequate remediation for their terrible losses. These examples were only prominent illustrations of the massive social costs of development wrongdoing resulting from decades of 'lawless development'.[47]

Second, the UN DRD's call for people and poverty-centred, participatory development was now complemented by the World Bank's 1990 *World Development Report: Poverty*, and the UNDP's widely acclaimed first *Human Development Report* of 1990. Both documents were contributing to a reconceptualisation of the objectives of development and the methods of measuring it.

In this context, Peter wrote, 'law [has] returned to centre stage' and ways must be found to impose an 'accountability' on development actors, notably IDAs, government agencies, and MNCs. The task of Cumberland Lodge 2 was to explore this need, and it did. Many of the

---

[42] Allott, 1984.

[43] Pellett, 1984.

[44] 'TWLS 1984,' Introduction.

[45] 'TWLS 1992,' Introduction.

[46] World Commission on Environment and Development.

[47] Dembo *et al*, 1986.

papers[48] were of a high quality, and quite responsive to Peter's challenge. Some papers explored the need to establish standards—both 'substantive' and 'processual'—drawn from IHRL, environmental law, and other sources. Much attention was paid to requiring and enabling participation in development processes, both as a means and an end in itself. Other papers focused on standards to prevent and remediate 'development wrongs', whether these were perceived as 'torts' or violations of human rights. Some focused on the need for creating new bodies of law to regulate IDA projects; the World Bank's recently adopted Operational Directives—for example, displacement and resettlement, indigenous people, environmental impact assessments—were cited as examples.

Institutional structures to enforce accountability to these standards were examined. There were interesting papers on the failures of the Indian legal system to provide justice for the poor as evidenced by the Bhopal litigation and, conversely on the Supreme Court's more recent efforts to facilitate 'social action litigation' on behalf of powerless, allegedly wronged peoples, and on the need to expand judicial jurisdiction to remediate wrongs proven. Another focus was on strategies to provide 'legal resources' to the poor. Other important papers focused on the potentialities of 'Ombudsman', institutions and on the use of NGOs as institutions to expose development wrongdoing and mediate between governments and aggrieved communities.

'The notion of accountability has been shown to have many facets', Peter concluded in his Introduction to the two TWLS volumes subtitled *Law, Accountability, and Development*. These are well worth a careful revisiting today, since they deal with issues which are still very much on the agenda.

Cumberland Lodge 3 in 2001 was convened by Peter to examine challenges confronting law and development in the new millennium, notably those produced by the 'globalisation' phenomena, but also by the recrudescence of ethnic and religious divisions, the faltering progress of 'democratisation'—characterised by the creation of 'formal' democracy without political freedoms and meaningful participation—and the continuing challenge of entrenched poverty in so much of the world. The papers in the present volume reflect some of these new concerns, and many illustrate the expansion of law and development into new fields as globalisation proceeds. Ironically globalisation also seems to lead us to revisit old topics: 'law and modernisation', the critical 'role of the lawyer'—and new kinds of dependency. However, I would like to complement the papers published here by noting briefly some of the Conference discussions on the continuing challenge of poverty, and the messages on that subject offered by two papers which were presented at Cumberland Lodge 3 but published elsewhere.

Certainly poverty reduction and human development remain, rhetorically at least, the overriding concern of the major IDAs and international community—as it has spoken through the series of recent World Conferences on development issues during the 1990s—and these subjects were certainly part of the Cumberland Lodge 3 agenda. Much attention was paid to the World Bank's three volume report of 2000 entitled *Voices of the Poor*—a project which had benefited from the considerable input from members of the UK's Department for International Development (DFID), some of whom attended Cumberland Lodge 3. As DFID's Clare Short and the World Bank's President Wolfenson noted in their joint introduction, the *Voices* project constituted 'an unprecedented effort to gather the views, experiences, and aspirations of more than sixty thousand poor men and women from sixty countries... Using participatory methods

---

48   'TWLS 1992,' Introduction.

the study presents very directly... [their] voices and [their perceptions of] the realities of their lives.'

Of course 'the poor' are in fact many different constituencies—small farmers, landless rural workers, marginal urban wage workers, petty traders, excluded minorities and women in all these capacities and as providers of household and child care. But the Report portrayed common themes which characterised the messages of all categories of the poor. First, *powerlessness*—for example, a lack of rights, access to justice, effective political representatives and intermediaries—and conversely a demeaning, vulnerability to the demands of landlords, employers, creditors, merchants, and officials supposedly responsible for community services such as police protection, health care, and schooling. Second, *discrimination*, grounded in ascribed social status, occupation, ethnicity or region, and above all gender. Third, *asymmetrical relations with the state* in the provision of public security, health, education, finance, distribution of water, agricultural services and worker protections, 'and even in the distribution of emergency relief' governmental departments are routinely 'experienced as corrupt, callous, and uncaring'. Fourth, the *fragmentation and deterioration of communities*—poor people increasingly lack local structures for sharing and collective self-help at a time when crime, violence, corruption, and political repression are becoming more and more pervasive. Yet governments seem to lack the political will to address these conditions. Thus, *disrespect for human dignity* seems to epitomise the experience and reality of poverty. As one 'voice' put it: 'Poverty is humiliation, being dependent, being forced to accept rudeness, insults, injustice, and indifference when we seek help.' It is this condition which must first be addressed.

It was suggested that the policy implications of *Voices* and other World Bank and UNDP[49] studies are profound—indeed, a recent conference of some of the World Bank's leading economists produced wide agreement that these studies have forced a major change in their discipline's conceptualisation of poverty and in the ways in which it should be 'assessed' and 'measured', and in the articulation of 'poverty reduction' or 'human development' objectives and strategies.[50] Thus 'poverty-centred' development is no longer dominated by 'economic analysis'. Particularly in the context of Africa, political and legal analysis of power-relations is critical.[51] Development, the Bank now tells us in its *World Development Report: 2000* is a 'holistic' concept entailing a 'comprehensive framework' of interrelated strategies concerned, for example, with: building 'civil society', 'social capital', 'organisational capacities', and the 'political power' among the poor; aggressive efforts by government and civil society organisations to free women from the often paralysing constraints of traditional forms of discrimination; reforming institutions and processes of governance to provide transparency, participation, accountability, and political responsiveness. These may well be the necessary first steps to provide poor people with enhanced access to key resources—such as markets, credit, secure land tenures, functional education of all sorts, and an effective health care system, which is also responsive to women's and children's needs—and with access to 'legal resources', courts, and pro-poor police services.

Patrick McAuslan's magisterial paper emphasised the importance of enhancing poor people's power and participation to confront the increasing pressures, produced by globalisation and growth measures, to make land a marketable commodity—the need to view this very difficult problem in political, as well as economic, terms and the need to create

---

[49] Boyle, 1993; Seidman, A, 1993; Paul, 1992; Anderson, 1993; Cottrell, 1993; Fox, 1993; Hatchard, 1993.
[50] Meir and Stiglitz, 2001.
[51] World Bank, 2001a, emphasising a 'political economy' approach to assessing poverty in Africa.

participatory land reform structures.[52] I hope my own paper complemented Patrick's by focusing on operational measures necessary to integrate human rights into most spheres of development policy-making and administration—the need to create new bodies of state law and IDA policies which require the promotion and protection of participation, equality, remediation and other rights as law governing development; the need to incorporate measurable 'rights realisation targets', into many different kinds of programs and projects; the sensitive 'political' implications of the legal duty to integrate which I believe is now clearly imposed by international law on both IDAs and governments—and rhetorically recognised by UNDP and other relevant UN agencies.

IN CONCLUSION

The UN Charter posits peace, human rights, and development as interrelated, basic objectives, and international law is clearly seen as the essential means to promote them.[53]

The creation of an international law of development (ILD) has hitherto been neglected. The importance of that project is the subject of an important recent paper by Peter, which was circulated, but regrettably not discussed at Cumberland Lodge 3.[54] The ILD, he argues, should occupy a central place in the international law of the future because it provides a means to integrate presently disparate parts of international law—for example, human rights and peacekeeping—into a more coherent whole. He notes the growing movement of international law away from the doctrine that it is a law regulating relations between states to the belief that it is, primarily, a law concerned with the welfare of people. This view certainly characterises the ILD if we accept the principle that development must be a 'people-centred', 'participatory' process, aimed at 'the realisation of a generalised human right to [human] development'. Thus development becomes a critical means to promote human rights and protect our global environment and access to the resources of our global commons. Development, emphasising the dignity, indeed sanctity, of the human person, creates a context of international co-operation conducive to peaceful resolution of conflicts within as well as between states.

Peter views the ILD as providing a potential 'highway to the future'—a project 'under construction', entailing many tasks beginning with the effective integration of environmental and human rights law into the ILD. So, too, the provisions of 'International Economic Law' must be harmonised with the humanistic principles of the ILD. One might also suggest that the ILD must refine, 'harden', and incorporate the present 'soft law' concepts of the 'Right to Democracy', and the 'Right to Good Governance'.[55] Perhaps it must also incorporate some elements of humanitarian law and international criminal law.[56]

Reflection on these challenges suggests that law and development has come a long way from the abstract, often sterile discourse of the 1970s and the confusion and pessimism which constrained Cumberland Lodge 1. Those of us who have muddled along in law and development work for four decades can be grateful for Peter's vision of the future, as well as his past contributions. I am sure new generations of scholars will also be mindful of this legacy.

---

[52]   McAuslan, 2001.
[53]   Paul, 2001.
[54]   Boutros-Ghali, 1995.
[55]   Slinn, 1999.
[56]   Franck, 1992; McAuslan, 1996.

REFERENCES AND BIBLIOGRAPHY

Allott, A, 'Development for what?—false gods and holy writ', in Slinn, P and Tristram, H (eds), *Third World Legal Studies* (Human rights and development), 1984, New York: ICLD, pp 1-9

Anderson, M, 'Litigation and activism', in Slinn, P (ed), *Third World Legal Studies* (Law, accountability and development: challenge and response—legal methodologies of accountability), 1993, New York: ICLD, pp 177-188

Ayers, R L, *Banking on the Poor: The World Bank and World Poverty*, 1984, Cambridge, MA: M I T University Press

Bainbridge, J, *The Study and Teaching of Law in Africa*, 1972, New York: ILC

Boutros-Ghali, B, 'Forword: Symposium on the United Nations: challenges of law and development'(1995) 36 Harvard International Law Journal 267-271

Boyle, A E, 'Environment and development: accountability through international law', in Slinn, P (ed), *Third World Legal Studies* (Law, accountability and development: challenge and response—legal methodologies of accountability), 1993, New York: ICLD, pp 95-106

Brietzke, P H, 'Development as a human rite', in Slinn, P and Tristram, H (eds), *Third World Legal Studies* (Human rights and development), 1984, New York: ICLD, pp 25-58

Bryde, B O, 'The reception of European law and autonomous legal development in Africa' (1978) 18 Law and State 21

Bryde, B O, *The Politics and Sociology of African Legal Development*, 1976, Frankfurt: Metzner

Cottrell, J, 'Courts and accountability: public interest litigation in the Indian high courts', in Slinn, P (ed), *Third World Legal Studies* (Law, accountability and development: challenge and response—legal methodologies of accountability), 1993, New York: ICLD, pp 199-213

D'Sa, R, 'The "Right to Development" and the New International Economic Order, with special reference to Africa', in Slinn, P and Tristram, H (eds), *Third World Legal Studies* (Human rights and development), 1984, New York: ICLD, pp 140-159

Dag Hammarskjöld Foundation, 'What now another development: the 1975 Dag Hammarskjöld report on development and international co-operation', in *Development Dialogue*, 1975, Upsala: Dag Hammarskjöld Foundation

Daniels, W E and Woodman, G, *Essays in Ghanaian Law*, 1976, Legon, Ghana: Faculty of Law

Dembo, D, Dias, C, Morehouse, W and Paul, J C N (eds), *The International Context of Rural Poverty*, 1986, New York: ICLD

Dias, C J and Paul, J C N, 'Lawyers', in Dias, C J, Luckham, R, Lynch, D O, and Paul, J C N (eds), *Lwyers in the Third World: Comparative and Developmental Perspectives*, 1981, New York: ICLD

Fox, H, 'Private law damages as a method of state accountability: the tort exception to state immunity', in Slinn, P (ed), *Third World Legal Studies* (Law, accountability and development: challenge and response—legal methodologies of accountability), 1993, New York: ICLD, pp 107-119

Franck, T M, 'The new development: can American law and legal institutions help developing countries?' (1972) Wisconsin Law Review 767

Franck, T M, 'The emerging right to democracy' (1992) 86 American Journal of International Law 46

Friedman, L, 'On legal development' (1969) 24 Rutgers Law Review 11

Friedman, W, 'The role of law and the function of the lawyer in the developing countries' (1963) Vanderbilt Law Review 181

Galanter, M, 'The modernization of law', in Weiner, M (ed), *Modernization: The Dynamics of Growth*, 1966, New York: OUP

Gardner, J A, *Legal Imperialism: American Lawyers and Foreign Aid in Latin America*, 1980, Madison: University of Wisconsin Press

Geraghty, T, 'People, practice, attitudes and problems in lower courts of Ethiopia' (1969) 6 Journal of Ethiopian Law 427

Ghai, Y P and McAuslan, J P W B, *Public Law and Political Change in Kenya*, 1971, Nairobi, Oxford: OUP

Ghai, Y P, 'Control and management of the economy: research perspectives on public enterprise', in Ghai, Y (ed), *Law in the Political Economy of Public Enterprise: African Perspectives*, 1977, New York: ICLD

Ghai, Y P, 'Notes towards a theory of law and ideology: Tanzania perspectives' (1976) 13 *African Law Studies* 31

Gower, L C B, *Independent Africa: The Challenge to the Legal Profession*, 1968, Cambridge, Mass: Harvard University Press

Gower, L C B, Johnstone, Q, and Stevens, R, *'Legal Education in Uganda: A Report to the Attorney General'*, 1969, Kampala: Ministry of Justice

Gutto, S, 'Responsibility and accountability of states, transnational corporations and individuals in the field of human rights to social development: a critique', in Slinn, P and Tristram, H (eds), *Third World Legal Studies* (Human rights and development), 1984, New York: ICLD, pp 175-186

Hager, LM, 'Training lawyers for development: the IDLI experience', in Hiller, J and Brietzke, P (eds), *Third World Legal Studies* (Teaching law and development), 1986, New York: ICLD, pp 57-62

Harding, A J, 'Public interest groups, public interest law and development in Malaysia', in Slinn, P (ed), *Third World Legal Studies* (Law, accountability and development: theories, techniques and agencies of development), 1992, New York: ICLD, pp 231-243

Harvey, W B, *Law and Social Change in Ghana*, 1962, Princeton: Princeton University Press

Hatchard, J, 'Developing governmental accountability: the role of the ombudsman', in Slinn, P (ed), *Third World Legal Studies* (Law, accountability and development: theories, techniques and agencies of development), 1992, New York: ICLD, pp 215-230

Havens, A E, 'Methodological issues in the study of development' (1972) Sociologia Ruralis 252-260

ICLD (International Center for Law in Development), 'Research priorities for another law' (1978) 2 Development Dialogue 115

ICLD, *Law and Legal Resources in the Mobilization of the Rural Poor for Self-Reliant Development, a Report to the International Foundation for Development Alternatives*, 1979, New York: ICLD

ILC (International Legal Center) Committee on Legal Services to the Poor in the Developing Countries, *Legal Aid and World Poverty: A Survey of Asia, Africa, and Latin America*, 1974, New York: ILC

ILC Committee on Legal Education in Developing Countries, *Legal Education in a Changing World: Report of the Committee on Legal Education in the Developing Countries*, 1975, New York: ILC

ILC, *Newsletters*, Nos 1-17, 1968-1975

ILC Research Advisory Committee on Law and Development, *Law and Development: The Future of Law and Development Research*, 1974, New York: ILC

ICJ (International Commission of Jurists), *African Conference on the Rule of Law*, Lagos, Nigeria, January 1961

ICJ, Rural Development, *Rural Development and Human Rights in South Asia*, 1982, Geneva

International Foundation for Development Alternatives, 'Report of a workshop on peoples' participation in development', No 4, *Dossier*, 1979, Geneva

Johnstone, Q, 'American assistance to African legal education', 1972, Tulane Law Review 657

Kibwana, K, 'Human rights and/or economic development: which way Africa?', in Slinn, P (ed), *Third World Legal Studies* (Law, accountability and development: challenge and response—legal methodologies of accountability), 1993, New York: ICLD, pp 43-55

Leys, C T, *Underdevelopment in Kenya: The Political Economy of Neo-Colonialism, 1964-1971*, 1975, London: Heinemann

Luckham, R (ed), *Law and Social Enquiry: Case Histories of Research*, 1981, New York: ICLD

Manase, W T, 'Grassroots education in Zimbabwe: successes and problems encountered in implementation by the Legal Resources Foundation of Zimbabwe' (1992) 36 Journal of African Law 11-17

McAuslan, P, 'Good governance and aid in Africa' (1996) 40 Journal of African Law 168-182

McAuslan, P, 'From Greenland's icy mountains, from India's coral strand: the globalization of land markets and its impact on national land law', presented at conference on Law and Development at Cumberland Lodge, June 2001

McNamara, R S, Address to the Board of Governors, 1977, Washington, DC : World Bank

Meier, G M and Stiglitz, J E (eds), *Frontiers of Development Economics: The Future in Perspective*, 2001, New York: World Bank and OUP

Merryman, J H, 'Comparative law and social change: on the origins, style, decline and revival of the law and development movement' (1977) 25 American Journal of Comparative Law 457-89

Myrdal, G, *Asian Drama: An Inquiry into the Poverty of Nations*, 1968, New York: OUP

Myrdal, G, 'The "soft state" in underdeveloped economies' (1977) 15 *U C L A Law Review* 1118

Nwabueze, B O, *Judicialism in Commonwealth Africa: The Role of Courts in Government*, 1977, London: C Hurst

Parkinson, F, 'The right to economic development in international law' (1984) *Third World Legal Studies* 120-128

Paul, J C N, 'Legal education and development planning: some notes on literature concerned with African experience', 1972, ILC Working Paper

Paul, J C N, 'American law teachers and Africa: some historical observations' (1987) 31 Journal of African Law 18-28

Paul, J C N, 'The human right to development: its meaning and importance', in Slinn, P (ed), *Third World Legal Studies* (Law, accountability and development: theories, techniques and agencies of development), 1992, New York: ICLD, pp 17-54

Paul, J C N, 'Globalization, poverty and integrating human rights into development: why and how', presented at conference on Law and Development at Cumberland Lodge, June 2001

Paul, J C N and Dias, C J, 'Introduction: contrasting paradigms of development', in Paul, J, and Dias, C (eds), *Third World Legal Studies* (Law in alternative strategies of development), 1982, New York: ICLD, p 1

Paul, J C N, Incorporating human rights into the work of the world summit for social development, 1995, American Society of International Law Issue Papers on World Conference, No 3, Washington, DC, 17-20

Paul, J C N, 'International development agencies, human rights and humane development projects' (1988) 17 Denver Judiciary International Law and Policy 67

Paul, J C N, 'The United Nations and the creation of an international law of development' (1995) 36 Harvard International Law Journal (Symposium on the United Nations: Challenges of Law and Development) 307-328

Pellett, A, 'The function of the right to development: a right to self-realization', in Slinn, P and Tristram, H (eds), *Third World Legal Studies* (Human rights and development), 1984, New York: ICLD, pp 129-139

Seers, D, 'The meaning of development' (1969) 11 International Development Review 2

Seidman, A, 'Participation and the law', in Slinn, P (ed), *Third World Legal Studies* (Law, accountability and development: challenge and response—legal methodologies of accountability), 1993, New York: ICLD, pp 1-11

Seidman, R B, 'Law and development: a general model' (1972) 6 Law and Society Review 311

Seidman, R B, *The State, Law, and Development*, 1978, London: Croom Helm

Seidman, R B, 'The fatal race: law-making and the implementation of development goals' in Slinn, P (ed), *Third World Legal Studies* (Law, accountability and development: theories, techniques and agencies of development), 1992, New York: ICLD, pp 79-98

Shivji, I G, *Class Struggles in Tanzania*, 1975, Dar es Salaam: Tanzania Publishing House

Shivji, I G (ed), *Limits of Legal Radicalism: Reflections of Teaching Law at the University of Dar es Salaam*, 1986, Dar es Salaam, Tanzania: Faculty of Law, University of Dar es Salaam

Singer, N, 'Modernization of law in Ethiopia: a study in process and personal values' (1970) 11 Harvard International Law Journal 73

Slinn, P and Snyder, F (eds), *International Law of Development: Comparative Perspectives*, 1987, Abingdon: Professional Books

Slinn, P and Read, J S (eds), *Law Reports of the Commonwealth*, published annually 1986 to 1989, Abingon: Professional Books (subsequently Butterworths)

Slinn, P and Hatchard, J, 'Towards an African Zimbabwean constitution?' in An-Na'im, A A (ed), *Third World Legal Studies* (Building constitutional orders in sub-Saharan Africa), 1988, New York: ICLD, 119-138

Slinn, P, 'A fresh start for Africa?'(1991) Journal of African Law 1-7

Slinn, P, 'Development and developing international and European law', in Benedek, W, Isak, H and Kicker, R (eds), *Essays in Honour of Konrad Ginther on the Occasion of his 65th Birthday*, 1999, Vienna: Peter Lang

Slinn, P, 'Development issues: the international law of development and global climate change', in Churchill, R and Freestone, D (eds), *International Law and Global Climate Change*, 1991, London: Graham and Trotman, pp 75-94

Slinn, P, 'La doctrine Britannique devant le droit international du développement', in Flory, M, Mahiou, A and Henry, J-R (eds), *La formation des Normes en Droit du Développement*, 1983, Paris: Editions CNRS, pp 105-108

Slinn, P, 'Protection of international norms and social development in Commonwealth countries', in Pellet, A and Sorel, J M (eds), *Le Droit International du Développement Social et Cultural*, 1997, Paris: L'Hermes, pp 225-230

Slinn, P, 'The contribution of the United Nations to the evolution of the principles of international development law', *Proceedings of the Seventh Annual Conference of the African Society of International and Comparative Law*, 1995, London: African Society of International and Comparative Law, pp 263-278

Slinn, P, 'The implementation of international obligations towards developing countries: equality or preferential treatment?', in Butler, W E (ed), *Control over Compliance with International Law*, 1991, Dordrecht, London: Martinus Nijhoff, pp 165-174

Slinn, P, 'Comparative approaches to the relationship between international law and development', in Slinn, P and Snyder, F (eds), *International Law of Development: Comparative Perspectives*, 1987, Abingdon: Professional Books, pp 27-39

Trubek, D M, 'Toward a social theory of law: an essay on the study of law and development' (1972) 82 Yale Law Journal 1

Trubek, D M and Galanter, M, 'Law and society: scholars in self-estrangement: some reflections on the crisis in law and development studies in the United States' (1974) Wisconsin Law Review 1062

'Twenty Years After', Conference at Arden House (NY) of Law Teachers Who Worked in Africa, September 26-28, 1986

(TWLS 1982) Paul, J and Dias, C (eds), *Third World Legal Studies* (Law in alternative strategies of development), 1982, New York: ICLD

(TWLS 1984) Slinn, P and Tristram, H (eds), *Third World Legal Studies* (Human rights and development), 1984, New York: ICLD

(TWLS 1985) Hiller, J and Brietzke, P (eds), *Third World Legal Studies* (Developing legal resources with the poor), 1985, New York: ICLD

(TWLS 1988) An-Na'im, A A (ed), *Third World Legal Studies* (Building constitutional orders in sub-Saharan Africa), 1988, New York: ICLD

(TWLS 1989) Reyntjens, P (ed), *Third World Legal Studies* (Pluralism, participation and decentralization in sub-Saharan Africa), 1989, New York: ICLD

(TWLS 1991) Cook, R (ed), *Third World Legal Studies* (Realizing the rights of women in development processes: women's legal entitlements to agricultural development), 1991, New York: ICLD

(TWLS 1992) Slinn, P (ed), *Third World Legal Studies* (Law, accountability and development: theories, techniques and agencies of development), 1992, New York: ICLD

(TWLS 1993) Slinn, P (ed), *Third World Legal Studies* (Law, accountability and development: challenge and response—legal methodologies of accountability), 1993, New York: ICLD

United Nations Development Programme, *Human Development Report – 1990*, 1991, New York: UNDP

United Nations Commission on Human Rights, *Report of the Secretary General* on Realization of Rights and International Dimension of Right to Development, E/CN, 4/1334, January 1979, Geneva

Vanderlinden, J, *Proceedings of the Conference on Legal Education in Africa*, 1968, mimeo, Addis Ababa

Weber, M, *On Law in Economy and Society*, Edited by Max Rheinstein, 1966, Cambridge, Mass: Harvard University Press

Woodman, G R, 'Land law and the distribution of wealth', in Daniels, W E and Woodman, G R, *Essays in Ghanaian Law*, 1976, Legon, Ghana: Faculty of Law

Woodman, G R, 'Constitutions in a world of powerful semi-autonomous social fields', in Reyntjens, P (ed), *Third World Legal Studies* (Pluralism, participation and decentralization in sub-Saharan Africa), 1989, New York: ICLD, pp1-21

Woodman, G R, 'Customary law, state courts, and the notion of institutionalization of norms in Ghana and Nigeria', in Allott, A and Woodman, G R (eds), *People's Law and State Law*, 1985, Dordrecht: Foris Publications, pp 143-163

World Bank (2001a), *African Poverty at the Millennium: Causes, Complexities and Challenges*, 2001, Washington, DC: World Bank

World Bank (2001b), *World Development Report 2001: Attacking Poverty*, 2001, Washington, DC: World Bank

World Commission on Environment and Development, *Our Common Future*, 1987, New York: OUP

Foreword

World Council of Churches, Commission on the Churches' Participation in Development, *Betting on the Weak: Some Experiences in People's Participation and Development*, 1976, Collection of Articles and Case Studies

CHAPTER 1

INTRODUCTION

John Hatchard and Amanda Perry-Kessaris[*]

COMPLEXITY

The papers in this volume divide neatly into three parts: theoretical developments, international practice and national practice. They reflect the diversity of issues addressed at the 2001 Law and Development conference under the broad theme of 'Complexity'—a point neatly encapsulated in the contribution by Harding and Carter:

> Whereas the UK government department involved in this area... prefers 'interventions' which are 'SMART' (short, measurable, achievable, realistic, and time-limited), the reality is that, for legal reform in most countries, effective intervention is more likely to be long-term, incalculable, uncertain, idealistic and continuing—such real-life complexities leave little room for neat acronyms.

... in inter-disciplinarity

A key task for any interdisciplinary field such as law and development is to determine what each discipline aims to gain from its interaction with the other. Law and development certainly seeks to ensure that development considerations are taken into account by lawyers, and that legal considerations are taken into account by those who study development. But is the aim to ensure that law merely begins to feature—if ever more regularly and prominently—on a list of development objectives, and vice versa; or is it to ensure that legal and developmental concerns are each so integrated into the domain of the other, that placing them on a list of objectives is no longer necessary? The contributions to Part 1 argue that, whatever our aims in consulting other disciplines, we must use them with caution.

In Chapter 2, David Kennedy argues that law is important as 'a distributional tool' for development—a way of implementing political choices between multiple economically efficient outcomes. But he is uneasy about the enthusiasm with which law, in particular the 'rule of law', has come to be seen 'as' development. 'The focus on rights, on constitutions, on government capacity or judicial independence may all be to the good—but without a sharp sense for how one is intending to affect the economy, it is hard to compare building the rule of law with leaving the economy to operate more informally, and hard to compare building the rule of law one way with building it another.' The promotion of 'the' rule of law—of formalism over informality in private relations, and of rule-based decision-making over discretion in private-public relations—is often unaccompanied by essential and 'more conventional questions of development policy and planning which demand decisions about distribution.' Kennedy concludes that: 'Much as we might wish it, there is no single "rule of law" whose establishment will generate development,' but we forget that because

[*] Professor John Hatchard is General Secretary of the Commonwealth Legal Education Association. Dr Amanda Perry-Kessaris is Lecturer in the Department of Law, Queen Mary, University of London, a.j.perry-kessaris@qmul.ac.uk.

'remembering would take us straight back to politics, economics and to the enduring dilemmas of development policy-making.'

Kennedy's concerns about unquestioning reliance on the neatly packaged law are mirrored by Amanda Perry-Kessaris' concerns about unquestioning reliance on neatly packaged economics in Chapter 3. She argues that the utility of any regulatory strategy is 'dependent upon the extent to which the regulation successfully affects the behaviour of a particular category of decision-maker.' But economics—the study of choice—has for decades presented a distinctly simplistic and unrealistic view of decision-making. Drawing on Paul Ormerod's work, Perry-Kessaris explains that 'contrary to conventional theory, decision-makers do not have a fixed idea of what they want; do not make choices in an isolation tank; and therefore, do not make predictable decisions.' This is because the preferences of individual decision-makers are not fixed. Rather they are informed by past decisions, by new information, or by the preferences of others—that is, trendiness. Since it is rarely possible to determine on which basis decisions will be made, predicting and affecting decisions is extremely difficult. Unable to deal with complex and interactive decision-making, economics is certain to fail in predicting and explaining such decision-making in different cultural contexts. This issue is of huge significance for the study of law and economic development, which seeks to find effective ways of harnessing and constraining the power of the market in vastly different environments. Perry-Kessaris concludes that those studying law and development should '[d]raw on other disciplines, but understand their limitations, and listen to the rebels within them.'

In Chapter 4, Ann Stewart applauds the new recognition of the importance of 'social—as well as economic—relations within families and local communities' in human development; and the resulting increase in attention devoted to 'local' justice—a subject which feminist legal theorists have addressed 'for some time'. However, Stewart is concerned that 'the local—which is recognised within feminist legal analysis as a gendered construct, as well as a space in which women seek gender justice—will be reconfigured through mainstream development and law approaches as a location wherein women access formal rights.' The local may come to be viewed 'as a place badly in need of formalisation to remove it from the messy world of culture into the pure world of abstract legal personality and rights, and the best way of achieving this will be attachment to the lowest rung on the justice system.' Local '"non state" or informal processes' may become 'over legalised, in an attempt to incorporate them into the formal institutions.' Although '[s]tate laws can assist women,' it is 'local and community level dynamics' which 'determine to what extent.' In particular, '[a]ttempts to transpose informal claims which are seen as legitimate—if contested—into formal rights can have unforeseen consequences' because those women who 'are not powerful may not be able to claim such rights.' Furthermore, 'competing social norms may not be displaced simply by the granting of a formal right.' In an echo of Kennedy's critique of law and development's current emphasis on formalisation, Stewart insists that 'it is always important to ask: why formalise? Will a legal right increase women's ability to claim entitlement?' Stewart concludes by arguing that 'feminist analyses of diversity and plurality offer ways forward to the wider development agenda; that diversity and plurality are part of 21st century legal systems not relicts of a bygone era'; and that a 'shift of emphasis within development policy to look beyond state institutional reform to agency at a local level provides an opportunity for feminist legal analysis to move from the margins.'

... in balancing the needs of the developed and the developing

As interlinkages between national economies become ever more obvious, a central concern for the study of development is to what extent any appreciation in the status of 'have nots' is dependent upon a depreciation in the status of 'haves.' To corrupt an old adage, if I teach you how to fish, will I still be able to eat forever? The first two contributions in Part 2 expose this tension through examinations of the bitterly contested fields of intellectual property rights and transfer of technology.

For Peter Muchlinski (Chapter 5), the degree to which developing countries rely on imported technology, and the importance of technology to economic and social welfare are such that the need to 'maintain' and 'strengthen' the 'preferential treatment for developing countries in relation to the transfer of technology' is not in doubt. 'The real question is how to operationalise this preference.' Importantly, contemporary efforts to resolve tensions over technology transfer take place in the context not of old-style regulatory models focused on the role of the state, but of the new market-based model. This model, best exemplified by the TRIPS Agreement, 'abandons the willingness to prohibit specific terms in technology transfer transactions that is characteristic of the "regulatory" approach, relying rather on competition rules to control abuses.'

Muchlinski stresses that the current reliance on a market-based approach to development does not entail a reduction in the importance of regulation—quite the contrary. Regulation retains a role because 'it is simply not sustainable to argue that... all transactions will always offer the most efficient allocation and distribution of information, resources, goods and services.' Again echoing the theme of inter-disciplinarity introduced in Part 1, he notes that we must begin to recognise the relevance to law and development of the study of regulation—'predominantly a domestic and public law oriented discourse' which must be adapted 'to a transnational public/private economic/social sphere'. In so doing, it 'is necessary to rise above a narrow liberalisation/privatisation agenda and develop ideas about how social issues might affect and inform the new transnational dimension of development oriented regulation.' In this way, debates over technology transfer can take account of the fact that the 'economic bias of earlier approaches has been supplemented to include a broader social, environmental and cultural conception of "development."' For example, he argues that technology transfer arrangements might be regulated, by voluntary arrangement or otherwise, using the emerging frameworks of 'corporate social responsibility' and 'human rights impact assessments.'

In Chapter 6, Philippe Cullet focuses the technology transfer debate on the specific tension between intellectual property rights over drugs and the human right to health. He notes that: 'Most proposals to improve access to drugs focus on ways to make drugs more affordable for patients in developing countries, without compromising the existing legal framework provided by TRIPS,' but that 'TRIPS does not have much to say concerning health.' Instead, it focuses on intellectual property rights holders, and views intellectual property rights as 'a vehicle to foster trade and not as a moral recognition for scientific or technological prowess.' Therefore TRIPS is 'not the only relevant legal framework that should dictate policies on access to drugs.' Cullet argues that the literature relating to the human right to health offers a useful, and frequently overlooked, avenue for debate. Cullet notes a 'lack of concurrence between intellectual property law and human rights law,' resulting from 'the fact that the intellectual property system has traditionally not been linked to socio-economic concerns.' However, in practice, the two fields are clearly linked. For example, if the introduction by a state of patents on medicines causes drug prices to rise, and the state takes no measures—such as subsidies—to offset these price rises, access to drugs will be reduced. This 'may amount to a violation of the ESCR Covenant', which protects the right to health.

Although Cullet accepts that 'the human right to health is clearly not a non-derogable right under present international law,' he insists that where intellectual property rights and the right to health conflict, and a hierarchy must therefore be established, 'international law indicates that human rights should generally take precedence.' The two rights need not always be presented as conflicting. Cullet argues that it is possible to interpret intellectual property rights in such as way as to give due recognition to the right to health—'for instance, by guaranteeing the "social dimensions of intellectual property,"' or by seeking to 'strengthen the criteria for obtaining a patent, in particular the requirement of non-obviousness.' But for developing countries to rely on 'loopholes or unclear language in TRIPS to foster the realisation of the right to health is unsatisfactory in that the central concern of health is consistently framed as an exception.' As a fundamental right, the right to health cannot simply be considered as an exception to property rights such as patents. Cullet concludes that, although 'the solution of giving primacy to human rights is unlikely to meet with the approval of all states, and would probably not stand if it came for adjudication in a WTO context,' it 'nevertheless seems adequate from a legal and ethical point of view.'

... in creating and learning the new rules of the game

Current debate presents two targets for the development process—catching up and moving forward. The last four contributions to Part 2 consider the complexities associated with moving forward in the tasks of learning and creating the new rules and institutions deemed necessary for development; and with catching up in the implementation of old rules and institutions.

In Chapter 7, Emmanuel Awuku notes that developing countries previously regarded competition law and policy as a tool for developed countries and their multinational companies dominate their developing country competitors. Many developing countries do not have laws or institutions necessary to promote free competition. However, developing countries have, by necessity, developed a new-found enthusiasm for competition law. The growth of cross-border transactions and the rise of liberalisation, deregulation and privatisation programmes have provided domestic stimulants for action in the field of competition. Nonetheless, Awuku stresses that the protection of competition presents major institutional challenges, and that 'even in the case of those countries that do [have strong, well-functioning and well-funded competition authorities], it took a considerable time until they assumed an important role.' Furthermore, markets 'characterised by a high level of state ownership and intervention... are less appropriate environments for the implementation of competition law, than market-oriented economies based on democracy and public participation, transparent and accountable government, efficient services, observation of human rights and the rule of law, and disapproval of corrupt practices.' Awuku concludes that, if developing countries are to create a competitive environment for business, they must be given technical assistance to introduce and improve competition authorities and legislation, the capacity of existing competition authorities must be strengthened, and the 'development impact of possible international agreements on competition laws and policy, including the possibility of special and preferential treatment of developing countries' must be considered.

The need for technical assistance to developing countries in the implementation of international economic law is further explored by Mary Footer in Chapter 8, specifically in relation to the World Trade Organisation (WTO). She explains that 'the functions and principles of the WTO are more ambitious' than those of the GATT, which it replaces. It creates a new international economic organisation which provides an institutional forum not only for trade negotiations and dispute resolution, but also for 'further normative developments in international trade law.' These developments require a 'vertical' expansion of international trade law, since 'WTO rule making now reaches more directly into the private conduct of natural and corporate entities, at national and regional levels.' Footer argues that vertical integration of international trade law in particular 'has implications for all WTO Members in a globalising economy, but it weighs most heavily on developing country governments,' which must spread their thin resources between 'drafting implementing legislation for market economy reforms' and implementing legal and institutional reforms necessary to achieve good governance, and respect for democracy, human rights and the rule of law. 'Thus, for many of them the implementation of WTO trade obligations is simply another item to add to the growing list of legal and institutional reforms that underpin neo-liberal development policy.' In recognition of the weight of the reform burden carried by developing countries, and '[f]or the first time in the history of the WTO, the Doha Declaration explicitly recognises that trade-related technical assistance (TRTA) and capacity-building are "core elements of the development dimension of the multilateral system"' and 'endorses a "New Strategy for WTO Technical Co-operation for Capacity-building, Growth and Integration".' Although she welcomes this pledge of support to developing countries, she retains a degree of scepticism, informed by past experience, of the extent to which such support is likely to be meaningful. Footer argues that TRTA can only be effective if it is integrated in countries' broader development strategies, and 'takes account of other competing development needs.' But she suspects that the extent and complexity of the institutional and legal reforms necessary—and thus the level of assistance required—have yet to be appreciated. But such assistance as is provided is 'by multilateral and bilateral donors is badly co-ordinated and, in some cases, inherently contradictory in its aims and objectives.' Furthermore, although 'capacity-building' is acknowledged as an essential component of the implementation of the trade framework, action is often restricted to the level of policy, rather than law. Implementation of trade obligations is made all the more complex by the fact that the trade law agenda was negotiated without substantive and effective involvement of developing countries; is often essentially a restatement of standards already existing in developed countries, and/or promoting their commercial interests; and is therefore viewed as an alien framework 'imposed upon' developing countries. Footer concludes with the warning that 'economic changes are creating both new forms of dependency for developed countries, and the potential for a symbiotic paring of private commercial interests and TRTA.'

In Chapter 9, David Salter shifts our attention to the problems associated with defining the new rules of the game, in an exploration of the recent moves in the OECD to identify and combat what it perceives to be 'harmful' tax competition. The OECD lists features commonly present in such jurisdictions—namely, lack of information exchange and transparency, and the absence of real commercial activity by investors. The OECD considers tax competition to be 'an inevitable and not necessarily objectionable consequence of the fiscal sovereignty.' However, it does object to 'predatory' tax practices which '[detrimentally] affect the location of... service activities, erode the tax base of other countries, distort trade and investment patterns and undermine fairness, neutrality and broad social acceptance of tax systems generally.' The OECD has therefore categorised certain jurisdictions as tax havens—and, depending on their response, as Uncooperative Tax Havens (UTHs)—and identified 'defensive measures that might be taken against UTHs.' According to Salter, the response of tax havens 'has been mixed.' Some have decided to 'enter into the necessary commitment with the OECD as soon as possible,' others have taken their chances with UTH status. Some states were indecisive about which way to sway, perhaps due to 'an uncertainty on the part of some tax havens about what precisely the OECD initiative expected of them.' Echoing some of Footer's comments on the WTO, Salter notes an unease amongst member and non-member states alike that the new rules of tax competition are being defined by one institution, the OECD. Although the OECD tends to encourage the view that its role is 'merely facilitative,' this 'ignores the reality of the considerable influence wielded by the OECD over both OECD and non-OECD member states and the political weight/authority with which OECD pronouncements are imbued.' However, according to Salter, 'it is conceivable that the strongest challenge to the legitimacy of the OECD initiative... will be mounted not against the OECD, but against those OECD member states that seek to impose the defensive measures' it recommends. For example, they might argue that those measures 'violate the GATT or GATS non-discrimination prohibitions, because they would not apply to OECD member states.'

Salter concludes that the 'ideal outcome' for the OECD—and perhaps even for tax havens—is for states to agree to comply with OECD recommendations. However, if not all tax havens comply, then the distinction between co-operative and uncooperative tax havens will become important and will have consequences for economic development. UTHs may be subjected to defensive measures and 'non-tax' measures by OECD member states, and may also 'lose non-essential economic assistance from other jurisdictions.' But on the upside, 'they will retain the characteristics that ensure their attractiveness to taxpayers.' For co-operative tax havens, the downside is that they are likely lose the economic benefits of 'income derived from geographically mobile activities.' Finally, internal support for the OECD initiative is not universal, so 'the tax havens might be best advised to bide their time and to seek to exploit divisions within the OECD ranks with a view, therefore, to ultimately retaining direct control over their own destiny.'

In Chapter 10, Philippe Sands traces the development of the concept of sustainable development as set out in international instruments, and applied in decisions of the ICJ and the WTO. Sands begins an analysis of the decision of the ICJ in the *Gabčíkovo-Nagymaros Case*, highlighting three points of note. 'First, the fact that it invokes "sustainable development" at all, indicates that the term has a legal function. Second, "sustainable development" is a "concept" and not a principle or a rule.' Third, this 'concept' 'has both a procedural/temporal aspect'—according to which the parties must reassess the environmental consequences of their actions, 'and a substantive aspect'—requiring the release of a 'satisfactory volume of water.' However, the Court did not elaborate as to the mechanisms for the former, or the definition of the latter. Sands argues that the pleadings of Hungary and Slovakia 'reflect the inherent malleability and uncertainty of the term' sustainable development. Hungary 'focused on the environmental aspect of the concept' of 'sustainable development,' and used it 'to justify its view that there should be no barrages.' By contrast, Slovakia focused on the '"developmental" elements' of the concept, and argued that it 'justified the opposite conclusion.' Finally the Court used 'the concept to achieve an accommodation of views and values whilst leaving to the parties the task of fleshing out the harder practical consequences.' It 'provided no further assistance as to the status of "sustainable development" in international law, or its practical consequences, beyond the fact that it was to fulfil a function of integrating the potentially competitive societal objectives of environment and development.'

In the *Shrimp Case*, the WTO Appellate Body was asked to assess the compatibility of domestic US laws with international trade law provisions. The Body noted that signatories to the 1994 WTO Agreement 'were "fully aware of the importance and legitimacy of environmental protection as a goal of national and international policy"' and that the Preamble 'explicitly acknowledges the objective of *sustainable development*.' This, says the

Appellate Body, 'is a "concept" which "has been generally accepted as integrating economic and social development and environmental protection."' Furthermore, the Board used the concept of 'sustainable development' to 'provide "colour, texture and shading" to the concept of an "unjustifiable discrimination" in relevant GATT provisions.' This then allowed the Appellate Body 'to reach out to... other, non-trade instruments to ascertain what are the minimum standards to be met' under the relevant GATT provisions before the US could take 'discriminatory measures' in the trade arena, in order to protect an environmental objective—here the conservation of sea turtles. It thus gave 'sustainable development' a 'procedural element'—in addition to the substantive element—'namely the requirement that appropriate diplomatic means—including those available within relevant multilateral agreements—be exhausted before unilateral measures may be taken.' Sands observes that '[b]oth the ICJ and the Appellate Body refer to sustainable development as a "concept,"' and 'treat it as having a status in international law, in the sense that it is invoked as part of a legal analysis to justify a legal conclusion.' However, '[n]either body explores its international legal status, whether as custom or convention law, or adds significantly to our sense of what it is or what role it has in the international legal order, beyond indicating that in normative terms it may have both procedural and substantive consequences.' Nonetheless, they seem to use the concept 'as a significant aid to assist in reaching fairly radical conclusions.' Sands argues that these are both 'far-reaching' decisions, breaking 'with prior international practise' and 'for which little, if any, international precedent can be found.' He concludes that sustainable development 'remains an elusive concept which essentially requires different streams of international law to be treated in an integrated manner,' and which 'aims at harmonisation and reconciliation with a view to avoiding "a state of normative anarchy"'. 'Although we remain unsure as to its nature, legal status, operation and consequences, these two cases indicate that... "sustainable development" has gained legal currency and that its consequences will be felt more rather than less widely.'

... in borrowing from others

In Part 3 we move to consider law and development debates at the national level. The first four chapters of Part 3 consider the complexities associated with borrowing laws and institutions from abroad.

In Chapter 11, Scott Newton explains that for transition economies that 'cannot afford and do not wish to go through the same process of slow and tentative development as the developed economies,' transplantation is commonly thought to be an efficient tool. But he questions the accuracy of our understanding of the transplantation process. 'To speak, as comparative lawyers typically do, of transplantation as "reception" is to obscure the political calculations and complex play of interests behind any modern instance of importing statutes (or concepts or provisions)'—'even if a jurisdiction decides to import a foreign law lock, stock, and barrel, it nonetheless must *enact* it, with all the sovereign political implications any enactment carries.' Whether they believe that transplantation processes ignore relevant cultural or social issues, or that it is a 'matter of economic rationality, and that market-enabling laws are largely culture-neutral', commentators 'habitually seem to wring the politics out of the account of 'transplantation.' They put aside 'matters of policy, such as the economic or social rationale for a particular piece of legislation' and 'questions about the substantive authority in the name of which a law is enacted,' and the degree to which the 'process embodies principles of deliberation, transparency and accountability.' Newton suggests that this narrow perspective finds favour in part because it allows the precise role of foreign advisers to go unchallenged. For him, the danger is that '[i]n transplantation as in transition, the emphasis on product over process works to privilege legality over legitimacy.'

Newton's survey of the history of the insolvency and pension laws reveals that 'two assumptions about transplantation require challenge.' First, is not clear 'that the market legal framework in Kazakhstan was in fact transplanted,' and second, it is not true that 'the result was achieved (and could only have been achieved) by reliance on foreign technical advisers.' The transition process 'necessarily entailed a high degree of adaptation of market-regulating legislation from elsewhere,' but foreign legislation was never simply copied. 'Rather, Kazakhstani legal scholars have studied foreign legal materials and drafted statutes drawing on them without reproducing them,' and model CIS legislation in particular 'has played a central role.' Echoing concerns expressed by other contributors in Part 2, Newton notes that foreign advisers have tended to be overly prescriptive and western-centric, and have largely failed to give adequate attention to Russian-language alternatives for reform. Instead they have preferred to believe that they are facilitating the '*replacement* of a failed legal experiment and parochial aberration (socialist law) by a proven success and putative global standard (market law)' often of American origin. Furthermore, they have wrongly promoted the view that the introduction of insolvency and pensions legislation is 'revolutionary', when in fact it can better—but less usefully, for those who seek a sense of 'urgency... , enabling them to realise ends that might otherwise have been frustrated'—be viewed as an 'incremental' change. Finally, 'the mutually reinforcing rhetoric of transition and transplantation, urgency and expertise, seems to serve indefinitely to defer matters of legitimation.' Newton concludes that '[w]hat legislative reconstruction needs is more politics, not less: the expansion of participation, the volubility of contest.'

In Chapter 12, Lakshman Marasinghe deliberates over the early stages of the transplantation process, exploring the various constitutional frameworks which Sri Lanka might adopt in order to resolve its ethnically-based conflict. He concludes that its current unitary constitutional structure—as inherited from colonial rule, and later adapted to allow a certain amount of decentralisation—does not 'provide a sufficient basis for a constitutional settlement of the Sri Lanka's ethnic problem.' He therefore looks outside of Sri Lanka for inspiration, to the federal model—used, for example, in Canada, Australia and the US—and the French bi-cephalous executive model.

Marasinghe argues that in the Sri Lankan government's view, it is non-negotiable that there shall be no 'mitosis of sovereignty'—that is, that island will not be divided 'into two separate states, both claiming to be independent and sovereign'. Although the separatist LTTE 'has not abandoned its quest for a sovereign state,' they have 'agreed to discuss the issue of what the final constitutional structure should be, and to that extent in their view the matter remains open.' Marasinghe believes that 'rather than pursuing their idea of a separate Eelam state, the LTTE might opt for a confederation,' under which independent sovereign states delegate their sovereignty to the centre. In Sri Lanka, this would involve establishing a separate state, but also going some way to appease the central government by rejoining as an equal confederate. However, this would involve a 'mitosis of sovereignty', with Eelam being free to retract the sovereignty it delegated to the centre at any time. '[T]he government may reject this line of constitutional development as the confederation model poses the in-built danger that it might be used as an alternative path to establishing a separate state Tamil state of Eelam.'

By contrast, the Australian/USA model of 'centrifugal federalism' may offer a plausible option to the two parties. Under this model, the flow of power is reversed, and powers 'move away from the central government and towards the regions.' The centre retains most of the powers, and there is 'devolution'—rather than mitosis—of sovereignty. The federal structure is flexible enough to allow 'greater latitude for power sharing' and the creation of 'co-ordinate', rather than 'subordinate' bodies. Marasinghe suggests that a close relationship between the centre and the regions might be fostered under a 'federal hybrid of a constitutional symbiosis' under which legislative and enforcement powers are separated and divided between the centre and the regions, forming a sort of 'constitutional hug'. This structure would be flexible enough to 'accommodate the French model of a divided slate of executive powers between the President and the Prime Minister.' The Presidency could be used to 'forge an axis with Parliament at the centre, and the regional bodies at the periphery' and the sovereignty of the federation could be 'shared among three distinct bodies—president and parliament at the centre, and the regions.' Importantly, this would open up 'a third avenue for engaging several ethnic and religious groups, as participants in the process of governing the island.'

In Chapter 13, Andrew Harding and Connie Carter make the case for borrowing the lessons, if not all of the content, of law and development in Singapore. They argue that 'rather like the psychiatrist who is good at diagnosing mental illness, but has no idea how mental well-being can come about other than through the absence of mental illness,' the '"law and development" movement has been unreasonably preoccupied with the problems rather than the solutions.' In particular, Harding and Carter are concerned that commentators and practitioners in the field are reticent to look for answers in existing success stories in East and South East Asia—perhaps because they fear that these countries are too unique to be relevant, or too far from the 'currently authorised version of law and development' to be acceptable. It seems that '[t]he more these countries develop economically the less they are seen as containing lessons or fields of study for law and development.' To illustrate the utility of examining experience in the region, they present the example of Singapore, arguing that '[n]o other society discussed in this book or elsewhere has made more thorough and successful use of law *for* development, at least if one defines development in purely economic terms.' They argue that Singapore takes a 'singularly "instrumentalist"' approach to law and development, with law 'seen primarily as an instrument of social engineering rather than as the expression of a particular balance of principles defined politically or culturally and regarded as the embodiment of a politically neutral justice.'

According to Harding and Carter, 'Singapore is too small and vulnerable to withstand the shock waves of a genuinely open society, and it must therefore maintain a rigid policy of social discipline and clearly defined, forcefully implemented, social objectives.' Using the example of labour law, the authors demonstrate that 'the Singapore model of law and development based on social and political discipline embodies a complex of interlocking elements.' Law is at the centre of this complex, and creates and/or enforces stability, equality, planning and discipline. These five elements are 'mutually reinforce[d]' by the economy, efficiency, development, unity and enforcement.

Contrary to some other contributions to the volume, they argue that 'the example of Singapore indicates clearly the advantages of formalisation. However, 'the very rigour of law enforcement and social engineering, and the inexorable subordination of everyone and everything to the common goal of economic development,' may have caused '[c]reativity, spontaneity, flexibility and intuitiveness' which are 'necessary for individual problem-solving skills and for finding the independent innovative solutions' to be 'inadvertently... "cloned out" of Singaporeans by the social engineers.' 'The complacency and docility that have replaced vibrancy, resilience and creativity might now in themselves be obstacles to continued successful development.' Harding and Carter conclude that the conditions of Singapore are too unique to repeat elsewhere. However, they do argue that 'there are many Singaporean devices, policies and legal instruments that could be adopted or adapted elsewhere to solve particular problems.'

... in securing broadly accessible justice

David McQuoid-Mason continues the theme of borrowing and transplantation in Chapter 14, this time at a regional level. He also introduces the further theme, echoed in the ensuing two chapters, of the complexities associated with securing access to the justice system for all members of society, and all subjects of contention.

McQuoid-Mason surveys the role of legal aid in the development of South Africa, and its implications for Nigeria. He acknowledges that the South African 'is by no means a perfect model for developing countries,' since it is much better resourced than many other African countries, including Nigeria. However, there 'are many parallels that emerge in respect of the delivery of legal services by the Legal Aid Council of Nigeria.' McQuoid-Mason suggests that '[i]n any country, the development and delivery of legal aid services depends upon a number of factors, including: the structure of the legal profession; the nature of the criminal justice system; the constitutional imperatives; the national legal aid structures; and the model of delivery used.'

Having outlined these aspects of the South African system, he draws a number of conclusions of relevance to both South Africa and Nigeria. First, he suggests that the best mechanisms for delivering legal aid services will be identified by reference to specific characteristics of the country in question—that is, 'the size and structure of the legal profession, the demands of the criminal justice system, their relevant constitutional imperatives, and the availability of adequate financial resources.' Second, he argues for the adoption of a 'holistic approach' to delivering legal aid services, using a combination of judicare, salaried lawyer and public defender models, and shaped by the level of demand for services. Echoing Marasinghe, he notes that several of the foreign models available cannot 'be directly transplanted from developed countries.' Third, he urges both South Africa and Nigeria to recognise that, in the context of limited human and financial resources, law students are 'a potentially valuable and inexpensive resource available to national legal aid structures.' Fourth, he suggests that Nigerian legal aid structures should follow the lead of South Africa and 'enter into co-operative legal aid arrangements with independent providers of legal services such as non-governmental public interest law firms.' Finally, 'national legal aid structures should work closely with para-legal advice offices as they are where people often first go for legal advice.'

In Chapter 15, Anton Cooray continues the theme of accessibility of justice, assessing the role of the judicial and administrative tribunals in environmental protection in Hong Kong. He notes that 'although the legislature began legislating for basic forms of environmental protection from the very beginning of its establishment in 1843, dedicated environmental legislation is a recent phenomenon.' The five major environmental laws (covering air pollution, water pollution, noise pollution, waste disposal and environmental impact assessment) form the backbone of environmental protection in Hong Kong. The system has adopted a 'pragmatic' rather than 'integrated' approach to environmental protection, 'enacting legislation dealing with specific areas of environmental concern.' Perhaps because they were 'passed at different times,' 'provisions relating to offences and to appeal matters are not uniform' and should be 'revised to achieve internal consistency.' Nonetheless, 'a fair degree of centralised policy formulation and implementation' is ensured 'by the conferment on the

Environmental Protection Department of enforcement and monitoring powers.' The five major environmental laws increased the role in litigation both of courts of law, and of administrative authorities such as the Environmental Protection Department, the Chief Executive of Hong Kong, and the Chief Secretary for the Environment and Food. Importantly, Cooray notes that many of the administrative bodies involved in environmental litigation do not provide public records of their decisions.

Turning to the ordinary law courts, Cooray explains that they have both supervisory (judicial review) and enforcement (criminal law) powers. With regard to the courts' criminal jurisdiction, Cooray argues that '[w]hile recognising the importance of protecting the environment at the cost of imposing some restrictions on fundamental rights, courts have been vigilant to see that no criminal prosecutions are instituted unless there is clear breach of the law.' Similarly, he notes that they have 'firmly held that mere technical irregularities in statutory notices and orders do not render such notices or orders invalid, so long as the alleged irregularities have not caused substantial injustice.' In dealing with judicial review cases, the 'courts have acted with restraint so as not to usurp the functions of the administration, but have not been slow to defend citizens' rights where the administration had been overzealous.'

Moving to the various environmental appeals boards, Cooray sets out a number of recommendations regarding administrative environmental decision-making made in board decisions. These cover matters such as the clarity of requirements in notices issued by administrative bodies to members of the public, and the need for those bodies to be more proactive—for example, by 'explaining to persons in breach of legislative provisions what could be done to regularise their activities such as by obtaining a licence.' Cooray is of the opinion that the specialist environmental appellate system 'is obviously a better safeguard than judicial review in many ways.' In particular, '[a]s administrative tribunals, environmental appeal boards are not only free of many procedural constraints that saddle legal proceedings, they are also free to examine the merits of the original decision, whereas judicial review is concerned with legality of administrative action.' Furthermore, members of the boards 'can bring to it a wide range of expertise, including legal expertise as its chairman has to be a lawyer qualified for appointment as a district judge.' However, Cooray notes an important failing of the ordinary courts and administrative boards—namely that they can only be used by a person or administrative body 'directly affected by an environmental decision.' Here the Ombudsman fills an significant gap, 'enabling the private citizen to institute a prosecution or to institute a civil action compelling the authority to exercise its enforcement powers.'

However, the Ombudsman's powers and jurisdiction are limited. Cooray therefore concludes that 'the next step in the development of environmental litigation in Hong Kong... appears to be provision for citizen suits,' and a 'serious examination of the extent to which citizens must be empowered to actively participate in environmental matters, not only by taking part in consultation processes, but also by ensuring that environmental laws and standards are properly implemented by direct involvement in enforcement.'

In Chapter 16, Beatrice Odonga-Mwaka considers the role of democracy in promoting access to justice for women at levels of the dispute resolution system in Uganda. She observes that since women 'are not only individuals but are members of family groups... [and] communities,' it is not possible to 'examine their individual rights without exploring their relationships with collective rights of groups to which they belong.' Furthermore, the various roles that women play in society—as 'daughters, single women, wives, mothers, childless or not, widows, aunts, grandmothers, in-laws'—can each give rise to conflict. There are a number of fora in which disputes involving women can be resolved, ranging from grassroots mediation to national court structures, which 'may often supplement each other in a way that caters for the needs and interests of differently situated women within complex relationships.'

Odonga-Mwaka goes on to analyse the impact on women of the introduction of democratic participation in Uganda following a 1986 military coup. On the question of whether women's concerns should be treated separately, or included in a broader list of issues facing society, Odonga-Mwaka observes that opinion is divided—on the one hand, inclusion in the national agenda may result in gender issues being 'subsumed' among other interests; on the other hand, it can 'be the key to ensuring that the issues are not marginalised.' The undemocratic nature of the introduction of democracy to Uganda increased the risk of marginalisation of women's concerns. 'Revolutionary struggles for a democratic government generally seek to liberate the whole society from the repression and brutality of a previous regime. It is the interests of the repressed as a whole that is expounded,' which 'often means that specific interests and identities are subordinated for the wider goal.' Revolution requires a sense of unity, and this requires that minority interests are set aside for a time'—perhaps with 'far reaching consequences for women.' However, Odonga-Mwaka is broadly positive about the outcome of revolution in Uganda.

A key reform under the new regime was the creation of elected Local Councils and Local Committee Courts at the village level, with direct links to regional and national level legislative, executive and judicial bodies. These 'grassroots' institutions have the advantages of being 'located within communities, require no legal expertise and are constituted wherever and whenever it is convenient, therefore cutting down on costs and time use.' The creation of new structures such as the Local Councils and Committee Courts in Uganda has 'created new ways of engagement, especially in providing solidarity and skills.' However, Odonga-Mwaka notes that the success of these institutions in improving the status of women can only be properly assessed by examining 'the involvement of women in the processes of the elections, their membership in the Councils and the extent of their use of the Committee Courts.' The introduction of affirmative action ensured not only that women came to be better represented in local and national institutions, but also that they were directly involved in the drafting of the new constitution for Uganda. In the process of constitutional drafting, '[w]omen got almost everything they asked for.'

'Women's alignment with the state is often necessary at the start of their struggle since the state has the machinery, resources and power to advance their cause.' But 'it is important to remember that in confronting indigenous structures and ideologues and practices, centres of power are located not only at the top policy level, but more so at grassroots level where attitudes and practices are more entrenched in the daily lived reality of people's lives.' In an attempt to achieve a balance between these competing concerns, the Ugandan state 'deliberately sought to work within the old structures to bring about changes within it, changes that would be appropriate to evolving customs and cultural practices.' In particular, the Local Council system rejects the rule followed in the traditional clan system that 'only kinship members could be part of the committee of decision-makers.' Instead, 'membership in the Council cuts across family and clan relationships' by making residence the criterion for standing for elections. 'Thus where tribes are mixed and living together in urban and rural communities, any person, including a non Ugandan can be a member of a Local Council. In areas where there are refugees as in southern Uganda with the Rwandese and Northern Uganda with Sudanese, one gets a mix of Local Council members.' In Odonga-Mwaka's personal experience, Uganda's women 'were divided along class, profession, experience and interests... and... working to keep the members united was one of the toughest challenges.' She concludes that '[a]t the end of the day, it is the group or groups that are discontented that must struggle for their cause,' but '[s]ometimes women in indigenous communities are the obstacles to the advancement of their own status.' Women must therefore begin by finding common ground across income, class, tribe and status.

PART 1

THEORETICAL DEVELOPMENTS

CHAPTER 2

'LAWS AND DEVELOPMENTS'

David Kennedy[*]

THE 'RULE OF LAW' *AS* DEVELOPMENT

Law and development is back—taught again in law faculties, the focus of policy initiatives at the leading development institutions, the subject of numerous books and conferences. Renewed interest in bringing law to bear in the struggle for development offers an opportunity to contest the distributive choices and market alternatives of development policy-making. Unfortunately, too often this has been an opportunity missed. The idea that building 'the rule of law' might *itself* be a development strategy instead encourages the hope that choosing law could substitute for the perplexing political and economic choices which have been at the centre of development policy-making for half a century. The legal regime offers an arena to contest those choices, but it cannot substitute for them. The hope that it might encourages people to settle on the particular choices embedded in one legal regime as if they were the only alternative.

The ideas about development which fuel contemporary interest in the law also seem to encourage the hope that law could simplify development policy-making, toning down its engagement with political and economic controversy. I encounter these ideas first in the classroom. In the First World settings where I have recently taught law and development, the field now draws numerous students from the broad centre-left of the political spectrum. Young people with humanitarian, progressive, generally cosmopolitan and internationalist sensibilities. The more technocratic specialists of the centre-right who flocked to the field in the eighties and early nineties seem to have retreated, or have come to express themselves in more restrained terms. But gone also are the social democratic internationalists of the fifties and sixties who inaugurated the field, and whose contributions we have celebrated here.

These contemporary students of law and development seem to share a mid-level conception of 'development policy'—neither a narrow matter of technical economic detail nor a broad vocabulary for political struggle, but something in between. In my experience, this is new. I may be idealising, but fifteen years ago, students of development policy in First World institutions were split between confident First Worlders for whom 'development' was a project of technical adjustment or economic management; and equally confident, if often angrier, students from developing societies for whom the term 'development' brought to mind the entire field of national—and international—political struggle. For both groups in those days, 'development' was a universal phenomenon. For the technocrats of the north, it meant the adjustment of developing societies to economic axioms of universal validity—growth is growth. For students from the south, development meant broad questions of political economy and social theory which must be confronted by all societies, regardless of their place in the world system—politics is politics.

[*]   Henry Shattuck Professor of Law, Harvard Law School. I would like to thank Duncan Kennedy and Scott Newton with whom I have taught law and development, David Trubek and Bob Meagher who first excited me about the field, and the extraordinary group of law and development students from whom I have learned so much in the last few years.

The last decade has chastened both groups. Today's First Worlders, in retreat from one-size-fits-all neo-liberalism, share an intuition that 'development' must mean something particular—to the specific market conditions of transitional or developing societies, and to the cultural setting of each national economy. They are often drawn to technical accounts of development's specificity—characteristic market failures in particular. Demand curves which don't slope gently off to the right, oligopolies, thin markets, peculiar information problems, transaction costs, sometimes even disparities in bargaining power. Third World students meet this intuition from the other direction—in flight from political generalities, they hope for a more technocratic development science. They aspire to participate in 'governance' rather than government, and are often drawn to more universal expressions of their political aspirations— human rights in particular.

For both groups, the economies and political systems of developing societies again seem to differ from those of the north and west—and to differ in ways which encourage attention to particular legal arrangements rather than universal economic or political theories. Development policy must be attuned to specific political, social and cultural conditions. Institutional issues are central. As politics and economics have become local, they seem to merge with the professional world of informed, empathetic and humble expertise. On the economic side, institutional economics, transaction cost problems and market failures are back. On the political side, attention to human rights, to cultural and social costs, to policy sequencing, planning, and the institutional mechanics of policy-making is in. All this places law, legal institutional building, the techniques of legal policy-making and implementation— the 'rule of law' broadly conceived—front and centre.

Unfortunately, however, this new interest in '*law and* development' is often accompanied by an ambition to leech the politics from the development process and to muddle the economic analysis. Students—like policy professionals—turn to law all too often in flight from economic analysis and political choice. As a teacher of 'law and development,' I start with the rather old-fashioned notion that development policy is a matter of both contestable political choices and sharp economic analysis—for neither of which is 'law' a substitute.

On the political side, I start from the idea that one makes policy to distribute—to give some people, groups, interests, more wealth, status, power, than they had before and to give other people less—and that law is interesting precisely as a distributional tool. To generate 'development' one needs to distribute in ways that will encourage development—get things into the hands of those whose return on their use will have the greatest multiplier effect. There are lots of different theories about how to do this—and they are economic theories. To count as a 'development policy,' a proposal needs to be rooted in an idea about how a distributional political choice will generate economic growth of whatever kind one considers likely to bring about 'development.' If development means more than a one-time growth spurt—means some sort of sustained, upward spiral, or some kind of socio-economic transformation—then one needs an idea about how a political choice will generate such a change. Where there turns out to be more than one equally efficient way to do this, the political choices among development policies become even more salient. There is politics, in other words, right at the start, in the distributive choices which underlie the aspiration for growth and development. This approach is, I admit, old fashioned—thinking about development as contestation about what should be distributed to and from whom in the service of economic growth and political vision. We might better call this 'rulership' than 'policy-making' or 'governance.'

Attention to the place of law in development often seems to bring with it a resistance to rulership—a flight from distribution and contestation. Partly this seems a retreat from the cold realisation that policy-making breaks eggs, imposes costs, *intervenes* in foreign places with a view to changing them. One encounters instead the vague sentiment that getting governance right, injecting the rule of law, enforcing human rights, will somehow bring a softer gentler development graciously in its wake. Partly the resistance to rulership arises from the intuition that political and economic debates about what development is and how to make it happen—questions to which the field has been host over the last half century—have not produced an *answer*. There is, it turns out, no technical consensus on how to bring about development. As a result, focus on politics or economics places the ruler in the awkward position of having to *choose*, to choose in a way which will have consequences for people, without clear guidance from a political consensus or economic theory. This makes people, particularly policy-makers who aspire to act from expertise, uncomfortable. The 'rule of law' promises an alternative—a domain of expertise, a programme for action, which obscures the need for distributional choices or for clarity about how distributing things one way rather than another will, in fact, lead to development. Unfortunately, this turns out to be a false promise. The focus on rights, on constitutions, on government capacity or judicial independence may all be to the good—but without a sharp sense for how one is intending to affect the economy, it is hard to compare building the rule of law with leaving the economy to operate more informally, and hard to compare building the rule of law one way with building it another.

In this, the focus on law as a development policy shares a great deal with other efforts to replace political and economic thinking with a general appeal to technical expertise and ideas about best practice. The result, by default or design, is a narrowing of the ideological range. Political choices fade from view—as do choices among different economic ideas about how development happens or what it implies for social, political and economic life. Where once there might have been ideological and theoretical contestation, there is a somewhat muddy consensus.

It need not be this way. One could focus on law in ways which sharpened attention to distributional choices and rendered more precise the consequences of different economic theories of development. In the days when people focused more overtly on economic theories of development, there were periods of contestation—and periods in which one or another idea drowned out all competitors. The neo-liberalism of the Washington Consensus was the last big theoretical consensus—chastening that idea by placing law and institutions in the picture might lead us back to more overt debates about economic strategy. But too often this is not the result—the turn to law has accompanied a chastening of the neo-liberal consensus, but in the name of vagueness rather than sharp economic debate.

Similarly, when development policy was understood in more overtly political terms, the result was often less contestation than ideological consensus—around a national import substitution idea in the fifties, or a free trade market shock idea in the nineties. Attention to the legal regime supporting these congealed ideological forms might heighten awareness of the choices involved in constructing either regime and help challenge the substitution of an ideological programme for political choice. But the precise opposite has more often been the case—attention to law has further muddied the waters, replacing attention to distributional and political alternatives with ideas about universal rights and technical judgments about 'the' appropriate legal regime for development. In a similar fashion, attention to the specifics of culture and place might lead us back to thinking about development policy as political choices among policy alternatives—but all too often attention to culture has led instead to hesitance about 'intervention' and policy-making, and to assessment of policy choices in a vague vocabulary of 'appropriateness' cut off from both political and economic analysis.

For me, attention to the role of law in development offers an opportunity to re-focus attention on the political choices and economic assumptions embedded in policy-making.

Elements in a legal order encode distributional choices and reflect economic and other ideological commitments. Their analysis could offer a retail level perspective on the stakes for economic and political contestation. Let me begin by affirming the centrality of law to development. Hernando de Soto, author of *The Mystery of Capital*—a book which quickly became a bestseller in development policy circles—is right to insist that 'capital' is a legal institution.[2] It is not just that you need a working legal regime to implement development policies—to collect tariffs, to manage monetary policy, to administer the state and so forth. de Soto rightly turns our attention to the background norms and institutions of ownership, exchange, money, security, risk, corporate form and so forth. Everything in a market is built on the back of norms, norms which remain, for the most part, in the background.

So far, so good. But it now gets more difficult... *what* law exactly? Is there 'a' rule of law suitable for development? Once we understand the centrality of law to capital formation and growth, can we simply inject 'the' rule of law as a development policy? It seems hard to deny the importance of some minimum national institutional functionality. But those who see the rule of law as a development strategy generally mean something more. Rather than the rule of law as a terrain for contestation, we have the rule of law as a recipe or readymade. There are two broad themes in the rule of law literature which sustain this sleight of hand, which position the rule of law as a substitute for politics and economics.

Those themes are formalisation and corruption—the notion that development requires a formalisation of law and the elimination of corruption. Each of these ideas has a long history in the rule of law literature, each suggests a set of tactics for policy-making. Each theme heightens the sense both that the rule of law can be injected without political choice, and that its implementation is a pre-condition to economic growth rather than a choice among alternative theories of development.

Each idea offers a rather simple vision of 'law,' which forgets much of what has become commonplace within the domain of legal theory for more than a century. It turns out that all the leading economic theories of development have implicit notions of what law is and what it can do. So do all the leading political ideas about how development should be defined and brought about. From a lawyer's point of view, these ideas about law expect the legal order to perform feats we know it rarely can accomplish, and expect law to remain neutral in ways we know it cannot. From inside the legal field, merging the 'rule of law' with formality and opposition to corruption seems a typical lay misunderstanding. Non-lawyers often think of law as a matter of neutral forms, or think of corruption as something easily defined and outlawed. Insiders to legal culture generally appreciate more readily the limits and alternatives of form, and the difficulty of defining or resisting corruption.

The surprising thing about 'law and development' today is the emergence of these simpler images within the legal field. Their presence suggests that some forgetting is going on. Part of what is forgotten is the range of possible legal arrangements, their association with alternative political and legal ideas, and their contestability. It is by unravelling these simplifying assumptions about the 'law' in 'law and development' that I hope we can return political and economic contestation to development policy-making.

---

[2]   de Soto, 2000.

FORMALISATION

Since at least Weber, people have asserted that 'formalisation' of entitlements, in one or another sense, is necessary for development. Necessary for transparency, for information and price signalling, to facilitate alienation of property, to reduce transaction costs, to assure security of title and economic return, to inspire the confidence and trust needed for investment, and so forth. From the start, formalisation has meant a wide variety of different things—a scheme of clear and registered title, of contractual simplicity and reliable enforcement, a legal system of clear rules rather than vague standards, a scheme of legal doctrine whose internal structure was logical and whose interpretation could be mechanical, a system of institutions and courts whose internal hierarchy was mechanically enforced, in which the discretion of judges and administrators was reduced to a minimum, a public order of passive rule following, a priority for private over public law, and more. These ideas are all associated with the reduction of discretion and political choice in the legal system, and are defended as instantiations of the old maxim 'not under the rule of man but of god and the law.'

It is easy to imagine, from the point of view of a particular economic actor, that formalisation in any of these ways might well enhance the chances for successful economic activity. A clear title may make it easier for me to sell my land, and cheaper for my neighbour to buy it. A clear set of non-discretionary rules about property, credit or contract might make a foreign legal culture more transparent to me as a potential investor. The reliable enforcement of contracts might make me more likely to trust someone enough to enter into a contract, and so forth. Indeed, it seems hard to imagine 'capital' except as a set of enforceable legal entitlements—a first lesson of law school is that property is less a relation between a person and an object than a relation between people with differing entitlements to use, sell, possess, or enjoy an object. All these themes are present in de Soto's book. The developing world is full of potential assets—but they have not been harnessed to productive use. Why? Because no one has clear title to them, nor are there predictable rules enforcing expectations about the return on their productive use.

The association of formalisation with development, however, has always seemed more problematic than this, also since at least Weber. For starters, it has also been easy to imagine, from the point of view of *other* economic actors, that formalisation in each of these ways might well eliminate the chance for productive economic activity. A clear title may help me to sell or defend my claims to land—but it may impede the productive opportunities for squatters now living there or neighbours whose uses would interfere with my quiet enjoyment. A great deal will depend on what we *mean* by clear title—which of the numerous possible entitlements which might go with 'title to property' we chose to enforce. Clear rules about investment may make it easy for foreign investors—but by reducing the wealth now in the hands of those with local knowledge about how credit is allocated or how the government will behave. An enforceable contract will be great for the person who wants the promise enforced, but not so for the person who has to pay up. As every first year contracts student learns, it is one thing to say stable expectations need to be respected, and quite another to say whose expectations need to be respected and what those expectations should legitimately or reasonably be. To say anything about the relationship between formalisation and *development*, we would need a theory about how assets in the hands of the title holder *rather than* the squatter, the foreign *rather than* the local investor, will lead to the sort of growth we associate with development.

The urge to formalise downplays the role of standards and discretion in the legal orders of developed economies. We might think here of the American effort to codify a 'Uniform

Commercial Code' to reflect the needs of businessmen—an effort which returned again and again to the standard of 'reasonableness' as a measure for understanding and enforcing contractual terms. We might remember Weber's account of the 'English exception'—the puzzle that industrial development seemed to come first to the nation with the most confusing and least formal system of property law and judicial procedure. Or we might think of Polyani's famous argument that rapid industrialisation was rendered sustainable, politically, socially and ultimately economically in Britain precisely because law slowed the process down.

The focus on formalisation downplays the role of the informal sector in economic life. It is not only in the post-transition economies of Eastern or Central Europe that the informal sector provided a vibrant source of entrepreneurial energy. The same could be said for many developing and developed economies. Think of the mafia, of the economic life of diasporic and ethnic communities. But think also of the 'old boys network,' the striking demonstrations in early law and society literature about the disregard businessmen in developed economies often have for the requirements of form or the enforceability of contracts. Think of routine debates within conventional schemes of contract about efficient breach, or within property about adverse possession. The informal sector is often an economically productive one. And there is also often security, transparency and reliability in the informal sector—the question is rather security for whom, transparency to whom?

The formalisation story downplays the range of possible formalisations, each with its own winners and losers. In a world with multiple potential stable and efficient equilibria, a great deal will depend upon the path one takes, and much of this will be determined by the choices one makes in constructing the system of background norms. Does 'being' a corporation mean having an institutional, administrative or contractual relationship with one's employees? With their children's day care provider? And so forth. Looking at the legal regime from the inside, we encounter a series of choices, between formality and informality, between different formalisations—each of which will make resources available to different people. What is missing from enthusiasm for the rule of law is both an awareness of the range of choices available *and* an economic theory about the developmental consequences of taking one rather than another path.

In a particular developing society, for example, it might be that the existing—discretionary, political, informal—system for allocating licenses or credit is entirely predictable and reliable for some local players even where it is not done in accordance with published rules. At the same time it might not be transparent to or reliable for foreign investors. This might encourage local and discourage foreign participation in this economic sector. We might well have a political theory of development which suggests that one simply cannot have access to a range of *other* resources necessary to develop without pleasing foreign direct investors. Or we might have an economic theory suggesting that equal access to knowledge favours investment by the most efficient user *and* that this user will in turn use the profits from that investment in ways more likely to bring about 'development,' perhaps based on a projection of how foreign, as opposed to local investors will invest their returns. But the need for such theories—which would themselves be quite open to contestation—is obscured by the simpler idea that development requires a 'formal' rule of law.

Interest in the rule of law as a development strategy gets in trouble when it replaces more conventional questions of development policy and planning which demand decisions about distribution. Traditional questions about who will do what with their surplus, how gains might best be captured and reinvested or capital flight eliminated. Or about how one might best take spillover effects into account and exploit forward or backward linkages. Or questions about the politics of tolerable growth and social change, about the social face of development itself, about the relative fate of men and women, rural and urban, in different stable equilibria, along different policy paths.

We might return to de Soto here for an example, although he is far from alone in his disinterest in the distributional choices one must make in designing a rule of law suitable for a policy of 'formalisation.' In discussing land reform, de Soto is adamant that squatters should be given title to the land on which they have settled to create useful capital by permitting them to eject trespassers. His implicit assumption that squatters will make more productive use of the land than the nominal current owners may well often be correct. But he provides no reason for supposing that the squatters will be more productive than the trespassers. Nor for concluding that exclusive use by one or the other group is preferable to some customary arrangement of mixed use by squatters and trespassers in the shadow of an ambiguous law.

None of these observations is new. Development planners and practitioners have long struggled with precisely these problems. The puzzle is how easily one loses sight of these traditional issues of political and economic theory when the words 'rule of law' come into play. There is something mesmerising about the idea that a formal rule of law could somehow substitute for struggle over these issues and choices—could replace contestable arguments about the consequences of different distributions with the apparent neutrality of legal best practice.

CORRUPTION

A second theme running through enthusiasm for treating the 'rule of law' *as* a development strategy is the desire to eliminate corruption. Like formalisation, the elimination of corruption is linked to development in a variety of ways. Eliminating corruption is promoted to avoid squandered resources, to promote security and predictability, to inspire confidence, eliminate price distortions and promote an efficient distribution of resources. These things will lead, in some way, to development. Many of the advantages of corruption run parallel to those of formalisation—eliminating corruption can seem much like eliminating judicial and administrative discretion. Indeed, sometimes 'corruption' is simply a code word for public discretion—the state acts corruptly when it acts by discretion rather than mechanically, by rule.

And it is not implausible to imagine that eliminating corruption will enhance the chances for some economic actors to make productive use of their entitlements. The state's discretion, including the discretion to tax, and even the discretion to levy taxes higher than those authorised by formal law, may spur some and retard other economic activity. As with formalisation more generally, however, it is also not difficult to imagine that other actors—including those who are collecting 'corrupt' payments—will in turn be less productive once corruption is eliminated. As with the replacement of discretion by form, it is necessary to link elimination of corruption to an idea about the likely developmental consequences of one rather than another set of economic incentives. A simple example would be: Who is more likely to productively reinvest the profits, the marginal foreign investor brought in as corruption declines, or the marginal administrator whose take on transactions is eliminated? In my experience, such questions are rarely asked, and yet their answer is not at all obvious. We are back to the need for a political and economic theory about which allocation will best spur development.

Enthusiasm for eliminating corruption as a development strategy arises from the broader idea that corruption somehow drains resources from the system as a whole—its costs are costs of transactions, not costs of the product or service purchased. Elimination of such costs lifts all boats. And such costs might as easily be quite formal and predictable as variable and discretionary. Here the desire to eliminate corruption goes beyond the desire for form— embracing the desire to eliminate all costs *imposed* on transactions which are not properly costs *of* the transaction. There are at least two difficulties here. First, the connection between eliminating corruption and 'development' remains obscure. Even if the move from a 'corrupt' legal regime to a 'not corrupt' regime produces a one time efficiency gain, there is no good economic theory predicting that this will lead to growth or development, rather than simply another stable low level equilibrium. More troubling is the difficulty of distinguishing clearly between the 'normal' or 'undistorted' price of a commodity and the 'costs' associated with a 'corrupt' or distortive process for purchasing the commodity or service.

Economic transactions rely on various institutions for support, institutions which lend a hand sometimes by form and sometimes by discretion. But the tools these institutions, including the state, use to support transactions are difficult to separate from those which seem to impose costs on the transaction. The difference is often simply one of perspective—if the cost is imposed on you it seems like a cost, if it is imposed on someone else for your benefit it seems like support for your productive transaction. Here the desire to eliminate corruption bleeds off in a variety of directions. But the boundary between 'normal' and 'distorted' regulation is the stuff of political contestation and intensely disputed economic theory. When the anti-corruption project suggests that the 'rule of law' always already knows how to draw this line, it fades into a stigmatising moralism, akin to the presentiment against the informal sector.

de Soto again provides a good illustration. He is adamant that the number of bureaucratic steps involved in formalising entitlements retards development, and he has been a central voice urging simplification of the bureaucratic procedures which he sees as mud in the gears of capital formation and commerce. Every minute and every dollar spent going to the state to pay a fee or get a stamp is a resource lost to development. This seems intuitively plausible. But there is a difficulty: When is the state supporting a transaction by formalising it and when is the state burdening the transaction by adding unnecessary steps or costs? The aspiration seems to be an economic life without friction, each economic act mechanically supported without costs. But forms, like acts of discretion, are not simply friction—they are choices, defences of some entitlements against others. Everything which seems friction to one economic actor will seem like an entitlement, an advantage, an opportunity to another. The point is to develop a theory for choosing among them.

Let us say we begin by defining corruption as the economic crimes of public figures— stealing tax revenues, accepting bribes for legally mandated services and so forth. Even here the connection to development is easier to assume than to demonstrate: Are these figures more or less likely to place their gains unproductively in foreign bank accounts than foreign investors, say? Even if we define the problem narrowly as one of theft or conversion it is still difficult to be confident that the result will be slower growth. Sometimes, as every first year property instructor is at pains to explain, it is a good idea to rearrange entitlements in this way, adverse possession being the most dramatic example. Practices one might label as 'corrupt' might sometimes be more efficient means of capital accumulation, mobilising savings for local investment. Moreover, rather few economic transactions are best understood as arms length bargains. It turns out, for example, that the lion's share of international trade is conducted through barter, internal administratively priced transactions, or relational contracts between repeat players. The line between tolerable and intolerable differences in bargaining power—between consent and duress—is famously a site for political contestation. And, just as sometimes what look like market distorting interventions can also be seen to compensate for one or another market failure, so what look like corrupt local preferences can turn out to be efficient forms of price discrimination.

But those promoting anti-corruption as a development strategy generally have something more in mind—a pattern of economic crimes which erodes faith in a government of laws in general or actions by public (or private) actors which artificially distort prices—unreasonable finders fees, patterns of police enforcement which protect mafia monopolies, things of that sort.

Here, the focus moves from the image of public officials taking bribes outward to actions which distort free market prices or are not equally transparent to local and foreign, private and public, interests. Corruption becomes a code word for 'rent-seeking'—for using power to extract a higher price than that which would be possible in an arms length or freely competitive bargain—and for practices which privilege locals. At this point, the anti-corruption campaign gets all mixed up with a broader programme of privatisation, deregulation and free trade (dismantling government subsidies and trade barriers, requiring national treatment for foreign products and enterprises). And with background assumptions about the distortive nature of costs exacted by public as opposed to private actors.

Here the project enters arenas of deep contestation. It has been famously difficult to distinguish administrative discretion which prejudices the 'rule of law' from judicial and administrative discretion which characterises the routine practice of the 'rule of law.' It has been equally difficult to distinguish legal rules and government practices which 'distort' a price from the background rules in whose shadow parties are thought to bargain. And there is no *a priori* reason for identifying public impositions on the transaction as distortions—costs of the transaction—and private impositions as costs of the good or service acquired. These matters might be disputed in political or economic terms. But the effort to treat corruption reduction as a development strategy substitutes a vague sense of the technical necessity and moral imperative for a 'normal' arrangement of entitlements.

It is easy to interpret the arrangement of entitlements normalised in this way in ideological terms. When the government official uses his discretionary authority to ask a foreign investor to contribute to this or that fund before approving a license to invest, that is corruption. When the investor uses his discretionary authority to authorise investment to force a government to dismantle this or that regulation, that is not corruption. When pharmaceutical companies exploit their intellectual property rights to make AIDS drugs largely unavailable in Africa while using the profits to buy sports teams, not corruption, when governments tax imports to build palaces, corruption.

Perhaps the most telling problem is the difficulty of differentiating some prices and transactions as 'normal' and others as 'distorted' by improper exercises of power when every transaction is bargained in the shadow of rules and discretionary decisions, both legal and non-legal, imposed by private and public actors, which could be changed by political contestation. This old American legal realist observation renders incoherent the idea that transactions, national or international, should be allowed to proceed undistorted by 'intervention' or 'rent-seeking.' There is simply no substitute for asking whether the particular intervention is a desirable one—politically and economically. In this sense, seeking to promote development by eliminating 'corruption' replaces economic and political choice with a stigmatising ideology.

THE LEGAL REGIME: SITE FOR CONTESTATION AND EXPERIMENTATION

Development strategy requires a detailed examination of the distributional choices effected by various legal regimes and rules to determine, as best one can, their likely impact on growth and development. It requires that we identify the choices which might lead to different development paths and compare them in social, political and economic terms. These choices cannot be avoided, even if we lack a strong consensus or decisive expertise about how to make them. One makes policy to distribute—by price, by administrative action—hoping to allocate resources to their most productive, most developmentally promising, use. It is unfortunate that there is no distributional recipe for development, but that is our situation. There are contending ideas, contending interests, contested theories, complex unknowables. Not knowing, we must decide. We might even experiment.

As a result, politics can't wait until later. Development is not a matter of 'growth plus' but of 'what growth how.' Of course, as we pursue any development path there will *also* be struggles about how to deploy resources for *other* objectives. But the struggle for development itself—the struggle to grow the pie in the first place—is also and unavoidably a place of political and economic choice. Choices which are contested. Building a legal regime involves choices, choices implicate distributive objectives which contribute to development in different ways. Sometimes, no doubt, increasingly formal rules would be a good idea. Sometimes less governmental discretion, sometimes more vigorous criminal enforcement, broader distribution of supply relationships, less local preference in contracting, all might be very helpful. But sometimes we would also expect the opposite.

The law is a terrain for this inquiry, not a substitution for it. There is no doubt that 'law' is central to development. The market rests on a set of legal arrangements. Formal arrangements and informal arrangements. Arrangements of public action and inaction. Of private and public entitlements. The rule of law is a collection of enforced distributions. Economic activity conducted on this foundation sometimes leads to growth, and sometimes to development. It seems completely plausible that different distributions will yield different economic results, and that attention to law in the development process would heighten our awareness of the choices available to us.

The emergence of the 'rule of law' as a development strategy has become a substitute for assessments of this sort. Opposing corruption leverages a shared moral opprobrium, promoting a formal rule of law leverages a common ethical commitment—harnesses them to legal and institutional changes which will strengthen some economic efforts and retard others while leaving their developmental consequences obscure. Much as we might wish it, there is no single 'rule of law' whose establishment will generate development. We know that. But we forget. Forget because remembering would take us straight back to politics, economics and to the enduring dilemmas of development policy-making.

REFERENCES

de Soto, H, *The Mystery of Capital: Why Capitalism Triumphs in the West and Fails Everywhere Else*, 2000, London: Bantam Books

CHAPTER 3

DECISION-MAKING IN A REGULATORY ENVIRONMENT: REPRESENTING THE BUTTERFLY

Amanda Perry-Kessaris[*]

'Policy-makers have long been encouraged to believe in the check-list mentality which lies at the heart of conventional economics. Do A, B and C, and the consequence *will* be X. But this offers merely the illusion of control rather than the reality.'[1]

Butterflies are paradoxically entrancing creatures. Their appeal lies in the contrast between the symmetry of their structure and markings on the one hand, and their errant flutterings on the other. But how do you effectively present the complexities of the butterfly? Do you efficiently pin it down and mount it on the wall? Do you loosely observe it in its natural habitat? Or do you adopt a middle course, perhaps popping it into the lepidopteran equivalent of the aviary?

For those who study the role of law in economic development, the behaviour of decision-makers presents a similarly seductive quandary. We are drawn to the contrast between their occasional rhythm and consistency on the one hand; and to their contrasting independence and entrepreneurial flair on the other. How do you effectively present the complexities of the decision-maker? Do you efficiently map them out in a series of equations based on strict and often unrealistic assumptions, in the manner of the traditional economist? Do you observe them more loosely in their natural habitat, in the manner of the anthropologist? Or do you adopt a middle course, considering them as organic beings framed by a mathematical cage?

These choices are central to the study of decision-making, which in turn is central to the study of regulation, which in turn is central to the study of law and economic development. If we are to harness or constrain the market for the purposes of promoting economic development, we must affect the decisions of those individuals who shape it.

This paper critically assesses some of the major contributions of the economic approach to the understanding of decision-making. Its aim is to highlight the utility and limits of the economic approach to the subject, with a view to encouraging a deeper level of co-ordination between the fields of regulation, law and development and economics.

REGULATORY TOOLS AND THE DECISION-MAKER

The importance of individual decision-making to law and economic development can be illustrated by reference to the example of a government wishing to ensure that its citizens have access to affordable, high quality telecommunication services. If we imagine, as is increasingly the case, that such services are to be provided by the private sector, then the government's involvement in the process will be that of referee of private sector decision-making, rather than that of direct provider. According to Baldwin and Cave, such a government might adopt any of six regulatory strategies in order to guide the behaviour of the private sector (Table 1).[2]

---

[*]   Lecturer, Department of Law, Queen Mary (London), Mile End Road, London E1 4NS, a.j.perry-kessaris@qmul.ac.uk.
[1]   Ormerod, 1998, xiii. Original emphasis
[2]   Baldwin and Cave, 1999, Chapter 4.

Table 1: Regulatory strategies and behaviour of decision-makers[3]

Tool	Nature	Example	Decision-maker initially affected
Financial incentive	Grants, subsidies, loans	Subsidy for rural telecommunications providers.	Regulated
Market forces	Harnessing competition between producers for benefit of consumers	Franchise auction of telecommunication licenses for affordability & quality.	Regulated
Command	Criminal sanction	Custodial sentence for failures in quality or cost (!)	Regulators
Direct action	Physical action by state	Close unaffordable/low quality provider.	Regulators
Information	Market empowerment of individuals	Affordability & quality league table.	Third parties
Protected rights	Legal empowerment of individuals	Consumer's right to value for money.	Third parties

The utility of each regulatory strategy is dependent upon the extent to which the regulation successfully affects the behaviour of a particular category of decision-maker. As Table 1 shows, the financial incentive strategy must directly affect the behaviour of telecommunications providers (the 'regulated') by making them choose to provide services to rural areas. The command strategy must directly affect the behaviour of members of government or quasi-governmental bodies (the 'regulators'), by making them choose to prosecute those who fail to reach quality or cost targets. The information strategy must directly affect the behaviour of members of the public ('third parties'), by making them the buy the cheapest and/or highest quality product.

The lesson to be draw from this highly simplified representation of the regulatory process is that successful regulation is dependent upon understanding how decision-makers actually make their choices, and how those choices can be influenced.[4] The contribution of economic theory to understanding this process is the subject of the following sections.

---

[3] Adapted from *ibid*.

[4] Obviously the command and information strategies should then indirectly affect the behaviour of the 'regulated' by making them choose not to break the quality and cost standards, in order to avoid prosecution; and making them reduce costs and increase quality, in order to retain customers; respectively.

THE TRADITIONAL VIEW: PERFECT DECISION-MAKING IN SPLENDID ISOLATION

Devoted as it is to the study of choice, economics is a natural reference point for approaching this question. It offers a clear set of tools with which we can attempt to predict and explain decision-making. It deals with inputs and outputs which appear to be measurable, thus lending themselves to experimentation and proof. This air of certainty which economic theory engenders is comforting. So comforting indeed, that economics has become a sort of unassailable lingua franca (although sometimes poorly translated or misunderstood) for the analysis of decision-making. This is particularly the case among international development organisations, which are dominated by economists, and are in many ways the leaders of modern law and development thinking and action.

Like most disciplines, economics has its rebels. Some exhibit many of the hallmarks of 'self-estrangement' that ushered in an era of hibernation in the field of law and development.[5] For example, in the introduction to *The Price of Onions*, former economic adviser to the Indian government Ashok Desai notes that '[e]conomists pretend to be like doctors: they claim to have cures for the ills of an economy, and formulae to help people earn more and work less. But no one can drop into an economist's clinic and buy a magic formula.'[6]

However, unlike their colleagues in law and development, most sceptical economists do appear to find overall solace in their discipline. Desai concludes his introduction on a more hopeful note, arguing that 'a smattering of economics enables one to see quite ordinary events in a more interesting light... It is a bit like scuba diving; seascapes look very different, more brilliant and colourful, if one dives with a mask than if one watches them from a boat.'[7] This image would be as damning as it is charming, if it were not for Desai's final remark that '[e]conomics helps one bring out the hidden meaning of day-to-day phenomena.'[8]

In the right hands, economics is indeed a colourful and interesting discipline. But its ability to describe, explain and predict messy reality, as opposed to clear abstraction, has always been the subject of vigorous debate. Some have argued that it is only in recent years, and only at the fringes, that economists have begun once again to focus their attentions specifically upon the challenge of dragging the analysis of decision-making into the real world.[9]

According to the traditional economic framework, our decision-makers (whether the regulator, the regulated or third parties) will choose their course of action on the basis of a cost-benefit analysis of all possible options. In theory, all the government need do is create a regulation which ensures that a decision-maker would derive more benefits than costs from acting in the desired fashion. In theory, the decision-maker will then make the desired choice.

Importantly, this neat traditional economic framework is dependent upon a number of strict assumptions. The first assumption is that decision-makers have fixed preferences—that is, they know how much they like apples and oranges, and they know how much they are willing to buy of each, depending on their relative availability and price. Other people's tastes will not affect an individual's preferences. Other important assumptions are that decision-

---

5   See Trubek and Galanter, 1974.
6   Desai, 1999, p ix.
7   *Ibid*, p xvii.
8   *Ibid*.
9   Ormerod, 1998, p 59 and Chapter 5.

makers make rational choices (although it is accepted that individuals do sometimes behave irrationally, the effects of these occurrences are assumed to cancel each other out); have the capacity, the desire and the necessary information to weigh up each possible course of action; and are guided by the sole aim of promoting their own welfare.[10]

Scholars in the field of law and economics apply this theory, including its assumptions, to the analysis of the relationship between law and economic behaviour. They argue that laws should be 'efficient'—that is, they should make it clear to decision-makers that the benefits of compliance outweigh the costs—if they are to successfully manipulate decision-making. But the validity of the assumptions on which traditional micro-economic theory, and spin-offs such as law and economics, are based has increasingly been called into question. So much so that it is unclear if we know enough about decision-making to regulate markets effectively.

THE INSTITUTIONALIST VIEW: IMPERFECT DECISION-MAKERS AND IMPERFECT INSTITUTIONS

A serious attack on the assumptions of traditional micro-economic theory came from the Institutionalist schools of economics. Neo-Institutional Economics in particular attacks economic theory for its unrealistic, narrow, over-mathematised and abstract view of the world. Institutionalists make two important qualifications to the traditional micro-economic theory favoured by the Chicago school.

First, they argue that in reality, decision-makers do not operate in isolation. In fact, their behaviour affects, and is affected by, the institutional environment. In particular, decision-makers take account of the 'search and information costs, bargaining and decision costs, and policing and enforcement costs,' associated with engaging in any transaction. As Coase explained, the role of the legal institutions is to reduce those costs as much as possible.[11]

But as Neo-Institutionalists argue, legal institutions may themselves add to transaction costs. For example, if a potential telecommunications provider is considering whether to enter into the market, they will weigh up the costs of applying (including institutional transaction costs, such as delays) against the benefits (such as obtaining a subsidy). If the costs of delays outweigh the benefits of obtaining the subsidy, they will not apply.[12] The importance of institutional transaction costs has been a major motivating force behind the legal reform agenda of development organisations, with the result that a vast array of developing country legal institutions have been subjected to transaction costs reducing measures.[13]

The second qualification introduced by Institutionalists is that decision-makers operate within the confines of 'bounded rationality'—that is, they are constrained by limited information and by their limited ability to analyse it.[14] As a result, their decisions may not succeed in maximising their welfare. Returning to our example, a potential telecommunications provider who does not have access to information about institutional

---

[10] See, for example, Cooter and Ulen, 1996, Chapter 2.

[11] Coase, 1988, pp 6-7.

[12] *Ibid*, pp 8-10.

[13] However, the lessons of transaction costs have not been uniformly learnt. For example, a 1996 study by the World Bank notes that programmes seeking to ensure factory compliance with environmental standards still fail to take account of the enforcement costs which the state must bear: Afsah, La Plante and Wheeler, 1996.

[14] See, for example, Katz, 1998, pp 231-33.

delays, or the capacity to calculate the benefits of a subsidy, it will not be factored in to decision-making.

Perhaps because its effects are difficult to quantify, the importance of bounded rationality has rarely been directly addressed in the international legal reform agenda. As the World Bank noted in a report on regulation of industrial pollution in developing countries, 'a regulatory approach based on inappropriate assumptions about information and transactions costs has distracted policy analysts from the real implementation issues in developing-country agencies.'[15] The report concludes that, 'the traditional emphasis on "appropriate instruments", while ultimately correct, is premature because most developing-country agencies have too many information and transactions costs problems to implement and instruments in a comprehensive manner.'[16]

BUTTERFLY ECONOMICS: IMPERFECT DECISION-MAKERS INTERACTING UNPREDICTABLY

A more radical assault on the underlying assumptions of traditional micro-economic theory comes from Paul Ormerod's study entitled *Butterfly Economics*. He attacks the traditional view of markets as a machine, arguing that it is more realistic to view markets as living organisms, operating at the brink of chaos.

Ormerod's most significant contribution for our purposes is to explore the impact of interactive decision-making upon the ability of governments to regulate the behaviour of economic actors. He argues that, contrary to conventional theory, decision-makers do not have *fixed* ideas (preferences) as to what they want; do not make choices in an isolation tank; and, therefore, do not make predictable decisions. In fact decisions are made either on the basis of past decisions, on the basis of new information, or on the basis of the decisions (expressions of preferences) made by others. It is rarely possible to determine on which basis decisions will be made, and therefore, what those decisions will be.

Importantly, the traditional economic approach only allows for the possibility that decision-makers interact in the narrowest of senses. Returning to our example, a potential telecommunications provider will weigh up the costs of applying (including the institutional transaction costs) against the benefits (including the possibility that they might be awarded a subsidy). Imagine that the greater the number of potential providers, the greater the institutional transaction costs (for example, delay) of applying for a subsidy. The cost of obtaining the subsidy will increase. Traditional economic theory allows for the possibility that the potential provider may be indirectly affected by the choice of others, to the extent that as the number of other decision-makers choose to apply, our decision-maker will be increasingly less likely to choose to apply. However, the traditional economic analysis does not allow for the possibility that a potential telecommunications provider might be directly encouraged or discouraged from applying, simply on the grounds that everyone else is doing it.[17] That is, traditional economic theory does not allow for the concept of trendiness.

The importance of trendiness, and the difficulty of predicting it, is the focus of Ormerod's work. According to Ormerod's model, our potential telecommunications providers might

---

[15]   Afsah, La Plante and Wheeler, 1996, s 4. The 'real implementation issues' are constraints relating to information, bureaucracy, human and technical resources: *ibid*, s 3.

[16]   *Ibid*, 1996, s 5.

[17]   Ormerod, 1998, p 61.

choose to enter the market (or not) either because that is what they have done before, or because they have some new information which appears to indicate that this now the correct choice, or because everyone else is doing it. Since we cannot predict on which basis an individual decision will be made, it is impossible to know how what their decision will be, and consequently impossible to develop strategies for guiding them to the 'right' decisions.

That the choice of one individual might affect the choices of others makes clear common sense. Why else would anyone wear a tie? What else can account for the dreaded rise of the mullet haircut? How else can one explain continued investment in a stock market which everyone agrees is overvalued (such as the recent unhealthy obsession with internet stocks); or the apparently arbitrary trouncing of products such as the Betamax video format by their technologically inferior rivals—in this case, VHS.[18] These outcomes are not rational, and are not based on economically 'good' information. They are, quite simply, trendy.

If interactive decision-making makes common sense, then why have economists ignored it for so long? In a chapter entitled 'Use the Maths, then Burn It', Ormerod argues that in the days before their discipline became over-mathematised, economists were much more willing to attempt to address the complexities of decision-making, despite the absence of the mathematical tools necessary to prove their conclusions. An important factor in the general failure of modern economics to consider interactive decision-making is that the mathematical tools necessary to deal with this possibility were not developed until the 1980s.[19] Similarly, Coase argued that most economists prefer to dwell in the fanciful world of 'blackboard economics'—that is, the kind of economics in which 'all the information needed is assumed to be available and the teacher plays all the parts,' and issues which do not lend themselves to such abstraction are ignored.[20] In his view, economists have little interest in or understanding of the institutions and individuals who make the choices, so that 'the rational utility maximiser of economic theory bears no resemblance to the man on the Clapham bus, or indeed, to any man (or woman) on any bus.'[21]

SOME PRELIMINARY LESSONS FOR LAW
AND ECONOMIC DEVELOPMENT

Putting aside the question of 'why?' and moving to the question 'who cares?', what lessons might the butterfly approach present for the study of law and economic development? If Ormerod's observations are correct, then regulating the market for the purposes of promoting economic development is more complicated than traditional economic theory would suggest.

As Table 2 indicates, the broad conclusion to be drawn from the butterfly approach is that in the short term, the prediction of individual choices and patterns of choice is often impossible.[22] Efforts at short term interventions and quick fixes are a false comfort.

It is important not to take this argument too far. When you heat a volume of gas, the individual atoms fly all over the place, and predictions of their individual movements are

---

[18] *Ibid*, pp 20 and 23.
[19] *Ibid*, Chapter 5. Ormerod's work relies on non linear probability which can be used to describe situations in which an increase in one dimension may result in either an increase, a decrease, or no change at all in the other dimension at any given time.
[20] Coase, 1988, pp 1, 8-10, 13-20 and 158.
[21] *Ibid*, pp 3-5.
[22] Ormerod, 1998, pp 182-203.

wrong—but the overall effect of a rise in pressure is correctly predicted by rules about the relationships between temperature, volume and pressure. So, just because individual actors do not follow nicely prescribed rules does not mean that we might not get useful predictions of the collective, average response.[23] We just need to be aware of the limitations of our predictions.

Patterns of choice *can* be predicted in the long-term. As a consequence, long-term approaches to regulation have a much higher chance of success. However, despite the fact that 'accurate short-term prediction is at best difficult and at worst impossible,' it is still the case that '[m]uch government intervention is motivated by specific, short-term ends, and depends crucially on the idea that the economy and/ or society is a predictable machine.' Add to this that '[s]mall changes can have big consequences and vice versa,' and that '[p]olicies can also have seemingly perverse effects,' and economics feels a lot less comforting.[24]

Table 2: Assumptions and conclusions of economic approaches to decision-making

Traditional	Institutional	Butterfly
Decision-makers:	Decision-makers:	Decision-makers:
Know what they want;	Know what they want;	Have the desire (but not always capacity or information) to weigh up costs & benefits of all options; and
Have the desire, capacity & information to weigh up costs & benefits of all options; and	Have the desire (but not always capacity or information) to weigh up costs & benefits of all options;	
	Try to make rational choices to promote their welfare; and	Try to make rational choices to promote their welfare; but
Always make rational choices which successfully promote their welfare.	Will attempt to take account of institutional transaction costs.	In fact choose on the basis of past choices, new information, or the choices of others.
Therefore: with the right mathematical tools, choices are broadly easy to predict and influence.	Therefore: with the right mathematical tools, and access to data about transaction costs, capacity and information, choices are fairly easy to predict and influence.	Therefore: with the right mathematical tools, patterns of choice can be predicted and influenced in the long-term; but in the short term, individual choices and patterns of choice are often impossible to predict and therefore influence.

---

[23] Thanks to my father, Chris Perry, for putting that point so nicely in an email.
[24] Ormerod, 1998, p xiii.

Ormerod's musings on butterflies raise the need for widespread and deep-rooted reassessment of the limitations of regulation. It also raises a number of questions of more specific interest to the field of law and economic development. In particular, if traditional economic theory is unable to deal with the more complex interactive version of decision-making proposed by Ormerod, it is certainly unable to deal with the possibility that such complex decision-making varies in different cultural contexts. This issue is of huge significance for the study of law and economic development, which seeks to find effective ways of harnessing and constraining the power of the market in vastly different environments.

Take the example of variations in levels of individualism among different societies. Geert Hofstede's Individualism Index tells us about the extent to which people in a range of cultures think of themselves primarily as an individual; or as a member of a group.[25] In a collectivist society, 'the personal relationship prevails over the task and should be established first'. By contrast, in an individualist society, 'the task is supposed to prevail over any personal relationships'.[26] Having made an investment in personal relationships, the collectivist has a foundation of understanding and trust on which to build. As a result, many things 'which in collectivist cultures are self-evident must be said explicitly in individualist cultures'. For example, 'American business contracts are much longer than Japanese business contracts'.[27]

When placed in the context of Ormerod's findings about decision-making, the distinction between individualist and collectivist societies provokes some fascinating questions. Might decision-makers in a more collectivist (rather than individualist) society be more likely to make 'interactive' choices. Is the likelihood that decision-makers will choose to follow the actions of others higher in more collectivist societies. If so, might the content of law become less important than societal norms? That is, will regulators decide not to prosecute, or consumers decide not to sue for compensation, simply because no one else is?

Hofstede notes that economics is essentially an 'individualist science' dominated by thinkers from 'strongly individualistic countries' such as the UK and USA. As a consequence, its 'assumptions are unlikely to apply' in collectivist societies, in which the interests of the group are placed above those of the individual.[28] The extent of the inapplicability of economic assumptions is a key area for future research by those concerned with the relationship between law and development.

BEWARE ECONOMISTS BEARING GIFTS

So, how do you effectively present the complexities of the decision-maker? Do you efficiently map them out in a series of equations based on strict and often unrealistic assumptions, in the manner of the traditional economist? Do you observe them more loosely in their natural

---

[25] Hofstede, 1997, pp 49-54. For more on the significance of Hofstede's findings for the study and practice of law and development, see Perry, 2002. IDV scores were based on responses to questions such as: 'Try to think of those factors which would be important to you in an ideal job; disregard the extent to which they are contained in your present job. How important is it to you to... Have a job which leaves sufficient time for your personal or family life... Have considerable freedom to adopt your own approach to the job' and so on. As Hofstede notes, these issues do not cover the full range of distinctions between individualism and collectivism in society. However, correlations between these IBM findings and studies of 'other characteristics of societies confirm (validate) the claim that this dimension from the IBM data does, indeed, measure individualism': *ibid*, pp 51-52.

[26] *Ibid*, p 67.

[27] *Ibid*, p 60.

[28] *Ibid*, p 72.

habitat, in the manner of the anthropologist? Or do you adopt a middle course, considering them as organic beings framed by a mathematical cage? Each course of action requires a trade-off. The key is to identify the nature and the significance of the trade-off, bearing in mind the specific task at hand.

An important rule for law and development is to treat claims of other disciplines to 'brilliant and colourful' revelations with caution. 'The predictive limits of empirical research favours an incremental, highly contextual approach to developing new legal initiatives intended to alter people's behaviour.'[29] Draw on other disciplines, but understand their limitations, and listen to the rebels within them.

REFERENCES

Baldwin, R and Cave, M, *Understanding Regulation: Theory, Strategy and Practice*, 1999, Oxford: OUP

Coase, R H, *The Firm, the Market and the Law*, 1988, Chicago: University of Chicago Press

Cooter, R and Ulen, T, *Law and Economics*, 2nd Edition, 1997, Reading, Massachusetts: Addison Wesley Longman

Desai, A V, *The Price of Onions*, 1999, New Delhi: Penguin Books India

Hofstede, G, *Cultures and Organizations: Software of the Mind*, 1997, New York: McGraw Hill

Ormerod, P, *Butterfly Economics*, 1998, London: Faber and Faber

Perry, A J, 'The relationship between legal systems and economic development: integrating economic and cultural approaches' (2002) 29:2 Journal of Law and Society 282

Rostain, T, 'Educating *homo economicus*: cautionary notes on the new behavioural law and economics movement' (2000) 34:4 Law and Society Review 973

Shakeb, A, La Plante, B and Wheeler, D, *Controlling Industrial Pollution: A New Paradigm*, World Bank Policy Research Working Paper No 1672, 1996, available at www.worldbank.org/nipr/work_paper/1672/index.htm.

Trubek, D and Galanter M, 'Scholars in self-estrangement: some reflections on the crisis in law and development studies in the United States' (1972) Wisconsin Law Review 1062

Wiener Katz, A, *Foundations of the Economic Approach to Law*, 1998, New York: OUP

---

[29]   Rostain, 2000, p 989.

CHAPTER 4

JURIDIFYING GENDER JUSTICE: FROM GLOBAL RIGHTS TO LOCAL JUSTICE

Ann Stewart[*]

The last two decades have seen a flowering of development strategies informed by the language of law. The impetus has come from many quarters but women's organisations and those concerned with the economic and social position of women have taken a particular interest in rights discourses.

While there have been activities at 'local', state and international levels, a substantial amount of energy has been dedicated to advocating the recognition of women's rights as human rights within the international arena. The sustained and varied campaigns have produced results.[1] I would argue that the recognition of women's rights as human rights is a success story, albeit a limited one.[2]

The basic premise of international law is that all women have public rights, irrespective of their position within their own societies. There have been many challenges to this liberal philosophy, not least from feminists and women activists who have argued against its essentialist[3] basis and therefore its lack of recognition of diversity. Many would argue that what has been achieved are formal individual rights which, in the face of economic neo-liberalism, are unable to protect against attacks on women's basic living standard—let alone produce substantive social justice.[4]

In the new millenium, the spotlight is moving to 'local' justice, as human rights and development discourses move closer together. Thus the capabilities approach[5] incorporates concepts of entitlement into both the rights and development frameworks. This approach also recognises that social—as well as economic—relations within families and local communities have a significant effect on human development.

Many issues are raised by this shift. First, how do different constituencies understand the local? Second, such a focus raises questions about the nature and role of nation states in an era of globalisation. Most accounts of globalisation focus on the importance of global markets and

---

[*] Reader in Law, School of Law, Warwick University.

[1] Women have their 'own' convention and enforcement mechanism. Gender issues are mainstreamed, albeit to a variable extent within the other treaty bodies. There is a special rapporteur on violence against women. Men have been convicted of war crimes against women. See: Charlesworth and Chinkin, 2000, for a detailed discussion of gender issues within international law and human rights law specifically; Connors, 2000, for a discussion of mainstreaming gender issues within the United Nations institutions.

[2] Charlesworth and Chinkin are less sanguine: 'women are on the margins of the international legal system. Their participation in the development of international legal principles is minimal and the international legal order appears impervious to the realities of women's lives. Although a specialised area of 'women's human rights law' is evolving, and occasionally women are acknowledged in 'mainstream' international law, by and large, whenever women come into focus at all in international law, they are viewed in a very limited way, chiefly as victims, particularly as mothers, as potential mothers, and accordingly in need of protection': Charlesworth and Chinkin, 2000, p 48.

[3] Essentialism is the notion that women have a fixed 'essence' or set of characteristics.

[4] See Nussbaum, 2000, for a discussion of the limitations of rights and the contribution that a capabilities approach can make, while Kiss, 1997, offers a robust defence of liberal rights although she recognises some of the criticisms.

[5] Sen, 1999; Nussbaum, 1999 and 2000.

their impact on localities, while ascribing a reduced role to the state.[6] Does a local focus represent a renewed interest in the problems for the poor associated with the implementation of state-based laws through the administration of justice institutions; or the discovery by wider constituencies than lawyers of what is known as legal pluralism, with its focus on 'non state' laws and its emphasis on cultural diversity? Third, what understandings of law underpin these developments? Are we witnessing a challenge to mainstream legal thinking from theories which would view law as embedded within social and economic processes?

Feminist legal activists and theorists working primarily in postcolonial societies have been tackling the issues associated with the 'local' for some time. Their work on customary and personal law systems and how they interact with state legal regimes have produced understandings of the complexities and costs of these interactions, as well as the controversies and dangers associated with attempts at change.[7] This has led to analyses of law which emphasise its power to construct meanings and its relationship to other regulatory frameworks. These approaches have been informed by feminist legal theorists generally, whose methods of analyses have broken out of the straightjacket of traditional legal scholarship.[8]

The legal scholarship which has informed international development strategies—known historically as technical legal assistance—has been firmly located within mainstream legal thinking. Although gender justice is recognised as being a matter of general policy concern, the current debate over the use of law does not address directly the analytical issues posed by feminist legal thinking. There is a danger that the local—which is recognised within feminist legal analysis as a gendered construct, as well as a space in which women seek gender justice—will be reconfigured through mainstream development and law approaches as a location wherein women access formal rights. This could lead to the local 'non state' or informal processes becoming over legalised, in an attempt to incorporate them into the formal institutions. This may prove problematic for women.

While there are dangers, there is also the potential for the self-critical, contextual thinking which informs much feminist legal scholarship to make an impact on the legal analysis which informs development agendas through the newly found interest in social and gender justice. There is some evidence that such an approach is developing.[9]

This will only be possible if gender analysis is 'mainstreamed' within the legal thinking of the organisations concerned, so that a gendered analysis not only informs access to justice issues but restructures law and governance analysis generally.

THE LOCAL[10]

The local is now being used in a variety of ways, and holds within it a range of meanings. As Rai points out the local 'has found a privileged place in the vocabulary of different groups concerned with issues of development and democracy.' She suggests there are several reasons for this. '[I]t allows a critique of nationalist agendas of political elites focused on major industrialization projects'; 'challenges the universalism of scientific discourses upon which the

---

[6]   Rai, 2002.
[7]   Stewart, 1996 and 2000a.
[8]   Naffine, 2002.
[9]   One World Action, 2001.
[10]   I am indebted to Upendra Baxi for his discussion of what constitutes the local: Baxi, 2002.

framework of modernization was built by pointing to the salience of local knowledge and paradigms'; 'allows people to participate in the economic and political life of their community'; and 'challenges authoritarianism by promoting decentralization and autonomy.'[11]

The local has been an important site for women activists, not only to argue for rights for women, but also to expose the limitations of the mainstream human rights approaches; to caution against over resort to their use; and generally to argue for a reconstruction of their content. Women from the South in particular have argued against essentialist constructions of women and for the recognition of diversity.[12] The local also has a strong association with the liberal concept of the 'private' sphere.

> International law operates in the public, male world. While it formally removes private concerns from its sphere, the international legal system nevertheless strongly influences them. One form of influence is the fact that private issues are left to national, rather than international, regulation. This means that laws concerning private matters, such as the family, can quite properly (from an international perspective) take account of cultural and religious traditions that may allow the domination of women by men.[13]

The foundation for critiques of analytical categories, which are portrayed as universal but based on western societal contexts, is rooted often in local experience. Thus it is very difficult to specify what is the 'private' domain in agrarian societies. Such analysis does not assist with an understanding of personal laws in rural India,[14] or the customary law systems of Andean peoples in Peru, or rural Shona in Zimbabwe.[15]

In addition to the local being used to critique and develop human rights frameworks, it has also been the site of women's legal activism. Much energy has also been devoted to legal literacy campaigns in specific localities usually defined as rural areas throughout the world. The sophistication of these campaigns varies considerably but they are usually focused on enabling women to use state enacted rights in conjunction with their international human rights.[16]

Some women's organisations, specialising in action research, have developed a 'grounded'[17] approach to law.

> Such an approach involves building up legal and social science knowledge which encompasses the practices and perceptions of women and men in Southern and Eastern Africa... In using grounded theory the aim is to engage empirical knowledge about gender relations and local practices and procedures... To do this legal researchers need to have first hand knowledge of local practices and procedures in the area they are researching.[18]

Finally, the local has been the site for the legal anthropologists and postcolonial legal historians who are associated with the legal pluralist school. I will return to a more detailed discussion of gendered constructions of local laws and legal pluralism in a later section.

---

[11] Rai, 2002, pp 207–208.

[12] Ali, 2000; Armstrong, 1993.

[13] Charlesworth and Chinkin, 2000, pp 56–57.

[14] See Patel, 2000.

[15] Maboreke, 1996.

[16] See Tsanga, 1997; Schuler and Kardirgamar–Rajasingham, 1992.

[17] Grounded theory is an iterative process in which data and theory, lived reality and perceptions about norms are constantly engaged with each other to help the researcher decide what data to collect and how to interpret it: Bentzon, Hellum, Stewart, Ncube and Agersnap, 1998, p 18.

[18] *Ibid*, 1998, p 25.

NEEDS, CAPABILITIES AND ENTITLEMENTS

Rai identifies the basic needs theorists as also having a particular interest in the local.[19] Basic needs theory, which developed in the 1970s, challenged development theory orthodoxy which concentrated on economic growth as the means to tackle poverty, and relied on wealth 'trickling down.' Theorists sought instead to link poverty to the inability of people to meet their basic needs, to link growth policies to income distribution policies. Basic needs approaches were concerned with all members of society, not just those involved in the labour market. Consequently, consumption within the family was brought into the analysis, and the individual's ability to articulate their needs became important.

While basic needs theory was not in favour with the powerful international financial institutions or national development agencies in an era of neo-liberal economics, we can see its influence in the human capabilities approach which has emerged into prominence in the last few years via the United Nations Human Development programme. This approach, pioneered by Amartya Sen, Jean Dreze and Martha Nussbaum, has steadily gained policy interest and is now informing discussions at the World Bank under the Presidency of James Wolfensohn.[20]

For Sen:

> Development can be seen... as a process of expanding the real freedom that people enjoy. Focusing on human freedoms contrasts with narrower views of development, such as identifying development with the growth of gross national product, or with the rise in personal incomes, or with industrialization, or with technological advance, or with social modernization.[21]

Sen links development to the removal of economic social and political unfreedoms, including intolerance, or overactivity of repressive states.[22] Freedom involves developing human achievements and capabilities. Poverty is a capability deprivation. 'In analyzing social justice, there is a strong case for judging individual advantage in terms of the capabilities that a person has, that is, the substantive freedoms he or she enjoys to lead the kind of life he or she has reason to value.'[23] This approach specifically addressed the capabilities of women, in particular the social and economic constraints they face. Nussbaum has developed Sen's analysis in relation to gender issues, addressing the way in which the specific minimum capabilities—which she deems essential for women—while rooted in specific social and economic contexts, can be 'squared' with universal human rights concepts.[24]

Sen argues that capabilities are met through the 'entitlements' which are either possessed by individuals (endowments) or are a product of market-based exchanges. The analysis directs attention 'to the processes through which individuals gain access to commodities and other resources (or fail to do so) which is said to depend on their socio-economic position and on the rules that render claims over commodities "legitimate".'[25] Sen recognises the role played by

---

[19] Rai, 2002.

[20] Sen was invited to give a series of lectures as a Presidential Fellow at the World Bank on his approach which led to the publication of *Development as Freedom* in 1999. Sen was asked to give the inaugural lecture at the World Bank seminar in June 2000 on Comprehensive Legal and Judicial Development: Towards an Agenda for a Just and Equitable Society in the 21st Century.

[21] Sen, 1999, p 3.

[22] *Ibid*.

[23] *Ibid*, p 87.

[24] Nussbaum, 1995, 1999 and 2000.

[25] Razavi, 1998, p 13.

legal rights in achieving capabilities through entitlement not only in the public sphere but also within the private sphere of the family.[26]

> The perception of individual contributions and appropriate entitlements of women and men play a major role in the division of a family's joint benefits between men and women. As a result, the circumstances that influence these perceptions of contributions and appropriate entitlements (such as women's ability to earn an independent income, to work outside the home, to be educated, to own property) can have a crucial bearing on these divisions.[27]

Women are no longer seen as the 'passive recipients of welfare enhancing help' but as 'active agents of change: the dynamic promoters of social transformations that can alter the lives of *both* women and men (original emphasis).'[28]

Capabilities analysis has two potentially positive advantages for those seeking gender justice. First, the analysis itself is 'gender friendly' with its recognition of the importance of social and economic processes including those within the family and its emphasis on individual agency. Second, legal analysis is imbricated within the development theory itself. Entitlements in Sen's work and capabilities in Nussbaum's have a close relationship to rights, concentrating on the basis for the claim within economic and social processes, rather than the right itself.[29]

Gore has argued that Sen's framework is excessively marketised and 'legalistic' in its understanding of the rules of entitlement,[30] because it is based on a positivist understanding of law as state-based. He argues for an extenuation of the focus 'to encompass not only state-enforced legal rules, but also socially-enforced moral rules which constrain *and* enable command over commodities' (original emphasis).[31] The approach therefore has the capacity to understand the plurality of local social and cultural norms—including those structured by local and 'personal' law—thus providing an opportunity for feminist legal analysis which has been based on analyses of plurality and difference to reach a wider audience.

However there are dangers. First, the theories of law which have traditionally informed development policy are not those associated with an embedded analysis of law. On the contrary, they have been associated with dominant neo-liberal economic policies which have fuelled the processes of globalisation. Second, claiming entitlements involves challenging structural constraints on the one hand and norms which are accepted as natural and self-evident (what Bourdieu refers to as doxa) on the other. This can be dangerous for women,[32] particularly for women living in postcolonial states. I will consider the dominant approach to law and governance in the next section, before returning to a discussion of women's position within the postcolonial state.

---

[26] Sen, 1999, p 191.
[27] *Ibid*, p 193.
[28] *Ibid*, p 189.
[29] Gore, 1993; Nussbaum, 2000.
[30] Gore, 1993.
[31] Razavi, 1998, p 13.
[32] *Ibid*, p 15.

STATE, LAW AND GOVERNANCE IN A GLOBALIZING WORLD

Globalisation is the subject of a very wide-ranging literature now which covers economic, political and cultural issues.[33] Here I am restricting my focus to those aspects of globalisation which are particularly important to an analysis of legal strategies and their role in development policies. These are set within the context of the rapid expansion of world markets, bolstered by the dominance of free trade and market liberalisation policies in the aftermath of the collapse of the Soviet Union. Western governments and the international financial institutions have expanded their spheres of action in the light of the far-reaching consequences of these events. Their growing influence and the expansion in world trade has stimulated or obliged Third World countries to liberalise their economies.

Globalisation has a significant effect on the nature and role of the national state. Some argue that the state is being marginalised in the processes whereby economic power is lost to global markets, and political power is being relocated within regional and global institutions. Others claim that the processes of globalisation are reorganising states, requiring states to facilitate the development of global markets and to manage the domestic economic and social consequences of this development. Thus states are implicated in more or less active ways in facilitating the global developments.

In the 1980s, as Tshuma points out, the two Bretton Woods institutions diagnosed the causes of the balance of payment and debt crises of many developing countries as 'largely endogenous. The state in developing countries had stunted economic growth through excessive and unwise interventions in the economy.'[34]

Faundez contends that '[f]rom leading protagonist in the development process, the state is now seen as a mere facilitator of market-based policies.'[35] Under structural adjustment lending policies initiated by the international financial institutions, countries were obliged to undertake legal and regulatory reform to fulfil the conditions of the loans.[36]

> There has been a comprehensive redefinition of the rules governing economic policy as virtually every country in the world incorporated the 'Washington consensus'[37] into its legislative framework. This new legislation provided the platform to launch major programmes of liberalisation, de-regulation and privatisation.[38]

'Law has been accorded a pre-eminent role in confining the state to its proper place...'[39] By the 1990s the Bank had reviewed its understanding of the role of the state and adopted its governance agenda. 'Failure to establish a predictable framework of law and government behaviour conducive to development or arbitrariness in the application of rules and laws' are signs of poor governance which can be 'cured by a strict adherence to the rule of law conceived as a system comprising abstract rules which are actually applied and institutions

---

[33] See Rai, 2002, chapter 3 for a summary and gendered analysis.

[34] Tshuma, 2000, p 9.

[35] Faundez, 2000, p 2.

[36] Tshuma, 2000, p 10.

[37] These include fiscal discipline, tax reform, market-determined interest rates, competitive exchange rates, trade liberalisation, opening up to foreign direct investment, privatisation of state enterprises, deregulation and legal security for property rights: World Bank, 2000, p 63.

[38] Faundez, 2000, p 3.

[39] Tshuma, 2000, p 7.

which ensure the appropriate application of such rules.'[40] The Bank concentrated on the formal indices of the rule of law, rather than venturing into substantive issues such as justice.

During the 1990s the Bank was concerned with governance and law reform only in so far as it relates to economic development. However, during that period it revised its view of what constituted good governance. 'A fundamental role of the Bank is to help governments work better in our client countries... the Bank must focus more of its efforts on building efficient and accountable public sector institutions—rather than simply providing discrete policy advice.'[41] Thus the focus had moved to the institutions upon which markets rest: law and property rights. 'Once the foundations of lawfulness are in place and where the institutional capabilities exist, the next stage is to address other parts of the legal system which strengthen property rights.'[42] The Bank maintains that the 'legal reforms it finances are technocratic and apolitical in character.'[43] '[T]he procedural version of law is intended to limit, as much as possible, the extent to which politicians and bureaucrats can use the law to tell individuals what to do and how to do it', although '[l]aws which purport to promote substantive values other than through the market are suspect as they are likely to be a smoke screen for self-serving group interests.'[44]

The Bank's institutional reform programmes were informed by the new institutional economics theory associated with North, which claims that economic performance hinges on institutions.[45] 'The key analytical concepts... are property rights, contracting and transaction costs.'[46] It is the role of the state to provide a suitable institutional framework to protect the first two and minimise the third. 'The Bank's legal sector institutional reform programme focuses on the enforcement of laws, the professionalization of interpretation and application of legal doctrine, the institutionalization of adjudicative processes, and the development of efficient legislative institutions... '[47] It is assumed that law can structure 'incentives' and that it 'therefore influences behaviour and economic performance.'[48] Intervention is directed at a strategic level, at state institutional reform.

By the end of the 1990s the focus of attention has moved to tackling poverty. The Bank has become far more aware of the difficulties associated with its approach to law and governance activities. First, measures focused on specific reforms and institutions such as the judiciary do not seem to have delivered the desired results in many instances.[49] Second, Faundez[50] contends that national governments are now aware of the need to extend the process of reform away from supporting core market functions to wider areas such as equal opportunities, gender

---

[40] *Ibid*, p 13.

[41] World Bank Governance and Public Sector Reform Website, 2002.

[42] Tshuma, 2000, p 14.

[43] *Ibid*.

[44] *Ibid*, p 17.

[45] 'Institutions include conventions, codes of conduct, norms of behaviour, statute law and common law, property rights and contracts. They may be formal or informal; and they may be created or they may develop over time': Tshuma, 2000, p 19.

[46] North, 1990, p 19. 'Property rights are social institutions that determine the value of an asset by setting the range of its productivity or exchangeability. Contracting is the process through which property rights are established, assigned or modified... Transaction costs are the costs associated with the creation, maintenance, or modification of institutions, such as property rights...': Tshuma, 2000, p 19.

[47] North, 1990, p 20.

[48] *Ibid*, p 21.

[49] This is evident from the World Bank's own assessment of its actions particularly in relation to Latin America: Messick, 1999; Thome, 2000.

[50] Faundez, 2000.

equality and land tenure systems. Third, faith in the ability of neo-liberal economics has faltered in some quarters as the ideology is challenged by a range of critics who point to the social and economic consequences for those who have been impoverished by the processes.

In its Comprehensive Development Framework,[51] the approach is more 'holistic and acknowledges the complexity of the development enterprise' and that 'national governments, in partnerships with civil society organisations, have the principal responsibility for the design and implementation of their country's development strategy.'[52] The World Development Report 2000/2001[53] recognises that strategies must consider social and political causes of poverty as well as economic. The market alone will not produce results.

'The legal system is thus no longer seen as a passive framework of rules, but as an instrument that can and should be used to respond to the needs and demands of the poor.'[54] The state is charged with the responsibility of providing the framework to enable citizens to gain a voice. Just laws and justice institutions are important in implementing this approach.

> Improving, facilitating and expanding individual and collective access to law and justice supports economic and social development. Legal reforms give the poor the opportunity to assert their individual and property rights; improved access to justice empowers the poor to enforce those rights. Increasing accessibility to courts lessens and overcomes the economic, psychological, informational and physical barriers faced by women, indigenous populations, and other individuals who need its services.[55]

The 2002 World Development Report again focuses on 'institution building for markets':[56]

> Weak institutions—tangled laws, corrupt courts, deeply biased credit systems, and elaborate business registration requirements—hurt poor people and hinder development ... Countries that systematically deal with such problems and create new institutions suited to local needs can dramatically increase incomes and reduce poverty. These institutions range from unwritten customs and traditions to complex legal codes that regulate international commerce.[57]

The aim is to reduce the institutional barriers which prevent the poor gaining access to markets. The scope of the institutional analysis has broadened to include the 'local.' To some extent we are seeing an interest in embedding the pro-poor capacities and entitlements approach within the development framework, moving the focus from ensuring that citizens can access justice through the formal judicial system to ensuring that entitlements can be claimed where they arise.[58] The focus of attention moves from a 'top down' reform of the state legal and judicial institutions to a 'bottom up' approach in which local institutions are recognised as key decision-making fora.

The World Bank is still relying on institutional analysis albeit more widely drawn. Other agencies seem more comfortable with approaches that incorporate processes. The UK's

---

[51] World Bank, 2000.

[52] Faundez, 2000, p 3.

[53] World Bank, 2001.

[54] Faundez, 2000, p 3.

[55] World Bank Legal and Judicial Reform (Access to Justice) Website, 2002.

[56] World Bank, 2002.

[57] World Development Report 2002 Website, 2002.

[58] 'In recent years, critics have argued that access-to-justice reform has largely conflated access to justice with access to the courts. Some seek to turn the debate from procedural access to substantive justice, shifting emphasis from guaranteeing the availability of lawyers or court procedures to producing social outcomes that are more fair and equitable. Greater access to the courts, they note, will not help the poor in a country where the laws entrench their social and economic exclusion': World Bank Legal Institutions of the Market Economy (Access to Justice) Website, 2002.

Department for International Development has a 'new focus on poverty reduction, a more people centred approach, and a strengthened focus on human rights. ... A strong thrust ... is to treat justice as a sector ... With linkages, the important ones are the process and procedural linkages, the informal/formal linkages, and holding institutions to account.'[59]

What understanding of law informs these developments? For some the resurgence of interest in using law to produce development has echoes of the earlier discredited[60] law and development movement[61] even though the dominant economic framework of neo-liberal economics provides a different context.[62] Faundez considers that there is more possibility of success because the role of the state is now limited to facilitating markets rather than social change.[63]

It is not clear whether there is a new understanding of law, and its contribution to economic development to inform the most current debates relating law to 'pro-poor' policy debates. Are we witnessing a move away from legal liberalism with its emphasis on formal legal systems and, many would argue, built in American legal system template? Such an analysis fits very uneasily, if at all, with an approach which moves beyond state institutions into local cultural and social processes. How are legal interventions to support the development of capacities at a 'local' level? Is law seen as contributing to the processes of impoverishment or as a means of tackling the outcome, poverty? Lawyers working within their traditional boundaries of positivist law are ill equipped to deal with these issues and we are witnessing considerable hesitancy over the development of legal strategies.

I argue that incorporating a gendered local focus into development practice based on the capacities approach has the potential to challenge the dominant approach to law which sees it as a technical tool deployed to support economic initiatives.

LEGAL METHOD, LEGAL PRACTICE AND FEMINISM

While the capabilities approach chips away at neo-liberalism and opens up a space for gendered analysis at a local level, feminist legal analysis in general challenges traditional legal method. The feminist analysis of plural regulatory regimes poses a particularly trenchant challenge to orthodox analytical jurisprudence.

Feminist legal scholars have been far more willing than most lawyers to undertake practical research to seek out the voices of women. They have adopted a range of techniques

---

[59] Gerry, 2001, p 26.

[60] Not all commentators take such a pessimistic view of the achievements of the Law and Development movement. See Richard Messick in his World Bank briefing note on the history of the Law and Development movement: World Bank Legal Institutions of the Market Economy (Law and Development Movement) Website, 2002. Tamanaha, 1995, is an optimist.

[61] 'The guiding assumption of the law and development movement was that law is central to the development process. A related belief was that law was an instrument that could be used to reform society and that lawyers and judges could serve as social engineers. As Merryman (1977) notes, not everyone subscribed to this view. A few participants in the movement argued that only minor changes could be effected through legal reforms, and others contended that law reform should follow broader changes in society; that is, that the proper aim of reform was to adjust the legal system to social and economic changes that had already taken place. But the dominant view of law and development practitioners and theorists alike, although still unproven, was that law reform could lead social change, that law itself was an engine of change': World Bank Legal Institutions of the Market Economy (Law and Development Movement) Website, 2002.

[62] Messick, 1999; Rose, 1998; McAuslan, 1997; Tshuma, 2000.

[63] Faundez, 1997.

from use of legal literacy campaigns, to action research using the 'grounded' research methods discussed earlier.

They have embraced interdisciplinary approaches and sought out methods pioneered in jurisdictions other than their own, adapted and then applied them locally. Consequently they have provided a wealth of information on the position of women in a wide variety of local contexts. They have ascertained the way in which women perceive and are perceived in the law. As Naffine points out 'the general purpose of legal feminism is to make sense of the many ways gender shapes law, to reveal the many ways that law, as a consequence, harms women, and to try to change law so that women are helped.'[64]

Much of this work has taken place outside the traditional academic institutions, within non-governmental organisations concentrating on gender and law issues. Feminist legal scholars struggle to have their research and analysis included within the academic world. This is not surprising given the general marginality of women within law and its institutions. As Naffine points out:[65]

> The theorists who still dominate the scholarly legal literature have simultaneously insisted on the autonomy and integrity of their law as a specific institution, and shown little interest in the precise location of their law vis-à-vis social and political and economic institutions: that is, the other institutions from which law is supposedly autonomous.

Feminist legal analyses 'reveal the precise ways in which socio-economic and legal power ... determine what can be said, ... and by whom, within these multiple and overlapping communities of legal meaning.'[66] Feminist legal method has treated the 'operation of law as if it were an alien life form... Feminists have therefore refused to accept the orthodox liberal argument that some parts of life with which law deals—the supposedly private, the natural, the sexual, the biological—are simply not the responsibility of law.'[67] Feminist analysis which recognises the embedded nature of law is resisted by legal scholars, who insist that legal personality is an abstraction and cannot be subjected to a gendered analysis.[68]

Most law faculties in postcolonial societies maintain a strong adherence to the dominant jurisprudential views including its emphasis on legal centralism. As Bentzon *et al* point out, within the law faculties in Southern and Eastern Africa 'a top down theoretical approach is retained.'[69] Staff members are aligned to the paradigm of Western law, rather than to indigenous systems of law.[70]

> Curriculum design is still predicated on the assumption that the imported Western law is universally applicable. If indigenous systems of law are covered... it is usually as discrete optional subjects. Customary law is often taught from a legal centralist perspective... despite the well accepted argument that Western law is moulded on the life experiences, rationales and interests of white, Western, middle-class males.[71]

Much of the work on understanding the reasons for women's exclusion from society, and the complex way in which regulatory regimes including law mould gender and power relations,

---

[64]   Naffine, 2002, p 72.
[65]   *Ibid*, p 74.
[66]   *Ibid*, pp 74–75.
[67]   *Ibid*, p 79.
[68]   *Ibid*.
[69]   Bentzon, Hellum, Stewart, Ncube and Agersnap, 1998, p 23.
[70]   *Ibid*.
[71]   *Ibid*, p 24.

is ignored. This leads to an overemphasis on the role of the state and state law as the medium through which to achieve change.[72]

GENDER, GOVERNANCE AND THE STATE

Third World feminism is intimately bound up with nationalism and its substantiation in the postcolonial state.[73] Feminist theories and strategies have been shaped by their connection with nationalist movements, 'a complicated relationship of sympathy and support, mutual use and mutual co-operation, and unacknowledged contestatory tension.'[74] 'Different visions of the future of the nation-state, and of its citizens, determined where women were positioned... in different political systems.'[75] In liberal political systems the rhetoric was of civic nationalism: citizenship tolerant of different groups, ethnicities and religious communities. Women were still 'regarded as markers of non secular group identities but at the same time became individualized citizens.'[76] 'In Marxist states the concept of citizenship was subsumed under the categories of class while cultural nationalism'[77] was absorbed into state ideologies concerning with constructing socialism.

Heng argues that '[t]he manipulation of women's issues as an ideological and political resource in Third World nationalist history commonly develops... into the manipulation of women themselves as a socio-economic resource in Third World nation states.'[78]

This leads to a 'troubled, complex and sometimes dangerous oppositional relationship to the contemporary Third World State.'[79] The authoritarian and interventionist nature of the state may channel feminist activity into informal networks and alliances. Due to this nationalist history, feminism has been obliged to adapt to the ambivalence of Third World nations to modernity. While the 'technological and economic machinery of modernization' are deemed essential, the 'cultural apparatus may be regarded as contaminating, dangerous and undesirable.'[80] Feminist activities can be damned easily by association with the foreign, and feminists are often obliged to structure their activities in such a way as to maintain legitimacy.[81]

The difficulty of maintaining legitimacy can be seen when women seek to exercise their rights as citizens. I have argued elsewhere that state-based legal strategies have been particularly difficult for women activists in postcolonial societies[82] when they have sought to exercise their formal rights to equality and non-discrimination under constitutional provisions. These activities provoke strong reactions which expose the gendered nature of citizenship in postcolonial states.

---

[72]   Manji, 1999, p 439.
[73]   Jayawardena, 1986; Alexander and Mohanty, 1997; Heng, 1997; Rai, 2002.
[74]   Heng, 1997, p 31.
[75]   Rai, 2002, p 40.
[76]   *Ibid.*
[77]   *Ibid*, p 41.
[78]   Heng, 1997, pp 31–32.
[79]   *Ibid*, p 32.
[80]   *Ibid*, p 33.
[81]   *Ibid.*
[82]   Stewart, 1996.

The present context of globalisation, wherein the nation state seems to be losing power to global markets and institutions on the one hand, and yet is facing increasing disruptions created by the localised impact of economic policies on the other, heightens many tensions within ruling elites and can provoke hostile responses to women's demands. These tensions can be heightened by the interventions of the international development agencies in heavily donor-dependent countries, if women activists are perceived as supporting agendas which 'interfere' with local norms or challenge local power structures.

LOCALITY, LEGAL PLURALISM AND LEGAL FEMINISM

We are witnessing a renewed interest in legal pluralism[83] with its concern for normative orders which overlap and interact with formal law and its institutional framework. Although a day to day reality for people living with pluralistic legal systems and a key area of feminist legal analysis and practice, this has, until recently, been a rather abstruse area of academic legal interest.

The context for this interest is being restructured in a number of ways. First, women are contributing to national development policy debates, so gender issues are no longer ignored. Second, as we have seen, governance and law issues are now on state level agendas, because of the imperatives of globalisation to open up markets, and because development agencies view broad-based institutional reform as important to the implementation of pro-poor policies. Third, policies of democratisation are leading to a reassessment of rural local governance institutions. Fourth, the capabilities approach recognises that family relations and, to a lesser extent, local community norms are important areas of policy concern, thus bringing 'private' law areas—that is, customary and personal laws—under the spotlight.

Feminists have demonstrated the ways in which familial and gender norms construct the terms upon which women and men enter and participate in the market and public life.[84]

> A similar concern is articulated by Gita Sen:[85] the need to move beyond the assumption that gender power relations at the local level are embedded in conjugal, intra-household relations alone. The structures of power that women confront at a local level... operate not only within the home, but also in the terrain of communities, local markets and the institutions of local government.[86]

Reform over land rights—which incorporate family and property relations in agrarian societies—provides a contemporary example of the controversies raised by the plurality of regulatory regimes through which women are obliged to negotiate. Historically, land in Eastern and Southern Africa was held in communal form by a clan or kinship group. Disposition was organised within and through this kinship network by elders. However, while these customary laws constructed the property relations within the clan, they were also used to challenge the objectives of the colonial state, which would have wished to exploit the

---

[83] 'Legal pluralism is usually defined as a situation in which two or more legal systems coexist in the same social system': Merry, 1988, p. 870. Interest in legal pluralism developed from the study of what is known as juristic (Griffiths, 1986) or classical (Merry, 1988) legal pluralism which is based on the dual legal systems created through European colonialism, general or imposed law for the 'public' arena, customary and personal laws for the 'private' sphere. These parallel legal regimes are all dependent on the state legal system: Merry, 1988, p 871; and Stewart, 2000a.

[84] Kabeer, 1994, p 61.

[85] Sen, 1998.

[86] Razavi, 1998, p 17.

land through private ownership and sale. Historical research has shown how the clans organised their resistance to these developments. The colonial state was obliged to rely on the chief's authority to regulate relations within rural areas, and in the end accepted as valid the definitions of land use and allocation promulgated as customary by the chiefs.[87] Thus the chiefs and the colonial state constructed an understanding of what was customary land tenure through the struggle to retain control over the land within the clan. By defending their custodianship over land, and preventing it from being turned into private property, the kin groups resisted state authority over them. However, at the same time they constructed customary laws which maximised gender hierarchies. Feminist anthropologists have argued that women lost rights in this process, and through the codification of customary law under colonialism. They also point to the ways in which women challenged and resisted attempts to reduce their rights, thus recognising that customary norms are malleable.[88] Nonetheless, because the system was based on status, it is generally argued that women were not recognised as 'fully acting subjects.'[89] Land was normally inherited not by a widow, but by a male relative of the deceased.

This history has an impact on the way in which the interaction between gender relations and customary practices are understood in the postcolonial era. The norms and local institutions within customary practices are seen by some as providing the basis for resisting wider exploitation, by others as impeding progress particularly for women. Lawyers generally adopt the latter position. They would seek to curtail or abolish them through state legislation which creates equal rights for women in line with international human rights provisions. However, those working within the women's law tradition associated with the Women and Law in Southern and Eastern Africa projects argue strongly for a grounded empirical approach, which seeks to ascertain present practice within localities and takes account of the interactions between family, customary and state normative orders.[90] Their work shows that customary norms are not fixed. They adapt to changing social and economic circumstances and are influenced by norms such as equality which are drawn from state laws.[91] The present norms are also often very different from those recognised by state courts as authentic customary practices. Generally there is no hierarchy of norms, rather contexts determine which are most powerful.

Anne Griffiths' research, based on extensive fieldwork on marriage, kinship relations and property rights in Botswana,[92] illustrates the nature and complexity of power relations, and the way in which gender relations interact. She argues persuasively that individuals must be seen as involved in networks which shape their world and channel their access to resources. These resources include the power to negotiate. She views individuals as social beings linked to networks with gendered attributes. These networks give rise to discourses. How individuals are situated in relation to the networks affects their power to construct the form of discourse which they can use to support their claims. Law—be it state, religious or customary—is a form of discourse and in specific contexts can be powerful. However it often works to exclude women who are not already powerful players. It does not of itself empower them. Other networks might render greater power to women to structure their claims.

---

[87]   Chanock, 1991.
[88]   Mbilinyi, 1988.
[89]   Whitehead, 1984.
[90]   Bentzon, Hellum, Stewart, Ncube and Agersnap, 1998.
[91]   Armstrong, 2000.
[92]   Griffiths, 1997.

These debates are being translated into policy discussions over land reform.[93] Tanzania provides an example of major differences over policy development. On one side are those who would seek to transfer responsibility for land transactions to the localities—to Village Assemblies—in an attempt to strengthen democratic control over land and implicitly limit the power of the state, which is perceived by the proponents of this approach to be pursuing policies designed to privatise land and favour foreign investors. On the other side are those who would retain power within the central state, because local control would impede development. The ferocity of the debates initially marginalised questions of gender justice, although eventually gender issues featured strongly. Some centralists argued that the 'localists' were not recognising the patriarchal power structures contained within the village structures, and were therefore limiting women's abilities to claim equal access to land. Their view was that customary land law should be abolished and replaced with legislative provisions securing women's individual rights to own and dispose of land. The localists argued that local institutions are potentially more democratic and open to contestation by women; that state-based rights, particularly those predicated on the development of a market will not provide substantive justice to poor women in rural areas. The Lands Act 1999 retained ultimate ownership of land in the central government, did not abolish customary land practices, but did provide equal rights for women to own land.[94]

Struggles over land rights are happening throughout the sub-Saharan region. We see similar tensions elsewhere.[95] Should power lie within the local institutions which will use customary laws and practices to determine ownership and distribution? Are women able to exercise agency within the local embedded social and economic contexts? Do individualised property rights at a state level provide women with the entitlements they need to argue for 'a field of one's own' and to maximise their capacities?

These are highly politicised issues and can have dangerous consequences for women. The shadow of the donor community is never far away in sub-Saharan Africa. Some constituencies benefit from the technical assistance of foreign experts employed by the donors, others receive financial assistance from donors to marshal evidence or prepare a position paper. Individualised state-based land rights may be seen as disrupting local social and family institutions in the pursuit of externally dominated policies. For instance, women's groups in Tanzania were accused of being used by the state to divide civil society, pursuing their own agenda of rights for women (informed by Western-based interests) which did not threaten the wider aim of introducing a free market in land and promoting foreign investment in local communities.[96] Tripp describes how the coalition campaigning for co-ownership rights in the land reforms in Uganda was accused of fronting Western interests.[97] In both countries there were attempts to relocate the issues relating to gender within inheritance and succession provisions (successfully in Uganda but not in Tanzania), thus moving them to the 'private' sphere.

---

[93] Razavi, 1998; Tsikata, 2001; Whitehead and Tsikata, 2001.

[94] I present a schematic view of the issues which greatly simplifies the range and complexity of the arguments. For a very detailed fully referenced account see Tsikata, 2001.

[95] See for instance Walker, 1998 for the South African context; Castillo, 2000, for Mexico; Kabeer, 1998, for South Asia.

[96] Tsikata, 2001.

[97] Tripp, 2000.

A POSITIVE CONCLUSION

I have charted the growing interest in the capabilities approach to development, with its recognition that capabilities need to be analysed within local contexts. We have seen that law plays a part in structuring entitlements, although the view of law held by the protagonists of this approach is informed by positivism. Generally the legal theoretical perspectives informing the international governance and law agenda reflect those held by mainstream analytical jurisprudential approaches. While law can be deployed as a technical tool, it retains its own internal 'integrity', with a discrete language unaffected by wider social, economic and political contexts. Dominant views of law are uneasy with the very concept of legal pluralism, and with the idea of a culture of law. Analyses of law based on law's power to construct meanings or its imbrication within specific cultural contexts are resisted.

There is therefore considerable uncertainty about how law is to be understood by development lawyers once the focus moves beyond state laws and institutions into other forms of normative orders. Once the analysis focuses on the interaction between the familial and local, social and cultural practices, issues of gender, not surprisingly, emerge—first, because the analytical framework is built upon gendered foundations; and second, because women become visible at the local level, and within 'non state' normative orders.

Thus the move to the local could be seen simply in the narrowest institutional reform terms of a need for all citizens including women to have access to state-based justice systems institutions. It could involve the adoption of the existing local informal dispute resolution processes as the panacea to women's legal problems, thus confining women to a particular space without recognising the relationships of power which structure the local.

One dangerous outcome of a new found interest in plural legal systems might be that there will be an over-juridification of gender justice issues. Attempts to transpose informal claims which are seen as legitimate—if contested—into formal rights can have unforeseen consequences. Women who are not powerful may not be able to claim such rights, and competing social norms may not be displaced simply by the granting of a formal right.[98] It is essential to recognise that local social contexts are diverse, and that cultural constructions of women's rights or customary rights affect women differently in different contexts. They will affect men and women in the same context differently. In some situations ambiguity may be strategically beneficial to women because it arouses less resistance.[99] State laws can assist women, but local and community level dynamics will determine to what extent.

It is always important to ask: why formalise? Will a legal right increase women's ability to claim entitlement? Not many 'technical legal experts' see the world in this way. There is a danger that they may view the local as a place badly in need of formalisation to remove it from the messy world of culture into the pure world of abstract legal personality and rights, and the best way of achieving this will be attachment to the lowest rung on the justice system. If that is the case a great opportunity will be lost.

The danger of over-juridification is closely associated with the position of women within postcolonial states. While states are to a greater or lesser extent facilitating global economic liberalisation policies, these are having profound effects on social and political relationships at a local level. The ambivalence of postcolonial states to modernism, seeking legitimacy through

---

[98]   Patel, 2000; Kabeer, 1998.
[99]   Razavi, 1998.

some agendas but wishing to maintain cultural hegemony in others, can undermine women's position and expose them to dangers.

More optimistically there is a possibility for more nuanced thinking on law, informed by feminist methods, to permeate throughout the legal agenda of development policy-makers. I would argue that feminist analyses of diversity and plurality offer ways forward to the wider development agenda; that diversity and plurality are part of 21st century legal systems, not relicts of a bygone era. A shift of emphasis within development policy to look beyond state institutional reform to agency at a local level provides an opportunity for feminist legal analysis to move from the margins.

The focus on the local has the potential to do this if the analysis of law is rooted in gendered approaches, which recognise that law is not a technical language and tool alone—rather it has the power to construct categories and identities. The local cannot be separated from the national and the international. Discourses of rights drawn from the international arena and of citizenship drawn from the nation state do permeate the local and can be deployed in some contexts by women in their claims for justice. At the same time, by rooting the pursuit of justice locally the range of regulatory regimes including the family which impact differentially on women and men are revealed and can be tackled in the search for gender justice.

REFERENCES

Alexander, M J and Mohanty, C T, *Feminist Genealogies, Colonial Legacies, Democratic Futures*, 1997, New York and London: Routledge

Ali, S S, *Gender and Human Rights in Islam and International Law: Unequal Before Allah, Unequal Before Man*, 2000, The Hague: Kluwer Law International

Armstrong, A, *Uncovering Reality: Excavating Women's Rights in African Family Law*, 1993, Harare: University of Zimbabwe Publications

Armstrong, A, 'Rethinking culture and tradition in southern Africa: research from WLSA', in Stewart, A (ed), *Gender, Law and Social Justice*, 2000 London: Blackstone Press

Baxi, U, 'Law, gender and secularism', Comments at the Siting Secularism Conference, Oberlin College, USA 19-22 April 2002

Bentzon, A W, Hellum, A, Stewart, J, Ncube W and Agersnap, T, *Pursuing Grounded Theory in Law: South-North Experiences in Developing Women's Law*, 1998, Oslo: Tano Aschehoug

Castillo, R A H, *National Law and Indigenous Customary Law: The Struggle of Justice of Indigenous Women in Chiapas, Mexico*, 2000, mimeo, Geneva: UNRISD

Chanock, M, 'Paradigms, policies, and property: a review of customary law of the land tenure', in Mann, K and Roberts, R (eds), *Law in Colonial Africa*, 1991, Portsmouth: Heinemann

Charlesworth, H and Chinkin, C, *The Boundaries of International Law: A Feminist Analysis*, 2000, Manchester: Manchester University Press

Connors, J, 'Mainstreaming gender within the international framework', in Stewart, A (ed), *Gender, Law and Social Justice*, 2000, London: Blackstone Press, pp 19-43

Faundez, J, 'Introduction: the ever-expanding governance agenda', in Faundez, J, Footer, M E and Norton, J J (eds), *Governance, Development and Globalization*, 2000, London: Blackstone Press

Faundez, J, 'Legal technical assistance', in Faundez, J (ed), *Good Government and Law: Legal and Institutional Reform in Developing Countries*, 1997, Basingstoke and London: Macmillan Press, pp 1-24

Gerry, A, 'Justice and poverty reduction', in *Making Justice Democratic*, 2001, London: One World Action

Gore, C, 'Entitlement relations and "unruly" social practices: a comment on the work of Amartya Sen' (1993) 29:3 Journal of Development Studies 427

Griffiths, A, *In the Shadow of Marriage: Gender and Justice in an African Community*, 1997, London and Chicago: University of Chicago Press

Griffiths, J, 'What is legal pluralism?' (1986) 24 Journal of Legal Pluralism 1

Heng, G, '"A great way to fly": nationalism, the state and the varieties of third-world feminism', in Alexander M J and Mohanty, C T (eds), *Feminist Genealogies, Colonial Legacies, Democratic Futures*, 1997, New York and London: Routledge

Jayawardena, K, *Feminism and Nationalism in the Third World*, 1986, London: Zed

Kabeer, N, *Reversed Realities: Gender Hierarchies in Development Thought*, 1994, London and New York: Verso

Kabeer, N, *The Conditions and Consequences of Choice: Concepts, Measures and Women's Empowerment*, 1998, mimeo, Geneva: UNRISD

Kiss, E, 'Alchemy or fool's gold? assessing feminist doubts about rights', in Shanley, M L, and Narayan, U (eds), *Reconstructing Political Theory: Feminist Perspectives*, 1997, Cambridge: Polity Press, pp 1-24

Maboreke, M, *The Betrayal of the Return to Self Project: The Resurgence of Zimbabwe's Ngozi Custom as a Case Study*, 1996, unpublished PhD thesis, University of Warwick

Manji, A, 'Imagining women's "legal world": towards a feminist theory of legal pluralism in Africa' (1999) 8:4 Social and Legal Studies 435

Mbilinyi, M, 'Runaway wives in colonial Tanganyika' (1988) 16 International Journal of Sociology of Law 1

McAuslan, P, 'Law, governance and the development of the market: practical problems and possible solutions', in Faundez, J (ed), *Good Government and Law*, 1997, Basingstoke and London: Macmillan Press

Merry, S E, 'Legal pluralism' (1988) 22:5 Law and Society Review 869

Messick, R E, 'Judicial reform and economic development: a survey of the issues' (1999) 14:1 World Bank Research Observer 117

Naffine, N, 'In praise of legal feminism' (2002) 22:1 Legal Studies 71

North, D C, *Institutions, Institutional Change and Economic Performance*, 1990, Cambridge: CUP

Nussbaum, M, *Sex and Social Justice*, 1995, Oxford: OUP

Nussbaum, M, 'Women and equality: the capabilities approach' (1999) 138:3 International Labour Review 227

Nussbaum, M, *Women's Capabilities and Social Justice*, 2000, mimeo, Geneva: UNRISD

One World Action, *Making Justice Democratic*, Seminar Report, 2001, London: One World Action

Patel, R, *Labour and Land Rights of Women in Rural India—With Particular Reference to Western Orissa*, 2000, unpublished PhD thesis, University of Warwick

Rai, S, *Gender and the Political Economy of Development*, 2002, Cambridge: Polity Press

Razavi, S, *Gendered Poverty and Social Change: An Issues Paper*, UNRISD Discussion Paper no 94, 1998, Geneva: UNRISD

Rose, C V, 'The "new" law and development movement in the post-Cold War era: a Vietnam case study' (1998) 32:1 Law and Society Review 93

Schuler, M and Kardirgamar-Rajasingham, S, *Legal Literacy: A Tool for Women's Empowerment*, 1992, Washington, DC: Women, Law and Development International

Sen, A, *Development as Freedom*, 1999, Oxford: OUP

Sen, G, *Engendering Poverty Alleviation: The Challenges and Opportunities in the 1990s*, 1998, mimeo, Geneva: UNRISD

Stewart, A (2000a), 'Personal and customary law', *International Encyclopaedia of Women*, 2000, London: Routledge

Stewart, A (2000b), 'The contributions of feminist legal scholarship to the "rights approach to development"', in Stewart, A (ed), *Gender, Law and Social Justice*, 2000, London: Blackstone Press, pp 3-18

Stewart, A, 'Should women give up on the state? the African experience', in Rai, S M and Lievesley, G (eds), *Women and the State: International Perspectives*, 1996, London: Taylor and Francis, pp 23-44

Tamanaha, B Z, 'The lessons of law-and-development studies' (1995) 89 American Journal of International Law 470

Thome, J R, 'Heading south but looking north: globalization and law reform in Latin America', in Faundez, J, Footer, M E and Norton, J J (eds), *Governance, Development and Globalization*, 2000, London: Blackstone Press

Tripp, A M, *The Politics of Women's Rights and Cultural Diversity in Uganda*, 2000, mimeo, Geneva: UNRISD

Tsanga, A, *Taking the Law to the People: The Case of Legal Education in Zimbabwe*, 1997, unpublished PhD thesis, Faculty of Law, University of Zimbabwe

Tshuma, L, 'The political economy of the World Bank's legal framework for economic development', in Faundez, J, Footer, M E and Norton, J J (eds), *Governance, Development and Globalization*, 2000, London: Blackstone Press, pp 7-27

Tsikata, D, *Land Tenure Reforms and Women's Land Rights: Recent Debates in Tanzania*, 2000, mimeo, Geneva: UNRISD

Walker, C, *Land Reform and Gender in Post-Apartheid South Africa*, 1998, mimeo, Geneva: UNRISD

Whitehead, A and Tsikata, D, *Policy Discourses on Women's Land Rights in sub-Saharan Africa*, 2000, mimeo, Geneva: UNRISD

Whitehead, A, 'Women and men; kinship and property: some general issues', in Hirschon, R (ed), *Women and Property—Women as Property*, 1984, London: Croom Helm

World Bank Governance and Public Sector Reform Website, 2002, www1.worldbank.org/publicsector

World Bank Legal and Judicial Reform (Access to Justice) Website, 2002, www4.worldbank.org/legal/leglr/access.html

World Bank Legal Institutions of the Market Economy (Access to Justice) Website, 2002, www1.worldbank.org/publicsector/legal/accesstojustice.htm

World Bank Legal Institutions of the Market Economy (Law and Development Movement) Website, 2002, www1.worldbank.org/publicsector/lega/ldmovement.htm

World Bank World Development Report 2002 Website, 2002, www.econ.worldbank.org/wdr/2391

World Bank, *World Development Report 1999/2000: Entering the 21st Century: The Changing Development Landscape*, 2000, Oxford: OUP

World Bank, *World Development Report 2000/2001: Attacking Poverty*, 2001, Oxford: OUP

World Bank, *World Development Report 2002: Building Institutions for Markets*, 2002, Oxford: OUP

PART 2

INTERNATIONAL PRACTICE

CHAPTER 5

TECHNOLOGY TRANSFER: SHIFTING MODELS OF LAW AND DEVELOPMENT

Peter Muchlinski[*]

In its original version, as presented at the Conference on Law and Development in the 21st century in June 2001, this paper aimed to answer a fairly narrow question: what changes have there been in the last 30 or so years in the approach taken to the issue of technology transfer in international economic agreements and other related instruments? That version was based on research undertaken by the author for UNCTAD, the fruits of which now appear in the UNCTAD paper *Transfer of Technology*, as part of the UNCTAD Series on issues in international investment agreements.[1] From that research, it became clear that a significant shift had occurred in the treatment of technology transfer which can be summarised as a move from a 'regulatory' to a more 'market-based' approach. This shift raises some fundamental questions that are of relevance to the wider issues surrounding the future direction that the field of law and development might take in the 21st century, and which were the focus of much debate at the Conference. In particular, it brings to the fore the need to understand the relationship between law as a tool of regulation, and the increased use of self-regulation through the market as possible methods of achieving development goals. On a more specific level, it raises the question whether the move towards the latter approach is likely to achieve the social and economic objectives that underlie the process of development better than the 'command and control' type of state-centred regulation favoured by earlier policy prescriptions. This paper aims to examine these wider issues, using technology transfer as a case study.

Technology transfer offers a good source of raw material for a critical re-evaluation of the role of law in the development process, especially as the transfer of technology to developing countries has been one of the most discussed areas of international economic relations in the past 30 or more years. The role of transnational corporations (TNCs) in the process of developing, applying and disseminating technology across national borders to such countries has generated especial interest. One result has been the institution of numerous policy initiatives at the national, regional and multilateral levels. These have, in turn, produced a significant number of legal provisions both in national law and in international instruments. Furthermore, since technology has always been important to economic and social well-being, its transfer has traditionally been treated as a core issue in the law and development agenda. In addition, technology is even more critical to development because of its important role of rapidly transforming all productive systems and facilitating global economic integration. Thus the effective generation, transfer and dissemination of technology to developing countries continues to be one of the most important economic and social questions to be tackled in an increasingly integrated global economy and society.[2]

---

[*] Professor of Law and International Business, Kent Law School. This paper draws on the author's manuscript which forms the basis of the UNCTAD publication *Transfer of Technology* in the UNCTAD Series on issues in international investment agreements. The author is a Principal Adviser to the UNCTAD Series. The views expressed here are those of the author and in no way represent the official policy of UNCTAD.

[1] UNCTAD, 2001b.

[2] *Ibid*, p 5.

The paper will consider the case of technology transfer, first by analysing the principal features of the international market for technology; and, second, by reviewing major changes to the treatment of this issue in international agreements and instruments. The paper will conclude by what lessons can be drawn case study by the field of law and development..

THE MARKET FOR TECHNOLOGY AND THE ROLE OF TNCS IN THE GENERATION, TRANSFER AND DIFFUSION OF TECHNOLOGY

Technology, which can be broadly defined as the technical, entrepreneurial and managerial knowledge that goes into the creation and provision of products or services,[3] may exist in non-proprietary forms that can be generally accessed, as, for example, in publicly available books or journals. However, the major concern that underlies the regulatory issues covered by the present paper focuses on proprietary technology—that is, technology that is capable of generating a profit for its owner. Thus, the first significant feature of the market for commercial technology is that such technology should be treated as the private property of its owner, not as a public good capable of general use at little or no cost to its user.[4] Commercial technology is usually commoditised through the application of intellectual property rights, which give the owner a legally determined monopoly over the use and disposal of that right, or by way of protected and restrictive contractual transfer as in the case of non-patentable know-how that is secret. This process of commoditisation may help to increase the value of the technology to its owner by creating relative scarcity through legally restricted access to it. However, not all types of useful knowledge are so treated. Thus, knowledge in agriculture, health sciences or services is relatively free from private claims based on intellectual property and should be more freely available.

The generation of commercial technology is closely bound up with the technological infrastructure of a country. This includes the public and private organisations which fund the development and adaptation of technology, the public and private research and development (R&D) organisations that conduct work on new and improved technology, the intermediaries who move the technology around the country and across its borders and the users who apply the technology in their business activities or who are the end consumers of products incorporating the technology in question. Consequently, the states that possess the more developed systems for generating, delivering and using technology are likely to be the leading sources of proprietary technology.[5]

TNCs are strongly influential in the operation of national and international technological infrastructures. They can be found operating at each stage of such a system in the most technologically advanced economies of the world. That this should be so stems from the fact that one of the main ownership specific advantages of TNCs is their ability to 'produce, acquire, master the understanding of and organise the use of technological assets across national boundaries'.[6] Consequently, TNCs are a major force in shaping international markets for technology, particularly on the supply side. Their influence on the demand side is also

---

[3] See further Muchlinski, 1999, pp 425–426.

[4] See further Muchlinski, 1999, pp 427–429 from, which the following paragraphs have been adapted and developed.

[5] See UNCTAD, 1999, pp 198–202

[6] Dunning, 1992, p 290. Professor Dunning observes that in the late 1980s MNEs were accounting for between 75percent and 80percent of privately undertaken R&D in the world.

significant, given that increasing amounts of international technology transfers occur between related enterprises.

Turning to the supply side, the world's major TNCs will seek to control commercial technology markets for maximum gain, exploiting their dominant position in such markets. However, the degree of control exercised by these firms may vary according to the type of technology involved. A distinction has been drawn between markets for 'conventional' technology, where the technology is sufficiently distributed for many firms from many countries to be able to supply it, and markets for 'high' technology, where the technology can be developed only by a few very large firms with very high R&D spending and where constant innovation is the basis for competitive success. Examples of the former include: footwear, textiles, cement, pulp and paper or food processing. Examples of the latter include: aerospace, electronics, computers, chemicals and machinery. The supply of technology in 'conventional' industries is said to be relatively competitive, given the stable and generally non-proprietary nature of the technology involved. By contrast, in 'high' technology areas competitive supply is likely to be restricted. Owners will guard the source of their competitive advantage, making their technology available only on restrictive terms favourable to the earning of a monopoly rent. Furthermore, such considerations may create a preference for internalised transfer of technology within the network of TNC affiliates, rather than an externalised transfer to unaffiliated licensees. In addition, the absence of viable alternative technology suppliers that could offer competition over the terms and conditions of transfer could exacerbate the risk of monopolistic pricing of the technology and its associated products and/or services. However, it would be a mistake to see all 'high' technology markets as uncompetitive on the supply side. For example, in the newer high technology industries, such as semiconductors or computers, the entry of smaller, innovative firms has stimulated choice in sources of technological supply, making for increased competition in that field, although in the long-term concentration can be predicted to occur. Furthermore, as 'high' technology matures into 'conventional' technology, new entrants into the field can be expected. The competitive situation on the supply side of a market for technology is not, therefore, a static phenomenon, and each industrial sector should be analysed on its own terms.

The demand side of the market will also be conditioned by the nature of the technological infrastructure present in the state where the recipient is situated. Thus a distinction can be made between conditions in technologically advanced recipient states and those in technologically less developed states. Conditions in the former are characterised by an ability to absorb technology effectively through advanced production systems, a highly trained workforce, high demand for the technology concerned and the ability to pay for it. Furthermore, technologically advanced recipients will be in a stronger position to bargain over the terms of supply. Alternative local sources of technology, which can compete with the technology on offer from outside, are more likely to exist. Moreover, there exists a greater likelihood that the purchaser will itself be in a strong position to condition the market, as where it is another major corporation operating at the same level of the market as the supplier, or where it is in a quasi-monopolistic position such as, for example, the postal and telecommunications authority of a major advanced country. In advanced countries the principal concern is that of ensuring the existence of workable competition even in highly concentrated technology markets. Thus competition law plays a significant role in the regulation of technology transfers to such countries.

By comparison, the absorption of proprietary technology in developing countries is more problematic. The absence of a sophisticated technological infrastructure has significant consequences for demand conditions. In particular, a high level of dependency on outside suppliers is created due to the lack of alternative, domestically generated technology caused by a relatively underdeveloped domestic industrial and R&D base. This creates a weak bargaining position which is exacerbated by the relative lack of information about technology caused by the absence of adequate numbers of skilled specialists who could evaluate the technology on offer. In such cases the technology owner is likely to enjoy a monopolistic position in relation to the recipient market and may be able to exact excessive prices and restrictions on the utilisation of the imported technology.

Consequently, the conditions of technology transfer will be determined by the needs of the TNC as an integrated enterprise. TNCs are among the main sources of new technology to developing countries. TNCs transfer technologies in two ways: *internalised* to affiliates under their ownership and control, and *externalised* to other firms.[7] *Internalised* transfer takes the form of direct investment and is, by definition, the preserve of TNCs. It is difficult to measure and compare directly the amounts of technology transferred in this manner. Measured by payments for royalties and licence fees, a substantial part of the payments is made between affiliates in the same firm. Furthermore, the trend towards the forging of strategic alliances between competing firms for the development and application of new technologies, has created networks within which technology is transferred, and has tended to blur the distinction between internalised and externalised technology transfer—although in strictly economic terms such transfer still takes place within a single economic enterprise, and so can be understood in terms of an internalised transfer.[8] *Externalised* modes of transfer by TNCs take a variety of forms: minority joint ventures, franchising, capital goods sales, licenses, technical assistance, subcontracting or original equipment-manufacturing arrangements. TNCs are not the only type of firm that can supply technology by this means. Purely national firms can do so as well. However TNCs are very important in high-technology areas and in providing entire packages, including not only the technology but management, marketing and other factors which can make the technology work to its best limits.[9] What determines the mode of technology transfer? According to the aforementioned UNCTAD study on *Transfer of Technology* this can be answered by reference to a number of variables. The most important of these are: *the nature of the technology*, in that internalised transfer is more likely in highly complex and fast moving technology areas so that the firm can retain control over its competitive advantage as the developer and owner of the technology in question; *the business strategy of the seller*, as where it has decided that a specified affiliate will obtain the exclusive global mandate to produce a particular product line; *the capabilities of the buyer*, in that an externalised transfer assumes the existence of a competent licensee, the absence of which may require an internalised transfer to a new affiliate (often at higher cost and risk than licensing to a third party) where projected demand for the product or service involved justifies such expenditure; *host government policies* which may demand the compulsory licensing of technology to local partners.[10]

From a purely commercial perspective, it may be desirable to allow TNCs a 'free choice of means' in determining whether to transfer technology internally or externally. However, from a development perspective there may be certain advantages and disadvantages stemming from the choice of transfer mode. Naturally this discussion assumes the possibility of a choice: where no suitable external recipient exists then an internalised transfer becomes the only feasible way forward. This can occur either through the establishment of a new affiliate in the

---

[7] See UNCTAD, 1999, p 203; Muchlinski, 1999, pp 431–432; UNCTAD, 2001b, pp 12–15.
[8] See Dunning, 1997, chapter 3.
[9] UNCTAD, 1999, p 203.
[10] UNCTAD, 2001b, p 13.

host country, or through the acquisition of a local firm that can be turned into a suitable recipient.[11] Given the existence of such a commercially feasible choice, the UNCTAD study lists a number of advantages and disadvantages to development from an internalised transfer.[12] The principal advantages would include: the provision of technology and financial resources; the possibility of expanding the technological base of the host economy; the use of advanced technology that may not be available through externalised transfer or the use of mature technology applied in an international production network; increased speed of transfer; and access to the technological assets of the TNC offering learning opportunities for the host economy. By contrast two major disadvantages of internalised transfer are highlighted: first, the host economy must pay for the entire 'package' brought by a TNC which, in addition to technology, may include brand names, finance, skills and management, which will raise the overall cost of the transfer—especially where local firms possess such capacities in which case internalised transfer will be more expensive than external transfer to local enterprises. Second, the retention of technology and skills within the network of the TNC may hold back deeper learning processes and spill-overs into the local economy, especially where the local affiliate is not developing R&D capabilities.

In the light of the above, where a choice exists between internal transfers to TNC affiliates or external transfers to local technology recipients, governments may wish to intervene to affect the terms of transfer as where incentives are offered to TNCs for the transfer of advanced technical functions.[13] Indeed, concerns over the monopolistic tendencies of suppliers in developing country technology markets provided a major justification for calls for greater regulation of international technology transfers in the interests of developing recipient countries. This gave rise to new kinds of legal regimes in the 1970s, pioneered by Japan, the Republic of Korea and the Latin American states,[14] based on specialised technology transfer laws; and to negotiations for an international Code of Conduct on Technology Transfer (the Draft TOT Code) under the auspices of UNCTAD,[15] which will be considered further below, alongside more recent developments.

Finally two further issues, raised by the recent UNCTAD study, should be considered in the context of technology transfer to developing countries. The first is that of technology diffusion. According to UNCTAD, the diffusion of technology and skills within the host economy is a major benefit to be gained from technology transfer. In response to the presence of TNCs, local firms and industries may become linked into the technological processes of those firms through what are often termed 'demonstration effects', as where local firms seek to imitate the technology applied by TNCs, and to compete with TNCs by improving their technological capabilities and raising productivity. Equally, diffusion can occur through co-operation between TNC affiliates and local suppliers and customers, stimulating technology spill-overs to vertically linked firms and service providers. Furthermore, labour mobility from foreign affiliates to local firms, particularly of highly skilled personnel, can stimulate technological development.[16] On the other hand, such spill-over effects may not be inevitable, as where the TNC closely guards its competitive advantage in its technology, whether through its retention within the TNC network, and/or through limited skills transfer to employees,

---

[11] UNCTAD, 2000a, pp 174–176.
[12] UNCTAD, 2001b, pp 14–15.
[13] UNCTAD, 2001b, p 15.
[14] See further Omer, 2001, pp 295–312.
[15] UNCTAD, 1985.
[16] UNCTAD, 2001b, pp 15–16.

and/or through restrictive terms in employee contracts, preventing them from revealing technical secrets or from working for direct competitors for a set period of time.[17]

Second, the UNCTAD study highlights some important development implications from the issue of technology generation. As reported by the study, more recent research suggests that TNCs may be more willing than in earlier decades to move their technological assets around the world so as to match them to immobile factors, and to forge new alliances and reorganise production relations.[18] This presents an opportunity for at least the more industrially advanced developing countries to take a more active part in the generation of new technology. However, the impact of foreign direct investment (FDI) on technology generation in developing countries has so far been limited. TNCs tend to centralise their R&D facilities in their home countries and a few other industrially advanced countries. On the whole, developing countries continue to attract only marginal portions of TNC affiliate research, and much of what they get relates to production (adaptation and technical support) rather than innovation. Thus, developing countries are more likely to focus on adapting existing 'conventional' technologies more effectively. Indeed, the majority of developing countries do not have the research skills or institutions to make it economical for TNCs to set up local R&D facilities.[19] On the other hand, a number of firms from developing countries are emerging that specialise in niches of opportunity in such areas as biotechnology, information technology or new areas of services.[20] Given the greater willingness on the part of TNCs to move their technological assets around the world, such enterprises may offer useful allies for TNCs, from both developed and developing countries, in the evolution of new technologies—a process hitherto not commonly encountered in developing countries, and itself raising the question of what constitutes a 'developing country' in an increasingly integrated global economy.

The preceding analysis shows that the market for technology remains one dominated by TNCs possessing proprietary technology. It is also a market in which developing countries may be able to make some headway as locations for specialised transfers aimed at generating new technology 'niches' in areas where they possess competitive advantages. However, for most such countries the likelihood of active involvement in the generation of new technology remains remote. The majority are still faced with the problem of attracting technology needed for development and with the fact that such technology is only likely to be present though internalised transfers within TNC networks with the advantages and disadvantages that such modes of transfer contain. Therefore, at the beginning of the 21st century, not much appears to have changed, as compared to the position in the latter part of the 20th century, in the relative position of dependency that developing countries find themselves in as regards access to technology which remains, on the whole, foreign generated, owned and transferred. It is against this background that the next section of the paper will consider the shift in policy over technology transfer that is identifiable from the contents of international economic instruments dealing with this issue.

---

[17] Muchlinski, 1999, p 432.

[18] UNCTAD, 2001b, pp 11–12; UNCTAD, 1999, p 200–201.

[19] UNCTAD, 2000a, pp 173–174.

[20] UNCTAD, 1999, p 196.

ENCOURAGING TECHNOLOGY TRANSFERS[21]

The encouragement of technology transfers to developing countries has been a recurrent issue in the international economic agenda of the last three decades. This area has seen some significant changes in the approach of international instruments that deal with technology transfer. At least three major approaches can be discerned. These can be termed the 'regulatory', 'market-based development' and 'intra-regional technology development' approaches. In addition environmental concerns have also contributed to the development of new practices in relation to the transfer of environmentally sound technology. Each will be considered in turn.

The 'regulatory' approach

This seeks to encourage increased transfers of technology through collaboration between, in particular, developed and developing countries.[22] It centres on the potentially unequal nature of the technology transfer transaction, especially where the recipient is an enterprise in a developing country, or where—as is more likely—a TNC affiliate in a developing country receives technology from the TNC group network by means of an internal transfer. The underlying rationale for provisions displaying this approach is to control the potentially adverse economic consequences of such transfers for the weaker party, which includes both the licensee in an external transfer and the developing host country in the case of all transfers. The 'regulatory' approach is characteristic of instruments concluded by developing countries in the 1960s and 1970s, of which the Andean Community's Decision 24 is the leading example.[23]

Thus, UN Declaration on the Establishment of the New International Economic Order (General Assembly Resolution 3201 (S-VI)) requires respect for the principle of 'giving to the developing countries access to the achievements of modern science and technology, and promoting the transfer of technology and the creation of indigenous technology for the benefit of the developing countries in forms and in accordance with procedures which are suited to their economies'.[24] This principle is given some form by the Programme of Action on the Establishment of a New International Economic Order (General Assembly Resolution 3202 (S-VI)), which asserts that all efforts should be made: to formulate an international code of conduct for the transfer of technology corresponding to the needs and conditions prevalent in developing countries; to give improved access on the part of developing countries to modern technology; to adapt that technology to their needs; to expand significantly the assistance from developed to developing countries in R&D programmes and in the creation of suitable indigenous technology; to adapt commercial practices governing technology transfer to the requirements of developing countries and to prevent the abuse of rights of sellers; and to promote international co-operation and R&D in exploration and exploitation, conservation and the legitimate utilisation of natural resources and all sources of energy. In addition, the Programme of Action envisages, as part of the agenda for the regulation and control over the

---

[21] This section draws extensively on the author's manuscript which forms the basis of UNCTAD, 2001b, pp 44–70.

[22] *Ibid*, p 44.

[23] UNCTAD, 1996, Volume II, p 454. Decision 24 was superseded by Decision 220, which was in turn superseded by Decision 291 of 21 March 1991 which now represents Andean Community policy in this area: *ibid*, Volume II, p 447.

[24] UNCTAD, 1996, Volume I, p 50.

activities of TNCs, an international code of conduct for TNCs which would aim *inter alia* 'to bring about assistance, transfer of technology and management skills to developing countries on equitable and favourable terms'.[25] In a similar vein, the Charter on the Economic Rights and Duties of States (General Assembly Resolution 3281 (XXIX)) provides in Article 13(4) that, 'All States should co-operate in research with a view to evolving further internationally accepted guidelines or regulations for the transfer of technology, taking fully into account the interests of the developing countries.'[26]

Following on from these policy-making UN Resolutions, the draft UN Code of Conduct on Transnational Corporations contained a general provision on technology transfer that exemplifies the 'regulatory' approach to this issue. By paragraph 36 of the Code, TNCs are placed under the following duties: to conform to the technology transfer laws and regulations of the countries in which they operate; to co-operate with the authorities of those countries in assessing the impact of international transfers of technology in their economies and consult with them regarding various technological options which might help those countries, particularly developing countries, to attain their economic and social development; in their transfer of technology transactions—including intra-corporate transactions—to avoid practices which adversely affect the international flow of technology, or otherwise hinder the economic and technological development of countries, particularly developing countries; to contribute to the strengthening of the scientific and technological capacities of developing countries, in accordance with the policies and priorities of those countries, and to undertake substantial R&D activities in developing countries and make full use of local resources and personnel in this process.[27] The Draft Code of Conduct ends by referring to the applicability of the relevant provisions of the Draft TOT Code for the purposes of the Draft Code of Conduct, thereby emphasising the supremacy of the specialised code in relation to issues concerning technology transfer.

The regulatory approach can also be discerned in the draft provisions of the TOT Code. The draft TOT Code addressed the issue from various perspectives: the legitimatisation of specific domestic policies to promote the transfer and diffusion of technology; rules governing the contractual conditions of transfer of technology transactions; special measures on differential treatment to developing countries; and measures that would strengthen international co-operation.[28] The approach was to concentrate on the supply-side of the market and to remedy constraints to the acquisition of technology by developing countries caused by the domination of the international technology market by TNCs. In particular, it was proposed to liberalise trade in technology and to introduce guidelines on the terms and conditions of transfer of technology to developing countries. This approach concentrated on the transfer of technology *per se*, rather than on its diffusion.

The 'market-based development' approach

The 'regulatory' approach has been overtaken by other developments exemplified by the 'market-based development' approach.[29] Here the technology transfer transaction is not necessarily seen as one between unequal parties. Rather, the private property character of the

---

[25]   *Ibid*, pp 53–54.
[26]   *Ibid*, p 64.
[27]   *Ibid*, pp 168–169.
[28]   See Roffe and Tesfachew, 2001, pp 381–404; UNCTAD, 1999, p 222, Box VII.10.
[29]   See UNCTAD, 2001b, pp 44–45.

technology is stressed and the TNC which owns the technology is seen as being free to transfer it by whatever means it sees fit. However, given the potential inequality of market power between the owner and recipient of the technology, this freedom for the TNC is subject to certain obligations not to abuse its market power, whether in the case of an external transfer to a licensee or in the course of internal transfers within the TNC network. In addition, this approach recognises the potential asymmetry between developed and developing countries in the market for technology transfer, and so includes provisions that seek to encourage co-operation and assistance for developing countries in evolving their own technological base and R&D facilities, and the granting of incentives to TNCs by their home countries so as to encourage technology transfer to developing countries. Thus, it abandons the willingness to prohibit specific terms in technology transfer transactions that is characteristic of the 'regulatory' approach, relying rather on competition rules to control abuses.

The 'market-based development' approach is characteristic of more recent agreements and finds its fullest expression in the TRIPS Agreement.[30] It is best exemplified by the technology transfer related provisions of the TRIPS Agreement and by its competition provisions. These will now be studied in turn, with additional discussion of other related international agreements and instruments displaying a similar policy.

Technology transfer provisions

Articles 7 and 8 of the TRIPS Agreement provide that the protection of intellectual property rights (IPRs) should contribute to the promotion of technological innovation, and the transfer and dissemination of technology, to the mutual advantage of producers and users of technological knowledge and in a manner conductive to social and economic welfare, and to balance of rights and obligations. This policy is further developed in Article 66 (2) of the TRIPS Agreement whereby '[d]eveloped country Members shall provide incentives to enterprises and institutions in their territories for the purpose of promoting and encouraging technology transfer to least developed country Members in order to enable them to create a sound and viable technological base'. This is to be reinforced through an obligation, under Article 67, for developed country Members to provide, on request and on mutually agreed terms and conditions, technical and financial co-operation in favour of developing and least developed country Members in order to facilitate the implementation of the TRIPS Agreement.

A similar approach can be found in the Energy Charter Treaty, the General Agreement on Trade in Services (GATS) and the recently revised OECD Guidelines for Multinational Enterprises. Thus Article 8 of the Energy Charter Treaty calls upon signatories 'to promote access to and transfer of technology in the field of energy technology on a commercial and non-discriminatory basis to assist effective trade in Energy Materials and Products and Investment and to implement the objectives of the Charter subject to their laws and regulations, and to the protection of Intellectual Property rights.' This provision continues by requiring the signatories to eliminate existing, and to create no new, obstacles to the transfer of technology in this field.[31]

In the field of services, Article IV (1) (a) of the GATS Agreement recognises that, in order to increase the participation of developing countries in world trade, further negotiations should be pursued to strengthen their domestic services capacity, their efficiency and competitiveness, '*inter alia* through access to technology on a commercial basis.' Furthermore,

---

[30] UNCTAD , 1996, pp 337–371; see further Roffe, 2000, pp 397–413.
[31] UNCTAD, 1996, Volume II, p 553–554

developed country Members should establish contact points with developing and least developed country Members to supply information concerning, among other things, the availability of services technology.[32] In relation to the objectives set out in Article IV of the GATS, Article XIX makes clear that developing country Members are able to make the liberalisation of market access to foreign service providers subject to conditions that aim to achieve those objectives. Thus a degree of developing host country regulation over entry conditions is accepted where this is likely to enhance the given country's access to technology. Finally, the GATS Annex on Telecommunications obliges developed country Members, where practical, to make available to developing countries information on telecommunications services and developments in telecommunications technology to assist in strengthening their domestic telecommunications services sector.

The OECD Guidelines for Multinational Enterprises also broadly follow a market-based development approach. Thus chapter VIII of the Guidelines encourages enterprises to adopt, where practicable, practices that permit the transfer and rapid diffusion of technologies and know-how, with due regard to the protection of IPRs.[33] Although the Guidelines do not specifically mention developing countries, given that enterprises are expected to '[c]ontribute to economic, social and environmental progress with a view to achieving sustainable development',[34] the Guideline on Science and Technology can be read with the special needs of developing host countries in mind. This is reinforced by the OECD's Commentary on the Science and Technology Guideline which states that access to technology generated by multinational enterprises is 'important for the realisation of economy wide effects of technological progress, including productivity growth and job creation, within the context of sustainable development'.[35] Accordingly, when the Guidelines refer to the need for enterprises to 'perform science and technology development work in host countries to address local market needs, as well as employ host country personnel in a [science and technology] capacity and encourage their training, taking into account commercial needs' they can be understood as introducing development oriented considerations that ought to be taken into account by enterprises when determining their science and technology policy. This is reinforced by paragraph 1 of chapter VIII which states that enterprises should: 'Endeavour to ensure that their activities are compatible with the science and technology (S &T) policies and plans of the countries in which they operate and as appropriate contribute to the development of local and national innovative capacity.'

Arguably, the OECD Guidelines do not, in fact, adopt a pure market-based approach, in that they envisage an element of regulation in this field. However, it should not be forgotten that the Guidelines are voluntary and that they leave a wide measure of discretion to TNCs as to how they will discharge their science and technology obligations.

The adoption of a market-based approach to technology transfer issues can also be discerned in the various co-operation agreements concluded by the European Union (EU) with developing countries. Thus the Fourth Lomé Convention of 1989 contained numerous commitments on the part of the EU to assist in the transfer and acquisition of technology by the developing states parties to the Convention in a variety of fields including agricultural and industrial co-operation, energy and tourism.[36] The more recent Cotonou Agreement of 2000

---

32 GATS, Art IV (2) (c) in UNCTAD, 1996, Volume I, p 290.
33 OECD, 2000, p 26.
34 *Ibid*, p 19.
35 *Ibid*, p 52.
36 See UNCTAD, 1996, Volume II, p 385.

revises this approach, further emphasising the market led policy on technology transfer. Accordingly, by Article 23 (j), co-operation between the EU and developing contracting parties in the field of economic sector development includes the development of scientific, technological and research infrastructure and services, including the enhancement, transfer and absorption of new technologies. This is to be achieved in the context of the general policy behind the Cotonou Agreement to encourage developing country parties to integrate more fully into the global economy. Of particular relevance also is the commitment of all parties, in Article 46, to ensuring an adequate and effective level of protection of IPRs and other rights covered by the TRIPS Agreement. This includes *inter alia* an agreement to strengthen co-operation over the preparation and enforcement of laws and regulations in this field, the setting up of administrative offices and the training of personnel. In a similar vein, agreements concluded between the EU and Latin American economic integration groups contain a commitment to economic co-operation that includes the encouragement of technology transfer.[37]

Finally, although almost all BITs are silent on the question of technology transfer, it should be noted that the most recent Dutch Model Agreement of 1997 states in its Preamble that 'agreement upon the treatment to be accorded to investments [by the nationals of one Contracting Party in the territory of the other Contracting Party] will stimulate the flow of capital and technology and the economic development of the Contracting Parties... '[38] Thus the Dutch Model Agreement makes a clear connection between the promotion and protection of investors and their investments, and the stimulation of technology transfer. In that sense, it could be said that such a policy may be seen as part of the market-based development approach, as it aims for the creation of market conditions conducive to increased investment which, in turn, may lead to increased transfers of technology as part of the investment process.

Competition related provisions

Notwithstanding the aforementioned specific provisions on technology transfer, the main thrust of the TRIPS Agreement is centred on the belief that the encouragement of technology transfer is best achieved in an environment where IPRs are fully protected as private commercial property and where the market for technology is maintained in as competitive a condition as possible.[39] As pointed out above, earlier attempts at the multilateral regulation of technology transfers concentrated on defensive measures that could remedy dysfunctions in the international market for technology. Today, however, defensive measures are less in favour on the grounds that market imperfections are seen to be best addressed by measures aimed at improving the contestability of such markets. Hence competition policy acquires a greater significance than interventions that seek to modulate forcibly the conditions under which technology transfer takes place.[40]

The main interface between the generation, transfer and diffusion of technology and competition law relates to the control of restrictive business practices (RBPs) in licensing agreements—one of the major objectives of the unfinished TOT Code. The Draft TOT Code contained a more specific treatment of RBPs in relation to technology transfer in its Chapter 4.

---

[37]　See Framework Agreement for Cooperation Between the EU and the Cartagena Agreement and its Member Countries, 1993; EU–MERCOSUR Interregional Co-operation Agreement 1993, Arts 11(2) and 16(2) (b) (cooperation in technology transfer in the field of telecommunications).

[38]　UNCTAD, 2000b, Volume V, p 333.

[39]　UNCTAD, 2001b, pp 63–64 on which this paragraph is based.

[40]　UNCTAD, 1999, p 222; UNCTAD, 2001b, pp 70–79, on which the following paragraphs are based.

This part of the Draft Code was to prove one of the hardest to negotiate and, indeed, the failure to agree on its terms was a major reason for the eventual non-adoption of the Code. This was due to the then continuing disagreement between developing and developed country models of technology transfer regulation.[41] The former wished to take an economic regulation oriented approach which concentrated on the review of clauses in technology licensing agreements with a view to the prohibition of those clauses seen as inimical to the development process and/or likely to take advantage of the weaker bargaining position of the local technology recipient. The latter saw the issue primarily as one of ensuring effective competition in the transfer of technology. Accordingly only those clauses that could be seen as unreasonable restrictions on the freedom of the recipient to compete, or which placed unreasonable restraints on the competitive freedom of third parties, would be regulated. These two policy goals do not necessarily produce the same results. For example, a reasonable tie-in clause, requiring the technology recipient to obtain supplies of inputs from the technology transferor that would otherwise not be available in the open market at the same price or quality, might be acceptable on a competition-based analysis, but may be seen as a barrier to the development of local supply chains in the context of a developing country economy.[42] On the other hand there was general agreement over the list of practices that should be subject to regulation. These included: grant-back provisions, challenges to validity, exclusive dealing, restrictions on research, restrictions on the use of personnel, price fixing, restrictions on adaptations, exclusive sales or representation agreements, tying arrangements, export restrictions, patent pool or cross-licensing agreements and other arrangements, restrictions on publicity, payments and other obligations after expiration of industrial property rights and restrictions after expiration of arrangements. However, there remained disagreement on the text relating to some of these practices, namely export restrictions, publicity restrictions and restrictions after expiration of arrangements.

As can be seen from the developed country position over chapter 4 of the Draft TOT Code, the second, market-based, approach to RBPs and technology transfer has existed for some time. However, this approach has been used in more recent international instruments, suggesting that the debate which occurred in relation to chapter of the Draft TOT Code has moved in the direction of a competition approach based on the test of the reasonableness of particular restrictive terms and conditions.[43] In particular, under Article 8 (2) of the TRIPS Agreement, States may adopt such measures as may be needed 'to prevent the abuse of intellectual property rights by right holders or the resort to practices which unreasonably restrain trade or adversely affect the international transfer of technology' provided that these are consistent with other provisions of the Agreement such as, for example, the non-discrimination provisions. This policy is reiterated in Article 40 and of the TRIPS Agreement which adds, as examples of the types of practices that may be controlled, exclusive grant back conditions, conditions preventing challenges to the validity of IPRs and coercive package licensing. Article 40 adds that members shall enter, on request, into consultations with other Members in cases where such abuses of rights are suspected. The new competition oriented rules that the TRIPS Agreement has introduced have made many instruments used in the past by the then newly industrialising countries difficult to apply.[44] Specialised technology transfer laws are perhaps the best example here.[45] On the other hand there is scope for competitiveness

---

[41] Blakeney, 1989, pp 141–150; Muchlinski, 1999, p 445.

[42] Muchlinski, 1999, pp 433–436.

[43] See Roffe and Tesfachew, 2000, p 397.

[44] UNCTAD, 1999, p 223.

[45] Muchlinski, 1999, pp 446–449.

oriented strategies to be adopted by developing countries to improve their ability to assimilate and develop technology.[46]

Turning to other agreements and instruments, the NAFTA regime follows a similar approach to that in TRIPS. Thus Article 1704 of NAFTA states that the Parties are free to specify, in their domestic law, 'licensing practices or conditions that may in particular cases constitute an abuse of intellectual property rights having an adverse effect on competition in the relevant market. A Party may adopt or maintain, consistent with the other provisions of this Agreement, appropriate measures to prevent or control such practices or conditions'.[47] Furthermore, it should be noted that the OECD Guidelines for Multinational Enterprises recommend that enterprises should, 'when granting licenses for the use of intellectual property rights or when otherwise transferring technology, do so on reasonable terms and conditions and in a manner that contributes to the long-term development prospects of the host country'.[48] Thus the Guidelines supplement State rights to control RBPs in the field of IPRs with an exhortation that TNCs police their own negotiating practices and avoid the use of unreasonable terms and conditions.

Interestingly, the Guidelines go beyond a pure market-based competition analysis and also mention the development prospects of the host country. Though ambiguous as to its precise meaning, this formulation suggests that development concerns may be relevant when determining whether certain terms are reasonable or not. As the Commentary to the Guidelines asserts, not only should TNCs ensure that the terms and conditions on which they sell or license technology are reasonable, but also they may want to consider how they can improve the innovative capacity of their international subsidiaries and subcontractors and add to the local scientific and technological infrastructure, and how they may usefully contribute to the formulation by host governments of policy frameworks conducive to the development of dynamic innovation systems.[49] Such considerations will no doubt have an impact on what terms and conditions might be regarded as reasonable or unreasonable in the context of a sale or licensing of technology to a recipient in a developing host country.

Finally, in relation to competition related provisions dealing with technology transfer, it should be noted that BITs concluded by the United States and, more recently, Canada contain a clause specifically permitting technology transfer requirements where these are imposed by the courts, administrative tribunals or competition authorities of the host contracting party to remedy an alleged violation of competition laws.[50] A similar clause is to be found in NAFTA Article 1106 (1) (f) which prohibits any Party from imposing or enforcing any commitment related to the establishment, acquisition, expansion management, conduct or operation of an investment of an investor of a Party or a non-Party in its territory to transfer technology, a production process or other proprietary knowledge to a person in its territory, except when the requirement is imposed or the commitment or undertaking is enforced by a court, administrative tribunal or competition authority to remedy an alleged violation of competition laws or to act in a manner not inconsistent with other provisions of the Agreement.[51] Article 1106 (2) goes on to exempt, from the prohibition in paragraph (1) (f), any measure that requires an investment to use a technology to meet generally applicable health, safety or

---

[46] See UNCTAD, 1999, pp 223–228.

[47] North American Free Trade Agreement (NAFTA), 1993.

[48] OECD, 2000.

[49] *Ibid*, Commentary on Science and Technology, paragraph 54.

[50] See Canada/Philippines Agreement 1995, Art V(2)(e); US Model BIT 1994, Art VI (e).

[51] UNCTAD, 1996, Volume III, p 75.

environmental requirements though such measures will be subject to the prohibition on discrimination contained in the national treatment and most-favoured-nation treatment provisions of NAFTA. The NAFTA provisions were followed *verbatim* in the Canada-Chile Free Trade Agreement 1996 Article G-06 (1) (f) and (2).[52]

The above approach to the issue of technology transfer performance requirements was taken as a starting point for the formulation of a clause on this matter in an alternative International Agreement on Investment prepared by the Consumer Unity and Trust Society (CUTS) of India for the UNCTAD Round Table between Ambassadors and NGOs on a Possible Multilateral Framework for Investment jointly organised with the United Nations Non-governmental Liaison Service in Geneva on 10 June 1998. Thus Article IV (1) (f) and (2) of this instrument reproduce, in essence, the same provisions as are found in NAFTA and the other agreements mentioned above. However there is one significant difference: Article 4 (7) declares that, 'Notwithstanding anything contained in paragraph 1, a Contracting Party shall be free to adopt a measure otherwise prohibited by that paragraph for compelling social or economic reasons'.[53] CUTS explains this proviso by reference to the fact that many countries would find a harsh set of obligations in this area difficult to accept. Furthermore, 'a prohibition against requiring a foreign investor to transfer its specialised technology to local citizens would, in effect, mean that the level of technology in the host country would remain stagnant for all times to come. If the host country extends certain benefits, it should, in its turn, be allowed to derive benefits also.'[54] Thus the CUTS formulation offers an alternative approach based on a degree of regulation that is broader than that accepted by the North American formulation, which restricts regulatory intervention to competition-based or health, safety and environmental technology transfer requirements.

Finally, an alternative formulation, which preserves the full discretion of the host country to impose performance requirements, concerning *inter alia* technology transfer at the point of entry, is provided by the Asian-African Legal Consultative Committee Draft Model Agreement 'B' for Promotion and Protection of Investments. By Article 3(ii) thereof:

> The investment shall be received subject to the terms and conditions specified in the letter of authorisation. Such terms and conditions may include the obligation or requirement concerning employment of local personnel and labour in the investment projects, organisation of training programmes, transfer of technology and marketing arrangements for the products.

This approach is consistent with the regulatory model of technology transfer provisions discussed above.

The significance of environmental issues

An important variation to the 'market-based development' approach may be seen to be emerging in relation to environmental issues. Provisions for the transfer of environmentally sound technology to developing countries are increasingly common in international environmental agreements.[55] For example, the UN Framework Convention on Climate Change and its Kyoto Protocol contain specific provisions with regards to transfer and development of technology. These instruments have as their starting point the free commercial transfer of technology by TNCs, but subject to the need to ensure that such transfers are not harmful in

---

[52] UNCTAD, 2000b, Volume V, pp 82–83.
[53] *Ibid*, Volume V, p 420.
[54] *Ibid*, p 421.
[55] See further UNCTAD, 2001a, pp 41–50.

environmental terms and that TNCs are encouraged to transfer environmentally sound technologies to developing countries which may otherwise have no opportunity to use them. Thus, Article 19 of the Energy Charter Treaty encourages the sharing of technical information on environmentally sound technologies and the transfer of such technologies subject to the adequate and effective protection of IPRs. Equally, the UN Biodiversity Convention of 1992 establishes a link between 'appropriate' access and utilisation of genetic resources, on the one hand, and 'appropriate' transfer of relevant technology to developing countries (including those subject to patents and other intellectual property rights), on the other hand. This link is expressly acknowledged as part of the objectives of the Convention, which are:

> The conservation of biological diversity, the sustainable use of its components and the fair and equitable sharing of the benefits arising out of the utilisation of genetic resources, including by appropriate access to genetic resources, and by appropriate transfer of relevant technologies taking into account all rights over those resources and to technologies, and by appropriate funding.

Indeed, the Convention goes further in the text and uses mandatory language providing that the parties must provide and/or facilitate access for, and transfer to, other parties, 'technologies that are relevant to the conservation and sustainable use of biological diversity or make use of genetic resources and do not cause significant damage to the environment'.[56]

The 'intra-regional technology development' approach

This third approach has been adopted in regional economic development agreements between developing countries.[57] These agreements differ from the 'regulatory' model in that they concentrate on the encouragement of intra-regional technology development and transfer, whether through regional industrial policies or through the establishment of specialised regimes for regional multinational enterprises. They do not deal as such with technology transfer by investors from outside the region. Neither can these agreements be seen as examples of the 'market-based development' approach in that they are firmly committed to the development of member country sponsored industrial development policies. However, they may be closer in spirit to this approach as these regional agreements do not subject the inward transfer of technology by investors from outside the region to strict regulatory controls. Provisions encouraging the development and transfer of technology by enterprises operating within the region may be divided into two main groups: general provisions stressing co-operation in areas relevant to the development and transfer of technology within the region and specialised provisions establishing regional multinational enterprises, which, in turn, have an obligation to develop technology and transfer it across the region.[58]

LESSONS FOR THE DEVELOPMENT OF 'LAW AND DEVELOPMENT'

We have seen earlier that the provisions of international economic agreements, and related instruments that have dealt with technology issues, display a shift in focus, offering a range of approaches to such issues. These approaches have been characterised as falling within two main categories: first, a regulatory model, which seeks to control the conditions under which

---

[56] Biodiversity Convention 1992, Art 16(1).

[57] UNCTAD, 2001b, pp 68–70.

[58] For examples see *ibid*.

IPRs are protected and technology is transferred and which aims to protect the weaker party to the transfer, typically a technology recipient in a developing country; and second, a market-based development model, which stresses the need to maintain as high a degree of freedom for technology owners to exploit their advantages in this area as they see fit, subject only to competition-based regulation.[59] Furthermore, under this model, host countries are largely restricted in the nature and extent of performance requirements that they might impose in relation to the generation, transfer and diffusion of technology. Of course, these approaches are not mutually incompatible and it is possible to envisage a mixed approach which combines elements of regulation and market freedom. This is the case, it seems, in relation to the treatment of TNC obligations arising out of the science and technology policies followed by the countries in which they operate and as regards the transfer of environmentally sound technology. Furthermore, though competition controls may be seen as part of the market-based development approach, they undoubtedly offer a discretion to host and home countries alike to act with a light or heavy touch in their regulation of the possible anti-competitive effects of technology transactions undertaken by TNCs.[60]

So, what lessons does this empirical study suggest for the field of law and development? The first is the need to maintain an interdisciplinary perspective on law and development issues. When judged in the light of the realities of the market for technology, the shift towards a market-based development approach may be more rigorously and critically assessed. It displays a mismatch between market reality and market freedom which, by contrast, the older regulatory approach did acknowledge through its acceptance for the need to regulate technology transfer transactions. Equally, such an approach can point out the weakness of excessive state involvement in the control of market transactions and instruct as to the limitations of the older approach.

Second, the market-based approach does not envisage a total rejection of regulatory policies: clearly the emphasis is on a duty of technical assistance and co-operation on the part of developed countries and TNCs in the field of technology transfer, as exemplified by some of the aforementioned provisions in international instruments and agreements. The question raised here concerns whether the approach to this duty, adopted by existing instruments and agreements, is enough. As pointed out by Maskus, in his valuable study of the TRIPS Agreement, the obligations in Articles 66 and 67 thereof have offered little in practice to developing countries, while at the same time they have been expected to take on significant obligations in relation to the protection of IPRs, notwithstanding the grant of transitional periods to these countries.[61] Thus there may be a need to introduce a more demanding regime of co-operation in the area of technology generation, transfer and diffusion in the next round of negotiations over TRIPS.

Third, the shift to market-based approaches in relation to technology transfer does not dispel the insight of earlier concepts of developing country dependency that lie at the heart of the principle of 'common but differentiated responsibility',[62] a basic principle of an 'International Law of Development' (IDL) used in numerous instruments to ensure that the

---

[59] Advocates of stronger IPRs claim that increased protection together with adequate enforcement mechanisms would increase FDI flows and associated technology transfer to developing countries (see Beier, 1980). However, empirical evidence is rather mixed. Some researchers suggest that stronger IPRs are likely to have a positive impact on FDI while others are more cautious: See, for example, UNTCMD, 1993; Ferrantino, 1993; Kondo, 1995, Mansfield, 1994.

[60] UNCTAD, 2001b, p 83.

[61] Maskus, 2000, pp 225–226. See also De Feyter, 2001, pp 99–100.

[62] See Slinn, 1999, p 309.

special needs of developing countries are recognised. The case-study confirms that developing countries continue to be economically dependent on imported technology; and raises the question of the need to maintain and (as suggested above) strengthen the concept of preferential treatment for developing countries in relation to the transfer of technology. That much should not be in issue. The real question is how to operationalise this preference. It was suggested above that it may be necessary to impose stronger obligations of co-operation on developed countries in this area. In this regard the Doha Ministerial Conference decided that the mandatory obligation in Article 66(2) to assist the least developed countries in the transfer of technology should be strengthened through a monitoring mechanism. This is based on reports, submitted by the end of 2002 by developed country Members, on the functioning in practice of the incentives provided to their enterprises for the transfer of technology under Article 66(2). These reports will then be subject to review by the TRIPS Council and updated annually.[63]

Another possible avenue of reform might be to reconsider the use of transitional periods as a technique for offering more flexible approaches to developing and least developed country obligations. The current approach in TRIPS is to provide for general periods of transition without detailed consideration of the actual situation faced, in relation to IPR protection and technology transfer, by specific developing and least developed country Members. This may need to change, so that a less arbitrary case-by-case approach can be adopted in determining the precise length of the required transitional period. After all, not every developing country will face the same conditions in its transitional period, and different countries may find it relatively easier or harder to comply with the obligations in the Agreement, even within the established transitional periods.

Fourth, the repositioning of IDL towards a more holistic concept of development, integrating economic and social issues, is beginning to be reflected in technology transfer instruments. The inclusion of environmental concerns in technology transfer provisions may be seen as evidence of this trend. There is, no doubt, room for other social issues to be included in the future. One possible new area concerns the reform of technology transfer provisions in the light of the emergent principles of corporate social responsibility, which may include respect for the development objectives of developing countries in which firms operate, as suggested by the OECD Guidelines. Another possible issue concerns the use of human rights impact assessments in the examination of technology transfer transactions, aimed at determining whether the transaction in question enhances or detracts from the human rights concerns of the people affected by it. For example, the recent debate over the availability of patented drugs to control the symptoms of HIV/AIDS infection in developing countries raised these kinds of issues in the context of the right to health and life of the sufferers who needed the drugs, but who were not gaining access to them as a result of the patent rights exercised by the pharmaceutical companies that had developed the drugs in question.[64] The importance of this matter was re-emphasised by the adoption of the WTO Declaration on the TRIPS Agreement and Public Health at the Doha Ministerial Meeting on 14 November 2001.[65] This accepts that the TRIPS Agreement must be interpreted and implemented in a manner supportive of WTO Members' rights to protect public health and to promote access to medicines for all.[66]

---

[63] Doha Ministerial Conference, 2001, para 11.2.
[64] See further Joseph, 2001.
[65] WTO, 2001.
[66] *Ibid*, para 4.

Finally, the above discussion points to a more general theme that will play an increasingly important role in the future evolution of law and development, namely, how to deal with the re-emergence of regulatory questions out of the market-based approach to development. In relation to the subject matter of this study, the Doha Declaration contains a significant statement. By paragraph 22, which outlines the programme of work on the clarification of specific investment issues, it is made clear that '[a]ny framework should reflect in a balanced manner the interests of home and host countries, and take due account of the development policies and objectives of host governments as well as their right to regulate in the public interest.'[67] This raises the challenge of what is meant by a *'right to regulate'* in a global market environment, especially in the case of a developing or least developed country.

The present study identifies at least four areas of regulation that appear to be accepted in a market-oriented technology transfer regime: environmental protection, the need to maintain competition, co-operation in national science and technology policies and technical assistance and incentives to enterprises, offered by home countries of TNCs, aimed at enhancing technology transfer. To this may be added, as issues for future elaboration, the strengthening of preferential treatment for, in particular, the least developed countries and the introduction of social/human rights impact assessments of technology transfers.

In some ways this could be seen as a return to the old 'regulatory' agenda. However, that would not be wholly accurate. That agenda was born out of a specific historical context which was characterised by recent decolonisation, the prior existence of an international IPR regime elaborated by and for the developed countries only, and calls for greater respect for national sovereignty and economic self-determination for developing countries. The contemporary environment is, by contrast, characterised by a growing historical distance from colonial rule, significantly increased integration of the global economy through the operations of transnational capital markets and TNCs, the continuing domination of technology markets by the latter and a growing realisation of the inadequacy, not only of direct state involvement in the economy, but also of unregulated markets, such as the international market for technology, which display limits on free competition and may lead to resultant market failure which will adversely affect developing countries in particular. It is against this background that a new regulatory agenda is evolving.

The implications of these matters for the wider progress of law and development lie, arguably, in the need for the subject to adapt and evolve new methodologies for articulating a development oriented theory of regulation as it operates in the contemporary transnational context. This requires, as a first step, the recognition of the relevance of the existing literature on 'law and regulation' to law and development'.[68] The second step is to learn lessons from that literature and adapt these to actual development issues. That would require another paper—if not a series of papers!—and cannot be undertaken here. However, certain points can be made: first it is necessary to adapt what is predominantly a domestic and public law oriented discourse to a transnational public/private economic/social sphere;[69] second, it is necessary to rise above a narrow liberalisation/privatisation agenda and develop ideas about how social issues might affect and inform the new transnational dimension of development oriented regulation; third, it is necessary to concentrate further on co-operation, information

---

[67] Doha Ministerial Conference, 2001.

[68] See further Ogus, 1994, and Baldwin and Cave, 1999, for an introduction to this literature. See too Baldwin, Scott and Hood, 1998; Bratton, McCahery, Picciotto and Scott, 1996; and Picciotto and Campbell, 2002.

[69] On which see further the papers in Picciotto and Campbell, 2002.

transfer and monitoring systems at the transnational level, as these may be the essential facilities through which genuine development oriented policies can be put into effect.

As can be seen from the preceding discussion, the case of technology transfer is a rich example from which lessons can be learnt for the progress of law and development in general and IDL in particular. The social and economic changes that have challenged the original model of IDL do not lead to the conclusion that IDL is dead. Rather, they show that the issues traditionally addressed by IDL continue to give rise to practical questions that must be answered. Indeed, many of the inequalities that gave rise to the moral impetus behind IDL have not disappeared—they might even have become more pressing. If that is so, then the need remains for a global law relating to the equitable distribution of productive resources—in which the transfer of technology is a central issue—and to the promotion of ethical behaviour on the part of both state and non-state actors involved in the development process. That need can be filled by a progressive and responsive 'International Development Law' as a part of a wider area of law and development.

REFERENCES

Baldwin, R and Cave, M, *Understanding Regulation*, 1999, Oxford: OUP

Baldwin, R, Scott, C and Hood, C, *A Reader on Regulation*, 1998, Oxford: OUP

Beier, F K, 'The significance of the patent system for technical, economic and social progress' (1980) 11 *International Review of Industrial Property and Copyright Law* 563

Biodiversity Convention 1992 (1992) 31 ILM 818

Blakeney, M, *Legal Aspects of Technology Transfer to Developing Countries*, 1989, Oxford: ESC Publishing

Bratton, W, McCahery, J, Picciotto, S and Scott, C, *International Regulatory Competition and Co-ordination*, 1996, Oxford: Clarendon Press

Bulajic, M, *Principles of International Development Law*, 1986, Dorderecht: Martinus Nijhoff

Canada/Philippines Agreement 1995 in UNCTAD, *BITs in the Mid 1990s*, 1998, Geneva: UNCTAD

De Feyter, K, *World Development Law*, 2001, Antwerp: Intersentia

Doha Ministerial Conference *Implementation-Related Issues and Concerns* Decision of 14 November 2001 WTO Doc WT/MIN(01)/17 20 November 2001

Doha Ministerial Conference *Ministerial Declaration* 14 November 2001 WTO Doc WT/MIN(01)/DEC/1 20 November 2001.

Dunning, J H, *Alliance Capitalism and Global Business*, 1997, London: Routledge

Dunning, J H, *Multinational Enterprises and the Global Economy*, 1992, Wokingham: Addison-Wesley

EU-MERCOSUR Interregional Co-operation Agreement 1993

Ferrantino, M J, 'The effect of intellectual property rights on international trade and investment' (1993) 129:2 Weltwirtschaftliches Archiv 300

Framework Agreement for Co-operation Between the EU and the Cartagena Agreement and its Member Countries 1993 in UNCTAD, *International Investment Agreements: A Compendium* Volume V, 2000, New York and Geneva: United Nations

General Assembly Resolution 51/240 *An Agenda for Development*, 20 June 1997

Joseph, S, 'The "third wave" of corporate human rights accountability: parmaceuticals and human rights' paper presented at the 'Human Rights and Global Challenges Conference' Castan Centre for Human Rights, Monash University, 10-11 December 2001

Kondo, E K, 'The effect of patent protection on foreign direct investment' (1995) 29:6 Journal of World Trade 97

Mansfield, E, 'Intellectual property protection, foreign direct investment and technology transfer', *Discussion Paper*, No 19, 1994, Washington, DC: The World Bank and International Finance Corporation

Maskus, K, *Intellectual Property Rights in the Global Economy*, 2000, Washington, DC: Institute for International Economics

Muchlinski, P T, '"Basic needs" theory and "development law"', in Snyder, F and Slinn, P (eds), *International Law of Development: Comparative Perspectives*, 1987, Abingdon: Professional Books

Muchlinski, P T, *Multinational Enterprises and the Law*, 1999, Oxford: Blackwell Publishers

New York Agreement Relating to the Implementation of Part XI of the Law of the Sea Convention (1994) 33 ILM 1309

North America Free Trade Agreement (NAFTA) (1993) 32 ILM 605

OECD, *The OECD Guidelines for Multinational Enterprises*, 2000, Paris: OECD

Ogus, A, *Regulation*, 1994, Oxford: Clarendon Press

Omer, A, 'An overview of legislative changes', in Patel, S J, Roffe, P and Yusuf, A (eds), *International Technology Transfer: The Origins and Aftermath of the United Nations Negotiations on a Draft Code of Conduct*, 2001, The Hague: Kluwer Law International

Picciotto, S and Campbell, D (eds), 'New directions in regulatory theory' (2002) 29:1 Journal of Law and Society Special Issue

Roffe, P, 'The political economy of intellectual property rights—an historical perspective', in Faundez, J, Footer, M and Norton, J J (eds), *Governance, Development and Globalisation*, 2000, London: Blackstone Press

Roffe, P and Tesfachew, T, 'The unfinished agenda', in Patel, S J, Roffe, P and Yusuf, A (eds), *International Technology Transfer: The Origins and Aftermath of the United Nations Negotiations on a Draft Code of Conduct*, 2001, The Hague: Kluwer Law International

Slinn, P, 'The international law of development: a millenium subject or a relic of the twentieth century?', in Benedeck, W, Isak, H and Kicker, R (eds), *Development and Developing International and European Law*, 1999, Frankfurt: Peter Lang

Snyder, F and Slinn, P (eds), *International Law of Development: Comparative Perspectives*, 1987, Abingdon: Professional Books

UN Declaration of the Right to Development, UNGA Resolution 41/128, 4 December 1986

UNCTAD (1985), *Draft International Code of Conduct on the Transfer of Technology*, 1985, UN Doc TD/CODE TOT/47, 20 June 1985 in *International Investment Agreements: A Compendium* Volume 1, 1996, New York and Geneva: United Nations

UNCTAD (1996), *International Investment Agreements: A Compendium* Volumes II-II, 1996, New York and Geneva: United Nations

UNCTAD (2001a), *Environment*, Series on issues in international investment agreements, 2001, United Nations: New York and Geneva

UNCTAD (2001b), *Transfer of Technology*, UNCTAD Series on issues in international investment agreements, 2001, New York and Geneva: UNCTAD

UNCTAD, *World Investment Report 1999*, 1999, New York and Geneva: United Nations

UNCTAD (2000a), *World Investment Report 2000*, 2000, New York and Geneva: United Nations

UNCTAD (2000b), *International Investment Agreements: A Compendium* Volumes IV and V, 2000, New York and Geneva: United Nations

United Nations Convention on the Law of the Sea 1982, UN Doc A/CONF.62/122, (1982) 21 ILM 1261

United Nations, *An Agenda for Development: Report of the Secretary-General*, UN Doc A/48/935, 6 May 1994

UNTCMD *Intellectual Property Rights and Foreign Direct Investment* (1993) UN Doc ST/CTC/SER A/24

US Model Bilateral Investment Treaty 1994 in UNCTAD, *BITs in the Mid 1990s*, 1998, Geneva: UNCTAD

WTO, Declaration on the TRIPS Agreement and Public Health at the Doha Ministerial Meeting on 14 November 2001, WTO/MIN(01)/DEC/W/2, available at www.wto.org

CHAPTER 6

PATENTS AND HEALTH IN DEVELOPING COUNTRIES

Philippe Cullet[*]

'By January 1, 2005, developing countries must provide patents for new pharmaceutical products... Nothing is more controversial in TRIPS.'[1]

The link between patents on medicines and the human right to health has become a subject of central concern at the international level, as exemplified by the recent debates at the 2001 WTO ministerial conference.[2] International attention has focused in large part on the HIV/AIDS crisis, and the question of access to drugs for patients in those developing countries most affected by the epidemic.[3] The issue of access to drugs is acute in the case of HIV/AIDS, but is of general concern in most developing countries. It is also related to broader issues, such as the patentability of drugs and the human right to health.

Current debates take place in the context of the Agreement on Trade-Related Aspects of Intellectual Property Rights (TRIPS) provisions relating to the patentability of medicines.[4] Most proposals to improve access to drugs focus on ways to make drugs more affordable for patients in developing countries, without compromising the existing legal framework provided by TRIPS. This imposes the introduction of process and product patents on drugs in all WTO member states. There is, for instance, a growing body of literature concerning differential pricing and related mechanisms which fall within the patent system. While differential pricing, gifts by pharmaceutical companies or special contracts to supply the drugs cheaply to specific countries are important, it is necessary to place the question of access to drugs in a broader context. TRIPS is not the only relevant legal framework that should dictate policies on access to drugs. In fact, TRIPS does not have much to say concerning health, while there is a whole body of work concerning the human right to health which tends to be overlooked in current debates.

This article examines the context in which the debates concerning access to drugs arise. The first section examines the question of access to drugs from the point of view of intellectual property rights. The second focuses on human rights and the right to health in particular. Finally, the third section examines some of the theoretical and practical issues facing developing countries striving to implement both their intellectual property and human rights obligations.

---

[*] Lecturer, Law Department, School of Oriental and African Studies, University of London, pcullet@soas.ac.uk.
[1] World Bank, 2001, p 137.
[2] See 'Doha Health Declaration', 2001.
[3] Over 95percent of people living with HIV/AIDS are in developing countries. See 'Drug Price Report', 2001.
[4] 'TRIPS Agreement,' 1994.

ACCESS TO DRUGS AND THE GLOBAL INTELLECTUAL PROPERTY RIGHTS REGIME

Intellectual property rights, in particular patents, are deemed to provide the necessary incentives for research and technological development in some fields. Patents are time-bound monopoly rights. They derogate from the principle of free trade by offering exclusive rights to an inventor to use the invention, and to stop others from using it without his/her consent. The rationale for granting patents is the need to reward an inventor. In practice, this translates mainly into a right to commercialise the invention, and to stop others from commercialising it. The exception to the free trade rule is balanced with a limit on the duration of the right, and by forcing the inventor to disclose the invention, so that society at large benefits from scientific advancement.

The intellectual property rights system and health

Patents generally constitute an incentive for the development of the private sector in areas where they are granted. In the pharmaceutical sector, the private sector health industry finds them indispensable.[5] The argument in favour of patents on drugs focuses on the fact that the pharmaceutical industry spends more than any other industry on research and development (R&D) and that, while the development of new drugs is a costly process, it is relatively easy to copy an existing drug.[6] The patent system thus allows firms to charge prices that are higher than the marginal price of production and distribution to the first generation of patients, who are expected to absorb the cost of developing the drug. It is only after the product loses patent protection that competition among generic versions can bring the price closer to the marginal cost. One important factor to be taken into account in the case of drugs is that the price of drugs under patents may differ more significantly from the marginal price than in other sectors, because the demand for pharmaceuticals tends to be rather price-inelastic.[7]

Despite the private industry's plea for patent protection, a number of countries have traditionally restricted the patentability of drugs on public policy grounds. In fact, many developing countries provided either no patent protection or partial protection in the pharmaceutical sector, in large part because health was considered a basic need which should be protected from full commercialisation.[8] Although patents on drugs are now the norm in OECD countries, some countries—including countries with significant interests in the pharmaceutical sector such as Switzerland—introduced product patents on drugs relatively recently.[9]

In recent years, there have been wide-ranging debates concerning the potential contribution of the introduction of patents in developing countries to the development of drugs related to specific tropical diseases. One of the perceived benefits of the introduction of drug patents in all WTO member states is that it should give incentives to the private sector pharmaceutical industry to undertake more R&D in finding cures for diseases common in

---

[5] See, for example, Scherer 2000/1.

[6] See, for example, Bale, 1998; and Cueni, 1999.

[7] See, for example, Barton, 2001.

[8] 'WHO Policy Perspective', 2001.

[9] For Switzerland, see Loi fédérale sur les brevets d'invention, 1954 and Amendment of 1976.

developing countries.[10] However as the World Bank noted, if patent protection has the capacity to raise incentives marginally, it may also support considerably higher prices.[11]

The issue of patent protection in the health sector has proved increasingly divisive. This is in part linked to the fact that there is a significant tension between the pharmaceutical industry's aim to recoup its investments, and governments' interests in containing health care costs. Further, from a theoretical point of view, it remains uncertain whether the intellectual property right system is in fact an incentive to invent. For instance, Professor Barton finds that the intellectual property right system generally favours large firms over small ones, and in the final analysis stifles innovation rather than promoting it.[12] He argues that it is possible that the intellectual property system contributes to an unnecessarily concentrated industrial structure.[13]

Controversies at the theoretical and practical levels concerning patents on drugs have led to the search for alternatives. A number of proposals focus on making the patent system more 'health friendly', by searching for ways to keep the existing system in place and seek arrangements from within. These include focusing on some of the 'traditional' exceptions allowed in patent law such as compulsory licensing. In recent times, significant attention has also been given to differential pricing.[14]

Access to drugs and patents

Access to drugs is one of the fundamental components of the human right to health.[15] It is of specific importance in the context of the introduction of patents on drugs, because patents have the potential to restrict access. Accessibility generally refers to the idea that health policies should foster the availability of drugs to all those who need them at affordable prices.[16] First, this implies a strong link between access to drugs and poverty. Second, about one third of the world's population does not have access to basic drugs, a proportion which goes beyond 50percent in the worst off regions of Africa and Asia.[17] Third, a large proportion of people in developing countries do not have access to medical insurance and mostly pay for drugs themselves.[18] Since price is a major issue affecting access, it is significant that most theoretical models of the impacts of patents show that patented drugs are more expensive than generics.[19] However, patents are not the only factor influencing access,[20] since even cheap generic drugs may not be affordable for people below the poverty line. Access in these situations requires further measures such as public subsidies or price control measures. Finally, the sheer scope of the problem of access to drugs can be highlighted with the case of HIV/AIDS. A consortium of international organisations has estimated that less than 10percent

---

[10] Agrawal and Saibaba 2001.

[11] World Bank, 2001.

[12] Barton, 1999.

[13] *Ibid.*

[14] On compulsory licensing and differential pricing, see below.

[15] See, for example, Commission on Human Rights, 2001b.

[16] Velásquez and Boulet, 1998. See also United Nations Development Programme, 2001, p 3 estimating that about 2 billion people do not have access to low-cost essential drugs.

[17] See, for example, Velásquez, 2000/1.

[18] See, for example, World Health Organization and World Trade Organization Secretariats, 2001.

[19] See, for example, Dumoulin, 2000/1.

[20] See, for example, 'Drug Price Report,' p 5, stating that factors related to affordability include: patents, limited volume, limited competition, import duties and tariffs, local taxes and mark–ups for wholesaling, distribution and dispensing.

of the people living with HIV/AIDS in developing countries have access to antiretroviral therapy. This proportion goes down to about 0.1percent in Africa.[21]

The introduction of process and product patents in developing countries is likely to significantly influence access to drugs in most countries. Some of the main impacts will include price hikes, negative impacts on local pharmaceutical industries and a greater emphasis on private sector research and development in this field. These are likely to collectively cause a decrease in the accessibility and affordability of drugs. A comparison of the prices of similar drugs in India and other countries clearly indicates the benefits of a restrictive patent regime for end-users.[22] With regard to research, it is unlikely that the redistribution of resources to the private sector will trigger the development of more drugs specifically related to the needs of the poor. In fact, as noted by the WHO, of the 1,223 new chemical entities developed between 1975 and 1996, only 11 were for the treatment of tropical diseases.[23]

The TRIPS Agreement and access to drugs

The main vehicle for the introduction of patents on pharmaceuticals in developing countries is TRIPS. TRIPS generally seeks to provide minimum levels of intellectual property protection in all WTO member states. In other words, all WTO member states must accept standards of protection which are generally equivalent to a consensus position among developed countries. In the field of patents, the final agreement imposes the patentability of inventions, whether products or processes, on all fields of technology.[24] TRIPS is, as its name implies, concerned mainly with the interests of intellectual property rights holders. Further, intellectual property in TRIPS is mainly seen as a vehicle to foster trade and not as a moral recognition for scientific or technological prowess. Despite the very 'technical' nature of the agreement, TRIPS has significant impacts beyond the trade and intellectual property areas. However, the linkages between intellectual property, environmental management and human rights are not given much prominence in the WTO context.

TRIPS is by any account a treaty of major importance. From the point of view of developed countries, it is seen as one of the most significant achievements of the Uruguay Round.[25] For developing countries, TRIPS is significant because of the impacts it will have on the process of economic development, and on the realisation of fundamental human rights, such as the right to food and health.[26] As far as health is concerned, TRIPS will be an important vector in bringing about major changes to the health sector, especially in countries which rejected product and/or process patents on drugs. Indeed, the introduction of product and process patents in the pharmaceutical sector implies a fundamental change of orientation for countries such as India, which prohibited product patents on pharmaceuticals; and even more for countries such as Brazil, where no patents were available in this field prior to the Uruguay Round. In particular, the new regime will have important implications in countries like India where the domestic pharmaceutical industry owes its current status largely to the existing

---

21 *Ibid.*
22 See, for example, Chaudhri, 1997, p 6.
23 'WHO Policy Perspective'.
24 'TRIPS Agreement', Art 27(1).
25 See, for example, 'Special 301 Report', 2001, p 4.
26 TRIPS is also more significant in practice than many other international treaties because it provides rather strict obligations backed by a binding dispute settlement mechanism and associated sanctions. See Understanding on Rules and Procedures Governing the Settlement of Disputes, Art 22.

legal framework. These concerns are shared by the United Nations Development Programme (UNDP) which remarks that the existing potential of world technology to contribute to the eradication of poverty—for example, by giving access to the poor to essential drugs—is thwarted rather than helped by TRIPS, because it reinforces benefits to developers of inventions and not to society at large.[27]

Avenues to foster access within TRIPS

TRIPS introduces a relatively strict legal regime, especially as compared to some national laws in force before 1994 such as the 1970 Indian Patents Act. However, within the strict TRIPS framework of minimum standards of protection, there exist exceptions and qualifications that can be used to foster public policy goals such as access to essential drugs. TRIPS includes two general qualificatory provisions found at Articles 7 and 8. The first reminds member states that intellectual property rights regimes should contribute to the promotion of technological innovation and to the transfer and dissemination of technology 'in a manner conducive to social and economic welfare'.[28] It also recognises that the rights and obligations of patent holders should be balanced, thus acknowledging that limitations on intellectual property rights are a fundamental component of the regime. Article 8 specifically indicates that states can 'adopt measures necessary to protect public health and nutrition, and to promote the public interest in sectors of vital importance to their socio-economic and technological development'. However, Article 8 also mentions that these measures must be consistent with the provisions of TRIPS, thus limiting their scope. Indeed, it would be difficult to justify an exception not foreseen in TRIPS under Article 8, unless it is an exception to a right which is not protected under TRIPS.[29]

Exclusions to patentability and limitations of the right

Apart from the general qualificatory clauses at Articles 7 and 8, a number of important exceptions are found in the patents section itself. First, some exceptions to the scope of patentability are allowed.[30] For example, Article 27(2) allows states to restrict the patentability of inventions if they pose a threat to human life or health. However, the restriction on patentability is not acceptable if the law simply bans the exploitation of the invention. This would, for instance, prohibit a blanket restriction on product patents on pharmaceuticals.

Additionally, Article 30 permits states to limit the exclusive privilege granted through patent rights. However, this exception is also bound by several qualificatory provisions. First, there can only be 'limited exceptions' to monopoly rights; second, the exceptions should not 'unreasonably conflict' with the exploitation of the patent; and third, the exceptions should not 'unreasonably prejudice the legitimate interests' of the patent owner. Although the exceptions provided by Article 30 are bound by these qualificatory statements, the term 'limited exceptions' is not defined. This provision can therefore be used by countries to pursue public health goals. Indeed, that is exactly what the objectives clause of Article 7 requires in calling for a balance between the promotion of innovation and the transfer and dissemination of innovation, and for a balance of rights and obligations for the patent holder. This analysis is confirmed by a reading of the last part of Article 30, which shows that states must avoid

---

[27] United Nations Development Programme, 2000, p 83.

[28] 'TRIPS Agreement', Art 7.

[29] See, for example, Gervais, 1998, p 68.

[30] In principle, all inventions, whether product or processes, in all fields of technology are patentable. See 'TRIPS Agreement', Art 27.

'unreasonably' prejudicing the interests of patent owners, and at the same time must take into account the legitimate interest of third parties. On this basis, it may even be possible to argue that Article 30 permits states facing a severe HIV/AIDS crisis to provide exceptions to patent rights to fulfil the 'legitimate interests of third parties'—in other words, the interests of HIV/AIDS patients to have access to existing life-saving drugs. The major difference between Article 27(2) and Article 30 is that the latter does not allow states to reject the patentability of a given drug or other invention, only to regulate its use.

Compulsory licensing

The general exceptions of Articles 27(2) and 30 are supplemented by Article 31, which provides a regulatory framework for compulsory licensing. Compulsory licensing is permissible under TRIPS, but under strict conditions.[31] These include the following: compulsory licenses must only be issued on a case-by-case basis; states must first try to secure authorisation on commercial terms, unless there is a national emergency, or the state wants to make public non-commercial use of the invention; the term of the license must be limited to the purpose for which it is authorised, non-exclusive, and mainly to supply the domestic market; and the patent holder is entitled to 'adequate' remuneration and the decisions taken are subject to judicial review.

The compulsory licensing framework provides developing countries with tools to control some of the impacts of the introduction of patents, even where they are forced to extend patentability to new areas under Article 27. From the perspective of public health, a positive feature is that there is no limitation on the purposes for which compulsory licenses can be granted, thus giving member states significant leeway in framing public health and other public policy goals.[32] However, this remains limited insofar as Article 31 only allows the licensing of individual inventions. Clauses permitting the compulsory licensing of a whole class of products, such as drugs, would therefore be unacceptable.[33]

Further important features of Article 31 are the provisions concerning patent holder remuneration. While Article 31(h) calls for adequate remuneration, the context of Article 31 implies that this remuneration is necessarily below the cost of a normal license, since otherwise there would be no need for compulsion.[34] Article 31 also leaves states free to determine what constitutes a national emergency, as confirmed by the Doha declaration.[35] This is one of the clauses which may foster significant flexibility in TRIPS in the case of health emergencies such as HIV/AIDS. Indeed, African heads of state have proclaimed HIV/AIDS to be a state of emergency in the whole continent.[36] They have also specifically pointed out that they would use international trade regulations to ensure the availability of drugs at affordable prices.

Article 31(f) also addresses issues related to the working of the patent and importation. As specified under Article 28, the patent holder is not forced to industrially use the protected invention in the country where it is registered. Commercial use through imports is also

---

[31] See 'TRIPS Agreement', Art 31.

[32] As confirmed by the WTO Declaration on the TRIPS Agreement and Public Health, 2001.

[33] *Cf* 1970 Indian Patents Act, s 87 providing in derogation of the general regime that all food and medicine related inventions should be deemed to be endorsed with the mention 'license of right'.

[34] See, for example, Watal, 2001, p 325; and Weissman, 1996. Contra: Gervais, 1998.

[35] See 'Doha Declaration', 2001, s 5(c).

[36] Organisation of African Unity, 2001.

possible.[37] However, Article 6 specifically indicates that the question of parallel imports is not dealt with under TRIPS.[38] This leaves countries free to decide whether to take advantage of existing price differences in different countries around the world. In the case of compulsory licensing, countries can still take advantage of these provisions if they do not have the capacity to manufacture, or can find cheaper alternatives elsewhere. However, as noted above, Article 31(f) restricts countries from compulsorily licensing an invention to manufacture it mainly for exports. Articles 6 and 31(f) read together can thus be used by countries that have relatively high drug prices in their domestic market, or no manufacturing capacity to buy elsewhere.

Differential pricing

The question of parallel imports is directly linked to the issue of differential pricing. Differential pricing refers to the selling of drugs at different prices in different markets in order to take into account different levels of economic development and capacity to pay. In the case of drugs developed by northern multinational companies for diseases that exist both in developed and developing countries, the private sector pharmaceutical industry does not consider differential treatment to be controversial, since it does not affect their profits. At the same time, it is beneficial from the point of view of access in developing countries, since drugs can be sold without loss to the industry at a price equivalent or close to the marginal cost of production. Differential pricing fails to resolve two problems. First, the marginal cost of production may still be much more than what patients in developing countries can afford. Similarly, even if the price of a single dose is 'affordable', this may not be the case if a drug is to be taken for long periods of time. This implies that differential pricing is not sufficient in itself, and would have to be supplemented in many cases by subsidies. Second, where differential pricing results in low prices for developing countries, developed country private sector pharmaceutical companies will not have the necessary incentive to engage in R&D relating to developing country diseases.[39]

There is a definite tension in current proposals for differential pricing. On the one hand, differential pricing can only work satisfactorily from the point of view of intellectual property holders if markets are tightly segmented to prevent the leakage of differentially priced drugs to high-income markets.[40] This implies that there can be no parallel importation as provided under Article 6 of TRIPS if there is to be differential pricing, as markets must remain separate. On the other hand, Article 6 constitutes one of the instruments that developing countries can use to take advantage of different prices in different markets either due to different market conditions or to different intellectual property rights regimes. On the whole, Article 6 gives developing countries some flexibility within the patent system, while differential pricing with segmented markets gives this flexibility to intellectual property rights holders.[41]

---

[37] The definition of what amounts to 'working' the patent has changed over time and industrial use is not required any more. Cf Correa, 1999.

[38] On parallel imports, see generally Abbott, 1998.

[39] See, for example, Danzon, 2001.

[40] World Health Organization and World Trade Organization Secretariats, 2001.

[41] Cf Barton, 2001.

ACCESS TO DRUGS AND HUMAN RIGHTS

There are growing debates concerning the extension of patentability in the health sector because patents are often seen as being inimical to the realisation of the right to health for a majority of poor people in developing countries. In effect, one of the core issues is the lack of concurrence between intellectual property law and human rights law. This is due to the fact that the intellectual property system has traditionally not been linked to socio-economic concerns. The extension of patentability to sectors directly linked to the fulfilment of basic needs such as food and health requires a new look at the linkages between intellectual property and human rights. This section focuses specifically on the human right to health and its relationship to the intellectual property rights system.

The human right to health

The importance of a healthy life has generally been acknowledged at the domestic and international levels, and the right to health has been included as a human right in a number of international instruments. However, like other economic and social rights, it remains subject to frequent criticism for being vague in content and intersecting with too many other rights.[42] One of the most detailed pronouncements is found in the International Covenant on Economic, Social and Cultural Rights (ESCR Covenant) which recognises everyone's right to the 'enjoyment of the highest attainable standard of physical and mental health'.[43] The existence of a right to health—and other economic and social rights—implies obligations to respect, protect and fulfil that right. States are to refrain from interfering directly or indirectly with the enjoyment of the right, they should take measures to prevent third parties from interfering with the guarantees provided, and they should adopt appropriate legislative, administrative and other measures towards the full realisation of the right.[44]

The Covenant generally requires member states to take steps to the maximum of their available resources to progressively achieve the full realisation of the protected rights. It also indicates that these 'steps' should be taken through international assistance and co-operation, as well as by each state separately.[45] The Covenant thus clearly recognises that the full realisation of the rights may require more than domestic measures. It is symptomatic that the Committee on Economic, Social and Cultural Rights (ESCR Committee) has clearly indicated in its authoritative interpretation of the right to health that states have an obligation to facilitate access to essential health facilities, goods and services in other countries and to provide the necessary aid when required.[46] Further, states are to ensure that other international agreements they accede to do not adversely impact on the right to health. These are clear indications that states must, for instance, co-operate in making drugs available at affordable prices.

As expounded by the ESCR Committee, the core obligations of the right to health include the necessity to ensure the right of access to health facilities, especially for vulnerable or marginalised groups.[47] In the case of primary health care, this includes the promotion of a safe

---

42   Cf Fidler, 1999.
43   See ESCR Covenant 1966, Art 12. On the right to health, see generally Toebes, 1999.
44   See 'General Comment 14', 2000.
45   'ESCR Covenant'.
46   'General Comment 14', 2000.
47   Ibid.

and adequate food supply and proper nutrition; an adequate supply of safe water and basic sanitation; immunisation against the major infectious diseases; appropriate treatment of common diseases and injuries; and provision of essential drugs.[48] In the case of HIV/AIDS more specific elaborations of these obligations have been given. The World Health Assembly has, for instance, called on its member states to increase access to treatment and prophylaxis of HIV-related illnesses through measures such as ensuring provision and affordability of drugs.[49] The UN Human Rights Commission has gone in the same direction with its resolution on HIV/AIDS, stating that access to medication in this context is one fundamental element for achieving the full realisation of the right to the enjoyment of the highest attainable standard of physical and mental health.[50]

Apart from emphasising the importance of accessibility and affordability, the ESCR Committee has also indicated some circumstances in which the right to health will be considered to have been violated. These include the repeal of legislation necessary for the continued enjoyment of the right to health, and the adoption of legislation or policies manifestly incompatible with pre-existing domestic or international legal obligations in relation to the right to health.[51] Similarly there can be a violation of the obligation to respect the right to health if a state fails to take into account its legal obligations when entering into bilateral or multilateral agreements.[52]

Human rights and intellectual property rights

From the point of view of human rights instruments, the relationship between the intellectual property rights system and the realisation of human rights has not been given much consideration. However, unlike intellectual property law which has been conceived until recently entirely on its own, international human rights law has at least considered some of the relevant issues over the past few decades.

In fact, the ESCR Covenant includes a specific intellectual rights provision which recognises at Article 15(1)(c) everyone's right 'to benefit from the protection of the moral and material interests resulting from any scientific, literary or artistic production of which he is the author'.[53] It is important to understand the context within which intellectual property was included in human rights treaties. Sub-paragraph (c) was not present in the original draft Covenant of 1954. Article 15(1) only included two sub-paragraphs, which recognised everyone's right to take part in cultural life and the right 'to enjoy the benefits of scientific progress and its application'.[54] Article 15(1) was thus conceived mainly from the point of view of the 'end-users' of scientific inventions or cultural development. The original article did not even include an indirect reference to the interests of inventors or authors. Article 15(1)(c) must thus be read as an adjunction, and cannot prevail over the first two sub-paragraphs of the

---

48   See Declaration of Alma-Ata, Art VII.

49   World Health Assembly, 2000.

50   Commission on Human Rights, 2001.

51   'General Comment 14'.

52   See, for example, Intellectual Property and Human Rights – Statement of the Committee on Economic, Social and Cultural Rights, 2001 (CESCR IP Statement) para 12 stating specifically that 'any intellectual property regime that makes it more difficult for a State party to comply especially with its core obligations in relation to health, food, education or any other right set out in the Covenant, is inconsistent with the legally binding obligations of the State party.'

53   ESCR Covenant, Art 15(1)(c).

54   Draft Covenant on Economic, Social and Cultural Rights, 1954. Note that Art 15 was Art 16 in the 1954 draft. References in this chapter are all to Art 15.

article.[55] Further, Article 15(1)(c) refers only to 'authors'. Indeed, the rationale for the introduction of the amendment by Costa Rica and Uruguay was to protect authors against improper action on the part of publishers.[56] Uruguay argued that the lack of international protection allowed the piracy of literary and scientific works by foreign countries which paid no royalties to authors.[57] The idea was not to qualify the first two sub-paragraphs, but rather to highlight one specific problem.[58]

Article 15(1)(c) derives directly from Article 27(2) of the Universal Declaration.[59] The drafting history of the Declaration brings some more useful elements to the fore. First, the original Article 27 did not include a second paragraph.[60] This was added following an amendment proposed by Mexico on the basis of a similar provision included in the 1948 Bogotá Declaration.[61] In support of its submissions, Mexico argued that it was necessary to add to the rights already protected in the draft Declaration the rights of the intellectual worker, scientist or writer in order to protect all forms of work—manual and intellectual—on an equal basis.[62] France was one of the most active supporters of the proposal. Two elements of the French position must be noted. First, Professor Cassin had in mind both copyrights and patents. Second, his argument for including such a provision in the Declaration was that many scientists attached more importance to the spiritual side of their work, especially recognition, than to profits. He argued that patents and royalties were not enough, because they concentrated only on the material side.

It is notable that France was clearly thinking only of the 'traditional', individual scientist as an inventor, and of the need to protect and recognise her/his contribution. Further, Mexico and the other Latin American countries viewed the introduction of an intellectual property clause as a safeguard against predatory moves by foreign publishing houses. Finally, even though some countries made reference to scientific development and patents in the course of the deliberations, statements show that state representatives usually analysed the clause from the perspective of copyright only.[63]

Following the adoption of TRIPS, UN human rights bodies have progressively given more attention to the question of the impacts of intellectual property rights on the realisation of human rights. Among the political organs, the Sub-Commission on Human Rights adopted, for instance, a resolution in 2001 which recognises the existence of potential conflicts between the implementation of TRIPS and the implementation of economic, social and cultural rights.[64] Further, the ESCR Committee has embarked on the task of adopting a General Comment on the relationship between human rights and intellectual property. As an intermediary measure,

---

[55] For the text of the proposed amendment, see UN Doc A/C.3/L.636/Rev.1 (1957).

[56] Draft International Covenant on Human Rights, Report of the 3rd Committee, 1957.

[57] United Nations, Third Committee Summary Record of Meetings, 1957.

[58] Note that the amendment was accepted by 39 states including most Western European and Latin American countries and rejected by 9 countries from the communist bloc. Twenty–four countries abstained, including the United States. See Draft International Covenant on Human Rights, Report of the 3rd Committee, 1957.

[59] United Nations, Third Committee Summary Record of Meetings, 1957.

[60] See United Nations, Report of the Third Session of the Commission on Human Rights, 1948. Note that Art 27 of the final text was Art 25 in the draft Declaration. References in this chapter are all to Art 27.

[61] See American Declaration of the Rights and Duties of Man and United Nations, Art 13; Draft International Declaration of Human Rights – Mexico: Amendment to Article 25 of the Draft Declaration, 1948.

[62] United Nations, Third Committee Summary Record of Meetings, 1948.

[63] See, for example, the statements of the Dominican Republic supporting the amendment, UN Doc A/C.3/SR.799 (1957) and India which abstained, UN Doc A/C.3/SR.798 (1957).

[64] See Resolution 2001/21, 2001.

a statement on the matter was adopted in 2001.[65] Though non-binding on member states, this statement constitutes an important guide for an understanding of the human right to health in the TRIPS era.

The right to health in the TRIPS era

The introduction of process and product patents in developing countries is likely to significantly influence access to drugs in most countries. Some of the main impacts will include price hikes, impacts on local pharmaceutical industries and a greater emphasis on private sector research and development in this field. Together, these are likely to reduce accessibility and affordability of drugs. There is therefore a direct link between the patentability of drugs and the availability of medicines, the realisation of the right to health and ultimately the right to life. In other words, it is necessary to analyse the relationship between intellectual property rights and the human right to health.[66]

Since human rights instruments mention intellectual property, it is apt to examine whether intellectual property rights qualify as human rights. In fact, the debates of 1948 and 1957 clearly indicate that basic human rights treaties never intended to recognise the interests of authors (and even less inventors) as basic human rights.[67] Both the Universal Declaration and the first Covenant show that the basic claim they recognise is everyone's right to enjoy the fruits of cultural life and scientific development. The right of the individual author is subsidiary in the balancing of priorities. The implication is that human rights put the emphasis on societal benefits.[68] This is different from intellectual property rights instruments which focus mainly on the rights of authors, inventors and other legal entities claiming exclusive rights over an intellectual creation. The question of the balance of rights and obligations is included in TRIPS, but the interests of society at large come in more as an addition or even as an exclusion to the rights provided than as a integral part of the treaty. This is in contradistinction with human rights treaties which require the balancing act to be attempted from the perspective of society at large.

Significantly, the ESCR Committee comes to the same conclusion in its statement on intellectual property and human rights where it states that:

> The fact that the human person is the central subject and primary beneficiary of human rights distinguishes human rights, including the right of authors to the moral and material interests in their works, from legal rights recognised in intellectual property systems. Human rights are fundamental, inalienable and universal entitlements belonging to individuals, and in some situations groups of individuals and communities. Human rights are fundamental as they derive from the human person as such, whereas intellectual property rights derived from intellectual property systems are instrumental, in that they are a means by which States seek to provide incentives for inventiveness and creativity from which society benefits. In contrast with human rights, intellectual property rights are generally of a temporary nature, and can be revoked, licensed or assigned to someone else. While intellectual property rights may be allocated, limited in time and scope, traded, amended, and even forfeited, human rights are timeless expressions of fundamental entitlements of the human person.[69]

---

[65]   'CESCR IP Statement', 2001.

[66]   Cf United Nations Development Programme, 2000, p 84, mentioning that TRIPS raises issues of compatibility with human rights and international environmental law.

[67]   Sub-Commission on the Promotion and Protection of Human Rights, 2001.

[68]   Cf UN Doc E/CN.4/Sub.2/2001/13 (2001).

[69]   'CESCR IP Statement', 2001, s 6.

THE RIGHT TO HEALTH AND ACCESS TO DRUGS
IN THE 21st CENTURY

A series of major developments has taken place in recent years concerning access to drugs in developing countries. Of special importance are the adoption of TRIPS and the growing toll taken by HIV/AIDS, in particular in sub-Saharan Africa. While the impacts of TRIPS on the right to health have been debated, hardly any attention has been given to the relationship between TRIPS and the human right to health. This is due in part to the sectoral nature of international law, but also to the unresolved issues raised by potential problems of compatibility between two areas of the law. The general principle remains that developing countries should do their utmost to implement both the ESCR Covenant and TRIPS in such a way as to minimise conflicts. However, there are situations where they may not be completely eliminated. This section starts by examining developing countries' options within the TRIPS framework as it is understood after the Doha meeting. It then goes on to examine the ways in which potential conflicts between intellectual property rights and the human right to health could be resolved under international law.

Options to foster access to drugs

The previous section outlined some of the avenues that developing countries can use within the TRIPS context to foster better access to drugs, and the realisation of the right to health in general. The emphasis was on finding acceptable interpretations of TRIPS from the point of view of access to drugs, rather than on examining the question of the compatibility of TRIPS with the right to health. This enquiry must be pursued given that developing countries must implement TRIPS taking into account the existence of the ESCR Covenant.

A number of recent developments at the international level point towards the possibility for developing countries to act on the margins of TRIPS. This has been brought about mostly by the scale of the HIV/AIDS crisis and the extremely high price of existing medicines used to alleviate the disease. In fact, the extent of the crisis has been sufficient to trigger a US Executive Order which directs that measures taken by countries to promote access to HIV/AIDS medicines should not be challenged.[70] The failed challenges to the South African and Brazilian acts also indicate that even if the adopted measures are not strictly compliant with TRIPS, they are unlikely to be challenged again in the near future.[71] This is likely to be the case with most legislation seeking to foster better access to drugs for epidemics such as HIV/AIDS but not necessarily in other sectors.[72]

The question of the margin of appreciation that countries have in implementing TRIPS is an important issue, but focusing on this point tends to sideline more fundamental issues. Recent debates have focused mostly on the extent to which developing countries should be able to adapt the intellectual property rights system in situations where major problems have

---

[70] US Executive Order No 13,155, 2000. However, note that under this order, beneficiary countries can only benefit from its provisions if they provide adequate and effective intellectual property protection.

[71] Concerning South Africa, see *The Pharmaceutical Manufacturers' Association of South Africa et al vs The President of the Republic of South Africa et al.*, 1998 and *The Pharmaceutical Manufacturers' Association of South Africa et al vs The President of the Republic of South Africa et al*, 2001. Concerning Brazil, see Government of Brazil, 2001.

[72] The US indicated as it was challenging Brazil in the WTO that it made a clear distinction between the health and other sectors. See Special 301 Report, at 10. See also US Statement, 2001.

arisen. This does not deal with the question whether the introduction of process and product patents in all WTO member states is generally reconcilable with the measures that states must take to foster the realisation of the right to health.

There can be different solutions to the problem of reconciling the intellectual property rights system with the realisation of the human right to health. From an intellectual property rights perspective, since the patents system does not deliver all its stated gains in terms of incentives to innovation, it might be possible to strengthen the criteria for obtaining a patent, in particular the requirement of non-obviousness. This may reduce the misuse of patents from the point of view of the researchers and pharmaceutical companies which need easy access to previous research to further innovate.[73] This may also provide indirect gains to patients benefiting from the development of new medicines for diseases previously not curable.

The current status quo that has come about following the Brazilian and South African controversies and the Doha Declaration raises further issues. There is an international consensus that countries trying to deal with health emergencies such as HIV/AIDS will not be questioned in terms of their obligations under TRIPS. However, this leaves completely open a number of other issues. With regard to Brazil, while the US discontinued dispute settlement proceedings in the WTO, it is not at all clear if an international consensus exists that Brazil is free to grant compulsory licenses for any 'facts, among others, related to the public health, nutrition, protection of the environment, as well as those of primordial importance to the technological or social and economic development of this country'.[74] In the case of South Africa, Article 15(C)(a) of the Medicines Act clearly provides that patent rights can be overruled in some circumstances.[75] While the Act entered into force as adopted, it is unclear whether the most stringent provisions will in fact be implemented, and if so, whether implementation would go unchallenged. The theoretical acceptability of the Brazilian and South African laws thus does not necessarily indicate that all countries are entitled to deviate to such an extent from TRIPS.

From a broader perspective, it is clear that even if deviation from TRIPS is allowed as an exception in the case of some health emergencies, this remains an unsatisfactory response from the perspective of human rights. It is not possible to distinguish the realisation of the right to health from the eradication of poverty in general or the realisation of the right to food and water in general. If exceptions are warranted in the case of health, they should be extended to all basic needs. All sectors related to the fulfilment of basic needs should thus be granted exemptions.

On the whole, the fact that developing countries can use loopholes or unclear language in TRIPS to foster the realisation of the right to health is unsatisfactory in that the central concern of health is consistently framed as an exception. A fundamental right such as the right to health cannot be satisfactorily considered only from the point of view of exceptions to property rights like patents. This is confirmed by the approach to health taken by the Doha Declaration. While the Declaration provides gains for developing countries insofar as it extends possibilities for granting compulsory licenses, it does not amend TRIPS. A revision of TRIPS thus appears necessary so that principles in favour of access to drugs are included in the main provisions of the agreement rather than as exceptions.[76] However, an amendment to

---

[73] Barton, 1999.

[74] This constitutes the definition of 'public interest' under the Brazilian Presidential Decree on Compulsory Licensing 1999, Art 1.

[75] See Medicines and Related Substances Control Amendment Act 1997.

[76] As argued by the World Bank, 2001, p 148.

Article 27 TRIPS to compulsorily reduce the scope of patentability is unlikely in the near future, while a strengthening of TRIPS under the guise of the TRIPS-plus regime is possible. There is therefore a need to analyse TRIPS in its present form, and examine to which extent it is compatible with the existing human rights regime.

A human rights approach to patent rights: the case of health

As noted, there are potential tensions between TRIPS and the ESCR Covenant. In trying to find a solution to the question of the compatibility of the two, it is important to have in mind the overall framework that should guide a more technical legal analysis. From the narrow perspective of access to medicines, the challenge is to find ways to make sure that existing drugs are available at little or no cost to people who need them. More generally, the central concern that should guide the implementation of all international treaties concerning health directly or indirectly is the promotion of better health care.

From the standpoint of TRIPS, the question of health is one that can be tackled in some of the exceptions provided in Section 5 of TRIPS or in the two general qualificatory clauses of Articles 7 and 8. However, this falls short of providing a reasoned argument concerning the relationship between TRIPS and human rights. From the point of view of human rights, the link between the two fields was considered already in the drafting of human rights treaties. The general conclusion from the above analysis of human rights provisions is that the interests of the community at large generally prevail over those of the author. This does not imply a rejection of the interests of the author, simply their subordination to broader goals.

A human rights perspective on health neither entails an *a priori* rejection of all intellectual property rights in the field of health, nor provides another avenue for developing countries to claim preferential treatment. However, it leads one to question some of the tenets of intellectual property law. As noted, patent protection entails higher drug prices, while not ensuring that the most common diseases will attract the most research. This implies that even if patent protection can be justified in markets where all consumers can afford to pay—directly or indirectly—the price of patented drugs, this is not necessarily so in other situations. The issue of affordability of medicines is in large part, but not exclusively, a North-South question. In fact, from the point of view of human rights, full implementation must be judged against the level of implementation among the most disadvantaged and marginalised individuals and communities in each and every country. The issue is therefore not whether developing countries can afford patent rights in general, but whether the majority of their poor population will benefit.[77] One of the first steps in tackling the problems faced by the most disadvantaged sections of society would be to make sure that all essential medicines remain free from patent protection. This conceptual framework informed the rejection of product patents on drugs seen in the 1970 Indian Patents Act; and, to more limited degree, the attempt to provide an extensive definition of the public interest in the 1999 Brazilian decree on compulsory licensing.[78]

From a practical point of view, patents on drugs in developing countries are fraught with other difficulties. In a number of countries, most people pay for their own healthcare. Since a large part of the population does not have access to existing drugs today, any price rise tends

---

[77] Similarly, the fact that developed countries in general can 'afford' the costs involved in patent protected drug research, this does not imply that all individuals in those countries are in a position to benefit from the system.

[78] See India: Patents Act 1970; and Brazil: Presidential Decree on Compulsory Licensing, 1999.

to limit access for more people. The Indian example is useful. Today, millions of Indian people cannot afford drugs under a regime which denies product patents on pharmaceuticals. If prices are allowed to go even higher under TRIPS-mandated product patents, even fewer Indians will have access to drugs. From this perspective, the need is not for patent rights that lead to price rises, but for even lower prices to facilitate broader access to drugs.

In cases where compliance with TRIPS leads to reduced access to drugs in most developing countries, this might constitute a violation of the ESCR Covenant. Indeed, although Article 2 does not require immediate full implementation of the right to health, it does require states to take positive measures towards the fulfilment of the right.[79] The introduction of product patents could be construed as a 'deliberately retrogressive' measure.[80] This is due in part to the fact that patents provide incentives for the growth of the private sector, and the latter has not proven over time that it preferentially invests in the most common diseases of the poor.[81] One of the ways in which a state like India could offset the negative impacts of the introduction of product patents is by increasing subsidies so as to facilitate access to drugs by poor people despite higher prices.[82]

Fostering compatibility between human rights and intellectual property

The previous paragraphs highlight some of the problems that exist when trying to reconcile patents and the right to health, but do not address the way international law would solve a conflict in practice. International law does not provide a definite answer to the problem of conflicts between rules of different international treaties. However, there is a need for clear guidance to states that have to implement their human rights and TRIPS obligations.

Generally, states should refer to treaty law which provides broad rules of interpretation and envisages the matter of conflicts between different treaties. Given that they are bound to implement all their obligations, states must attempt to the maximum extent possible to reconcile all their international obligations, or at least to minimise conflicts.[83] International treaties are often sufficiently vaguely drafted to allow a states significant margin of appreciation in implementing them, and this provides an important tool to fully implement all their international obligations at the same time. Previous sections of this chapter show that reconciling patents on drugs and the right to health is only possible to a limited extent. In other words, reconciling the different commitments under TRIPS and the ESCR Covenant seems feasible only if states are allowed to adopt broad interpretations of TRIPS.

International law is to a large extent based on the principle that there is no hierarchy between sources of law and different areas of the law.[84] However, it is not free from any form of hierarchy. First, the UN Charter clearly states that it prevails over any other treaty signed by its member states.[85] But the Charter does not provide a clear answer to the question of conflicts between human rights and other treaty obligations.[86] Beyond the hierarchy recognised in the

---

[79] Committee on Economic Social and Cultural Rights, General Comment No 3, 2000.

[80] *Ibid.*

[81] See, for example, Wolf, 2001.

[82] This is the solution advocated by the World Bank which would rather see public funds used to purchase drugs or licenses rather than removing essential drugs from patentability. See World Bank, 2001, p 148.

[83] This derives from the rule *pacta sunt servanda.* 'Vienna Convention' 1969, Art 26.

[84] See, for example, Carreau, 2001.

[85] See UN Charter, Art 103.

[86] *Cf* Cot and Pellet, 1991.

Charter, the notion of *ius cogens* is relevant here.[87] It is today largely agreed that there are some fundamental principles and norms that states are not free to modify or abrogate.[88] These include, for example, the prohibition of slavery and crimes against humanity. The peremptory status of some other norms, such as the primacy of the respect for all human rights, remains unresolved.[89] At the time of the drafting of the Vienna Convention on the Law of Treaties, a number of states mentioned human rights in their enumeration of peremptory norms. Further, human rights treaties recognise the peremptory status of some specific rights.[90] However, while regional legal regimes such as the European Convention on Human Rights indicate an increasing recognition of the special nature of human rights, it is not yet possible to argue that all human rights are peremptory norms in general international law.[91]

It follows from this analysis that the human right to health is clearly not a non-derogable right under present international law. However, if some sort of a hierarchy had to be established between human rights and intellectual property rights, international law indicates that human rights should generally take precedence. The UN Sub-Commission on Human Rights drew this conclusion in its resolution on intellectual property and human rights when it noted the 'primacy of human rights obligations under international law over economic policies and agreements,' and called on states to ensure that the implementation of TRIPS should not negatively impact on the enjoyment of human rights.[92]

Overall, there seem to be a number of ways to resolve conflicts between the right to health and intellectual property rights, without resorting to a prioritisation between the two—for instance, by guaranteeing the 'social dimensions of intellectual property'.[93] However, in cases where prioritisation is necessary, human rights should be given more weight than intellectual property rights. This is a situation that some countries may face. If the introduction of patents on medicines, which implies higher prices for drugs, is not balanced with measures to offset price hikes, this is likely to lead to reduced access to drugs for people in developing countries who have to pay for their own drugs. This situation is particularly in evidence in countries like India which had specific restrictions on the patentability of drugs with a view to fostering better access to drugs. In this case, the dismantlement of a legal regime intended to foster better access to medicines is a step backwards in terms of the progressive realisation of the human right to health. Unless these changes are offset by other measures in other fields to promote better access to drugs, this may amount to a violation of the ESCR Covenant.

CONCLUSION

TRIPS is without doubt one of the most significant international treaties of the late twentieth century. In the field of health, it has and will have sweeping impacts in most developing countries. One of the complications from an international law point of view is that TRIPS does

---

[87] See, for example, Hannikainen, 1989. See also Koji, 2001.

[88] 'Vienna Convention' 1969, Art 53.

[89] Carreau, 2001.

[90] See, for example, International Covenant on Civil and Political Rights 1966, Art 4.

[91] Some authors agree, however, that human rights are *ius cogens*. See, for example, Hannikainen, 1989, p 429, noting that '[i]n my view there is no doubt that contemporary international law has reached a stage in which it has the prerequisites for the existence of peremptory obligations upon States to respect basic human rights.'

[92] Para 3 and 5 of Resolution 2001/21, 'Intellectual Property and Human Rights', 2001.

[93] 'CESCR IP Statement', s 18.

not arise in a vacuum, but in the context of a well-established human right to health, codified in one of the two main international human rights treaties.

The introduction of patents on drugs has provoked significant outcry in a number of developing countries where access to medicines is already abysmal. The justifications offered for the existence of patents as incentives to innovation often do not appear convincing to patients in developing countries, who see that R&D is overwhelmingly not invested in developing country-specific diseases. In other cases such as HIV/AIDS where drugs to alleviate the condition exist, the prices of these drugs—which are, for all practical purposes, life-saving—have been so high as to be unaffordable for all but the wealthiest individuals in developing countries.

The legal arguments concerning the relationship between human rights and intellectual property rights, and the practical debates concerning access to drugs in developing countries, both point toward the existence of potential conflicts between the introduction of patents on drugs in developing countries and the realisation of the right to health. Although states must endeavour as far as possible to reconcile their different international obligations, there seem to be some cases where the implementation of TRIPS directly implies a reduction in access to drugs, and thus a step back in the implementation of the right to health. This appears to be unacceptable under the ESCR Covenant, according to which countries in this situation would be expected to give priority to their human rights obligations. The solution of giving primacy to human rights is unlikely to meet with the approval of all states, and would probably not stand if it came for adjudication in a WTO context. It nevertheless seems adequate from a legal and ethical point of view.

REFERENCES

Abbott, F M, 'First report (final) to the committee on international trade law of the international law association on the subject of parallel importation' (1998) 1 J Int'l Econ L 607

Agrawal, P and Saibaba, P, 'TRIPS and India's pharmaceuticals industry' (2001) 36 Econ & Pol Wkly 3787

Amendment of 17 December 1976, *Recueil officiel des lois fédérales* 1977, 1997 (Switzerland)

American Declaration of the Rights and Duties of Man, reprinted in *United Nations, Human Rights—A Compilation of International Instruments* (Volume II: regional instruments), UN Doc ST/HR/1/Rev.5 Volume II, 1997

Bale, H E Jr, 'The conflicts between parallel trade and product access and innovation: the case of pharmaceuticals' (1998) 1 J Int'l Econ L 637

Barton, J H, *Differentiated Pricing of Patented Products*, 2001, CMH Working Paper Series Paper No WG4:2

Barton, J H, 'Intellectual property rights and innovation', in Imparato, N (ed), *Capital for our Time: The Economic, Legal, and Management Challenges of Intellectual Capital*, 1999, Stanford, CA: Hoover Institution Press

Brazilian Presidential Decree on Compulsory Licensing, Decree No 3201, 6 October 1999

Carreau, D, *Droit International*, 7th edition, 2001, Paris: Pédone

(CESCR IP Statement) 'Intellectual Property and Human Rights—Statement of the Committee on Economic, Social and Cultural Rights', 29 November 2001

Chaudhri, S, 'The evolution of the Indian pharmaceutical industry', in Felker, G (ed), *The Pharmaceutical Industry in India and Hungary—Policies, Institutions, and Technological Development*, 1997, Washington, DC: World Bank

Commission on Human Rights (2001a), 'Access to medication in the context of pandemics such as HIV/AIDS,' Resolution 2001/53, 23 April 2001

Commission on Human Rights (2001b), Resolution 2001/33, 'Access to medication in the context of pandemics such as HIV/AIDS', in *Report on the Fifty-Seventh Session*, 19 March-27 April 2001, UN Doc E/2001/23-E/CN.4/2001/167

Committee on Economic Social and Cultural Rights, General Comment No 3, 'The nature of states parties obligations (art 2, para 1 of the Covenant)', reprinted in Compilation of General Comments and General Recommendations Adopted by Human Rights Treaty Bodies, UN Doc HRI/GEN/1/Rev.4 (2000)

Convention on the Law of Treaties, Vienna, 23 May 1969, (1969) 8 ILM 679

Correa, C M, *Intellectual Property Rights and the Use of Compulsory Licenses: Options for Developing Countries*, Working Paper No 5, 1999, Geneva: South Centre

Cot, J-P and Pellet, A (eds), *La Charte des Nations Unies—Commentaire Article par Article*, 2nd edition, 1991, Paris: Economica

Cueni, T B, 'Industrial property protection—lifeline for the pharmaceutical industry,' in Cottier, T and Widmer, P (eds), *Strategic Issues of Industrial Property Management in a Globalizing Economy—Abstracts & Selected Papers*, 1999, Oxford: Hart

Danzon, P, *Differential Pricing for Pharmaceuticals: Reconciling Access, R&D, and Intellectual Property*, CMH Working Paper Series Paper No WG2:10, 2001

Declaration of Alma-Ata, 12 September 1978, reprinted in 'Report of the International Conference on Primary Health Care', 1978, Geneva: World Health Organization

(Doha Health Declaration) 'Declaration on the TRIPS Agreement and Public Health Ministerial Conference', Fourth Session, WTO Doc WT/MIN(01)/DEC/2 (2001)

Draft Covenant on Economic, Social and Cultural Rights, Commission on Human Rights, Report of the 10th Session, ECOSOC, 18th Session, Supplement 7, Doc E/2573-E/CN.4/705 (1954)

Draft International Covenant on Human Rights, Report of the 3rd Committee, UN Doc A/3764 (1957)

Drug Price Report: UNICEF-UNAIDS-WHO/HTP/MSF, 'Sources and Prices of Selected Drugs and Diagnostics for People Living with HIV/AIDS,' 2001

Dumoulin, J, 'Les brevets et le prix des médicaments' (2000/1) 45 Revue Internationale de Droit Economique

(ESCR Covenant) 'International Covenant on Economic, Social and Cultural Rights,' New York, 16 December 1966, reprinted in (1967) 6 ILM 360

Fidler, D P, *International Law and Infectious Diseases*, 1999, Oxford: OUP

(General Comment 14) Committee on Economic, Social and Cultural Rights, General Comment No 14, 'The right to the highest attainable standard of health', UN Doc E/C.12/2000/4 (2000)

Gervais, D, *The TRIPS Agreement—Drafting, History and Analysis*, 1998, London: Sweet & Maxwell

Hannikainen, L, *Peremptory Norms (Jus Cogens) in International Law—Historical Development, Criteria, Present Status*, 1989, Helsinki: Finnish Lawyers' Publishing

International Covenant on Civil and Political Rights, New York, 16 December 1966, (1967) 6 ILM 368

Koji, T, 'Emerging hierarchy in international human rights and beyond: from the perspective of non-derogable rights' (2001) 12 European J Int'l L 917

Loi Fédérale sur les Brevets D'invention, 25 June 1954, Recueil Officiel des Lois Fédérales 1955, 893 (Switzerland)

Medicines and Related Substances Control Amendment Act 1997 (Republic of South Africa) Government Gazette, 12 December 1997

Organisation of African Unity, Abuja Declaration on HIV/AIDS, Tuberculosis and Other Related Infectious Diseases, 27 April 2001, OAU Doc OAU/SPS/ABUJA/3 (2001)

Patents Act 1970 (India)

Presidential Decree on Compulsory Licensing, Decree No 3,201, 6 October 1999 (Brazil)

Resolution 2001/21, 'Intellectual property and human rights', United Nations Sub-Commission on Human Rights, UN Doc E/CN.4/SUB.2/RES/2001/21 (2001)

Scherer, F M, 'Le système des brevets et l'innovation dans le domaine pharmaceutique' (2000/1) Revue Internationale de Droit Economique 110

Special 301 Report: United States Trade Representative, *2001 Special 301 Report*, 2001

Statement of India, UN Doc A/C.3/SR.798 (1957)

Statement of the Dominican Republic, UN Doc A/C.3/SR.799 (1957)

Sub-Commission on the Promotion and Protection of Human Rights, *The Impact of the Agreement on Trade Related Aspects of Intellectual Property Rights on Human Rights*, UN Doc E/CN.4/Sub.2/2001/13 (2001)

The Pharmaceutical Manufacturers' Association of South Africa et al vs The President of the Republic of South Africa et al., Notice of Motion, High Court of South Africa (Transvaal Provincial Division), 18 February 1998

The Pharmaceutical Manufacturers' Association of South Africa et al vs The President of the Republic of South Africa et al., Joint Statement of Understanding, 2001

Government of Brazil, Press Communiqué, 25 June 2001

Toebes, B C A, *The Right to Health as a Human Right in International Law*, 1999, Antwerpen: Intersentia

(TRIPS Agreement) 'Agreement on Trade-Related Aspects of Intellectual Property Rights,' Marrakesh, 15 April 1994 (1994) 33 ILM 1197

UN Doc A/C.3/L.636/Rev.1 (1957)

Understanding on Rules and Procedures Governing the Settlement of Disputes, in General Agreement on Tariffs and Trade: Multilateral Trade Negotiations Final Act Embodying the Results of the Uruguay Round of Trade Negotiations, Annex 1A, Marrakesh, 15 April 1994, reprinted in (1994) 33 ILM 1125

United Nations Development Programme, *Human Development Report 2001*, 2001, Oxford: OUP

United Nations Development Programme, *Human Development Report 2000*, 2000, Oxford: OUP

United Nations, Draft International Declaration of Human Rights—Mexico: Amendment to Article 25 of the Draft Declaration, UN Doc A/C.3/266 (1948)

United Nations, Report of the Third Session of the Commission on Human Rights, UN Doc E/800 (1948)

United Nations, 3rd Committee Summary Record of Meetings, UN Doc A/C.3/SR.797 (1957)

United Nations, 3rd Committee Summary Record of Meetings, UN Doc A/C.3/SR.796 (1957)

United Nations, 3rd Committee Summary Record of Meetings, UN Doc A/C.3/SR.150 (1948)

US Executive Order No 13,155, 'Access to HIV/AIDS Pharmaceuticals and Medical Technologies' (2000) 65 Fed Reg 30

US Statement, TRIPS Council, June 2001, as sent to the IP-Health mailing list, ip-health@venice.essential.org on 21 June 2001

Velásquez, G and Boulet, P, 'Globalization and access to drugs: implications of the WTO/TRIPS Agreement', in *Globalization and Access to Drugs—Perspectives on the WTO/TRIPS Agreement 2*, WHO Doc WHO/DAP/98.9 (1998)

Velásquez, G, 'Médicaments essentiels et mondialisation' (2000/1) Revue Internationale de Droit Economique 37

Watal, J, *Intellectual Property Rights in the WTO and Developing Countries*, 2001, New Delhi: OUP

Weissman, R, 'A long, strange TRIPS: the pharmaceutical industry drive to harmonize global intellectual property rules, and the remaining WTO legal alternatives available to Third World countries' (1996) 17 U Pa J Int'l Econ L 1069

Wolf, M, 'The true price of saving lives: an international agreement to strengthen worldwide intellectual property rights on medicines is deeply problematic' *Financial Times*, 20 June 2001, available at www.ft.com

World Bank, *Global Economic Prospects 2002*, 2001, Washington, DC: World Bank

World Health Assembly, 'HIV/AIDS: confronting the epidemic', Resolution WHA53:14, 20 May 2000

World Health Organization and World Trade Organization Secretariats, Report of the Workshop on Differential Pricing and Financing of Essential Drugs, 8-11 April 2001, Høsbjør, Norway

World Health Organization, 'Globalization, TRIPS and access to pharmaceuticals' (WHO Policy Perspective) in *WHO Policy Perspectives on Medicines* No 3, 2001

WTO Declaration on the TRIPS Agreement and Public Health, Ministerial Conference—Fourth Session, WTO Doc WT/MIN(01)/DEC/2 (2001)

CHAPTER 7

INTERNATIONAL COMPETITION LAW AND POLICY IN DEVELOPING COUNTRIES

Emmanuel Opoku Awuku[*]

In the past, many developing countries regarded competition law and policy with suspicion—as just another tool for multinational companies, backed by the governments of their rich home countries, to break into the markets of the developing and least-developed countries. The general notion was that competition policy benefits multinational corporations—which have inherent advantages because of their scale and scope—over domestic firms, which will be wiped out in the heat of international competition.[1] However, with the growth of cross-border trade among states, the international economic system is undergoing revolutionary changes, and the issues of competition law and policy are featuring on multilateral and bilateral levels.

COMPETITION AT THE WTO

At the international level, the World Trade Organisation (WTO) Agreement also deals with competition issues. For example, the General Agreement on Trade in Services (GATS) recognises that anti-competitive business practices may restrain and thereby restrict trade, and provides for consultations aimed at eliminating anti-competitive business practices.[2] It also calls on each member to ensure that any monopoly supplier of a service in its territory does not, in supply of the monopoly services in the relevant market, act in a manner inconsistent with members' obligations under non-discrimination principles.[3] Similarly, the WTO Agreement on Trade Related Aspects of Intellectual Property Rights (TRIPS) took into account concerns, especially by developing countries, about anti-competitive practices involving the use of intellectual property rights.[4] Article 8(2) recognises that 'appropriate measures ... may be needed to prevent the abuse of intellectual property rights by right holders or the resort to practices which unreasonably restrain trade or adversely affect the international transfer of technology.' In particular, Article 40 deals with the control of anti-competitive practices in contractual licenses, and provides for consultations between member states and the supply of publicly available non-confidential information to the requesting member state. This area of the law is of particular relevance to the developing countries, whose bulk of technology transfer contracts is likely to involve foreign companies, and any enforcement action against alleged anti-competitive practices in these cases may require access to information outside their jurisdictions.

---

[*] Senior Programme Officer, Legal and Constitutional Affairs Division, Commonwealth Secretariat. EOAwuku@aol.com. The views expressed in the paper are those of the author alone and do not necessarily represent the views of the Commonwealth Secretariat. The fact of the author's employment with the Commonwealth Secretariat does not imply any endorsement of his views by the Secretariat.

[1] Centre for International Trade, Economics & Environment, 2002, p 1.

[2] General Agreement on Tariffs and Trade, Art IX.

[3] *Ibid*, Art VIII.

[4] World Investment Report, 1997, p 45.

The Set of Multilaterally Agreed Equitable Principles and Rules for Council of Restrictive Business Practices, adopted in 1980 by the United Nations Conference on Trade and Development (UNCTAD), sets out as an important objective to ensure that restrictive business practices do not impede or negate the realisation of benefits that should arise from the liberalisation of tariff and non-tariff barriers affecting world trade, particularly those affecting the trade and development of developing countries. It also seeks to attain greater efficiency in international trade and development, *inter alia* through promoting of competition, control of concentration of economic power, and encouragement of innovation. It aims to protect and promote social welfare in general, and the interest of consumers in particular. It calls upon governments to adopt, improve and effectively enforce appropriate competition legislation and implementation of juridical and administrative procedures.[5]

In the framework of the OECD, international co-operation in the field of competition policy has taken place since 1967 under successive versions of the Council Recommendations Concerning Co-operation Between Member Countries on Anti-competitive Practices Affecting International Trade. It calls on member governments to make best efforts with regard to the following aspects:

* Timely notification of the initiation of investigations to member countries whose interests may be affected;

* Co-ordination of actions when two or more member countries proceed against the same anti-competitive practice;

* Co-operation in developing or applying mutually satisfactory and beneficial remedies for dealing with anti-competitive practices, and, to that effect, supply each other with relevant information;

* Consultation when a country considers that an investigation by another country may affect its important interests, or when enterprises situated in another member country have engaged in anti-competitive practices that substantially adversely affect its interests, and giving sympathetic consideration to the views expressed by the affected country; and in this context

* Commitment to take whatever remedial action is considered appropriate.

It also recommends a set of detailed guiding principles for the implementation of notifications, exchanges of information, co-operation in investigations and proceedings, consultations and conciliation of anti-competitive practices affecting international trade.[6]

COTONOU PARTNERSHIP AGREEMENT

At the trans-regional level, members of the African, Caribbean and Pacific Group of States and the European Union agreed under Article 45 of the Cotonou Partnership Agreement that the introduction and implementation of effective and sound competition policies and rules are crucial to improve and secure an investment friendly climate, a sustainable industrialisation process and transparency in access to markets. To ensure the elimination of distortions to sound competition—and with due consideration to the different levels of development and

---

[5] *Ibid*, p 225.

[6] *Ibid*, p 223.

economic needs of each ACP country—the parties to the agreement undertake to implement national or regional rules and policies, including: the control and under certain conditions the prohibition of agreements between undertakings, decisions by associations of undertakings and concerted practices between undertakings which have as their object or effect the prevention, restriction or distortion of competition. The parties also agreed to reinforce co-operation in the area of competition policy with a view to formulating and supporting effective competition policies with the appropriate national competition agencies that progressively ensure the efficient enforcement of the competition rules by both private and state enterprises. The Agreement calls for special assistance in the drafting of an appropriate legal framework and its administrative enforcement with particular reference to the special situation of the least-developed countries.[7]

DEVELOPING AND LEAST DEVELOPED COUNTRY PRACTICE

The growth of cross-border transactions resulting from efforts to liberalise world trade and remove existing trade barriers has made it necessary to strengthen competition rules in international and trans-regional trade. Many developing and least-developed countries have moved towards market-oriented reforms, including the deregulation of the market system, prize liberalisation, and privatisation. In Zambia, for example, 241 of the 281 state-owned enterprises have been sold to the private sector. This required a competent competition authority to ensure that monopolies are not created in the process,[8] and to regulate subsequent competition in the market. In Ghana, the state telecom company has been privatised, new fixed-line operators have been allowed into the market, and the country was the first in Africa to embrace mobile telephony. However, the sector remains beset by squabbles, commercial bullying and political interference. The fundamental problem is that there is no strong independent regulator in place or a competition law to regulate the sector.[9]

These developments lead to a greater number of players in the national and international markets, and increased competition. Consequently, many developing countries are beginning to recognise the need of relevant competition law and policy as well as an institutional mechanism to reduce any restrictive trade or business practices, in order to ensure that mergers and take-overs do not result in undue concentration of economic power in big businesses, where these businesses make absolute profits at the expense of the consumers. The magnitude of this problem is shown by the operation of international cartels. The harmful effects of cartels are twofold: on the one hand, there are the visible results like higher prices and reduced supply; on the other hand, with even more serious implications for economic development, cartels use predatory tactics to exclude developing country producers from the markets. While international cartels, like the vitamins cartel, have been convicted and prevented from operating in the USA and Europe, they are still operating in developing countries. The issue is that the cartels have simply migrated towards those jurisdictions where they can get away without penalty. As a result of that, developing countries are suffering more than ever from such malpractice.[10]

---

7   ACP–EU Partnership Agreement, Art 45.
8   See Lipimile, 1999, p 35.
9   *The Financial Times*, p 5.
10 Centre for International Trade, Economics & Environment, 2002, p 14.

However, there are still many developing countries that do not have any sort of competition legislation in place. For these countries it is important to understand the nature of competition and how to regulate it. Competition is a dynamic concept, as it attempts to judge forms of industrial organisation and the policies of firms by reference to the extent to which they promote or hamper rivalry between businesses. It describes the kind of market pressure that must be exerted to penalise laggards, and to reward the enterprising—in this way to promote economic progress. It also reduces the number of players as the incompetent fall by the wayside.[11] In other words, competition allows the market to reward good performance and to penalise poor performance by producers. It thus encourages entrepreneurial activity and market entry by new firms, and also provides a stimulus for enterprises to become more efficient, to invest in the production of greater variety, or better quality.

The term competition policy is used in different contexts in different countries; it can be defined to include all policies relevant to competition in the market, which is made up of sectoral policies, including trade policy, industrial policy, regulatory policy and policies adopted by governments to address the anti-competitive policies of enterprises, whether private or public.[12] Competition law is only one element of competition policy. The main element of most competition laws in both developed and developing countries is to prohibit anti-competitive business practices, such as:

- Practices undertaken by a single firm (when a firm enjoys a dominant position);

- Anti-competitive mergers and acquisitions;

- Horizontal restraints—that is, arrangements between competitors to restrain competition—including price fixing, restraint of output, market allocation, import and export cartels, international cartels, conscious parallelism; and

- Vertical restraints—that is, anti-competitive arrangements between firms along the production-distribution chain—including exclusive dealing, reciprocal exclusivity, refusal to deal, discriminatory pricing, territorial restraint, and transfer pricing that may involve over-invoicing or under-invoicing of intermediate inputs between foreign affiliates.[13]

Competition law regulates the competitive behaviour of domestic and foreign firms with a view to protecting all firms operating in a territory, facilitating transparency and improving the investment atmosphere. Most competition laws have similar objectives, which are adopted to suit the different contexts and economic conditions of the country. These are to:

- Protect consumers from the undue exercise of market power;

- Protect economic efficiency, in both a static and dynamic sense;

- Promote trade and integration within an economic union or free trade area;

- Facilitate economic liberalisation, including privatisation, deregulation and the reduction of external trade barriers;

- Preserve and promote the sound development of a market economy;

- Promote democratic values, such as economic pluralism and the dispersion of socio-economic power;

---

[11] Mehta, 1999.
[12] International Trade Centre and Commonwealth Secretariat, 1999, p 286.
[13] United Nations, 1997, p 212.

- Ensure fairness and equity in marketplace transactions;

- Minimise the need for more intrusive forms of regulation or political interference in a free market economy; and

- Protect opportunities for small and medium-sized businesses.[14]

Competition law applies to all firms operating in a national territory and supplying a particular market, whether through domestic sales, imports, foreign affiliates or non-equity forms of foreign direct investment. They do not, in principle, discriminate between national and foreign firms or between foreign firms from different national or regional origins when it comes to competitive analysis. However, many competition laws make reference to such objectives as controlling the concentration of economic power, promoting the competitiveness of domestic industries, encouraging innovation, and supporting small and medium-size enterprises.[15]

Competition legislation applies to all sectors of economic activity unless special exemptions are made. However, countries should make careful use of exemption clauses. If, for example, the national development strategy of a country includes policies to promote small and medium-sized enterprises, disadvantage regions or groups, then these regions could be exempted from some of the provisions of competition law.[16] For example, section 5 of the Kenya Restrictive Trade Practice, Monopolies and Price Control Act 1990 exempts from its provisions trade practices which are directly and necessarily associated with the:[17]

- Exercise of exclusive or preferential trading privileges conferred on any person by an Act of Parliament or by the Government; and

- Licensing by the Government of participants in certain trades and professions.

In some countries, public sector enterprises are exempted from the competition law. In general, this runs counter to the aim of trying to create a competition culture within the country. In India, for example, the Monopolies and Restrictive Practice Act 1969 did not include public sector enterprises. However, the Act was amended in 1991 to make it applicable to the public sector.[18]

Different countries have developed different ways of dealing with anti-competitive practices. In Sri Lanka, for example, competition law is embodied in the Fair Trading Commission Act 1987.[19] This Act establishes the Fair Trading Commission for the control of monopolies, mergers and anti-competitive practices and for the formulation of a national price policy. The functions of the Commission include (a) to investigate into any matter relating to monopoly situations, possible mergers in the country, and the existence of any anti-competitive practices; (b) to examine any request on unreasonable increases in price of any article or any shortage that affects the market; and (c) to examine any complaint from competent authorities or business undertakings on variation of prices or charges. The Commission has the power to require maintenance of records and the furnishing of returns, to call for information, to authorise any officer to enter and inspect premises, and to hold inquires and investigations on any anti-competitive practices.

---

[14] *Ibid*, p 131.
[15] *Ibid*, 1997, p 190.
[16] Centre for International Trade, Economics & Environment, 2002, p 9.
[17] Restrictive Trade Practices, Monopolies and Price Control Act 1990 (Kenya), chapter 504.
[18] Centre for International Trade, Economics & Environment, 2002, p 10.
[19] Fair Trading Commission Act 1987.

In Zambia, the Competition and Fair Trading Act gives the courts jurisdiction to review anti-competitive trade practices, and any category of agreements, decisions and practices which have as their object the prevention, restriction or distortion of competition. The violation of the Act, any regulation or any directives as stated attracts a fine of up to ten million Kwacha or imprisonment for a term of up to five years.

The South Africa Competition Act 1998, which repealed the whole legislation on competition under the Maintenance and Promotion of Competition Act, provides for an independent Competition Commission that is subject only to the Constitution and the law of South Africa. It must be impartial and must perform its functions without fear, favour, or prejudice. The Commissioners appointed must not be seen to (a) engage in any activity that may undermine the integrity of the Commission; (b) participate in any investigation, hearing or decision concerning a matter in respect of which that person has a direct financial or any similar personal interest; and (c) make private use of, profit from, or divulge any confidential information obtained as a result of performing official functions. The Commission's functions include, for example, implementing measures to increase market transparency; implementing measures to develop public awareness of the provisions of the Act; investigate and evaluate alleged restrictive practices, abuse of dominant position, and mergers; refer matters to the Competition Tribunal, and appear before the Tribunal, as required by the Act; negotiate agreements with any regulatory authority to co-ordinate and harmonise the exercise of jurisdiction over competition matters within the relevant industry or sector, to ensure the consistent application of the principles of the Act; participate in the proceedings of any regulatory authority; advise, and receive advice from, any regulatory authority; and over time review legislation and public regulations, and report to the Minister concerning any provision that permits uncompetitive behaviour.

In Kenya, the Restrictive Trade Practices, Monopolies and Price Control Act is intended to encourage competition in the economy by prohibiting restrictive trade practices, and controlling monopolies, concentrations of economy power and prices. Section 16 provides for a Commissioner with powers to check and investigate alleged persons or firms who engage in restrictive trade practices. Section 17 of the Act requires the Commissioner to send reports together with recommendations to the Minister. Based on the recommendations submitted for action, the Minister may make an order requiring a person who is guilty of a restrictive trade practice to desist from that trade practice. The Act allows for appeal within 28 days to the Restrictive Trade Practices Tribunal under section 20. After the Restrictive Trade Practices Tribunal or High Court has pronounced its decision on an appeal, failure to comply with any portion of the Minister's orders shall be liable to imprisonment.[20]

Singapore does not have specific legislation on competition, competition board or commission. It relies on free competition to bring about a competitive market. This has served Singapore well over the years as its economy has proven to be one of the most competitive in the world. However, it recognise that as it promote the service sector, and privatises and liberalises former state monopolies, it allows competition into these sectors requiring adequate competition laws to ensure a level playing field for all. Although Singapore does not have umbrella competition laws, it does have competition provisions within sectoral legislation to ensure fair competition in the respective sectors.[21]

---

[20] See Restrictive Trade Practices, Monopolies and Price Control Act 1990, chapter 504.
[21] Interview with Wong Toon Joon, 18 July 2000, First Secretary (Economics) Permanent Mission of the Republic of Singapore to the UN in Geneva.

The majority of developing countries have not so far introduced national competition laws. In order to establish a national competition culture, an appropriate framework is required, including legal and institutional provisions. This means that the government would have to enact relevant legislation and delegate powers to a competition agency or regulatory body to check on public and private enterprises or any handicap that affects market operations. The established body would have to be independent from government and must be given appropriate enforcement powers to act as a tribunal.

It should be noted that there are few countries that have strong, well-functioning and well-funded competition authorities. It has taken a considerable time for existing competition institutions to assume an important role. So, it may well take newcomers to the regulation of competition many years to develop appropriate policies, and to establish the means to implement them fairly and effectively.[22] The implementation of specific elements of competition law and policy in developing economies must take into consideration the circumstances and the institutional endowment in a country. Markets characterised by a high level of state ownership and intervention such as price control mechanisms are less appropriate environments for the implementation of competition law, than market-oriented economies based on democracy and public participation, transparent and accountable government, efficient services, observation of human rights and the rule of law, and disapproval of corrupt practices.

In terms of co-operation, many developing countries are lagging behind developed countries, which have concluded bilateral co-operation and co-ordination agreements, for example between the United States and the European Union in 1991, and the Commonwealth Australian Trade Practices Commission and the Commonwealth New Zealand Commerce Commission in 1994. Similarly, Canada and the United States of America have an agreement on mutual legal assistance in criminal matters, including on anti-competitive practice, which was implemented in 1990. These agreements usually provide for notification by either party of enforcement activities affecting important interests of the other party and for the exchange of information, both of a general nature relating to competition policy in each country and relating to specific anti-competitive conduct. The agreements may contain provisions for co-operation and co-ordination of enforcement activities in situations where both parties have an interest in pursuing enforcement activities with regard to the situation.[23]

CONCLUSION

In conclusion, international consensus and co-operation, as well as adequate legislative and policy frameworks at the national level, are required to protect both businesses and consumers from anti-competitive practices that raise prices and reduce output. The WTO Working Group on Trade and Competition Policy argued that any competition law must be based on (a) principles relating to transparent and non-discriminatory application of competition law and policy, and (b) commitments to the prohibition of hard-core cartels.[24] A competition law must also be able to create provisions for an effective enforcement agency. That means that this agency will need broad powers to investigate enterprises' behaviour, including the authority to analyse the competitive effects of certain major types of Foreign Direct Investment and

---

22　WTO, 1997, p 212.
23　*Ibid*, p 53.
24　WTO, 2000.

international business transactions. The agency entrusted with the enforcement of competition law ought to be obliged to put fair competition and the maximisation of economic efficiency and consumer welfare above all other considerations. The rulings of competition authorities must be open to review by, or appeal to, the judiciary.[25]

Clear competition polices and their enforcement can contribute to sustainable economic development. A number of recommendations can be made to ensure that these benefits are achieved.[26]

First, it is necessary to provide assistance to those developing countries that do not yet have and are planning to develop a competition law to do so. This could be done by adopting the UN model law and the Framework for the Design and Implementation of Competition Law and Policy of the OECD, taking into account the economic conditions that exist in individual developing countries. Assistance could be in the form of helping to draft relevant legislation, establish enforcement agencies, training relevant staff, and developing appropriate enforcement procedures.

Second, it is essential to strengthen the capacities of existing competition law enforcement agencies in those developing countries whose competition laws provide for the establishment of a commission or board to oversee the observation of the provisions of the competition law and investigate any alleged breaches. This may include capacity building and staff training since well-trained staff with strong analytical skills are required to determine the economic consequences of potentially anti-competitive practices.

Third, UNCTAD's action in the fields of competition law and policy and consumer protection must be supported. This requires the continuation and, resources permitting, expansion of capacity-building in developing countries and economies in transition; helping authorities in creating a competition culture by educating the public at large, including the private sector; and studying the links between competition, competitiveness and development, as well as trade related aspects of competition.

Finally, it is important to conduct an in-depth study of the development impact of possible international agreements on competition laws and policy, including the possibility of special and preferential treatment of developing countries and dispute mediation mechanisms at bilateral, plurilateral and multilateral levels.

REFERENCES

ACP-EU Partnership Agreement, Cotonou, Benin, 23 June 2000

(TRIPS Agreement) Agreement on Trade Related Aspects of Intellectual Property Rights, The Results of the Uruguay Round, Geneva: World Trade Organisation 1994

Brusick, P, 'Countries reaffirm validity of UN competition code' (2000) 4:8 Bridges Newsletter (ICTSD), 8

Centre for International Trade, Economics & Environment, *Challenges in Implementing a Competition Policy and Law: An Agenda for Action*, 2002, India: CUTS

Competition Act (South Africa) 1998

---

[25] United Nations, 1997, p 215.
[26] Brusick, 2000, p 8.

Fair Trading Commission Act 1987 (Sri Lanka)

The Financial Times, 29 November 2000, p 5

Lipimile, G K, 'Deregulation, demonopolisation and privatisation: how to ensure consistency with competition: the Zambia experience of privatisation', presented at Pre-UNCTAD X Seminar on the Role of Competition Policy for Development in Globalizing World Markets, 14-15 June 1999, Geneva, available at www.unctad.org/en/doc/poitcdclpm14.en.pdf

Maintenance and Promotion of Competition Act 1979, as amended by Act No 88 of 1990 and government notices

Mehta, P S, 'Foreign direct investment, mega-mergers and strategic alliances: is global competition accelerating development or holding towards world monopolies?', presented at Pre-UNCTAD X Seminar on the Role of Competition Policy for Development in Globalizing World Markets, 14-15 June 1999, Geneva, available at www.unctad.org/en/doc/poitcdclpm14.en.pdf

OECD, 'Revised recommendation of the council concerning co-operation between member countries on anticompetitive practices affecting international trade', adopted by the Council at its 856th Session on 27 and 28 July 1995, C(95)130/FINAL, available at www.oecd.org/pdf/M00020000/M00020239.pdf

Restrictive Trade Practices, Monopolies and Price Control Act 1990 (Kenya)

International Trade Centre and Commonwealth Secretariat, *Business Guide to the World Trade System,* 1999, London: Commonwealth Secretariat

United Nations, *World Investment Report, Transnational Corporations, Market Structure and Competition Policy,* 1997, Geneva: United Nations

UNCTAD, 'The set of multilaterally agreed equitable principles and rules for the control of restrictive business practices', in UNCTAD, *The United Nations Set of Principles and Rules on Competition,* Geneva: UNCTAD, 1980, available at www.unctad.org/en/subsites/cpolicy/docs/CPSet/ibpc10rev20en.pdf

WTO, *Report (2000) of the Working Group on the Interaction Between Trade and Competition Policy to the General Council,* WT/WGTCP/4, 30 November 2000

WTO, *WTO Annual Report, Special Study on Trade and Competition Policy,* 1997, Geneva: WTO

TECHNICAL ASSISTANCE AND TRADE LAW REFORM POST-DOHA: BRAVE NEW WORLD

*Mary E Footer**

The establishment of the World Trade Organisation (WTO), in January 1995, signifies a turning point in international economic relations. Previously, international trade law was regulated by means of a complex set of treaty relations under the General Agreement on Tariffs and Trade (GATT) 1947 or by means of various practices of the GATT contracting parties. Under the WTO, nearly 145 countries are parties to a comprehensive body of trade rules known as the 'single undertaking' that emerged from the Uruguay Round of multilateral trade negotiations (MTN), which were held between 1986 and1994.[1] Henceforth, international trade has been conducted within an institutional setting since the Agreement Establishing the WTO (the WTO Agreement)[2] forms the constitutive act or charter for the WTO as an international organisation.

Already by 1980, the former GATT had evolved through seven rounds of MTN into a set of agreements that was remarkable for its 'complexity, variety and far-reaching scope.'[3] However, the mosaic of different treaty relations that dominated the former GATT also harboured its limitations.[4] In the face of growing international economic interdependence, the GATT contained rules that were substantively inadequate, out-of-date, or did not apply to all GATT contracting parties. It also lacked rules to discipline areas of non-tariff measures that distorted trade flows, particularly various forms of export restraints.[5] In addition, the GATT dispute settlement system was fragmented and for a brief period in the 1980s came under severe pressure, owing to several bitter US-EC disputes.[6]

Unlike its predecessor, the GATT, the functions and principles of the WTO are more ambitious. First, the WTO Agreement (besides its function as a constitution for world trade) together with the multilateral trade agreements which are annexed to it, lays down a code of conduct for world trade, by establishing a single set of rules and standards, to be applied by all WTO Members. Second, the WTO is a new international economic organisation, alongside the World Bank and the International Monetary Fund (IMF). Third, the organisation continues to provide a forum for ongoing trade negotiations involving tariff reductions/scheduling of service commitments and the development of new rules and disciplines. And fourth, it has become, during its brief eight-year history, the primary forum for the settlement of international trade disputes with a reasonably effective enforcement mechanism.

---

[*]   Deputy Director, Amsterdam Center for International Law and Member, Department of International Law, University of Amsterdam. This chapter draws upon an earlier version of a paper that was presented at the June 2001 Conference and has been published in a different form, as Chapter 23 in Faundez, Footer and Norton, 2000.

[1]   The term 'single undertaking' means that each WTO Member is expected to take on all WTO obligations in contrast to the Tokyo Round (1973-1979) Codes, whereby only signatories were bound.

[2]   The multilateral trade agreements, decisions, understandings are annexed to the WTO Agreement, p 19 et seq.

[3]   Jackson, 1980, p 26.

[4]   Roessler, 1985, pp 287-298.

[5]   Jackson, 1980, p 38.

[6]   Hudec, 1991, pp 129-177, especially at p 169.

The development of a broader institutional basis for the WTO means that the organisation has also evolved into the key forum for further normative developments in international trade law. At once WTO rule making fulfils Wolfgang Friedman's notions of the 'horizontal' and 'vertical' expansion of international law.[7] The results of the Uruguay Round MTN are evidence of a horizontal expansion of international trade law through transformation of the GATT 1947 into the present multilateral regime for trade in goods. It includes the gradual inclusion over time of trade sectors that were formally exempt from full GATT coverage (agriculture and textiles), as well as stricter disciplines on contingent protection measures (antidumping, subsidies and safeguards) and the introduction of rules and disciplines, where previously none existed (rules sanctioning the use of sanitary and phytosanitary measures, provided they are administered on a non-discriminatory basis). Additionally, some of the multilateral trade agreements focus on the application of rule making in new subject matter areas (trade in services and trade-related intellectual property rights).[8]

Similarly, international trade law has expanded vertically. WTO rule-making now reaches more directly into the private conduct of natural and corporate entities, at national and regional levels.[9] This has implications for all WTO Members in a globalising economy, but weighs most heavily on developing country governments that are already struggling to draft market economy legislation to improve their citizens access to world export markets and encourage foreign direct investment, as well introducing legal and institutional reforms to support good governance, democracy, human rights and the rule of law. For many, the implementation of WTO trade obligations is simply another item to add to the growing list of reforms that underpin a neo-liberal development policy which is 'organised around a set of "best practices" rules and institutions, derived from model market economies.'[10]

International trade law increasingly intrudes into domestic legal orders, requiring reform of substantive trade laws and practices. This is mirrored at the policy level where the 'parameters for much domestic policy-making are being set in international regional *fora*'.[11] It is this vertical expansion of international law, as it relates to the reform of trade laws in WTO developing country Members, with which this chapter is primarily concerned. The subject has become even more pressing with the new round of trade negotiations launched at the Doha Ministerial Meeting in November 2001,[12] and the call 'to place the needs and interests of developing countries at the heart of the Work Programme' set out in the Doha Declaration.[13] For the first time in the history of the WTO, this Declaration explicitly recognises that trade-related technical assistance and capacity-building are 'core elements of the development dimension of the multilateral system' and it goes on to endorse a 'New Strategy for WTO Technical Co-operation for Capacity-building, Growth and Integration'.[14]

The other main subject matter in this chapter concerns the link between technical assistance and capacity-building for trade law development, as set out in the Doha Declaration

---

[7] Friedman, 1964, pp 5, 6 and 9.

[8] See Fried, 2000, p 132.

[9] *Ibid*.

[10] Rittich, 2000, p 234. For an example of how this trend prevails in the donor community, see the 'Agenda and Issues for Discussion', together with the 'Background Papers' for the 'DAC Good Practices Workshop, 2000.

[11] See DAC Experts Meeting, 1998, p 5, para 12, giving Trade-Related Aspects of Intellectual Property Rights (TRIPS) and Trade-Related Investment Measures (TRIMs) as two such examples.

[12] Doha Declaration, 2001.

[13] *Ibid*, para 2.

[14] *Ibid*, para 38. See also 'New WTO Strategy', 2002.

in the Doha Development Agenda (as the Work Programme has become known),[15] where a call is made for more extensive co-operation with developing countries in mainstreaming trade in those countries. This linkage is better known as trade-related technical assistance (TRTA). Past experience has shown that, when it comes to the delivery of TRTA, scant attention has been paid to flanking policy issues and the need for an integrated approach that includes capacity-building measures. If it is to be effective then TRTA should place trade reform within a country's overall development strategy, taking account of other competing development needs, and ensuring that implementation of WTO rules and efforts to negotiate future trade disciplines make sense from a development perspective.[16]

In practice the reverse is often true. Although well-meaning, TRTA shows scant consideration of the far-reaching legal and policy implications which trade law reform raises within the overall development context. Additionally, legal technical assistance—as this type of TRTA is known—whether supplied by multilateral and/or bilateral donors is often badly co-ordinated and, in some cases, inherently contradictory in its aims and objectives. As a result of these two factors, trade law reform in developing countries is often no more than a reiteration and adaptation of developed countries' approaches to the implementation of substantive international trade law obligations.

The following contribution to the discussion on TRTA and trade law reform is designed around a number of different issues. In the next section I briefly review, from a historical and institutional perspective, the way in which the GATT has developed into the WTO, and the resulting effects it has had on normative processes within the new organisation. In the third and fourth sections I look at the changing nature of GATT/WTO law, and its effects on the implementation of basic trade rules and disciplines in developing countries. Then, in the fifth section, I consider the contribution of multilateral and bilateral technical assistance towards trade law reform in developing countries. I discuss the result of these efforts in the sixth section, before providing a summary and some conclusions from a post-Doha perspective in the final section.

THE WTO AND NORMATIVE PROCESSES

The WTO as a normative system originated in the GATT 1947, a multilateral agreement aimed at the reciprocal reduction of tariffs and supplemented by the drafting of 'general clauses' of obligation in order to complement any tariff-reduction agreement.[17] The GATT was negotiated as a multilateral treaty, not as an international organisation. It therefore (i) contained detailed provisions related to obligations of restricted use, (ii) was drafted in precise terms, and (iii) foresaw the possibility of dealing with bilateral protests relating to non-performance of specific treaty obligations. Work also continued during the mid-1940s on the charter for an International Trade Organization (ITO) which was completed at the Havana Conference.[18] It was originally intended that the ITO should contain precisely formulated legal rules, sometimes termed 'contractual' in character, which would be applied directly and without further elaboration by members.[19] The GATT treaty provisions would be revised to bring them into

---

15   *Ibid*, paras 38-41.
16   Prowse, 2002, p 2.
17   The general clauses were drawn from the draft charter for an International Trade Organization (ITO) and this drew on bilateral treaty clauses; see Jackson, 1997, p 38.
18   United Nations Conference on Trade and Employment, 1947-1948.
19   Jackson, 1969, p 12, citing Harry Hawkins.

conformity with the ITO and they would operate under the umbrella of the ITO, when the latter came into force. However, the ITO failed to materialise, due largely to the intransigence of the United States Congress in 1948 and the mid-1950s.[20]

This left the original 23 signatories to the GATT 1947 with the task of fulfilling the obligations set out in the multilateral treaty. The GATT established a favourable normative framework for future discussions without recourse to judicial proceedings or other outside agencies apart from—where necessary—mediation or diplomacy.[21] Additionally, primary GATT norms were to be found in treaty provisions that made no distinction between legal claims and other claims involving an impairment of reciprocity.[22]

The set of GATT provisions emerging from this process contains language may have been drafted in precise terms, but it is not always fully capable of implementation. Furthermore, it may be open to varying interpretations by implementing national authorities. This trend has been continued in the WTO context. WTO law comprises a matrix of primary and secondary norms, some of which are relatively normative—that is, contain substantive values that are open to clarification and interpretation as to their content. This has sometimes given rise to complications in the implementation of WTO obligations, especially in those jurisdictions where direct effect is normally given to treaty obligations.

Primary WTO norms are generally to be found in the substantive and procedural rules contained in the WTO Agreement and its annexed multilateral agreements. These include prescriptive and prohibitive norms, requiring WTO Member governments to undertake,[23] or abstain from,[24] certain action. The Uruguay Round introduced further primary norms allowing Members to pursue, or to refrain from, certain action—that is, the norms are permissive in character and deferential to differences in national legal rules and standards, provided that certain conditions are fulfilled.[25]

Secondary WTO norms provide for the possible extinguishment or modification of primary WTO norms.[26] They may specify the way in which those primary norms are ascertained—that is, through their performance; the way in which they are changed—that is, through procedure and practice; and the way in which they are remedied—that is, through adjudicative processes. The creation of secondary WTO rules can be observed at work in the business of WTO Councils and various WTO Committees, such as the adoption of a decision designed to implement specific provisions in a WTO Agreement,[27] or in the complaint

---

[20] Jackson, 1969.

[21] GATT, Arts XXII and XXIII.

[22] See League of Nations Memorandum 'Relating to the Pacific Settlement of International Disputes concerning Economic Questions in General and Commercial and Customs Questions in Particular'; also League of Nations 'Procedure for the Friendly Settlement of Economic Disputes between States,' p 4.

[23] An example is the national treatment standard: 'products … imported into the territory of any other contracting party shall be accorded treatment no less favourable than that accorded to like products of national origin…' (GATT 1994, Art III(4)).

[24] An example is the prohibition on quantitative restrictions: 'No prohibitions or restrictions other than duties, taxes or other charges … shall be instituted or maintained by any contracting party on the importation of any product of the territory of any other contracting party…' (GATT, Art XI).

[25] See, for example, the Agreement on Sanitary and Phytosanitary Measures (SPS) that builds on the language of the exception in GATT 1994, Art XX(b): 'Members have the right to take sanitary and phytosanitary measures necessary for the protection of human, animal or plant life or health, provided that such measures are not inconsistent with the provisions of this Agreement': SPS, Art 2.1.

[26] Wellens, 1994, p 7.

[27] See for example the adoption by the SPS Committee of a *Decision on the Implementation of Article 4 on Equivalence*, 2001, in order to 'make operational the provisions of Article 4 of the Agreement on the Application of Sanitary and Phytosanitary Measures'. It allows other states that serve as 'regulatory

procedures that exist in the WTO dispute settlement system where WTO obligations are interpreted and applied.[28]

For our purposes, the question is in what ways are these primary and secondary norms articulated—that is, given effect or implemented—in the national laws of WTO developing country Members? What modalities exist for their articulation and what are the constraints? It is to some of these questions that I now turn, in an attempt to expose the enormity of the problem that developing countries face with trade law reform in their domestic legal systems.

THE CHANGING NATURE OF GATT/WTO LAW AND ITS EFFECTS ON IMPLEMENTATION BY DEVELOPING COUNTRIES

The multilateral trade agreements annexed to the WTO Agreement mark a paradigm shift in international economic law rule making. The GATT 1947 and other international trade obligations[29] were largely concerned with border measures in the form of tariff and non-tariff barriers, but the Uruguay Round multilateral trade agreements increased the quantity and scope of regulatory obligations beyond the border.[30] Even with special concessions—such as longer transitional periods—developing countries are grappling with legislative and institutional reform of trade laws on an unprecedented scale.

Previously one of the primary ways of bringing developing countries more fully into the GATT-fold was to support trade promotion, an activity that was (and still is) largely stimulated through the activities of the Geneva-based International Trade Centre UNCTAD/WTO (ITC).[31] Little thought was given to ways of assisting with legislative or institutional implementation of trade obligations.[32] Nevertheless, implicit in the single undertaking of the Uruguay Round MTN is the fact that *all* Members are required to bring their laws and regulations into conformity with their WTO obligations,[33] which means being fully engaged in the process of regulating for trade in national legal systems.

---

bodies' to come up with alternative means of achieving the same regulatory goals. Upon the request of an exporting Member, an importing Member is under a duty to explain the objective and rationale behind an SPS measure, to clearly identify the risks that the relevant measures are intended to address and to indicate the appropriate level of protection that the SPS measures are designed to achieve. See further Marceau and Trachtmann, 2002.

[28] By adhering to the WTO Agreement and its annexes, Members recognise that one of the purposes of dispute settlement is 'to clarify the existing provisions of those agreements in accordance with the customary rules of interpretation of public international law': DSU, Art 3.2. However, the process must not lead to the creation of new primary rules: 'Recommendations and rulings of the DSB cannot add to or diminish the rights and obligations provided in the covered agreements': DSU, Art 3.2, final sentence.

[29] Principally, the various Codes which were developed within the framework of the Tokyo Round.

[30] See 'WTO Matrix on Regulatory Obligations'.

[31] More recent attempts to do the same, although presented in a different fashion, include the USAID seed-funded project for a self-financed and locally driven network of African entrepreneurs. See the report for USAID: Management Systems International, 2000, presented to DAC Good Practices Workshop, 2000.

[32] Another deeply troubling aspect for developing countries is their sense of 'growing protectionism in the developed countries as exhibited in tariff peaks, tariff escalation and non-tariff barriers' as well as 'the misuse and abuse of ... antidumping, countervailing and sanitary and phytosanitary measures' despite attempts of developed countries to promote developing countries' integration into the global economy. See Government of Egypt, 1999.

[33] This general obligation rests on *all* WTO Members: 'Each Member shall ensure the conformity of its laws, regulations and administrative procedures with its obligations as provided in the annexed Agreements': WTO Agreement, Art XVI(4).

Many developing country Members were 'sponsored' into the GATT by the former colonial power with which they maintained preferential trading relations.[34] Consequently, they did not go through the full working party examination process that acceding WTO Members currently face. This resulted in many of them, especially sub-Saharan African countries, becoming GATT contracting parties, and subsequently WTO Members, without knowing anything of substance about the GATT, without fully applying GATT provisions and without including trade in their overall programme of economic development.

Now such countries find themselves faced not only with fulfilling unprecedented obligations in the field of international trade to reduce trade barriers, by offering deeper tariff cuts on a range of manufactures and removing import substitution measures, but also they must implement significant legal reforms in a wide variety of areas connected to their WTO obligations, including providing for administrative and judicial procedures. An example of the latter is reform of customs laws and procedures in order to take account of customs valuation and to provide an appropriate institutional infrastructure to conduct appeals brought by importers. Besides this, developing country Members are under pressure to carry out other essential reforms in order to create an enabling business environment in the domestic economy and attract investment (for example by introducing technical standards, sanitary and phytosanitary standards or strengthening intellectual property laws).[35]

The actual process of trade law reform in developing countries is located within the broader context of globalisation. Generally, globalisation refers to discernible policies and trends associated with the liberalisation of markets and the process of functional integration between widely dispersed economic activities, which are characteristic of those markets. Where globalisation differs from internationalisation is that the former is characterised by the intensification of cross-border production, sale and distribution of goods and services with only marginal reference to the local, while the latter is embedded in processes of national economic production and the spread of economic activities across national boundaries.[36] Moreover, the processes of technological and informational convergence drive globalisation whereas internationalisation functions through more familiar modes of communication, which are largely transnational and supported by formal and informal institutional processes.

DEVELOPING COUNTRIES AND TRADE LAW REFORM

It is recognised that in order for any type of law reform to function well in a market economy certain basic requirements must be met. Some of these include: 'a supply of market-friendly laws, adequate institutions to implement and enforce them, and a demand for those laws from market participants.'[37] Additionally, in certain instances institutional reform may be a prerequisite for successful economic change.[38] Where trade law reform differs from other types of law reform in a market economy is that, instead of being aimed at private transactions that

---

[34] All that a developing country had to do was certify that it had 'full autonomy in the conduct of its external commercial relations and of the other matters provided for in this [General] Agreement': GATT, Art XXVI:5(c). This process is no longer open to acceding WTO Members; see Blackhurst, Lyakurwa, and Oyejide, 1999, at 34 footnote 15.

[35] Finger and Schuler, 1999, p 1.

[36] For some definitions see: Reinicke, 1997; cited in Tshuma, 1999, p 129; and Oloka-Onyango and Udagama, 2000, at pp 3-4.

[37] Gray, 1999, p 62.

[38] Ibid, p 63, where she notes that 'legal reform deals with process as well as substance, and in this sense it diverges from economic policy'.

rely on property, contract and company law, it seeks to codify norms and standards at the national level that have been negotiated and agreed upon internationally.[39] What are some of the particular constraints that developing countries face in respect of trade law reform?

Implementation of WTO norms in the domestic arena is no easy task for any government, given the quantity, scope and breadth of such rules.[40] In developing countries the task is made more difficult by the perception that trade law reform is imposed upon them by the major trading powers. This is partly attributable to the fact that many developing countries either did not participate effectively, or did not participate at all, in the WTO negotiations in which the rules were agreed. Thus, no solid sense of 'ownership' of those rules has emerged among them.[41]

There is evidence that is was only some of the higher income developing countries—such as Argentina, Brazil, Costa Rica, India, Korea and Mexico—that had the capacity to engage substantively on a wide range of trade reform issues addressed during the Uruguay Round. For example, the African Economic Research Consortium (AERC) has evaluated the participation of a large number of sub-Saharan African countries in rule making at the international level and found it to be minimal. AERC has attributed this to three main factors. First, many African countries failed to forge links between Geneva-based delegations (even where they existed) and the governments at home. Second, there was no established process to involve relevant ministries with issues of importance to them, which were being negotiated in Geneva (for example national health and agriculture ministries in the negotiations on sanitary and phytosanitary standards and agricultural trade respectively). Third, the private sector, particularly the business community, has been minimally involved in trade negotiations of particular interest to them.[42]

Not surprisingly, instead of the demand for new trade laws from market participants, as law reform dictates, the reverse is true. The legislative reform and implementation processes in those countries have been unable to rally behind them the potential winners of trade liberalisation—for example, the traders who might save money from improved customs operations, or producers and exporters who might be able to export more if standards were upgraded to an international level.[43] Instead, scepticism often creeps in and implementation is viewed as something that will help others in a distant land. Moreover, any attempts by fellow WTO Members to force implementation by bringing claims for non-implementation in the

---

[39] Fried remarks upon 'the "inter-permeability" of national and international rules': 2000, pp 134-135.

[40] For an overview of the process in some developed and higher income developing countries see Jackson and Sykes, 1997. Chung notes that international treaties are normally self-executing but 'given the scope and magnitude' of legislative action needed to implement the WTO Agreements, a special implementing law was passed by the Assembly for the first time in the constitutional history of Korea: 1997, p 374. Almost exactly the same considerations prevailed in Costa Rica, another 'self-executing' country, although political considerations prevailed too: see Echandi, 1997, pp 399-439. As for the sheer quantity of existing legislation that may need amending, see Fried, who cites Canada's *WTO Implementation Act* as amending 29 different federal statutes in order to bring Canada's domestic laws and regulations into conformity with its international treaty obligations under WTO Agreements: 2000, p 135.

[41] Finger and Schuler, 1999, pp 3-4, who note that 'ownership of the rules is an important element in the functioning of any system of rules ... such as the WTO, where the central organisation has limited power to enforce'.

[42] Ogunkola, 1999. As an indicator of the lack of involvement by sub-Saharan countries, Ogunkola observes that less than three percent of the written proposals, comments etc. circulated at the WTO during the Uruguay Round negotiations, were submitted by sub-Saharan countries: 1999, p 3.

[43] Finger and Schuler, 1999, p 5.

WTO dispute settlement mechanism may simply reinforce the impression that the WTO rules are imposed exogenously, for the benefit of those elsewhere.[44]

An example of the lack of engagement by developing country Members in the multilateral rule making process is to be found in primary WTO norms that permit countries to apply certain health and safety standards (under the SPS Agreement), provided this is not done in a discriminatory or arbitrary manner and that measures do not constitute a disguised restriction on trade. Developed countries already apply standards that either comply with or exceed relevant international conventions, and some have been leaders in establishing those international conventions, which generalise their countries' practices and standards. Consequently, for the vast majority of developed countries, whose systems are compatible with international conventions—or *vice versa*—the SPS Agreement means that they simply have to apply their domestic regulations fairly at the border.[45]

However, if developing country Members should seek to apply their own domestic standards, they could be faced with the additional and larger obligation of having to apply internationally sanctioned standards in their domestic economies.[46] For them it is clear that effective implementation of the SPS Agreement will depend on adopting new laws and regulations and on upgrading existing systems—or installing new ones—either of which must meet world-class standards. To some this is no more than 'industrial country practice, writ generic—the advanced countries saying to the others *Do it my way!*'[47]

A further prerequisite for law reform is that there should be adequate institutions to implement and enforce new or amended rules, including the possibility of interpreting and applying them fairly. As with any type of economic law reform, the reform of trade laws calls for 'substantial and mutually reinforcing legal reform', supported by 'a range of institutions' including courts, administrative tribunals, or appeal boards.[48] These institutions must be set up or adapted from existing institutional structures, and this takes time. The enabling environment for trade law reform, which these institutions represent, also entails the purchase and installation of equipment, the development of relevant judicial and administrative procedures and the provision of adequate training programmes for local personnel in order to develop knowledge and experience in the application of trade laws domestically.

I believe that too little consideration is being given to the far-reaching legal and policy implications of such reform within the overall development context. While the Doha Development Agenda and the related proposals on TRTA go some way towards addressing these so-called 'capacity-building' issues they are not nearly comprehensive enough. In fact, in many developing countries such endeavours are more likely to occur in the realm of trade policy rather than trade law development. The situation may be complicated by a multiplicity

---

44 This view is reflected in heated debates between developing and developed countries in 2000 and 2001 in the WTO General Council, Council for Trade in Goods and Dispute Settlement Body over the expiry of the transitional periods in TRIMs for developing countries, and the eventual recourse by the US and the EU to WTO dispute settlement procedures in respect of some developing countries. See *inter alia* Meeting of the General Council of 3 and 8 May 2000, ss 8, 32-42, paras 130-190, and Annex I on *Draft General Council Decision on Implementation-Related Issues to be Included in Chairman's Statement* and Annex II on *TRIMs Transition Period Issues*. More recently, WTO Members adopted a *Decision on implementation-related issues and concerns* at the Doha Ministerial Meeting. The matter was noted but no further specific extension periods were granted; instead the Council for Trade in Goods is called upon 'to consider positively' requests from least-developed country Members under TRIMs, *ibid*, paras 6.1 and 6.2.

45 Finger and Schuler, 1999, p 15.

46 *Ibid.*

47 From the transcript of a statement by World Bank economist: Finger, 1999.

48 Seidman, Seidman and Wälde, 1999, p 11.

of institutions ranging across different ministries and government departments, largely concerned with addressing trade policy issues rather than strictly legal ones, and making co-ordination difficult.

With WTO membership comes the responsibility of trying to make sense of it all, not only from a policy perspective[49] but also in locating trade law reform within a proper legal and institutional framework. And this can only be achieved where there are sufficient inputs of knowledge and skills from a broader spectrum of stakeholders—trade analysts, legislative drafters (including parliamentary draftspersons), economists and planners coupled with private sector and civil society inputs. There are examples in developing countries of inter-ministerial committees being established in order to grapple with the finer points of policy co-ordination at the national level, but it is unclear whether this reaches into all of the law making and regulatory functions.

At the policy level, Blackhurst, Lyakurwa and Oyejide, in their study of sub-Saharan African countries' participation in the WTO,[50] have noted that often an inter-ministerial committee is pitched at the highest level of government. In some cases, as in Nigeria, it is restricted to the federal government level, thereby neglecting inputs of state and local government authorities. In others, the inter-ministerial committee fails to take into account important stakeholders from the private sector (Kenya is an exception), or it operates through a mix of formal and informal mechanisms that draw upon Chambers of Commerce, Manufacturers' Associations, etc. In some Francophone West African countries like Benin, Cameroon, Côte d'Ivoire and Senegal, much of the underlying trade policy discussion takes place in meetings that are centralised in an Economic and Social Council.

Aside from the policy dimension, national regulators, judges and other officials—such as customs officers or patent examiners—find themselves having to enact trade laws and implement rules through a myriad of different local government agencies and institutions, many of which must be specially established for that purpose. While the actual mode for implementing primary and secondary WTO norms differs in each country dependent upon its constitution and legal system, it appears that the sheer scale of domestic implementation—even in those countries where international obligations are directly applicable—mitigates towards a raft of amending legislation that reaches deep into domestic systems. As Finger and Schuler point out, 'the scope of what the WTO regulates is narrower than the scope of what must be done to make development sense out of implementation'.[51] How are developing country Members coping with vast legal and institutional reform programmes? Before attempting to answer this question, we turn, in the following section, to review the contribution of TRTA to the process of trade law reform.

---

[49] Susan Prowse makes this point in her paper, 2002. She proposes an 'issues-based approach' to developing country participation in trade reform, under which transition requirements and sequencing for implementing obligations would be customised, taking account of a country's overall development strategy and competing demands on its resources. Associated costs and technical assistance requirements would also be calculated. This approach would take account of other national development strategies including the Policy Reduction Strategy Papers (PRSPs) and the United Nations Development Assistance Fund (UNDAF) undertakings by that same developing country.

[50] Blackhurst, Lyakurwa and Oyejide, 1999, p 11.

[51] Finger and Schuler, 1999, p 3.

THE CONTRIBUTION OF TECHNICAL ASSISTANCE TO TRADE LAW REFORM

As might be expected, constraints on human and financial resources, coupled with the strict implementation deadlines contained in many of the WTO Agreements, mean that reform of trade laws may be hurried, not fully understood and insensitive to the local social and economic environment. By 1996, a joint report by UNCTAD/WTO cited weaknesses in the human and physical infrastructure and institutional capacity related to trade as part of the bigger problem in implementing WTO Agreements in many developing countries.[52] The WTO itself has conducted a needs assessment, on the basis of a questionnaire, among least-developed countries in 1999 and come up with similar findings.[53] As might be expected, poor infrastructure and lack of resources are key impediments to the capacity of developing country Members to benefit from technical assistance support by developed countries and international institutions.[54]

There are a number of additional points to note. First, TRTA of any sort is voluntary. Several WTO Agreements suggest that developed country Members furnish technical assistance to developing country members 'that so request' it.[55] However, these provisions do not contain commitments to deliver technical assistance that are binding on developed country Members. If anything they are to be conducted on a 'best efforts' basis, and only if the assistance is specifically sought. Well before the Doha Ministerial Meeting of November 2001, a variety of technical assistance activities and programmes were provided on a continuing basis by international organisations, including the WTO, UNCTAD, the International Trade Centre (ITC) and the World Bank together with some bilateral donor assistance.

Second, the political climate has changed since the adoption of the Doha Declaration in which the issues of TRTA and capacity-building are explicitly taken up[56] but the fact remains that much of the legal technical assistance being supplied by multilateral and bilateral donors is badly co-ordinated and, in some cases, inherently contradictory in its aims and objectives. As Susan Prowse notes, trade development has been the limited province of a number of 'policy interventions and support measures by multilateral agencies and partner countries'.[57] The result is that 'bilateral donor involvement has correspondingly been narrow' and 'has been delivered, frequently randomly, indiscriminately and more often than not on a stand-alone basis'.[58]

The problem of poor co-ordination is addressed at two levels in the first two paragraphs of the section on technical co-operation and capacity building in the Doha Declaration. At the local level, WTO Members have instructed the Secretariat to co-ordinate with other relevant

---

[52] UNCTAD/WTO, 1996. See also OECD Policy Brief, 2001, p 3 on 'Why help develop capacity to trade?'

[53] Subcommittee on Least-Developed Countries, 1999.

[54] Economists typically list this as a 'supply-side constraint'. See Michalopoulos, 2001, pp 91–96, who concentrates on the lack of analytical skills, institutional capacity, and adequate regulatory regimes in many developing countries. Staffing levels, quality and resources in institutions responsible for drafting and implementing laws are often inadequate, and parliamentary committees often lack time to consider new bills.

[55] SPS, TBT, and Customs Valuation Agreement as well as TRIPS all contain such provisions. Some examples include SPS, Art 9; TBT, Arts 11 and 12(7); Agreement on Implementation of Article VII of the GATT 1994 (Customs Valuation Agreement, or CVA), Art 203; and TRIPS, Art 67.

[56] Doha Declaration, paras 38–41.

[57] Prowse, 2002, p 5.

[58] Ibid.

agencies in order to 'support domestic efforts for mainstreaming trade into national plans for economic development and strategies for poverty reduction'.[59] This is an express reference to the current thinking on delivery of TRTA, which should be conducted within the development context and where possible taking account of flanking policy reduction measures, as set out in the IMF-World Bank Policy Reduction Strategy Papers (PRSPs). The only problem here is that some but not all developing countries (mostly LDCs) can be accounted for under the PRSPs.

At the international level, the WTO Secretariat is called upon to co-ordinate the delivery of TRTA with bilateral donors through the OECD Development Assistance Committee (the DAC, see below) and with relevant international and regional intergovernmental institutions in order to establish a coherent policy framework and timetable for delivery.[60] Additionally, the WTO Director General is called upon to examine ways of enhancing two existing inter-agency technical assistance programmes (see below).[61]

While the Doha Development Agenda foresees an increase in the scope and delivery of TRTA and capacity-building endeavours, it is by no means certain that this will be specifically applied to trade law reform. I turn now to consider how such technical assistance has been delivered prior to Doha, first from the multilateral agencies and intergovernmental institutions, followed by some comments on the bilateral donor involvement in trade law development through the efforts of the OECD's Development Co-operation Directorate (DCD) and, more specifically, the DAC.

Technical assistance from multilateral agencies

In the case of the WTO, the Secretariat's capacity to deliver sufficient, high quality technical assistance programmes to developing country Members over a long period of time has consistently been hampered by serious budgetary constraints.[62] The reason for this has been that the expanded work programme of the WTO in relation to developing countries, including issues arising predominantly from implementation of the WTO Agreements, have drawn heavily upon the small budgetary allocation to the Secretariat by WTO Members for this purpose. Just prior to the Doha Ministerial Meeting the WTO Secretariat was covering as much as 90percent of its technical assistance requirements through extra-budgetary resources—that is, by drawing on trust funds provided by a few Member governments.[63] This type of funding presents enormous difficulties for the efficient and predictable planning of TRTA since the funds do not form part of the regular WTO budget and allow little room for co-ordination between the various donors and agencies.

The Doha Development Agenda Global Trust Fund (DDAGTF) was established following a decision of the WTO General Council in December 2001, with the purpose of raising funding for WTO TRTA in excess of CHF 15 million. However, such funds are not to be drawn from the regular budget, but rather raised externally. The primary means of doing this has been

---

[59] Doha Declaration, para 38.

[60] *Ibid*, para 39.

[61] *Ibid*.

[62] New WTO Strategy, p 5 and Annex IX.

[63] Some examples of developed and developing country Members that have provided trust fund money to the WTO for technical assistance activities in recent years include: Australia, France, Japan, the Netherlands, Norway, Poland, Singapore, Hong Kong, China, the UK and the US. See further Secretariat Note 2000, p 27.

through a pledging conference held in March 2002.[64] At the same time, the WTO's entire technical co-operation programme[65] has been revised.

Henceforth, the focus of the WTO's technical assistance is on six levels of action, mandated by the Doha Declaration.[66] The last of these, under Section (iv) is the 'annual Secretariat-wide Technical Co-operation Plan, to be delivered mainly by the WTO Secretariat (and to an extent in co-ordination with multilateral agencies with related competence)'.[67] TRTA and capacity-building will be aimed primarily at government policymakers and negotiators. No mention is made of lawmakers (parliamentarians), or the more specialist technicians, such as legal draftspersons. Indeed, there is no specific legal focus, despite the fact that legal issues such as rule implementation and WTO dispute settlement are included among the 22 separate headings under which technical assistance will be delivered.

As noted above, two technical assistance programmes established prior to the Doha Ministerial Meeting, and which have a particular focus on the lower-income developing countries, will be continued. The first is the 'Joint Integrated Technical Assistance Programme' (JITAP) begun in 1998. This capacity-building programme is run by the three Geneva-based organisations (WTO, UNCTAD and ITC) in those eight selected LDCs and other African countries. Local co-ordination among the Geneva institutions is to be promoted through National Steering Committees, with technical counterparts in each country to oversee implementation. Once again, this is primarily a trade policy capacity-building programme, and does not include specific inputs on trade law reform.

Integrated framework

The second is the 'Integrated Framework for Trade-Related Technical Assistance to Least Developed Countries' (the Integrated Framework),[68] which has brought together six co-operating international agencies (the Geneva organisations, plus the IMF, World Bank and UNDP), and flows directly from the First WTO Ministerial Meeting in Singapore in 1996. The Integrated Framework was established in October 1997 at a WTO High Level Meeting for least developed countries (both WTO Members and non-Members). Its aim is to provide a mechanism whereby trade policy, TRTA and capacity-building can be articulated within a broader development context. The Integrated Framework has come under criticism for being slow and cumbersome to implement, partly because it operates through a system of round tables involving all six agencies, donors and least developing country partners; and partly because there is limited capacity in least developed countries to present coherent, co-ordinated and integrated programmes on trade and poverty reduction capable of eliciting support.[69]

A number of recommendations were made for improving and redesigning the Integrated Framework at a meeting of the heads of the six agencies in July of 2000.[70] A Pilot Scheme was

---

[64]   The Doha Development Agenda Global Trust Fund (DDAGTF) has superseded the role of individual trust fund financing although monies deposited in the DDAGTF are still voluntary contributions and are being built up through pledging (see WTO Pledging Conference for the DDAGTF held in Geneva on 11 March 2002).

[65]   Coordinated WTO Secretariat Annual Technical Assistance Plan 2002. WTO Secretariat TA Plan, 2002.

[66]   Doha Declaration, paras 16, 21, 24, 26, 27, 33, 38-40, 42 and 43.

[67]   WTO Secretariat TA Plan 2002, p 4. WTO has forged links with regional development banks in the delivery of TRTA through Memoranda of Understanding with the Inter-American Development Bank (27 February 2002), with the Arab Monetary Fund (3 May 2002) and with the Asian Development Bank (9 May 2002).

[68]   For further details see the website of the Integrated Framework at www.ldcs.org.

[69]   For some of these points and the full review, see Rajapathirana, Lusthaus, and Adriene, 2000.

[70]   Decision of the Subcommittee on Least-Developed Countries, 6 July 2001.

set up in February 2001[71] to (i) initiate work on 'mainstreaming' a trade integration strategy into least-developed countriey (LDC) development plans and poverty reduction strategies including PRSPs, for countries that chose to do so; (ii) establish a trust fund; (iii) set out a co-ordinated, sequenced and prioritised programme of technical assistance and capacity-building for each country; and (iv) establish a steering committee, to improve governance of relations amongst LDCs, donors, and the core agencies. The Pilot Scheme has been applied to Cambodia, Madagascar and Mauritania and there are plans for its expansion, post-Doha.

There are a few points to note in connection with the operation of the Integrated Framework. It only extends to LDCs—not to developing countries as a whole. Second, it is not obvious that the programme is directed at any specific elements of trade law reform, and thus it is too early to assess its impact in those countries to which it applies. Third, there is a conceptual problem with the Integrated Framework in linking trade and poverty reduction, not least because not all LDCs have prepared PRSPs.[72] Fourth, from a resource point of view the IMF and World Bank are the two agencies with the most resources but neither has trade as a key policy, whereas the three agencies that do—the WTO, UNCTAD and ITC—have very few resources.

Commonwealth Secretariat

The Commonwealth Secretariat—a less formal body—is aware of the enormous dearth of legal and technical knowledge and skills among policy-makers, legislative drafters and other government officials in implementing reform of trade laws in Commonwealth developing countries. Its Legal and Constitutional Affairs Division has sought to evaluate the actual technical assistance needs of Commonwealth developing countries in implementing primary and secondary WTO norms, over a two-year period between 1996 and 1998, by holding a series of conferences in each of four major geographical areas of the Commonwealth.[73] Participants were drawn from ministries relating to trade and commerce and to law and justice, as well as from attorney generals' chambers. They also included patent and trademark officials. Participants filed country reports to the Commonwealth Secretariat as to their progress in implementation, and their legal technical assistance needs.

Unfortunately, lack of funds has made it impossible for the Secretariat to follow up on the majority of requests it received. Even so, it was heartening to discover that many of the national inter-ministerial committees formed to implement the WTO agreements contained a broad representation of stakeholders and were working reasonably well in co-ordinating the legal and institutional reform programmes across ministerial lines.

More recently the Commonwealth Secretariat has been active in the field of training, having entered into a joint training venture with the WTO Training Institute. While laudable, this form of TRTA has so far been limited to providing an extra two weeks of follow-up for Commonwealth participants on the WTO's Trade Policy Course, run on a regular basis for developing country government officials and policymakers by the WTO Training Institute in Geneva. However, participants on the specialist 'Familiarisation Programme'—a training programme tailored to the specific needs of Commonwealth WTO Members—benefit from

---

[71] Decision of the Subcommittee on Least-Developed Countries, 12 February 2001, in which it adopted the 'Integrated Framework—Proposal for a Pilot Scheme', 16 February 2001.

[72] See Michalopoulos, 2001, pp 96-99, who comments on this aspect at 98 along with broader remarks about the whole programme.

[73] A total of five conferences were held: one for TRIPS in Livingstone, Zambia, 1996; and one each for general WTO implementation in Port-of-Spain, Trinidad and Tobago, 1997; Auckland, New Zealand (for the Pacific Region), 1997; Colombo, Sri Lanka, 1998; and Arusha, Tanzania, 1998.

concentrating on writing briefing papers for their governments on a subject currently on the WTO agenda.[74]

Technical assistance from bilateral donors

There has been considerable movement on the bilateral donor front between 1997 and 2002, as is evident from the OECD Development Assistance Committee (DAC) reports. In 1997, DAC Members[75] asked the DCD at the OECD to prepare a survey of bilateral trade-related technical assistance projects of OECD Members.[76] Then in March 1997, a DAC Informal Experts Meeting on Capacity Development for Trade identified key points related to integrating developing countries in a globalising world economy. The emphasis was on strengthening the supply-side capacities of developing countries in order to increase their competitive advantages by means of trade promotion; improvements to infrastructure, public and private sector human and institutional capacities; and streamlining market access. Additionally, the report promoted comprehensive and integrated approaches by donors to capacity development for trade in developing countries.[77]

Eighteen months later, following a report by Professor John Whalley[78] and the start of the multilateral Integrated Framework initiative for LDCs, a small but vital addition was made to the so-called DAC Development Partnership Strategy at the November 1998 DAC Experts Meeting on Capacity Development for Trade. Trade development should be demand-driven by developing countries, locally owned and reflect donor co-ordination.[79]

Even so, trade and development form an uneasy alliance for the bilateral donor community. Donor field representatives often lack any trade policy skills or awareness, especially when it comes to a country's obligations for implementation of primary and secondary WTO norms and standards.[80] Additionally, not all bilateral donors are focusing on trade development as part of their development co-operation policy, even if they are members of the DAC and the DAC Informal Experts Group on Capacity Development for Trade. Chief among the DAC members that do pursue such policies are the UK,[81] Switzerland[82] and the European Union. The latter has brought development fully into its Directorate General for Trade, partly in response to the need—following the signing of a successor agreement to the

---

74 See 'First Edition of the Commonwealth Secretariat WTO's Familiarization Programme', 2001.

75 The DAC is the principal body through which the OECD deals with development co-operation issues and provides a forum for the major bilateral donors to work together. Currently the DAC comprises the following donors: Australia, Austria, Belgium, Canada, Denmark, Finland, France, Germany, Ireland, Italy, Japan, Luxembourg, the Netherlands, New Zealand, Norway, Portugal, Spain, Sweden, Switzerland, UK, US, the Commission of the European Communities. The IMF, UNDP and the World Bank are permanent observers to the DAC.

76 'Survey of DAC Members' Co-operation for Capacity Development in Trade' DCD/DAC(97).

77 DAC Experts Meeting, 1998.

78 Professor Whalley's report: 'Building Poor Countries' Trade Capacity', November 1998, is appended to the Summary of the DAC Experts Meeting, 1998, pp 13-36.

79 See 'Summary of the DAC Experts Meeting', 1998, pp 9-10.

80 *Ibid*, p 10.

81 See the UK Government's White Paper 'Eliminating World Poverty: A Challenge for the 21ˢᵗ Century' which *inter alia* is geared to assisting developing countries with domestic reform of their trade and investment laws and their participation in the related multilateral bodies, especially the WTO, available at www.dfid.gov.uk.

82 See Swiss Agency for Development and Co-operation, 2000, with a plan of action broken down into 15 objectives, split into 47 proposals for action and 150 measures for implementation with dialogue covering *inter alia* the Bretton Woods institutions, the WTO and relations with transition economies.

Lomé IV Agreement in 2000 (the ACP-Cotonou Agreement)—to better articulate the trade and aid policies of ACP-Lomé countries within the multilateral trading system.[83]

But donors may nonetheless be wary of providing technical assistance for reform of trade laws and policies in developing countries either because they threaten vested interests in their established export markets, or because they are potentially contrary to their domestic interests.[84] There are two discernible trends. First, there is a reported increase in outsourcing of manufacturing processes (sometimes through export processing zones) and services (notably processing of financial records and flight reservation systems) by large OECD companies to developing countries on grounds of cost.[85] Moreover, OECD companies may ask their governments to provide technical assistance to developing countries in order that the latter can deal with antidumping petitions made against their own goods imported to the OECD, or to support restrictions on exports by developing countries of textiles and apparel—despite requirements for the phasing out of safeguards under the new Agreement on Textiles and Clothing (ATC).

Second, there has been an increase in technical assistance directed towards areas of trade law reform of interest to bilateral donors, key among them being reform of intellectual property law towards compliance with international norms and standards. Whalley notes that 'teams of lawyers have travelled to countries, designed new intellectual property regimes and discussed their implementation'.[86] Despite the high costs involved with the design and operation of such systems—such as establishing and maintaining trade mark registrations and equipping and training an entire team of patent examiners—it is a favoured target for donor funds because of 'the tangibility of the technical assistance' and pressure from commercial interests in the donor countries. Similar explanations are to be advanced for the amount of technical assistance provided by bilateral donors to legislative and institutional reform programmes in developing countries in the areas of customs valuation and health and safety standards.[87]

The overall conclusion that can be drawn from the above is that economic changes are creating both new forms of dependency for developed countries, and the potential for a symbiotic paring of private commercial interests and TRTA. A contributory factor in the equation is that the type of technical assistance on offer for trade law reform is of relatively recent origin and is not yet embedded in mainstream development policy. Instead, it is rather *ad hoc* and is not necessarily geared to implementing the matrix of regulatory obligations arising from the WTO Agreements.[88] Above all, it lacks co-ordination although this objective may be intrinsically difficult to achieve in the field of trade and development where export promotion objectives may vie with development objectives in the technical assistance programmes of many donors, or as van Hove and Lecomte note in their 1999 study of ACP countries, 'donors may feel more like competitors than potential partners'.[89]

---

83   A new treaty was signed at Cotonou, Benin on 23 June 2000, available at http://www.europa.eu.int/ comm/development/cotonou/index_en.htm.

84   Prowse makes the same observation in her paper: 2002, p 6.

85   Whalley, 2000, p 20.

86   *Ibid*. Many lawyers who have conducted drafting and implementation missions on the TRIPS Agreement have done so on behalf of the World Intellectual Property Organization in Geneva. See 'WIPO's Legal and Technical Assistance to Developing Countries for the Implementation of the TRIPS Agreement from January 1, 1996 to June 30, 2000', August 2000, where it is noted that 111 developing countries and regional organisations have been recipients of legislative advice in this period.

87   See Finger and Schuler, 1999, p 35.

88   See 'WTO Matrix on Regulatory Obligations…'.

89   Van Hove and Lecomte, 1999.

Notwithstanding the obvious problems, the DAC has moved forward in its collective endeavour to put trade on the development agenda. Already at the DAC Informal Experts Meeting in 1998, the Committee called for further research and dialogue on trade capacity issues. As of May 2000 the DAC has aimed to develop a set of good practices in capacity development for trade. As preparatory background material for the May 2000 meeting, a set of four case studies were submitted by two independent experts, relating to two African countries (Ghana and Senegal), one Latin American country (El Salvador) and one South East Asian country (Vietnam).[90] The case studies do not dwell on any specific aspect of trade law reform, but instead address more mainstream issues of trade capacity and donor responses.

At the policy level, the DAC Development Partnership Strategy, as its name suggests, strongly supports co-operation and partnership between donors and recipients in the field of trade, including internal policy coherence and better co-ordination. There is also a more general move within the DAC to encourage DAC members to 'untie' aid and this extends to technical assistance programmes. Significantly, in April 2001 a High Level Meeting of the DAC endorsed a set of 'Guidelines' aimed at strengthening trade capacity for development.[91] The DAC Guidelines, while emphasising the contribution of trade liberalisation to development, recognise the need to support the beneficial integration of developing countries into the multilateral trading system through trade policy-makers and donor support.[92] While laudable, the DAC Guidelines do not specifically address trade law reform or the necessity of embedding trade reform in the legal systems of developing countries.

REITERATION, ADAPTATION AND TRADE LAW REFORM: THE DEVELOPING COUNTRY DILEMMA

As the studies of both Finger and Schuler and Whalley demonstrate, there has been some attempt to address the capacity of developing countries in implementing their trade-related legal and regulatory obligations. This includes the drafting, amendment and modernisation of laws and regulations in order to make them compliant with international norms and standards, especially in the areas of customs valuation, health and safety standards and intellectual property rights.

There is also a discernible trend towards the use of 'model laws' for trade law reform in developing countries, a common feature in market economy law reform. The model law is particularly useful for the introduction of new law, where none previously existed or where considerable modernisation is required. Often model law is either a mere template which has been tried and tested elsewhere for its consistency with international norms and standards, or a product of an international norm or standard setting body. Thus, on its face it is an ideal tool for achieving another objective of several of the WTO Agreements—harmonisation. In view of scarce resources and the limited time frames for implementation contained in many WTO Agreements there would seem to be some justification for using it in developing countries. Moreover, a model law often has the advantage of internal consistency and a history of

---

[90] The four reports are to be found in the Annexes to the 'Background Papers' to the 'DAC Good Practice Workshop, 2000'.

[91] *Guidelines on Capacity Development for Trade in the New Global Context*, 23 May 2001. At the same time the UK Department for International Development (DfID) issued a companion document: DfID, 2001.

[92] See also New WTO Strategy, p 4.

implementation and interpretation elsewhere.[93] The adoption of model laws by developing and transition economy countries (together with adherence to major international economic and commercial treaties) is sometimes seen by lending agencies and donors as an indication of a country's commitment to the reform process in the global economy.

An example of copying is found in what the World Intellectual Property Organization calls 'draft laws on intellectual property subjects'. These model laws cover seven substantive areas of intellectual property rights, and related rights,[94] as found in the TRIPS Agreement and many other major international intellectual property conventions. The reform of more procedural laws relating to customs valuation follows internationally recognised norms and standards which are promoted in developing countries by the Brussels-based World Customs Organization.

Yet, in essence the process of using model law in trade law reform is essentially a process of reiteration and adaptation of the laws of developed countries in the multilateral trading system. This process is mutually reinforcing as long as consultants and experts from developed countries, or international standard setting bodies, are involved with the implementation of primary and secondary WTO norms through advising on draft legislation, or actually undertaking the drafting. What is often forgotten is that those WTO developed country Members (and OECD DAC members) have benefited from the introduction of legal and regulatory reforms in their domestic legal systems at earlier stages of their economic development on an incremental basis, rather than within the space of five or ten, as dictated by the WTO Agreements. They have had therefore had plenty of time to adjust their domestic trade laws to the local environment—an opportunity not afforded most developing country Members.

This should be borne in mind, along with a number of other drawbacks when applying the model law process to trade in developing countries. We have already observed that many developing countries failed to rally support for the introduction of new rules and regulations in trade, in order to comply with WTO obligations, because their governments were insufficiently involved at the rule making stage and thus there is a lack of ownership.

Additionally, the time frames for implementation by developing countries and LDCs of trade law reform are sufficiently short as to exclude the possibility of underpinning the drafting process with an 'adequate legislative theory'.[95] That is, the legislative drafter will not be able to take account of both 'existing rules,' and 'also the relevant factors in the country-specific circumstances within which role-occupants act'.[96] This approach is contextual in character and country specific. In many ways it parallels the 'issues-based approach' towards trade policy reform that Susan Prowse proposes in her work.[97]

---

[93] See Webb, 1999, pp 33-52, at 42 where he advocates the use of model laws developed by institutions; *viz* UNCITRAL for international sale of goods, international transport and storage of goods, banking and international payments, government procurement and arbitration, or draft laws produced by UNCTAD relating to conflict of laws and competition. Wälde and Gunderson, 1999, pp 67-95, argue in somewhat contradictory fashion for legal transplants in the form of copying (including model law) for liberalising economies, as a matter of expediency, but call for such legislation to remain sensitive to underlying socio-economic forces. Their compromise solution is to 'create interim law for, around and subsequent to individual major transactions'.

[94] These are patents, industrial designs, trademarks for goods and services (including collective marks), geographical indications, layout-designs (topographies of integrated circuits), copyright and related rights and protection against unfair competition. Some countries also receive model laws on utility model certificates (or petty patents) upon request.

[95] Seidman and Seidman, 1996, p 11.

[96] Rule occupants means the 'addressees of the rules', *ibid*, p 12.

[97] Prowse, 2002, pp 12-15.

The hasty introduction of model laws may only reinforce the lack of local ownership over the national implementation of WTO norms; and further alienate rule occupants—or addressees—by failing to take account of that country's specific resource constraints, particularly where subjective interests, values and ideologies are involved. A potential example of this is to be found in the domestic implementation of the 'built-in' agenda item of Article 27(3)(b) TRIPS whereby *all* WTO members must legislate in their domestic legal systems for patents, plant variety protection, a *sui generis* system or a mixture thereof. It is true that the provision—still under review—leaves considerable flexibility to individual governments with respect to the scope of that legislation such as to permit coverage of plant variety protection (PVP), indigenous knowledge or even the protection of farmers' rights under a PVP scheme. In addition, countries may also consider imposing limitations on any rights given to commercial breeders that would satisfy one of the TRIPS provisions, such as the *ordre public* exemption and morality exceptions that conform to Articles 27(2) and 30 of the TRIPS Agreement respectively.

Nevertheless, there is increasing evidence that developing country Members are seeking the easy way out—adopting model PVP legislation conforming with either the 1978 or 1991 version of the International Convention on the Protection of Plant Varieties[98] without necessarily considering whether it is adapted to their local social and cultural environment.[99] Such legislation is often drafted with the technical assistance from bilateral donors, under one form of development aid package or another, and the consultative processes that such PVP legislation would normally call for—involving various sectors of indigenous peoples, local farmers and entrepreneurs—may be ignored in the interests of time, efficiency and achieving a tangible result.

The dilemma for WTO developing country Members is that they may be ill-served by model laws and various other forms of copying, even thought they fulfil the obvious demands of speedy implementation, uniformity and consistency. In essence, such models constitute no more than the reiteration and adaptation of developed country approaches to the implementation of substantive international obligations, which are borne of different traditions and experiences, and cannot fully take care of the specific developing country requirements and levels of social and economic development.[100] However, in reality, where technical assistance for building capacity on trade in developing countries is available from multilateral agencies and bilateral donors, the opportunity for developing countries to influence the process may be limited indeed.

SUMMARY AND CONCLUSION

This contribution has focused on the WTO and reform of trade laws in developing countries, with particular attention to the articulation of primary and secondary WTO norms in the

---

[98] The Union Internationale pour la Protection des Obtentions Végétales was established by the International Convention for the Protection of New Varieties of Plants, 2 December 1961, and was revised on 10 November 1972, 23 October 1978, and 19 March 1991, with the 1978 amendments entering into force on 8 November 1981 and the 1991 amendments on 24 April 1998. Countries that are parties to either the 1978 or 1997 versions usually enact plant variety protection (PVP) laws that are either (i) in accordance with UPOV; (ii) substantially in accordance with UPOV; or (iii) a hybrid system of laws that did not substantially follow the system of UPOV.

[99] India is the latest country to join UPOV on 31 May 2002 under the terms of UPOV's 1978 Act, *Economic Times*, 2002.

[100] The same argument can be made in the case of trade reform generally; see Prowse, 2002.

domestic legal systems, noting the constraints that developing countries face in implementing such laws due to the scope and coverage of the multilateral agreements. It has also focused on the new linkages that have been established between technical assistance and trade reform, as a result of the Doha Declaration.

The most immediate issue that many developing and least developed countries face is the implications of the vertical expansion of international trade law beyond the border. As a result of their membership of the WTO, they are under an obligation to implement a wide range of international trade obligations in their domestic legal systems in a relatively short space of time. The enthusiasm for such implementation may be lacking or difficult to muster, especially where there is a perceived lack of ownership of the rules because of insufficient developing country involvement in the rule making process during the Uruguay Round. In turn, this may affect the law reform process in those countries, not only at the level of substantive implementation of primary and secondary WTO norms, but also at the level of institutional reform.

Developing countries lack infrastructure, and human and financial resources and are thus reliant on technical assistance for trade law reform. It has been observed that although TRTA may be forthcoming, both from multilateral agencies and bilateral donors, it may be inherently contradictory, poorly co-ordinated and supply-driven rather than demand-driven. It is also difficult to ascertain the extent to which bilateral donor assistance for trade is dedicated to legal and institutional reform. What is certain is that very few developed countries have so far added trade to their mainstream development co-operation policy and may be reluctant to do so because it would threaten vested commercial interests in their own constituencies.

Where reform of trade laws has been most consistently carried out in developing countries it is mostly in the areas of intellectual property protection, customs valuation and with respect to health and sanitary standards. There is also a discernible trend towards the use of model laws as an efficient means of conducting trade law reform in some developing countries, even though it rarely takes account of the local environment and the relevant level of development of the developing country.

The Doha Declaration establishes a clear link between TRTA and capacity-building initiatives for developing countries within the overall context of trade reform. However, the main focus is on policy initiatives and not law reform. In fact, unless developing countries are given the type of legal technical assistance that is so urgently required in order to provide a sustainable legal and institutional framework for implementing their WTO commitments at the domestic level, the process of copying through models laws, based on internationally derived norms and standards, will continue to leave their mark. If the objectives of the Doha Declaration on TRTA and capacity-building are to have any effect then real efforts must be made to assist with trade law reform in developing countries and to embed such reform in mainstream development policy.

REFERENCES

(CVA) Agreement on Implementation of Article VII of the General Agreement on Tariffs and Trade), entered into force 1 January 1995, Annex 1A to the Marrakesh Agreement Establishing the World Trade Organization, opened for signature 15 April 1994, 1867 UNTS 3, (1994) 33 ILM 1125

(DAC Experts Meeting 1998) Summary of 'Informal DAC Experts Meeting on Capacity Development for Trade', held on 23-24 November 1998, Doc DCD/DAC(99) 13, available at www.oecd.org/dac/

(Doha Declaration) *Ministerial Declaration*, adopted on 14 November 2001 at the Fourth Session of the WTO Ministerial Conference, Doha, 9-14 November 2001, WT/MIN(01)/DEC/1, 20 November 2001

(New WTO Strategy) Note by the WTO Secretariat, *Technical Co-operation for Capacity-building, Growth and Integration: The New WTO Strategy*, February 2002

(TBT) Agreement on Technical Barriers to Trade, entered into force 1 January 1995, Annex 1A to Marrakesh Agreement Establishing the World Trade Organization, opened for signature 15 April 1994, 1867 UNTS 3, 33 (1994) ILM 1125

(WTO Agreement) Agreement Establishing the World Trade Organization, *The Results of the Uruguay Round of Multilateral Trade Negotiations: The Legal Texts* 1994, Geneva: GATT/WTO Secretariat, pp 6-18

(WTO Matrix on Regulatory Obligations) 'Matrix on regulatory obligations and other implications of the Uruguay round agreements', Note by the Secretariat, Addendum, to the WTO Committee on Trade and Development, Second Session, 28 June 1995, WT/COMTD/W/6/Add.1

(DAC Good Practices Workshop, 2000) DAC OECD Workshop 'Towards good practices for donors on capacity development for trade,' 29-30 May 2000, DCD/DAC (2000) series 2000, Paris: OECD, available at www.oecd.org/dac/

'First edition of the Commonwealth Secretariat WTO's familiarization programme', *WTO News; 2001 Press Releases*, No 262, 17 December 2001

'Survey of DAC members' co-operation for capacity development in trade,' DCD/DAC(97)

'WIPO's legal and technical assistance to developing countries for the implementation of the TRIPS Agreement from January 1, 1996 to June 30, 2000', WIPO/TRIPS/2000/1, August 2000

(Customs Valuation Agreement, or CVA) Agreement on Implementation of Article VII of the general Agreement on Tariffs and Trade, 1994

(SPS) Agreement on Sanitary and Phytosanitary Measures, entered into force 1 January 1995, Annex 1A to the Marrakesh Agreement Establishing the World Trade Organization, opened for signature 15 April 1994, 1867 UNTS 3, 33 (1994) ILM 1125

(TRIMs) Agreement on Trade-Related Investment Measures, entered into force 1 January 1995, Annex 1A to the Marrakesh Agreement Establishing the World Trade Organization, opened for signature 15 April 1994, 1867 UNTS 3, 33 (1994) ILM 1125

(TRIPS) Agreement on Trade-Related Intellectual Property Rights, entered into force 1 January 1995, Annex 1A to the Marrakesh Agreement Establishing the World Trade Organization, opened for signature 15 April 1994, 1867 UNTS 3, 33 (1994) ILM 1125

Blackhurst, R, Lyakurwa, B and Oyejide, A, 'Improving African participation in the WTO', Paper commissioned by the World Bank for a Conference at the WTO, 20-21 September 1999, available at www.worldbank.org

Chung, M S, 'Implementation of the results of the Uruguay Round Agreements: Korea', in Jackson, J H and Sykes, A O (eds), *Implementing the Uruguay Round*, 1997, Oxford: Clarendon Press

(WTO Secretariat TA Plan 2002) *Co-ordinated WTO Secretariat Annual Technical Assistance Plan 2002*, WT/COMTD/W/95/Rev.3, 8 March 2002

Decision of the Subcommittee on Least-Developed Countries, 'Review of the integrated framework: communiqué from heads of the six core agencies', 6 July 2001, WT/LDC/SWG/IF/2, 12 July 2001

Decision of the Subcommittee on Least-Developed Countries, 12 February 2001, WT/LDC/SWG/IF/13, 16 February 2001

Echandi, R, 'The Uruguay Round Agreements: constitutional and legal aspects of their implementation in Costa Rica', in Jackson, J H and Sykes, A O Jr (eds), *Implementing the Uruguay Round*, 1997, Oxford: Clarendon Press

Economic Times (New Delhi) 1 June 2002

Faundez, J, Footer, M E and Norton, J J (eds), *Governance, Development, Globalization*, 2000, London: Legal Research Centre/Blackstone Press

Finger, J M and Schuler, P, 'Implementation of Uruguay Round commitments: the development challenge', Background Study for the WTO on-line Conference 'Developing Countries and the Millennium Round', Trade and Development Centre, World Bank and the WTO, 11-19 October 1999 (draft, 5 September 1999), available at www.itd.org/wb/devfor.htm

Finger, J M, presented at 'Developing Countries and the New Round of Multilateral Trade Negotiations', Harvard University, 5-6 November 1999

Fried, J T, 'Governance in the global age: a public international law perspective', in Porter, R B and Sauvé, P (eds), *Seattle, the WTO, and the Future of the Multilateral Trading System*, 2000, Cambridge, MA: Center for Business and Government, John F Kennedy School of Government, Harvard University, pp 131-141

Friedman, W, *The Changing Structure of International Law*, 1964, New York: Columbia University Press

Government of Egypt, 'G-15 Symposium on Globalization and its Economic and Social Impacts', Cairo, 22-23 November 1999, submitted to the WTO Ministerial Conference, Seattle, 30 November-3 December 1999, WT/MIN(99)/14, 1 December 1999

Gray, C W, 'Reforming legal systems in developing and transitional countries', in Seidman, A , Seidman, RB and Wälde, T (eds), *Making Development Work: Legislative Reform for Institutional Transformation and Good Governance* 1999, The Hague, London, Boston: Kluwer Law International

Guidelines on Capacity Development for Trade in the New Global Context 23 May 2001, DCD/DAC (2001) 5/Final, 23 May 2001

Hudec, R E, *Enforcing International Trade Law: The Evolution of the Modern GATT Legal System* 1991, Salem, NH: Butterworth

Jackson, J H and Sykes, A O (eds), *Implementing the Uruguay Round* 1997, Oxford: Clarendon Press

Jackson, J H, 'The birth of the GATT-MTN system: a constitutional appraisal' (1980) 12 *Law and Policy in International Business* 21, reproduced in J H Jackson, *The Jurisprudence of GATT & the WTO* 2000, Cambridge: CUP, p 34

Jackson, J H, *The World Trading System: Law and Policy of International Economic Relations*, 1997, Cambridge, MA, and London: The MIT Press

Jackson, J H, *World Trade and the Law of the GATT*, 1969, Indianapolis: Bobbs-Merrill

League of Nations, 'Procedure for the friendly settlement of economic disputes between states' Off. No C.57.M.32.1932.II.B

League of Nations Memorandum 'Relating to the pacific settlement of international disputes concerning economic questions in general and commercial and customs questions in particular' Off No E.666.1931.II.B.I

Marceau, G and Trachtmann, J P, 'TBT, SPS and GATT: A map of the WTO law of domestic regulation', in Petersmann, E-U (ed), *WTO Jurisprudence 1995-2001: Law and Dispute Settlement Practice of the World Trade Organization*, 2002, The Hague: Kluwer Law International

Meeting of the General Council of 3 and 8 May 2000, WT/GC/M/55, 16 June 2000

Michalopoulos, C, *Developing Countries in the WTO*, 2001, Houndmills, Basingstoke: Palgrave

(Secretariat Note 2000) Note by the Secretariat to the WTO Committee on Trade and Development on concerns regarding special and differential treatment provisions in WTO agreements and decisions, WT/COMTD/W/66, 16 February 2000

OECD Policy Brief, *Trade and Development in the New Global Context: the Capacity Dimension*, 2001, Paris: OECD, available at www.oecd.org

Ogunkola, E O, 'African Capacity for Compliance and Defence of WTO Rights', Paper for African Economic Research Consortium (AERC)-Sponsored Conference on Africa and the World Trading System, Yaounde, Cameroon, 17-18 April 1999

Oloka-Onyango, J and Udagama, D, 'The Realization of Economic, Social and Cultural rights: Globalization and its impact on the full enjoyment of human rights', Preliminary report to the UN Economic and Social Council Sub-Commission on the Promotion and Protection of Human Rights, 52nd Session, Doc E/CN/4/Sub.2/2000/13, 15 June 2000

Prowse, S, 'Mechanisms for Trade-Related Capacity-building and Technical Assistance After Doha', Paper prepared for the World Bank Roundtable on 'Informing the Doha Process: New Trade Research for Developing Countries', Cairo, 20-21 May 2002

Rajapathirana, S, Lusthaus, C and Adriene, M-H, 'Review of the Integrated Framework for Technical Assistance for Trade Development to Least Developed Countries' 6 June 2000, Washington, DC, in 'Report of the Review of the Integrated Framework' to the Working Group on Least-Developed Countries/Integrated Framework, WT/LDC/SWG/IF/1, 29 June 2000

Reinicke, WH, 'Global public policy' (1997) 76:6 Foreign Affairs 127-138

Report for USAID of the Case Study: East African Enterprise Network, Southern African Management Systems International, 'Enterprise Network, West African Enterprise Network,' 2000, Management Systems International, Washington, DC, OECD Doc DCD(2000)10/ANN5

Rittich, K, 'Transformed pursuits: the quest for equality in globalized markets' (2000) 13 Harvard Human Rights Journal 221-233

Roessler, F, 'The scope, limits and function of the GATT legal system' (1985) 8 World Economy 287-298

Seidman, A, Seidman, R B and Wälde, T, 'Building sound national legal frameworks for development and social change', in Seidman, A, Seidman, R B and Wälde, T (eds), *Making Development Work: Legislative Reform for Institutional Transformation and Good Governance*, 1999, The Hague, London, Boston: Kluwer Law International

Seidman, A and Seidman, R B, 'Drafting legislation for development: lessons from a Chinese project' (1996) 44 American Journal of Comparative Law 1

SPS Committee, *Decision on the Implementation of Article 4 on Equivalence*, Doc G/SPS/19, 25 October 2001

Subcommittee on Least-Developed Countries, 'Third Progress report on the follow-up to the high level meeting', WT/COMTD/LDC/W/13, 24 February 1999

Swiss Agency for Development and Co-operation, 'Switzerland's North-South Relations in the 1990s' (2000), available at http://194.230.65.134/dezaweb2/home.asp

Tshuma, L, 'Hierarchies and government versus networks and governance: competing regulatory paradigms in global economic regulation' (1999) Law, Social Justice and Global Development, available at http://elj.warwick.ac.uk/global/issue/199-1/hierarchies

UK Department for International Development (DfID), *Building Trade Policy Capacity in Developing Countries and Transition Economies: A Practical Guide to Planning Technical Co-operation Programmes*, 2001, London: DfID, available at www.dfid.gov.uk

UK Government White Paper, 'Eliminating World Poverty: A Challenge for the 21st Century', available at www.dfid.gov.uk

UNCTAD/WTO, *Strengthening the participation of developing countries in world trade and the multilateral system* TD/375/Rev.1, 1996, Geneva: UNCTAD/WTO

United Nations Conference on Trade and Employment, Havana, Cuba, 21 November 1947-24 March 1948, UN Doc E/Conf.2/78

Van Hove, K and Lecomte, S H B, *Aid for Trade Development: Lessons for Lomé V*, ECDPM Discussion Paper No 10, August 1999, Maastricht

Wälde, T W and Gunderson, J L, 'Legislative reform in transition economies: Western transplants: a short-cut to social market economy status?', in Seidman, A, Seidman, R B and Wälde, T (eds), *Making Development Work: Legislative Reform for Institutional Transformation and Good Governance*, 1999, The Hague, London, Boston: Kluwer Law International

Webb, D, 'Legal system reform and private sector development in developing countries', in Seidman, A, Seidman, R B and Wälde, T (eds), *Making Development Work: Legislative Reform for Institutional Transformation and Good Governance*, 1999, The Hague, London, Boston: Kluwer Law International

Wellens, K C, 'Diversity in secondary rules and the unity of international law: some reflections on current trends' XXV (1994) Netherlands Yearbook of International Law 3-37

Whalley, J, 'Building poor countries' trade capacity', November 1998, DCD/DAC(99)13, Annex I, to the Summary of the DAC Experts Meeting, 1998

WTO Decision on implementation-related issues and concerns, 14 November 2001, WT MIN(01)/DEC/17, 20 November 2001

CHAPTER 9

THE OECD AND TAX COMPETITION: THE LAST RIGHTS FOR TAX HAVENS?

*David Salter**

When I was invited to participate in the proceedings of a conference with the theme 'Law and Development in the 21st Century' held in June 2001 I felt that, in view of my interest in taxation, it would be appropriate to present a paper that, in some respect, exhibited the role of taxation in development.[1] I also believed that this goal would be best served by eschewing an approach that focused on the intricacies and idiosyncrasies of national tax systems, and by favouring, instead, one that adopted an international/supra-national perspective.

In the event therefore, my paper, which this essay largely reproduces, initially sought to give an overview of the recent initiative of the OECD to identify and combat what it perceived to be 'harmful' tax competition. The paper then concentrated, in this context, on the position of those jurisdictions[2] characterised and subsequently named by the OECD as tax havens deemed to be engaged in 'harmful' tax competition. I pursued this latter inquiry in the belief that it would have a certain poignancy and relevance for some, and hopefully all, of the sponsors of the conference, because a high proportion of those jurisdictions designated as tax havens by the OECD for the purposes of the initiative are members of the Commonwealth.[3] As I have indicated, I will tread a similar path in this essay.

THE OECD INITIATIVE: AN OVERVIEW

The origin of this initiative lies in a May 1996 Communiqué, in which Ministers of the OECD member states called upon the OECD to 'develop measures to counter the distorting effects of harmful tax competition on investment and financing decisions and the consequences for national tax bases... '. Two years later, in response to this request, the OECD's Committee on Fiscal Affairs produced a report entitled 'Harmful Tax Competition—An Emerging Global Issue' (the 1998 Report). It was approved by the OECD Council on 9 April 1998.[4] The Council also instructed the Committee on Fiscal Affairs to continue its work in this area.

---

*   Senior Lecturer in International Economic Law, School of Law, Warwick University.

[1]   The conference was sponsored by the British Institute of International and Comparative Law, the Commonwealth Legal Education Association, the International Third World Legal Studies Association, and the Law Department, School of Oriental and African Studies, University of London.

[2]   The term 'jurisdiction', for present purposes, includes states and fiscally sovereign territories.

[3]   It should not be assumed, however, that only tax havens engaged in 'harmful' tax competition are 'targeted' by the initiative. As will be seen, the initiative also covers 'harmful' preferential tax regimes in OECD and non-OECD member states.

[4]   When approval was given to the 1998 Report by the OECD Council, Luxembourg and Switzerland abstained. A statement by each of these states is annexed to the report.

The 1998 report

Preliminary issues

At the outset, several preliminary—and yet fundamental—issues arise. These can be framed in a series of questions as follows: what does the OECD mean for the purposes of the 1998 Report by 'harmful' tax competition?; what prompted the 'recent' interest of the OECD in 'harmful' tax competition?; and is the OECD the proper forum for assessing what constitutes 'harmful' tax competition and for proposing what measures might be taken to counter it?

Each of these questions is addressed to some extent in the 1998 Report, and therein the treatment of the first two is inextricably linked. Thus, no all embracing definition of 'harmful' tax competition is proffered in the report—rather it would seem that 'harmful' tax competition is perceived as a phenomenon generated by the negative effects of globalisation, and that those negative effects may themselves be constituent elements of—or promote practices commensurate with—'harmful' tax competition. These notions are portrayed in the 1998 Report as follows:[5]

> Globalisation has... had the negative effects of opening up new ways by which companies and individuals can minimise and avoid taxes and in which countries can exploit... new opportunities by developing tax policies aimed primarily at diverting financial and other geographically mobile capital. These actions induce potential distortions in the patterns of trade and investment and reduce global welfare... these schemes can erode national tax bases of other countries, may alter the structure of taxation (by shifting part of the tax burden from mobile to relatively immobile factors and from income to consumption) and may hamper the application of progressive tax rates and the achievement of redistributive goals. Pressure of this sort can result in changes in tax structures in which all countries may be forced by spillover effects to modify their tax bases, even though a more desirable result could have been achieved through intensifying international co-operation. More generally, tax policies in one economy are now more likely to have repercussions on other economies.
>
> ... [W]here the interaction of tax systems is exploited by the enactment of special tax provisions which principally erode the tax base of other countries, the spillover effects on the other countries is not a mere side effect, incidental to the implementation of a domestic tax policy. Here the effect is for one country to redirect capital and financial flows and the corresponding revenue from the other jurisdictions by bidding aggressively for the tax base of the other countries. Some have described this effect as poaching as the tax base belongs to the other country. Practices of this sort can appropriately be labelled harmful tax competition as they do not reflect different judgements about the appropriate level of taxes and public outlays or the appropriate mix of taxes in a particular economy, which are aspects of every country's sovereignty in fiscal matters, but are, in effect, tailored to attract investment or savings originating elsewhere or to facilitate the avoidance of the other countries taxes.

From these extracts it can be inferred that the OECD's apparent concern is not with tax competition *per se* between jurisdictions, which is an inevitable and not necessarily objectionable consequence of the fiscal sovereignty. Nor is it concerned with tax competition generally, because its focus is on income derived from 'geographically mobile activities', such as financial and other service activities. The concern is rather, broadly speaking, with tax practices that '[detrimentally] affect the location of financial and other service activities, erode the tax base of other countries, distort trade and investment patterns and undermine fairness,

---

5   OECD Committee on Fiscal Affairs to the OECD Council, 1998, paras 23 and 29.

neutrality and broad social acceptance of tax systems generally'.[6] In other words, the pre-occupation is with tax practices that may be deemed to be, individually or collectively, predatory and hence unacceptable, and further, as will be seen, with such practices as perpetrated by tax havens and by those jurisdictions operating harmful preferential tax regimes.

The issue of the acceptability or otherwise of a tax practice or practices in this respect, of course, brings into play the third question set out above—that is, is the OECD the proper forum for assessing what constitutes 'harmful' tax competition and for proposing what measures might be taken to counter it? In this regard, the 1998 Report seeks to explain the OECD's particular interest in the area of tax competition in general terms reminiscent in some respects of the founding objectives of the OECD set out in Article 1 of the OECD Convention 1960.[7] Thus, the 1998 Report states:[8]

> ... The Report recognises that there are limitations on unilateral or bilateral responses to a problem [harmful tax competition] that is inherently multilateral, and identifies ways in which governments can best establish a common framework within which countries could co-operate individually and collectively to limit the problems presented by countries and fiscally sovereign territories engaging in harmful tax practices.

> ...The OECD believes that the progressive liberalisation of cross-border trade and investment has been the single most powerful driving force behind economic growth and rising living standards. The Organisation seeks to safeguard and promote an open, multilateral trading system and to encourage adjustments to that system to take into account the changing nature of international trade, including the interface between trade, investment and taxation. The Committee [on Fiscal Affairs] believes that the proposals set out in this Report...will further promote these objectives by reducing the distortionary influence of taxation on the location of mobile financial and service activities. If governments can agree that these location decisions should be driven by economic considerations and not primarily by tax factors, this will help move towards the level playing field which is so essential to the continued expansion of global economic growth.

> ... the fact that tax competition may lead to the proliferation of harmful tax practices and the adverse consequences that result... show that governments must take measures, including intensifying their international co-operation, to protect their tax bases and to avoid the world-wide reduction in welfare caused by tax-induced distortions in capital and financial flows.

These words suggest that the OECD's role in identifying and proposing means to counter 'harmful' tax competition should be viewed as merely facilitative. Hence, the onus is on individual or collective action (within the co-operative framework envisaged in the extracts above) against those jurisdictions engaging in harmful tax practices. Superficially, it is difficult to refute this construction. This is because from a strictly legal standpoint the OECD itself simply does not have the legal capacity to take steps to counter 'harmful' tax competition, nor can it prescribe what action(s) its members should take.

But, of course, this narrowly focused approach ignores the reality of the considerable influence wielded by the OECD over both OECD and non-OECD member states and the

---

[6] *Ibid*, para 4.

[7] Article 1 of the OECD Convention 1960 provides that the OECD shall promote policies designed: to achieve the highest sustainable economic growth and employment and a rising standard of living in Member countries, while maintaining financial stability, and thus to contribute to the development of the world economy; to contribute to sound economic expansion in Member as well as non-member countries in the process of economic development; and to contribute to the expansion of world trade on a multilateral, non-discriminatory basis in accordance with international obligations.

[8] OECD Committee on Fiscal Affairs to the OECD Council 1998, paras 4, 8 and 37.

political weight/authority with which OECD pronouncements are imbued (especially, when those pronouncements are couched in terms of recommendations[9]). Such practical considerations are fundamentally important in this sphere. After all, jurisdictions are responsible for harmful tax practices, and it is envisaged in the 1998 Report that actions taken under the auspices of the framework provided by the OECD will be directed against such jurisdictions by other jurisdictions, usually states. In this context, therefore, the most telling aspect of the 1998 Report is not the recognition of an abstract notion of 'harmful' tax competition and the articulation of general propositions that may be used to clarify its constituent elements. It is rather the depiction of the characteristics with which jurisdictions deemed capable of engaging in 'harmful' tax practices/competition are imbued, and the accompanying recommendations as to action that might be taken to counter 'unacceptable' tax practices undertaken by the jurisdictions so identified. As intimated above, the 1998 Report, in relation to depiction, refers generically to tax havens and to those jurisdictions that operate harmful preferential tax regimes. Neither classification means much without elaboration. This is provided in Chapter 2 of the 1998 Report. This chapter purports to set out the key (and other) factors that may be used, in the context of the report, to identify tax havens and harmful preferential tax regimes respectively. In other words, the factors that enable tax havens and harmful preferential tax regimes (wherever they may be located) to attract (unjustifiably) geographically mobile activities such as financial and other service activities, and, thereby, to practise 'harmful' tax competition. The essence of these factors is considered in the next section of this essay with primary emphasis, in view of the previously stated overall focus of this essay, placed on the characterisation of tax havens.

Tax havens and harmful preferential tax regimes

Chapter 2 of the Report purports to provide practical guidance in identifying tax havens and in distinguishing between acceptable and harmful preferential tax regimes. It does this, initially, by drawing a distinction between tax havens and harmful preferential tax regimes, and by alluding to their likely respective inclinations towards fiscal co-operation with other jurisdictions or otherwise. These matters are encapsulated in the following extracts:[10]

> ... a useful distinction may be made between, on the one hand, countries that are able to finance their public services with no or nominal income taxes and that offer themselves as places to be used by non-residents to escape tax in their country of residence [tax havens] and, on the other hand, countries which raise significant revenues from their income tax but whose tax system has features constituting harmful tax competition [states which have potentially harmful preferential tax regimes].

> ... In the first case, the country has no interest in trying to curb the 'race to the bottom' with respect to income tax and is actively contributing to the erosion of income tax revenues in other countries. For that reason, these countries are unlikely to co-operate in curbing harmful tax competition. By contrast, in the second case, a country may have a significant amount of revenues which are at risk from the spread of harmful tax competition and it is therefore more likely to agree on concerted action.

Thereafter, whilst acknowledging that 'many factors may contribute to the classification of the actual or potential effects of tax practices as harmful', the chapter concentrates on those factors—fiscal or otherwise—that the OECD considers may be used for the purposes of the

---

[9]   Chapter 3 of the 1998 Report contains nineteen recommendations that are related to counteracting 'harmful tax competition':*ibid*, Chapter 3.

[10]   *Ibid*, paras 42 and 43.

1998 Report to identify tax havens and harmful preferential tax regimes. In this identification process, a distinction is discernible between 'key' and 'other' factors. Many of the latter, although not all, are tax-specific and are discussed primarily in relation to the identification of harmful preferential tax regimes, and hence are beyond the scope of this essay.[11] As to the 'key' factors, however, the report perceives there to be a certain degree of congruence. Thus, there is a similar and essential pre-requisite for tax havens and harmful preferential tax regimes. In the case of tax havens, this is the imposition of no or nominal taxes on income derived from geographically mobile activities, whilst in harmful preferential tax regimes it is the imposition of a low or zero effective tax rate on income derived from such sources.[12]

In the context of tax havens, the report suggests that a jurisdiction which requires no or nominal taxation, whist offering or being perceived to offer itself as a place where non-residents can escape tax in their country of residence, may be identified in some cases as a tax haven. In practice, however, many tax havens will also exhibit, to some extent, the other 'key' factors specified in the report as being indicative of a tax haven. These 'key' factors, together with the primary and necessary pre-condition of no or nominal taxation, are itemised and described in the 1998 Report as follows:[13]

> *...Lack of effective exchange of information*
>
> Tax havens typically have in place laws or administrative practices under which businesses and individuals can benefit from strict secrecy rules and other protections against scrutiny by tax authorities thereby preventing the effective exchange of information on taxpayers benefiting from the low tax jurisdiction.
>
> *...Lack of transparency*
>
> A lack of transparency in the operation of the legislative, legal or administrative provisions is another factor in identifying tax havens.
>
> *...No substantial activities*
>
> The absence of a requirement that the activity be substantial is important since it would suggest that a jurisdiction may be attempting to attract investment or transactions that are purely tax driven.

In fact, these factors, in conjunction with certain other factors—for example, the absence of exchange controls and political stability—characterise what many would recognise as the archetypal or classical tax haven. This is an impression which, as will be seen, proved to be generally well founded when the OECD subsequently named as tax havens those jurisdictions that it deemed to exhibit some or all of these 'key' factors to an extent sufficient to warrant their designation.

Unlike tax havens, harmful preferential tax regimes do not have such a distinctive 'persona'. This may explain why the substantive treatment of such regimes in Chapter 2 of the 1998 Report is prefaced by the following generalised statement as to their purpose and likely sphere of operation:[14]

> These regimes generally provide a favourable location for holding passive investments or for booking paper profits. In many cases, the regime may have been designed specifically to act as a

---

[11] These factors, insofar as they relate to harmful preferential tax regimes, are set out in: *ibid*, paras 68-79.

[12] 'A zero or low effective tax rate may apply because the rate itself is very low or because of the way in which a country defines the tax base to which the rate is applied': *ibid*, para 61.

[13] *Ibid*, p 23, Box I.

[14] *Ibid*, paras 57 and 58.

conduit for routing capital flows across borders. These regimes may be found in the general tax code or in administrative practices, or they may have been established by special tax and non-tax legislation outside the framework of the general tax system.

The preferential tax regimes discussed in this part of the Report are usually targeted specifically to attract those economic activities which can be most easily shifted in response to tax differentials, generally financial and other service activities. Such tax regimes can be particularly successful if targeted to attract income from base company activities and from passive investment rather than income from active investment. The existence of these preferential tax regimes may encourage the relocation of activities for which there is little or no demand or supply in the host country's domestic market. In many cases the scheme is merely a conduit and absent the regime the investment flow would be unlikely to go through the country providing the regime.

Thereafter, the consideration of harmful preferential tax regimes in the report follows a pattern that is similar, but not identical, to that adopted in relation to tax havens. Thus, the potentiality of a particular regime to be 'harmful' is founded on an overall assessment of certain specified 'key' and 'other' factors. As with tax havens, one of the 'key' factors is stated to be a 'necessary starting point'. In this instance, as has already been intimated, it is the imposition of a low or a zero effective tax rate. The report envisages that a harmful preferential tax regime will be characterised by this factor coupled with one or more of the other 'key' factors (and, where relevant, with any of the 'other' factors[15]). The other 'key' factors are 'ring-fencing' of the regime, lack of transparency and lack of effective exchange of information.[16] For present purposes, only the former calls for any comment in that it graphically conveys a notion that is often central to the existence of a harmful preferential tax regime—namely, that of a 'system within a system' in a state. The 1998 Report refers, in this respect, to such a regime, where ring-fencing occurs, being partly or fully insulated from the domestic markets of the sponsoring state, and points out that the consequence of such 'ring fencing' is to protect this state from its own preferential regime to the detriment of the tax bases of other jurisdictions. In practice, the operation of ring-fencing is frequently evidenced by the exclusion of taxpayers resident in the sponsoring state from the benefits offered by the preferential regime.

The remainder of the 1998 Report (Chapter 3) focuses on ways in which harmful tax competition conducted by tax havens and harmful preferential tax regimes may be counteracted. The early part of this chapter re-iterates a viewpoint expressed at the beginning of the report,[17] namely that jurisdictions may take unilateral and/or bilateral action, but that multilateral steps are essential because 'co-ordinated action is the most effective way to respond to the pressures created in the new world of global capital mobility'. It then puts forward various recommendations (nineteen in total) that approach the problems associated with harmful tax competition from different perspectives. Some of these recommendations are specifically targeted, and may lead to unilateral and/or bilateral action. Thus, the Report states:[18]

Some of them [the recommendations] are aimed at encouraging countries to refrain from adopting practices constituting harmful tax competition. Others are aimed at offsetting the benefits for taxpayers of certain forms of harmful tax competition. Still others address the issue indirectly by focusing on tax avoidance and tax evasion, on the basis that many forms of harmful

---

[15] For the reasons given above, consideration of these factors (set out in: *ibid*, 1998, paras 68-79), lies beyond the purview of this piece.

[16] See *ibid*, p 27, Box II.

[17] *Ibid*, para 4.

[18] *Ibid*, para 94.

tax competition are aimed at taxpayers willing to engage in tax evasion ([for example,] using bank secrecy provisions to avoid paying tax in the source or residence country) or tax avoidance ([for example,] using certain offshore regimes).

Further and not surprisingly, some of these specific recommendations have a direct bearing on tax havens—for example, the first recommendation exhorts OECD member states either to adopt controlled foreign corporation rules (if such rules do not already exist) or to ensure that existing rules are applied in a manner consistent with the goal of curbing harmful tax practices.

However, without seeking to diminish the significance of such recommendations for tax havens, a more fruitful line of inquiry for the purposes of this essay and one that provides a convenient 'bridge' between the 1998 Report and material subsequent events (that are to be considered shortly) can be found elsewhere. That inquiry involves a number of recommendations the purported purpose of which is 'to intensify international co-operation in response to harmful tax competition'.[19] These recommendations embody what the report regards as the most important elements in a co-ordinated multilateral response to the problems of harmful tax competition. They are described as follows:[20]

> The adoption of a set of Guidelines…intended to ensure that [OECD] Member countries refrain from adopting preferential tax regimes constituting harmful tax competition and gradually eliminate those harmful preferential tax regimes that currently exist;[21]

> The creation of a subsidiary body of the Committee [on Fiscal Affairs], the Forum on Harmful Tax Practices, to allow… for an on-going discussion of experiences with the problems posed by tax havens and harmful preferential tax regimes and of the effectiveness of measures taken in response to such practices. The Forum will monitor the implementation of the Recommendations set out in the earlier sections of this Chapter and the accompanying Guidelines as well as:

> The preparation of a list of jurisdictions constituting tax havens; and

> The development and active promotion of principles of Good Tax Administration relevant to counteracting harmful tax practices.

These words make clear the pivotal role envisaged for a Forum on Harmful Tax Practices in the co-ordinated response to harmful tax competition in relation to both tax havens and harmful preferential tax regimes. However, it is also evident from these words that the critical 'element' from the perspective of those jurisdictions likely to qualify as tax havens in accordance with the criteria in Chapter 2 of the 1998 Report was the recommended creation of a Forum on Harmful Tax Practices with a remit that included the drawing up of a list of such tax havens.

In due course, the Forum on Harmful Tax Practices was established, and, as recommended, it was given, within its range of responsibilities, the sensitive and politically charged role of listing those jurisdictions that could be classified as tax havens for the purposes of the 1998 Report. This aspect of the Forum's work is obviously a central concern of this essay, and it is considered in the next section. The following section is also important, because it marks the point from which this essay adopts a narrower focus, and concentrates, in accordance with its professed purpose, on the position of tax havens in the context of the OECD initiative.

---

[19] *Ibid*, recommendations 15-19, pp 53-59.
[20] *Ibid*, para 139.
[21] The Guidelines are set out in: *ibid*, pp 56-57, Box III.

The forum on harmful tax practices

The 1998 Report stated that the completion of the list of tax havens would be a 'priority task' for the Forum on Harmful Tax Practices[22] ('the Forum'), and it recommended that the Forum be mandated to establish the list, for the purposes of the Report, within one year of its first meeting.[23] So, how did the Forum approach this 'priority task', and what was the outcome— that is, which jurisdictions (and how many) were identified, within the parameters laid down by the report, as tax havens?

Useful guidance on these matters is provided in the first report of the progress made by the Forum in its various spheres of operation. This was presented by the Committee on Fiscal Affairs to the OECD Council in June 2000, and it is entitled *Towards Global Tax Co-operation: Progress in Identifying and Eliminating Harmful Tax Practices* ('the 2000 Report'). There are several discrete sections in the 2000 Report that deal with the process of 'identifying' tax havens for the purposes of the OECD initiative. The first of these[24] explains the approach followed by the Forum in relation to 'the evaluation of jurisdictions under the tax haven criteria.'[25] It is apparent that the so-called evaluations were founded upon an in-depth factual review of those jurisdictions that appeared to the Forum to have the potential to satisfy the 'tax haven criteria'. Pertinent facts were assembled in the following way:[26]

> Starting from published sources, the Forum identified an initial grouping of 47 such jurisdictions [that is, jurisdictions that appeared to satisfy the tax haven criteria]. These jurisdictions were asked to submit information pertinent to the application of the tax haven criteria in the context of their facts and circumstances. The Forum examined, discussed, and reviewed this information, using a series of bilateral contacts (under the auspices of small Study Groups comprised of Forum members) and through multilateral consultations with the Forum itself. The Study Groups prepared factual jurisdiction reports with input from, and in many cases agreement by, the jurisdictions as to the factual accuracy of the reports.

Such information was the basis upon which the Forum decided that the following 35 jurisdictions met the 'tax haven criteria':[27]

Andorra	The Maldives
Anguilla	The Marshall Islands
Antigua and Barbuda	Monaco
Aruba	Montserrat
The Bahamas	Nauru
Bahrain	Netherlands Antilles
Barbados	Niue

---

[22] *Ibid*, para 145.

[23] *Ibid*, Recommendation No 16, p 57. This time scale was endorsed by the OECD Council in its approval of the 1998 Report: *ibid*, p 71.

[24] See OECD Committee on Fiscal Affairs to the OECD Council, 2000, paras 7–9.

[25] For the factors that may be relied upon to identify a tax haven for the purposes of the OECD initiative—that is, 'the tax haven criteria': see above.

[26] OECD Committee on Fiscal Affairs to the OECD Council, 2000, para 8.

[27] The Forum's evaluations to this effect were made in November 1999. Thereafter, they were presented to the Committee on Fiscal Affairs in January 2000 and confirmed by the Committee in May 2000. The OECD Council endorsed the evaluations in June 2000.

Belize	Panama
British Virgin Islands	Samoa
Cook Islands	The Seychelles
Dominica	St Lucia
Gibraltar	St Christopher & Nevis
Grenada	St Vincent & the Grenadines
Guernsey/Sark/Alderney	Tonga
Isle of Man	Turks & Caicos
Jersey	US Virgin Islands
Liberia	Vanuatu
Liechtenstein	

In the light of the foregoing discussion in this essay, it might be reasonable to expect, without more, that the listing of these jurisdictions would act as a catalyst for the type of unilateral, bilateral and/or concerted action contemplated by the 1998 Report. However with regard to the latter, the 2000 Report states, immediately prior to the publication of the list, that the 'listing is intended to reflect the technical conclusions of the Committee [on Fiscal Affairs] only and is not intended to be used as the basis for possible co-ordinated defensive measures'.[28] The 2000 Report suggests that the reason for this statement is that in the course of the evaluation process conducted by the Forum it became apparent that a number of the jurisdictions under review were interested in the possibility of co-operating with the OECD with a view to eliminating harmful tax practices.[29] It is conceivable that the extent of such interest was a surprise to the OECD,[30] but, be that as it may, it was a level of interest that prompted the following significant change of emphasis on the part of the OECD:[31] 'In response to this *development* [the extent of the interest in co-operation], the Committee [on Fiscal Affairs] believes that a *process* should be *established* to *promote co-operation and positive changes* to comply with the principles of the 1998 Report.' (Emphasis added.)

The 2000 Report sees the most positive outcome of this co-operative process as a commitment by jurisdictions on the list of tax havens to adopt a 'schedule of progressive change' to eliminate harmful tax practices within the same time scale as that accepted by those jurisdictions that had agreed 'advance commitments,'[32] namely the end of December 2005. The nature of this commitment is described as follows:[33]

> A jurisdiction making this commitment (a scheduled commitment) will develop with the Forum an acceptable plan within 6 months of having made the commitment, describing the manner in

---

28 See OECD Committee on Fiscal Affairs to the OECD Council, 2000, para 17.

29 In fact, prior to the publication of the 2000 Report, six jurisdictions (Bermuda, the Cayman Islands, Cyprus, Malta, Mauritius and San Marino) entered into an 'advance commitment' to eliminate their harmful practices by the end of December 2005. Consequently, these jurisdictions were not on the list in the 2000 Report of jurisdictions that met the 'tax haven criteria'. The other six jurisdictions identified in the initial grouping of 47 jurisdictions (Brunei, Costa Rica, Dubai, Jamaica, Macao and Tuvalu) were also not on the list, because they were found not to satisfy the 'tax haven criteria'.

30 The 2000 Report simply states that '[t]he extent of the interest in co-operation was not fully foreseen at the time that the 1998 Report was presented to Ministers'.

31 See OECD Committee on Fiscal Affairs to the OECD Council, 2000, para 18.

32 See footnote 29 above.

33 OECD Committee on Fiscal Affairs to the OECD Council, 2000, para 21.

which the jurisdiction (a co-operative jurisdiction) intends to achieve its commitment, the timetable for doing so, and milestones to ensure steady progress, including the completion of a concrete and significant action during the first year of the commitment. The jurisdiction must also agree to a standstill during the period of the commitment—that is, not to enhance existing regimes that the Forum finds constitute harmful tax practices; not to introduce new regimes that would constitute harmful tax practices; and to engage in an annual review process with the Forum to determine the progress made in fulfilling its commitment and to assess the use being made of its existing regimes.[34]

The 2000 Report contains 'incentives' that encourage entry into a 'scheduled commitment'. First, there is an acknowledgement that if a jurisdiction on the list of tax havens enters into a commitment to eliminate its harmful tax practices this may lead to adverse economic consequences for that jurisdiction.[35] In this respect, the report states that the OECD will work with other organisations to see how best to assist a co-operative jurisdiction in re-structuring its economy. Second, there is an incentive for such a jurisdiction to avoid the stated consequences of a less than ideal outcome of the co-operative process—that is, where, notwithstanding consultation and dialogue with the Forum, it fails to enter into a 'scheduled commitment' and persists in its harmful tax practices. In this circumstance, the report provides that the initial consequence is that the jurisdiction is to be placed on an OECD List of Uncooperative Tax Havens. Thereafter, the report contemplates that the jurisdiction may be subjected to defensive measures taken by OECD member states that fall, to use the language of the report, within '[t]he range of possible defensive measures identified to date as a framework for a common approach with regard to Uncooperative Tax Havens.'[36] Such possible defensive measures are specified in the report, and, whilst clearly not intended to be exhaustive, they provide a daunting prospect for an uncooperative tax haven. Some sense of the potential import of these measures may be gleaned from the following briefest of outlines of each of the measures:

(a)   Denial of deductions, exemptions, credits or other allowances relating to transactions with Uncooperative Tax Havens (UTHs) or to transactions taking advantage of their harmful tax practices;

(b)   Requirement of comprehensive information reporting rules for transactions involving UTHs or exploiting their harmful tax practices, with substantial penalties for inaccurate reporting or non-compliance;

(c)   Adoption of controlled foreign corporation rules, or, if such rules already exist, their adaptation to ensure that they curb harmful tax practices;

(d)   Denial of exceptions that may otherwise apply to penalties in respect of transactions involving entities organised in UTHs or taking advantage of their harmful tax practices;

---

34   In November 2000, the OECD supplemented this statement with the publication of a document entitled '[The] Framework for a Collective Memorandum of Understanding on Eliminating Harmful Tax Practices' ('The Memorandum of Understanding'). This document sets out the steps (expressed in the form of terms and timetables) that the OECD wishes jurisdictions identified as tax havens to follow in order to show a commitment to eliminate harmful tax practices. For example, the timetable envisages that by December 2001 such a jurisdiction would have adopted a detailed plan showing how by December 2005 it will achieve transparency and effective exchange of information and eliminate any regime that attracts business without substantial business activity.

35   In the absence of similar commitments by the other named tax havens, it might be expected that geographically mobile activities would be moved elsewhere with a corresponding loss of income derived from such activities.

36   OECD Committee on Fiscal Affairs to the OECD Council, 2000, para 35.

(e)   Denial of a foreign tax credit or participation exemption in relation to distributions that are sourced from UTHs or to transactions that exploit their harmful tax practices;

(t)   Imposition of withholding taxes on certain payments to UTH residents;

(g)   Enhancement of audit and enforcement activities with respect to UTHs and transactions taking advantage of their harmful tax practices;

(h)   Extension of domestic defensive measures to transactions with UTHs and to transactions exploiting their harmful tax practices;

(i)   Refusal to enter into comprehensive income tax conventions with UTHs, and the possible termination of existing conventions;

(j)   Denial of deductions and cost recovery for fees and expenses in relation to establishing or acquiring entities incorporated in UTHs;

(k)   Imposition of transactional charges and levies on certain transactions involving UTHs.[37]

The breadth of these measures is self-evident, and it is not difficult to imagine the likely impact upon a UTH of such measures (or a package thereof) if implemented by OECD member states. Perhaps the only solace for a UTH lies in the foreknowledge of the type of measure(s) that might be taken against it. This may in itself enable a UTH, in some instances, to anticipate the generic nature of the measures that it may face in due course, and, if possible, to adapt its practices accordingly. However, the utility of this foreseeability may diminish in time as further defensive measures are identified by the Committee on Fiscal Affairs and the scope of the defensive measures that may be taken is expanded to encompass what the 2000 Report refers to as 'non-tax measures'.[38]

TAX HAVENS: ISSUES ARISING FROM THE OECD INITIATIVE AND SUBSEQUENT DEVELOPMENTS

It is probably something of an understatement to say that the general response to the most important aspects of the OECD initiative for present purposes, namely the categorisation of certain jurisdictions as tax havens and the suggested defensive measures that might be taken against UTHs, has been mixed.[39] However, the somewhat tentative nature of this statement is prompted by the belief that such response, especially and most importantly from those jurisdictions named as tax havens, is in fact difficult to quantify and assess. In this respect, any attempt to gauge, in particular, the reaction of the named tax havens is bound to be influenced by the following two points and the uncertainty that they engender.

First, in view of the OECD's declared aim in the 2000 Report to promote a co-operative process between itself and the named tax havens,[40] it is a response that is likely, at any given time and for some time, to be in a state of flux. For example, the number of tax havens willing to embark on such a co-operative path will vary from time to time, as will the degree and extent of any co-operation. Entrenched views at both ends of the spectrum are possible. For

---

[37]   Only two of these defensive measures (c & i) appeared as recommendations in the 1998 Report.

[38]   OECD Committee on Fiscal Affairs to the OECD Council, 2000, para 36.

[39]   Although, it is fair to say that headlines accompanying some commentaries published shortly after the publication of the 2000 Report would suggest that the response was fairly unequivocal. See, for example, *The Financial Times*, 4 July 2000 and 7 July 2000.

[40]   See above.

those tax havens willing to co-operate, the course of action to be taken is clearly to enter into the necessary commitment with the OECD as soon as possible. For those unwilling to co-operate, there is the prospect of inclusion on the list of UTHs, and the possible implementation of defensive measures by OECD member states. But where there is uncertainty, dialogue would seem to be the sensible course—a course perhaps similarly apt for representatives of tax havens, who decried the OECD's stance regarding tax havens in the 2000 Report and its imposition of defensive measures as an imperialist attempt to exert control over their affairs[41] but who determined on reflection that they may be prepared after all to contemplate some degree of co-operation.[42]

Second, in view of the on-going nature of the co-operative process and its inherent sensitivity, there is likely to be little case-specific information in the public domain unless and until a particular tax haven makes the commitment needed to satisfy the OECD that it should not be placed on the list of UTHs.

Notwithstanding these difficulties, it is nevertheless apparent that several salient issues (which may, indeed, in some instances have coloured a particular named tax haven's response) have come to the fore. The initial issue relates to an uncertainty on the part of some tax havens about what precisely the OECD initiative expected of them.[43] This alleged difficulty was addressed to some extent by the OECD in the document entitled '[The] Framework for a Collective Memorandum of Understanding on Eliminating Harmful Tax Practices'. It will be recalled that it was published in November 2000, and that it is intended for use as a basis for the framing of a tax haven's commitment to transparency, non-discrimination and effective co-operation.[44] The Head of Fiscal Affairs at the OECD, Jeffrey Owens, has also sought, subsequent to the publication of the 2000 Report and when writing in a personal capacity, to clarify the scope, objectives and implications of the OECD initiative. He wrote:[45]

> The work of the OECD on harmful tax practices is concerned primarily with establishing effective exchange of information and transparency for tax purposes on a global level so that tax administrations can prevent and detect violations of the civil and criminal tax laws...

> The OECD project has been mischaracterised as seeking to harmonise taxes at a high rate, as forcing countries to alter their tax structures, and as attacking legitimate tax planning undertaken through legal means. These mischaracterisations are not correct... The focus on transparency and exchange of information make clear that the project is concerned primarily with the illegal tax practice (from a civil or criminal perspective) of failing to report income, and accordingly with regimes that facilitate this practice.

The search for clarity and better understanding of the OECD initiative has also been enhanced by the emergence since the publication of the 2000 Report of two deliberative bodies to facilitate aspects of the co-operative process. These bodies are the OECD Global Forum on Taxation and the OECD-Commonwealth Working Group on Harmful Tax Practices respectively. The former was established following a meeting held in Paris shortly after the publication of the 2000 Report at which OECD member and non-member states discussed

---

[41] See *The Financial Times*, 26 June 2000.

[42] Indeed, two commentators, Richard M Hammer (Chairman, Committee on Taxation and Fiscal Policy, Business and Industry Advisory Committee to the OECD) and Jeffrey Owens (Head, Fiscal Affairs, OECD), indicate that 32 of the 35 jurisdictions identified as meeting the 'tax haven criteria' have contacted the OECD seeking further co-operative dialogue: Hammer and Owens, 2001, p 3.

[43] See, for example, a view to this effect attributed to a Guernsey official in *The Financial Times*, 4 August 2000.

[44] See footnote 34, above.

[45] Owens, circa 2000.

matters pertaining to a global response to harmful tax competition. Its purpose is to foster multilateral dialogue with a view to promoting global co-operation on tax matters, and, most pertinently at the present time, in relation to harmful tax competition. The origin of the latter probably lies in the more parochial concern of the Commonwealth for those of its members named as tax havens in the 2000 Report.[46] However, its immediate antecedent is an agreement reached by the OECD and Commonwealth countries in January 2001 to seek to achieve global co-operation on harmful tax practices through dialogue founded on support for transparency, non-discrimination and effective exchange of information. The subsequently devised remit of the working group reflects this ethos.[47] Thus, the working group is invited, in the context of the agreement, to look for mutually acceptable political processes that facilitate the making by a jurisdiction of a commitment to eliminate harmful tax practices, and also to consider how to make the Global Forum on Taxation literally global in terms of representation and perspective.

Other salient issues have tended to relate to a single aspect of the OECD initiative—namely, whether or not it can be regarded as legitimate. One of the principal contentions favouring illegitimacy—that is, that the OECD is not the proper forum for determining what constitutes 'harmful' tax competition—and how it should be dealt with has already been considered above. Some of the other contentions supportive of the same view are more rhetorical than convincing. So there would seem to be little merit, again as already discussed, in the view that the OECD itself is seeking to impose sanctions on tax havens in due course, or that it wishes to compel tax havens to change their tax systems. In fact, it is conceivable that the strongest challenge to the legitimacy of the OECD initiative may be prospective rather than immediate, and that it will be mounted not against the OECD, but against those OECD member states that seek to impose the defensive measures specified in the 2000 Report. It has been argued that such a challenge might be sustained on the basis that several of those defensive measures—for example, the imposition of transactional charges and levies on certain transactions—may violate the GATT or GATS non-discrimination prohibitions, because they would not apply to OECD member states.[48] Of course, it remains to be seen how subsequent events unfold, and, consequently, whether action on this basis becomes a reality.

THE WAY AHEAD

For the OECD, the ideal outcome of its initiative in relation to those jurisdictions identified as tax havens in the 2000 Report is, presumably, a commitment by each of those jurisdictions to eliminate their particular harmful tax practices with the consequence that tax administrations are then better placed to counter breaches of civil and criminal tax laws. In a way, it might be argued that the tax havens would also 'benefit' from the same outcome, because if all of them make the requisite commitment to the OECD some degree of equilibrium will be achievable in respect of their fiscal competitiveness.

The reality may, however, prove to be different. If, notwithstanding the various avenues available for dialogue and discussion, it proves to be impossible to persuade all the tax havens to co-operate then the distinction between co-operative and uncooperative tax havens will come into play. This may have economic/developmental consequences for both types of tax

---

[46] A perusal of the list of tax havens in the 2000 Report shows that in the region of two thirds of the jurisdictions named are members of the Commonwealth.

[47] The working group comprises representatives from the Commonwealth, Caricom, the Pacific Island Forum and OECD member states.

[48] See Scott, 2001, pp 2146-2147.

haven. UTHs run the risk of being subjected by OECD member states to some or all of those defensive measures that such status may attract (see above) and/or to the unspecified 'non-tax' measures referred to in the 2000 Report. They may also lose non-essential economic assistance from other jurisdictions.[49] However, presumably, by resisting compliance with the OECD initiative, they will retain the characteristics that ensure their attractiveness to taxpayers. On the other hand, whilst UTHs still exist, co-operative tax havens are likely to witness a rapid diminution in the levels of income derived from geographically mobile activities with a consequent adverse effect on the economies of those jurisdictions. It will be recalled that the OECD has offered to examine how best to assist co-operative tax havens in restructuring their economies, but it should not be forgotten that the tax havens named in the 2000 Report are, by and large, small jurisdictions where the room for manoeuvre in this respect may be restricted.[50]

Finally, it is possible, of course, that the 'success' or otherwise of the OECD initiative may not turn on the reaction of tax havens to it, but rather on the response of OECD member states. It has already been seen that the OECD was unable to secure the unanimity of its members in relation to the 1998 Report. More recently, representatives of the Bush Administration, particularly the Treasury Secretary, Paul O'Neill, have expressed reservations about the initiative.[51] In these circumstances, the tax havens might be best advised to bide their time and to seek to exploit divisions within the OECD ranks with a view, therefore, to ultimately retaining direct control over their own destiny.

REFERENCES

(1998 Report) OECD Committee on Fiscal Affairs to the OECD Council, *Harmful Tax Competition—An Emerging Global Issue*, 1998, Paris: OECD

(2000 Report) OECD Committee on Fiscal Affairs to the OECD Council, *Towards Global Tax Co-operation: Progress in Identifying and Eliminating Harmful Tax Practices* 2000, Paris: OECD

(Memorandum of Understanding) 'Framework for a collective memorandum of understanding on eliminating harmful tax practices', available at www.oecd.org/media/M0Urev20novR1.pdf

Hammer, R M and Owens, J, *'Promoting Tax Competition'*, 2001, available at www.oecd.org/daf/fa/harm_tax/harmtax.htm

OECD Convention, Paris, 1960

Owens, J, *Promoting Fair Tax Competition*, published circa 2000, previously available at www.oecd.org/daf/fa/harm_tax/harmtax.htm

Scott, C, 'OECD "Harmful" tax competition move may violate WTO obligations, expert says' (2001) 22:18 Tax Notes International 2146-47

The Financial Times, 'US assailed at OECD meeting on tax havens... ', 18 May 2001

---

[49] See OECD Committee on Fiscal Affairs to the OECD Council, 2000, para 36.

[50] It should also be remembered that many of these jurisdictions may be affected by two other current supra-national initiatives, namely the investigation by the Financial Stability Forum into the role of Offshore Financial Sector banks in the world's financial system and that of the Financial Action Task Force into money laundering.

[51] See, for example, *The Financial Times*, 11 May 2001; *The Financial Times*, 18 May 2001.

The Financial Times, 'US move jeopardises tax haven reform', 11 May 2001

The Financial Times, 'Dependencies may escape tax blacklist', 4 August 2000

The Financial Times, 'OECD takes aim at "harmful" tax havens', 7 July 2000

The Financial Times, '"Tax exile islands" hostile to OECD reform', 4 July 2000

The Financial Times, 'Nowhere to hide', 26 June 2000

INTERNATIONAL COURTS AND THE APPLICATION OF THE CONCEPT OF 'SUSTAINABLE DEVELOPMENT'

Philippe Sands[*]

In 1992, at the United Nations Conference on Environment and Development (UNCED), States adopted the Rio Declaration on Environment and Development. Principle 27 of the Rio Declaration states:

> States and people shall cooperate in good faith and in a spirit of partnership in the fulfilment of the principles embodied in this Declaration and in the further development of international law in the field of sustainable development.

The language of Principle 27 is premised on the view that even at the time of its adoption there existed a body of 'international law in the field of sustainable development'. However, Principle 27 does not indicate the content of that law, in particular whether it is procedural or substantive or both, or where its content may be identified. Shortly after the adoption of the Rio Declaration a group of independent legal experts sought to identify its content, on the basis of a review of legal and policy instruments and the international practice of States (which was then, and remains now, somewhat limited). The group concluded that:

> The concept of 'sustainable development' is now established in international law, even if its meaning and effect are uncertain. It is a legal term which refers to processes, principles and objectives, as well as to a large body of international agreements on environmental, economic and civil and political rights.[1]

I have previously sought to review what these processes, principles and objectives might be. My conclusion was that 'international law in the field of sustainable development' coalesced around:

> a broad umbrella accommodating the specialised fields of international law which aim to promote economic development, environmental protection and respect for civil and political rights. It is not independent and free-standing of principles and rules, and it is still emerging. As such, it is not coherent or comprehensive, nor is it free from ambiguity or inconsistency. The significance of the UNCED process is not that it has given rise to new principles, rules or institutional arrangements. Rather, it endorses on behalf of the whole of the international community (states, international institutions, non-governmental actors) an approach requiring existing principles, rules and institutional arrangements to be treated *in an integrated manner*.[2]

At the time of writing the term 'sustainable development' had not been the subject of international judicial consideration. Subsequently, 'sustainable development' has found expression in a number of new international instruments and is regularly invoked to support all manner of positions which states seek to justify. 'Sustainable development' has also now been invoked before bodies charged with resolving international disputes, including the ICJ and the Appellate Body of the World Trade Organisation. The purpose of this short chapter is to consider what, if anything, the jurisprudence of those two bodies has added to our understanding of 'sustainable development'.

---

[*] Professor of Laws at University College London and Global Professor of Law at New York University Law School.

[1] See Foundation for International Environmental Law and Development, 1994.

[2] See Sands, 1994, p 379 (emphasis added).

INTERNATIONAL COURT OF JUSTICE

Before the ICJ the concept of 'sustainable development' received its first thorough airing in the case concerning the Gabèíkovo-Nagymaros project, between Hungary and Slovakia.[3] The case concerned a dispute over whether or not to build two barrages on the Danube shared by Hungary and Czechoslovakia. In 1977, by treaty, the two countries had agreed to build two barrages which would then be jointly operated. The 1977 Treaty envisaged the diversion of waters from the Danube, where it was a boundary river, onto Czechoslovak territory and the operation of a the dual system of barrages by 'peak-power' (rather than 'run-of-river' mode). Construction began and proceeded more slowly than had been originally envisaged. In the mid-1980s political opposition in Hungary focused on the environmental aspects of the barrage as a means of achieving broader political change.

In May 1989, great public pressure led Hungary to suspend work on large parts of the project. The two countries sought to reach an agreement as to how to proceed. Both were intransigent and committed to different approaches. Czechoslovakia took the view that the barrages posed no serious threat to the environment, Hungary was certain they would lead to significant environmental harm to water supplies and to biodiversity. Absent an agreed resolution of the problem, and in the face of Hungary's refusal to continue work on the project, in 1991 Czechoslovakia proceeded unilaterally to implement what it termed a 'provisional solution' (referred to as 'Variant C'), comprising a single barrage on the Czechoslovakian side, but requiring the diversion of some 80percent of the shared water and its territory. It argued that this was justified by the 1977 Treaty which, in effect, gave it rights over that amount of water for the purposes of operating a barrage on its side. As 'Variant C' proceeded in late 1991 and early 1992 Hungary took the view that it had no option but to terminate the 1977 Treaty, which apparently provided the sole basis upon which Czechoslovakia claimed to be able to proceed to its unilateral and provisional solution. In May 1992 Hungary purported to terminate the 1977 Treaty. This complicated situation was made no easier when, in January 1993, Czechoslovakia split into two countries, with the Czech Republic and Slovakia agreeing as between themselves that Slovakia would succeed to ownership of the Czechoslovak part of the project. In the meantime, in October 1992 Czechoslovakia had dammed the Danube and diverted over 80 per cent of the waters of the Danube into a bypass canal on Slovak territory. In April 1993, largely under the pressure of the Commission of the European Communities, Hungary and Slovakia agreed to refer the matter to the ICJ.

The Court was presented with an opportunity to address a wide range of international legal issues, including the law of treaties, the law of state responsibility, the law of international watercourses, the law of the environment, and the inter-relation of these areas. The Court was specifically asked to address three questions posed by the parties. What did it rule?

First, it found on the facts that Hungary was not entitled in 1989 to suspend or terminate—on environmental grounds—work on the joint project. Second, it ruled that Czechoslovakia (and subsequently Slovakia) was not entitled to operate from October 1992 a unilateral solution diverting the Danube without the agreement of Hungary (although it ruled that construction prior to operation was not unlawful). Third, the Court went on to say that

---

[3]   *Gabèíkovo-Nagymaros Project Case (Hungary v Slovakia)*, p 7 ff. The Court had previously referred to Principle 24 of the Rio Declaration on Environment and Development in its *Advisory Opinion on the Legality of the Threat or Use of Nuclear Weapons*, p 242.

Hungary was not entitled in May 1992 to terminate the 1977 Treaty, which remained in force. As to the future, the Court indicated the basis for co-operation and agreement which it hoped the Parties might pursue, suggesting that the preservation of the *status quo*—one barrage not two, jointly operated, no peak power—would be an appropriate solution, in effect rewriting the 1977 Treaty. It was in relation to future arrangements that the majority of the Court invoked the 'concept of sustainable development' to suggest a way forward. Specifically, what it said was this:

> Throughout the ages, mankind has, for economic and other reasons, constantly interfered with nature. In the past this was often done without consideration of the effects upon the environment. Owing to new scientific insights and to a growing awareness of the risks for mankind—for present and future generations—of pursuit of such interventions at an unconsidered and unabated pace, new norms and standards have been developed, set forth in a great number of instruments during the last two decades. Such new norms have to be taken into consideration, and such new standards given proper weight, not only when States contemplate new activities, but also when continuing with activities begun in the past. *This need to reconcile economic development with protection of the environment is aptly expressed in the concept of sustainable development.*[4]

The Court followed this by concluding, in the same paragraph of the Judgment, that

> For the purposes of the present case, this means that the Parties together should look afresh at the effects on the environment of the operation of the Gabčíkovo power plant. In particular they must find a satisfactory solution for the volume of water to be released into the old bed of the Danube and into the side-arms on both sides of the river.

At least three aspects of what the Court said are to be noted. *First*, the fact that it invokes 'sustainable development' at all indicates that the term has a legal function. *Second*, 'sustainable development' is a 'concept' and not a principle or a rule. And *third*, as a 'concept' it has both a procedural/temporal aspect (obliging the parties to 'look afresh' at the environmental consequences of the operation of the plant) and a substantive aspect (the obligation of result to ensure that a 'satisfactory volume of water' be released from the by-pass canal into the main river and its original side-arms). The Court does not, however, indicate the content of the procedural/temporal requirement (for example does this require a formal or informal environmental impact assessment? And if so, according to what standards?) or the factors for determining whether the volume of water flowing in the Danube would be said to be satisfactory.

Paragraph 140 is cryptic, to say the least. During the course of written arguments both sides had invoked 'sustainable development' to justify their positions.[5] The pleadings will repay a careful study, since they reflect the inherent malleability and uncertainty of the term. Hungary invoked 'sustainable development' to justify its view that there should be no barrages, whereas for Slovakia the 'concept' justified the opposite conclusion, namely that 'sustainable development' could only be achieved if both barrages envisaged by the 1977

---

[4] *Ibid*, p 78, para 140 (emphasis added).

[5] See, for example, Slovakia: 'It is clear from both the letter and the spirit of these principles that the overarching policy of the international community is that environmental concerns are not directed to frustrate efforts to achieve social and economic development, but that development should proceed in a way that is environmentally sustainable. Slovakia submits that these have been, and are today, the very policies on which the G/N Project is based': Counter-Memorial, para 9.56. In reply, Hungary takes the opposite view to support its argument that the G/N Project is unlawful: 'Well-established ... operational concepts like 'sustainable development' ... help define, in particular cases, the basis upon which to assess the legality of actions such as the unilateral diversion of the Danube by Czechoslovakia and its continuation by Slovakia': Hungarian Reply, para 3.51.

Treaty were constructed. It might be said that Hungary focused on the environmental aspect of the concept whilst Slovakia focused on its 'developmental' elements. For its part the Court invokes the concept to achieve an accommodation of views and values whilst leaving to the parties the task of fleshing out the harder practical consequences. The Court appears to use the concept to build a bridge, justifying a conclusion other than that which would tend to flow directly from its earlier reasoning and conclusions, namely that with its finding that the 1977 Treaty remained in force Hungary ought logically to be required to construct the second barrage at Nagymaros.[6] To be clear, the Court did not rely exclusively on 'sustainable development' to justify this conclusion, having found as a matter of fact that Slovakia itself had conceded that no second barrage was now necessary.[7] 'Sustainable development' was used to fortify that conclusion and provide some guidance as to its consequences.

Beyond paragraph 140, the Court provided no further assistance as to the status of 'sustainable development' in international law, or its practical consequences, beyond the fact that it was to fulfil a function of integrating the potentially competitive societal objectives of environment and development. Perhaps some assistance as to what the Court might have had in mind may be gleaned from the Separate Opinion of Judge Weeramantry, who joined in the majority judgment, and whose hand may have guided the drafting of paragraph 140. According to Judge Weeramantry the *Gabèíkovo/Nagymaros* case offered a unique opportunity for the application of the 'principle' of sustainable development, focusing attention 'as no other case has done in the jurisprudence of the Court, on the question of the harmonisation of developmental and environmental concepts'.[8] The principle fulfilled a harmonising and reconciling function, requiring development and environment to be treated in a balanced way to avoid 'a state of normative anarchy.'[9]

> It is thus the correct formulation of the right to development that that right does not exist in the absolute sense, but is relative always to its tolerance by the environment. The right to development as thus refined is clearly part of modern international law. It is compendiously referred to as sustainable development.[10]

Judge Weeramantry traces the emergence of 'sustainable development', noting its roots in the early 1970s, through to the 'considerable endorsement' which it has received from all sections of the international community and which amounts to 'a wide and general recognition of the concept'.[11] For him the principle of sustainable development is 'a part of modern international law by reason not only of its inescapable logical necessity, but also by reason of its wide and general acceptance by the global community',[12] and has 'a significant role to play in the resolution of environmentally related disputes',[13] providing 'an important principle for the resolution of tensions between two established rights'[14] within the fields of human rights, state

---

[6] Or, as two other authors have put it: 'What is perhaps more remarkable, however, is that the Court, despite its endorsement of a treaty regime that smacked of unsustainability, went on to invoke sustainable development in order to miraculously salvage something from a sinking ship': Stec and Eckstein, 1997, p 47.

[7] 'Equally, the Court cannot ignore the fact that, not only has Nagymaros not been built, but that, with the effective discarding by both parties of peak power operation, there is no longer any point in building it': *Gabèíkovo-Nagymaros Project Case (Hungary v Slovakia)*, 1997, p 76, para 134.

[8] *Ibid*, p 90.

[9] *Ibid*.

[10] *Ibid*, p 92.

[11] *Ibid*, p 93.

[12] *Ibid*, p 95.

[13] *Ibid*.

[14] *Ibid*.

responsibility, environmental law, economic and industrial law or other matters. It reaffirms, he says, 'in the area of international law that there must be both development and environmental protection, and that neither of these rights can be neglected'.[15] Judge Weeramantry notes also that the concept of sustainable development is one recognised in traditional legal systems.[16] In sum, it is 'not merely a principle of modern international law. It is one of the most ancient of ideas in the human heritage. Fortified by the rich insights that can be gained from millennia of human experience, it has an important part to play in the service of international law'.[17]

These words provide some illumination of the place which 'sustainable development' may have in the international legal order, but do not indicate with any degree of precision how reconciliation or harmonisation are to be achieved or how, on the facts of this case, one barrage rather than two might better achieve the objective of 'sustainable development'. This of course is not a criticism, but rather a comment on the difficulties posed for the judicial function of measuring and then balancing competing objectives. In this sense the term 'sustainable development' appears useful as a means of bridging two views without necessarily having to provide close reasoning as to method or outcome.

WTO APPELLATE BODY

By way of contrast, the approach of the ICJ may be compared with that of the Appellate Body of the World Trade Organisation in the subsequent case concerning the import prohibition imposed by the United States on Certain Shrimp and Shrimp Products from India, Malaysia, Pakistan and Thailand, on the grounds that they were harvested in a manner which adversely affected endangered sea turtles.[18] In 1987 the United States had issued regulations (pursuant to its 1973 Endangered Species Act) requiring all United States registered shrimp trawl vessels to use approved turtle excluder devices (TEDs) in specified areas where there was a significant mortality of sea turtles in shrimp harvesting. TEDs allowed for shrimp to be harvested without harming other species, including sea turtles. The United States regulations became fully effective in 1990, and were subsequently modified to require the general use of approved TEDs at all times and in all areas where there was a likelihood that shrimp trawling would interact with sea turtles. In 1989 the United States enacted Section 609 of Public Law 101-162, which addressed the importation of Certain Shrimp and Shrimp Products. Section 609 required the United States Secretary of State to negotiate bilateral or multilateral agreements with other nations for the protection and conservation of sea turtles. Section 609(b)(1) imposed (not later than 1 May 1991) an import ban on shrimp harvested with the commercial fishing technology which may adversely affect sea turtles. Further regulatory guidelines were adopted in 1991, 1992 and 1996, governing *inter alia* annual certifications to be provided by harvesting nations. In broad terms, certification was to be granted only to those harvesting nations which provided documentary evidence of the adoption of a regulatory programme to protect sea turtles in the course of shrimp trawling. Such a regulatory programme had to be comparable to the programme of the United States, with an average rate of incidental taking of sea turtles by their vessels which should be comparable to that of the United States vessels. The 1996 guidelines further required that all shrimp imported into the United States had to be

---

[15]   *Ibid*.
[16]   *Ibid*, p 98.
[17]   *Ibid*, pp 110 and 111.
[18]   Appellate Body of the World Trade Organisation AB-1998-4, 12 October 1998.

accompanied by a shrimp exporter's declaration attesting that the shrimp were harvested either in the waters of the nation certified under Section 609, or under conditions that did not adversely affect sea turtles, including through the use of TEDs. From a WTO perspective the difficulty was that the United States was, in effect, applying its conservation laws extraterritorially to activities carried out within—or subject to the jurisdiction of—third states. This, of course, raises an issue of general international law, namely the circumstances (if any) in which a state may apply its conservation measures to activities taking place outside its territory or jurisdiction, including by non-nationals. The United States sought to justify its actions on the grounds that the sea turtles it was seeking to protect were recognised in international law as being endangered.

The United States legislation was challenged by India, Malaysia, Pakistan and Thailand. At first instance a WTO Panel concluded that the import ban applied on the basis of Section 609 was not consistent with Article XI:1 of GATT 1994 and could not be justified under Article XX of GATT 1994.[19] The United States appealed to the WTO Appellate Body, invoking in particular Article XX(g) to justify the legality of its measures. Article XX(g) permits, as an exception to the GATT rules, measures 'relating to the conservation of exhaustible natural resources if such measures are made effective in conjunction with restrictions on domestic production or consumption'. In appraising Section 609 under Article XX of GATT 1994 the Appellate Body followed a three-step analysis. *First*, the Appellate Body asked whether the Panel's approach to the interpretation of Article XX was appropriate; and it concluded that the Panel's reasoning was flawed and 'abhorrent to the principles of interpretation we are bound to apply.'[20] *Second*, the Appellate Body asked whether Section 609 was 'provisionally justified' under Article XX(g). Invoking the concept of 'sustainable development', it found that it was so justified.[21] And *third*, it asked whether Section 609 met the requirements of the chapeau of Article XX, concluding that it did not because the US actions imposed an 'unjustifiable discrimination' and an 'arbitrary discrimination' against shrimp to be imported from India, Malaysia, Pakistan and Thailand. It is in relation to the second and third steps that the Appellate Body invokes the principle of 'sustainable development', as an aid to interpretation.

The Appellate Body's approach is premised upon an application of the 'customary rules of interpretation of public international law' as required by Article 3 (2) of the Understanding on Rules and Procedures Governing the Settlement of Disputes (DSU), which rules 'call for an examination of the ordinary meaning of the words of a treaty, read in their context, and in the light of the object and purpose of the treaty involved'.[22] It is these customary rules which the Panel failed to apply, leading to the conclusion at step one that the Panel's approach was flawed.

It is then in relation to step two that the Appellate Body initially invokes the principle of sustainable development, in determining whether the measures taken by the United States are 'provisionally justified'. As a 'threshold question' the Appellate Body has to decide whether Section 609 is a measure *concerned with* the conservation of 'exhaustible natural resources', in the face of the argument that the term refers only to finite resource such as minerals, and not biological or renewable resources such as sea turtles (which, it was argued, fall to be covered by Article XX(b)). This argument was rejected by the Appellate Body. It ruled that Article XX(g) of GATT 1994 extends to measures taken to conserve exhaustible natural resources,

---

19   WT-DS58/R of 15 May 1998.

20   Paras 112-124, at 121.

21   Paras 125-145.

22   See note 18, para 114.

whether living or non-living, and that the sea turtles here involved 'constituted "exhaustible natural resources" for the purpose of Article XX(g) of the GATT 1994'.[23] In reaching that conclusion, it stated that Article XX(g) must be read by a treaty interpreter 'in the light of contemporary concerns over the community of nations about the protection and conservation of the environment'.[24] Referring to the Preamble to the 1994 WTO Agreement, the Appellate Body noted that its signatories were 'fully aware of the importance and legitimacy of environmental protection as a goal of national and international policy' and that the Preamble 'explicitly acknowledges "the objective of *sustainable development*"'.[25] This, says the Appellate Body, is a 'concept' which 'has been generally accepted as integrating economic and social development and environmental protection'.[26] According to the Appellate Body this conclusion is supported by modern international conventions and declarations, including the UN Convention on the Law of the Sea.[27] It follows that the sea turtles at issue were an 'exhaustible natural resource' and they were highly migratory animals, passing in and out of the waters subject to the rights of jurisdiction of various coastal states on the high seas.[28] The Appellate Body then observes:

> Of course, it is not claimed that all populations of these species migrate to, or traverse, at one time or another, waters subject to United States jurisdiction. Neither the appellant nor any of the appellees claims any rights of exclusive ownership over the sea turtles, at least not while they are swimming freely in their natural habitat—the oceans. We do not pass upon the question of whether there is an implied jurisdictional limitation in Article XX(g), and if so, the nature or extent of that limitation. We note only that in the specific circumstances of the case before us, there is a sufficient nexus between the migratory and endangered marine populations involved and the United States for the purpose of Article XX(g).[29]

The concept of 'sustainable development' is not expressly invoked to justify this potentially far-reaching conclusion as to the nexus between the sea turtles and the United States. Nevertheless, the concept appears to inform that conclusion, apparently establishing the necessary link between the interest of the United States in the proper conservation of a distant natural resource located from time to time outside its jurisdiction, and the finding that Section 609 is 'provisionally justified' under Article XX(g). Although the Appellate Body claims that it does 'not pass upon the question of whether there is an implied jurisdictional limitation in Article XX(g)', its conclusion appears hardly consistent with such a limitation. Between the lines, then, the concept of 'sustainable development' (and the need to integrate economic and social development and environmental protection) appears to have been implicitly invoked to extend (by interpretation) the jurisdictional scope of Article XX(g). If this is correct then 'sustainable development' has a significant substantive element. This marks a significant move away from the approach of the earlier Tuna Dolphin panels and an opening which could,

---

[23] *Ibid*, paras 131 and 134.

[24] *Ibid*, para 129.

[25] *Ibid*.

[26] *Ibid*, para 129, at note 107 and accompanying text. The Preamble to the WTO Agreements provides *inter alia* that 'the Parties to this Agreement, recognising that their relations in the field of trade and economic endeavour should be conducted with a view to raising standards of living, ensuring full employment and a large and steadily growing volume of real income and effective demand, and expanding the production of and trade in goods and services, while allowing for the optimal use of the world's resources in accordance with the objective of sustainable development, seeking both to protect and preserve the environment and to enhance the means of doing so in a manner consistent with their respective needs and concerns at different levels of economic development ...'

[27] *Ibid*, para 130, citing UNCLOS 1982, Art 56(1)(a).

[28] *Ibid*, paras 132 and 133.

[29] *Ibid*, para 133.

depending on your perspective, either strengthen global environmental objectives or contribute to unwarranted interferences by one state in the affairs of another.

Having found that the US measures are 'provisionally justified' the Appellate Body then moves on to the third step of its analysis, namely whether Section 609 is consistent with the requirements of the chapeau to Article XX. In my view the Appellate Body rightly concludes not, because the measures are applied in an unjustifiable and arbitrarily discriminatory manner. Of interest, however, is the fact that the Appellate Body invokes 'sustainable development' again, this time in the context of its conclusion that Section 609 is an 'unjustifiable' discrimination.[30] In the introduction to this part of its analysis, the Appellate Body revisits the Preamble to the WTO Agreement, noting that it demonstrates that WTO negotiators recognised 'that optimal use of the world's resources should be made in accordance with the objective of sustainable development' and that the preambular language, including the reference to sustainable development:

> ... must add colour, texture and shading to our interpretation of the agreements annexed to the WTO Agreement, in this case the GATT 1994. We have already observed that Article XX(g) of the GATT 1994 is appropriately read with the perspective embodied in the above preamble.[31]

In support of the relevance of 'sustainable development' to the process of interpretation of the WTO Agreements, the Appellate Body then invokes the Decision of Ministers at Marrakech to establish a Permanent Committee on Trade and Environment. That Decision refers, in part, to the consideration that 'there should not be ... any policy contradiction between ... an open, non-discriminatory and equitable multilateral trading system on the one hand, and acting for the protection of the environment, and the promotion of sustainable development on the other ...'.[32] The Appellate Body notes that the terms of reference for the establishment by this Decision of the Committee on Trade and Environment, which makes further reference to the concept of sustainable development, specifically refer to Principles 3 and 4 of the Rio Declaration on Environment and Development.[33]

This is all by way of introduction. There is no further reference to the concept of sustainable development, at least explicitly. Why then has it been invoked by the Appellate Body? No clear answer can be given to that question. However, it appears that 'sustainable development' informs the conclusion that the United States' measures constituted an unjustifiable discrimination: Section 609 established a rigid and unbending standard by which United States officials determined whether or not countries would be certified, and whilst it might be quite acceptable for a government to adopt a single standard applicable to all its citizens throughout that country, it was not acceptable, in international trade relations, 'for one WTO member to use an economic embargo to require other Members to adopt essentially the same comprehensive regulatory programme, to achieve a certain policy goal, as that in force within that Member's territory, without taking into consideration different conditions which may occur in the territories of those other Members'.[34] Shrimp caught using identical methods to those employed in the United States had been excluded from the US market solely

---

[30] Sustainable development is not invoked or referred to justify the conclusion that s 609 constitutes an 'arbitrary discrimination'.

[31] *Ibid*, para 153.

[32] *Ibid*, para 154.

[33] Principle 3 of the Rio Declaration provides that 'the right to development must be fulfilled so as to equitably meet developmental and environmental needs of present and future generations'. Principle 4 states, 'In order to achieve sustainable development, environmental protection shall constitute an integral part of the development process, and cannot be considered in isolation from it'.

[34] *Ibid*, para 164.

because they had been caught in waters of countries that had not been certified by the United States, and the resulting situation was 'difficult to reconcile with the declared [and provisionally justified] policy objective of protecting and conserving sea turtles'.[35] This suggested that the United States was more concerned with effectively influencing WTO members to adopt essentially the same comprehensive regulatory regime as that applied by the United States to its domestic shrimp trawlers. Moreover, the United States had not engaged the appellees 'in serious, across-the-board negotiations with the objective of concluding bilateral or multilateral agreements for the protection and conservation of sea turtles, before enforcing the import prohibition'.[36] The failure to have *a priori* consistent recourse to diplomacy as an instrument of environmental protection policy produced 'discriminatory impacts on countries exporting shrimp to the United States with which no international agreements [were] reached or even seriously attempted'.[37] The fact that the United States negotiate seriously with some but not other members that exported shrimp to the United States had an effect which was 'plainly discriminatory and unjustifiable'. Further, different treatment of different countries' certification was observable in the differences in the levels of efforts made by the United States in transferring the required TED technology to specific countries.[38] Moreover, the protection and conservation of highly migratory species of sea turtles demanded 'concerted and cooperative efforts on the part of the many countries whose waters [were] traversed in the course of recurrent turtle migrations'.[39] Such 'concerted and cooperative efforts' were required by *inter alia* the Rio Declaration (Principle 12), Agenda 21 (paragraph 2.22 (i)), the Convention on Biological Diversity (Article 5) and the Convention on the Conservation of Migratory Species of Wild Animals. Further, the 1996 Inter-American Convention for the Protection and Conservation of Sea Turtles provided a 'convincing demonstration' that alternative action was reasonably open to the United States, other than the unilateral and non-consensual procedures established by Section 609.[40] And finally, whilst the United States was a party to the 1973 Convention on International Trade in Endangered Species of Wild Fauna and Flora (CITES), it had not attempted to raise the issue of sea turtle mortality in relevant CITES Committees, and had not signed the Convention on the Conservation of Migratory Species of Wild Animals or the 1982 UNCLOS or ratified the 1992 Convention on Biological Diversity.[41]

The concept of 'sustainable development' appears to have been invoked to provide 'colour, texture and shading' to the concept of an 'unjustifiable discrimination' in the chapeau of Article XX. That in turn allows the Appellate Body to reach out to these other, non-trade instruments to ascertain what are the minimum standards to be met before discriminatory measures such as those to be found in Section 609 may be justified under Article XX. In this way 'sustainable development' has—beyond its substantive use in relation to the meaning of Article XX(g)—a procedural element, namely the requirement that appropriate diplomatic means—including those available within relevant multilateral agreements—be exhausted before unilateral measures may be taken.

---

[35] *Ibid*, para 165.

[36] *Ibid*, para 166.

[37] *Ibid*, para 167.

[38] *Ibid*.

[39] *Ibid*, para 168.

[40] *Ibid*, para 170. The 1996 Convention establishes obligations to reduce harm to sea turtles and encourages the appropriate use of TEDs (Art IV(2) (h)). It also provides expressly that in implementing the Convention the parties shall act in accordance with the WTO Agreement, including in particular the Agreement on Technical Barriers to Trade and Article XI of GATT 1994 (Art XV).

[41] *Ibid*, para 171 and note 174 (and accompanying text).

CONCLUSIONS

To what extent is a reader of these two decisions enlightened about *sustainable development*? Both the ICJ and the Appellate Body refer to sustainable development as a 'concept'. Both treat it as having a status in international law, in the sense that it is invoked as part of a legal analysis to justify a legal conclusion. Neither body explores its international legal status, whether as custom or convention law, or adds significantly to our sense of what it is or what role it has in the international legal order, beyond indicating that in normative terms it may have both procedural and substantive consequences. And yet both bodies apparently use 'sustainable development' as a significant aid to assist in reaching fairly radical conclusions. For the ICJ 'sustainable development' contributes to the construction of the bridge across which the majority travels to justify its conclusion that although the 1977 Treaty between Hungary and (Czecho)Slovakia requires the construction of two barrages and remains in force, it does not now require Hungary to participate in the building of a second barrage. In effect, 'sustainable development' is utilised by the Court to assist in rewriting the 1977 Treaty, to justify an interpretative conclusion which would not on its face be an outcome of its earlier prior analysis. The emergence of 'sustainable development' is a post-Rio fundamental change of circumstances which was not present in 1989 so as to justify Hungary's original suspension of works.

For the Appellate Body, 'sustainable development' provides the 'colour, texture and shading' to permit interpretation of the GATT 94 text which legitimately permits one state to take measures to conserve living resources which are threatened by actions in another state, subject to a need to exhaust multilateral diplomatic routes which may be available. This too is a far-reaching conclusion which breaks with prior international practise and for which little, if any, international precedent can be found.

From these two cases it appears, then, that 'sustainable development' remains an elusive concept which essentially requires different streams of international law to be treated in an integrated manner.[42] In the words of Judge Weeramantry, it aims at harmonisation and reconciliation with a view to avoiding 'a state of normative anarchy'. The jurisprudence of those two bodies has not added greatly to our understanding of 'sustainable development': we do not know with a great deal more certainty what it is, or what international legal status it has, or in what precise way it is to be made operational, or what consequences might flow from its application.[43] What we do know is that two important international judicial bodies have been prepared to invoke it to justify or support conclusions with consequences which challenge some basic tenets of traditional international law and are potentially far-reaching. At the very least, these two cases indicate that the 'concept' or 'principle' of 'sustainable development' has gained legal currency and that its consequences will be felt more rather than less widely. One can therefore expect 'sustainable development' to be relied upon in other fora, perhaps to justify the integration of environmental considerations into foreign investment protection agreements (for example in the context of ICSID proceedings) or the integration of developmental considerations into the application of human rights norms.

---

[42] See more generally Sands, 1998.

[43] See also Boyle, 1997, p 18, noting that the International Court's treatment of 'sustainable development' left open two very large questions, namely whether the Court could review development proposals on the ground that they were not sustainable, and whether the principle had an *erga omnes* character.

REFERENCES

AB-1998-4, 12 October 1998, 33 (1999) ILM 118

Advisory Opinion on the Legality of the Threat or Use of Nuclear Weapons [1996] ICJ Reports 226

Agreement on Technical Barriers to Trade and Article XI of GATT 1994

Appellate Body of the World Trade Organisation Decision on Shrimp and Shrimp Products AB-1998-4, 12 October 1998, (1999) 33 ILM 118

Boyle, A E, 'The *Gabèíkovo-Nagymaro*: new law in old bottles' (1997) 8 Yearbook of International Environmental Law 13

Counter Memorial of Slovakia in the *Case Concerning the Gabèíkovo-Nagymaros Project* (Hungary/Slovakia), 5 December 1994, available at the Library of the International Court of Justice

Foundation for International Environmental Law and Development, 'Report of the consultation on sustainable development: the challenge to international law' (1994) 3 Review of European Community and International Environmental Law 1

Gabèíkovo-Nagymaro Project Case (Hungary v Slovakia) [1997] ICJ Reports 7

Sands, P, 'International law in the field of sustainable development' (1994) LXV BYIL, 303

Sands, P, 'Treaty, custom and the cross-fertilisation of international law' 3 (1998) Yale Hum Rts Dev L J, available at http://diana.law.yale.edu/yhrdlj/vol01iss01/sands_philippe_article.htm

Stec, S and Eckstein, G, 'Of solemn oaths and obligations: environmental impact of the ICJ's decision in the case concerning the *Gabèíkovo-Nagymaros Project*' (1997) 8 Yearbook of International Environmental Law 41

WT-DS58/R of 15 May 1998

PART 3

NATIONAL PRACTICE

CHAPTER 11

POST-COMMUNIST LEGAL REFORM: THE ELISION OF THE POLITICAL

*Scott Newton**

INTRODUCTION

Legal transplantation is a term that has come to be used for the borrowing or importing of legislative models, concepts, approaches or even statutory language from another jurisdiction, typically via the offices of experts in the borrowed law.[1] In Kazakhstan, as in the other so-called 'transitional' states of the former USSR, it acquires special force, in the context of the wholesale re-configuration of the legislative framework from one supporting a planned economy, to one supporting a market.[2] This re-configuration is supposed by definition to have required some form of transplantation, and with it some degree of assistance from foreign lawyers. Indeed, the concept of 'transplantation' in prevalent thinking appears to be linked to (if not required by) that of 'transition', as instrument of choice against the background of globalisation. In turn, the employment of this pair of concepts for analytic and prescriptive purposes tends to mask the subordination of the political requirements of legitimacy to the technical requirements of legality in the legislative reform process in places like Kazakhstan.

This chapter looks at the salience of transplantation and transition, and their implications for the relation of legality to legitimacy, in two very substantial recent items of commercial legislation in Kazakhstan, the Insolvency Law of 21 January 1997 and the Pension Law of 20 June 1997. Both exemplify the 'architectural' dimension of new commercial legislation in the post-communist states—the fashioning of complex new regulatory institutions, as distinct from the dimension of basic legal rules.[3] Both have been regarded as legal transplants. Both

* Lecturer in the Laws of Central Asia, School of Oriental and African Studies. The author was director of the USAID commercial law training project from 1996-2000 and director of the USAID commercial law drafting project from 1998-2000. He has also served as adviser to the Minister of Justice of Kazakhstan and consultant to the World Bank-funded Legal Reform Project Unit at the Ministry of Justice. Where a specific reference for a point in the narrative drafting history of the two laws considered here is not provided, the author is relying on his own knowledge, and all translations are his. The arguments and conclusions elaborated herein are entirely the author's and in no way reflect the views of USAID, the World Bank, or the Government of Kazakhstan or any officials thereof. He wishes to thank the following individuals for their time and assistance: Kuliash Iliasova, Vladimir Ivlev, William Baldridge, Erlan Osipov, Iskander Zhanaidarov, Maidan Sulemeinov, Anatoli Matiukhin, Susan Marks.

1 A good recent summary of transplantation with emphasis on the transition states is supplied by Waelde and Gunderson, 1999, pp 84-90.

2 Law in Kazakhstan as elsewhere in the post-Soviet realm has been viewed as the fulcrum of sweeping economic, political, and social transformation. It has been understood by all actors in the process—government officials, legal scholars, foreign advisers—in classic Weberian terms as the means and the medium for reconfiguring the basic institutions of society—the formalised sets of roles, functions, rules, procedures, and practices by which social, economic, and political relations are organised, conducted, and regulated. The burden thus placed on law in Kazakhstan has been enormous. Participants, commentators, and analysts have for the most part simply assumed that law was up to the task. A critique of legal instrumentalism as such in the command-to-market transformation is beyond the ambitions of this chapter.

3 The attention to the architectural or legal-institutional dimension is by way of corrective to the emphasis on private law in much of the discussion of 'market transition.' The defining feature of a modern economy is its administrative framework—the complex of regulatory institutions for the

are held to represent milestones on the road to transition. Both have been found wanting in some technical particulars, and have undergone subsequent amendment. And both raise important questions about legitimacy—about the process by which they became the law of the land.

It is generally assumed that the states of the former Soviet Union (fSU) were obliged to transplant, because they had inherited a legal system with no legal basis for the vast array of transactions and types of commercial activity found in any modern industrialised economy— everything from home mortgages to company debentures—and had no choice but to provide that basis by copying from other jurisdictions. According to one analysis, '[w]hat is indisputable is that for the legal systems of Central and Eastern Europe, *transplantation is a reality*. Because transition economies cannot afford and do not wish to go through the same process of slow and tentative development as the developed economies in order to achieve their modern legal and regulatory structures, they must, to a large extent import them.'[4]

But the question whether a project of legal transplantation has in fact been attempted in jurisdictions such as Kazakhstan is a very loaded one. For even if a jurisdiction decides to import a foreign law lock, stock and barrel, it nonetheless must *enact* it, with all the sovereign political implications any enactment carries. Thus, the very term 'transplantation,' biased toward the technical, masks the political realities, for 'legal transplantation' is always necessarily a species of the genus legislation. To speak, as comparative lawyers typically do, of transplantation as 'reception' is to obscure the political calculations and complex play of interests behind any modern instance of importing statutes (or concepts or provisions).

Even where commentators and analysts adopt a critical rather than descriptive approach, they habitually seem to wring the politics out of the account of 'transplantation.' Two views seem to prevail. One is that legal 'transplantation' ignores cultural or social context and widens the fissure inherited from state socialism between official, state law and 'actually existing' popular understandings and practices. The other is that transplantation is a matter of economic rationality, and that market-enabling laws are largely culture-neutral. For the first proposition, legal reform permitting a market to develop and flourish is contingent on background cultural and social factors; for the second, it is primarily a technical matter of proper statutory formulation. In neither view is it a political matter of the contested allocation of social goods. Both views share the premise that what counts is the product enacted, not the process of enactment.

By focusing on 'transplants,' and looking primarily to legislative text, commentators concentrate on questions about the functioning of a law. Will the transplant 'take'? Will the actors whose conduct it is intended to govern internalise the relevant norms? They thus bypass the more interesting questions which look instead to the circumstances in which the law comes into being at all. What does the process of drafting, proposing, revising, and adopting this law reveal about policy and its (national and transnational) horizons? What does it reveal about the background theory of the political genesis of law, and law's relation to society? What does it say about the play of interests and factions, both local and foreign (including especially bilateral and multilateral donors)? Whose law is it anyway—who has made it? Why, and to what end?

---

market in goods and services (banking, insurance, finance). The preoccupation with basic rules of market relations (civil codes, for example, which define and elaborate the fundamental categories of civil actors and the types of civil relationships they may legally form) seems to reflect the dominant neo-liberal, laissez-faire thinking about the post-communist transition.

[4] Dahan and Dine.

In transplantation as in transition, the emphasis on product over process works to privilege legality over legitimacy. Those who do the work of legislative reform in Kazakhstan tend to observe a certain logic of preference, according to which legality comes before policy, which in turn precedes legitimacy. Legal commentators also seem to reflect this. Both interveners and domestic actors in Kazakhstan have exhibited a tendency to treat the process of legislative reform primarily in legal-formal terms. That is to say, they are preoccupied with the internal consistency of a proposed law, its harmony with other applicable legislation, the quality of its draftsmanship, its fidelity to the designated economic function, and its legal capability to compel, prohibit, enable, organise or regulate the behaviour or practice which is its object. Matters of policy, such as the economic or social rationale for a particular piece of legislation, its function in the system of allocating goods and regulating relations, are often accorded secondary significance. Likewise put aside are questions about the substantive authority in the name of which a law is enacted, about the political grounding (presumably democratic grounding) of the process by which the law comes to be, and about the degree to which that process embodies principles of deliberation, transparency and accountability. But can the legitimacy of a novel legal regime be secured purely on the basis of its formal legality, particularly in the uncertain circumstances of post-Soviet states? In Kazakhstan, which saw the previous system come down around its ears without immediately discernible cause like a natural catastrophe, and which had independence thrust upon it, the nature of authority is precisely what seems to remain unsettled.

Attention to process and politics brings to the fore the issue of *dramatis personae*, which serves as a leitmotiv in the discussion below. The role of foreign interveners (experts and donors), and ideas about that role, are indispensable elements in the generally accepted concept of transplantation, shared by its partisans and critics. It is also a very prominent feature of the landscape of legal reform across the fSU, as measured by funding levels and the quantity and variety of legal technical assistance projects and personnel. In Kazakhstan, the United States Agency for International Development (USAID) and the International Bank for Reconstruction and Development (World Bank) offered extensive technical assistance in the development of both the insolvency and pension schemes discussed below.

Some, especially legal sociologists and anthropologists, urge that one of the foremost reasons for the failure of 'transplants' to take root is slavish adherence on the part of government drafters to the (inappropriate) prescriptions of foreign advisers. Others argue that transplants fail because of insufficient fidelity to foreign models. Yet the role of foreign advisers is surely more complicated and more ambiguous than either assessment suggests— and governments are certainly just as capable as Odysseus's sailors of stopping their ears. The intent or aims of advisers often diverge dramatically from their actual functions in the genesis of new legislation.

In sum, close examination of the law-creating process in these two particular cases can restore the political in all its dimensions and reveal some of the ways in which an alliance between the concepts or categories of 'transplantation' and 'transition' has hitherto obscured those dimensions. Such an examination can also reveal the tension between technical legality and political legitimacy as an important aspect of 'state law' in transition states which makes its enforcement, acceptance, and practical significance so distinctly problematic.

LEGAL REFORM IN KAZAKHSTAN AND THE DRAFTING PROCESS

The drafting process in Kazakhstan begins when the Prime Minister's office prepares an annual legislative agenda before the start of the parliamentary session in September. Laws are then drafted by working groups, organised by the ministry or agency which is charged by the Prime Minister's office with responsibility for preparing a draft statute. The bulk of basic Kazakhstani commercial legislation was drafted in the period 1995 to 1997. At that time, working groups for a number of especially important laws, including the bankruptcy law, were staffed by academic consultants whose services were paid for by a World Bank technical assistance loan. Since then, the pace of legislative activity has appreciably slowed and working groups have been staffed almost exclusively by government lawyers (along with a very few donor-funded local consultants).

Law on bankruptcy[5]

Insolvency legislation was targeted early in the post-Soviet period as an essential step towards a functional legal underpinning for the market. The Government recognised that an orderly procedure for the disposition of insolvent companies and market exit was a necessary component of commercial stability and predictability and a particular need in the course of market transition, in order to enable assets to be massively re-deployed to more productive uses than previously. Once enterprises were deprived of state subsidisation and thrown on their own resources and profit-making capacities, they were free to fail. The result was an insolvency explosion, for which regulation was clearly required. Insolvency legislation has been in fairly continuous flux. An initial insolvency law was adopted in 1992. A more substantive presidential decree on the subject was then promulgated in 1995, in tandem with the provisions of the civil code. However, these measures proved largely ineffectual. A vanishingly small number of insolvency cases were adjudicated under them: none at all in 1993 and 1994, 33 in 1995, and 4 the following year. The third law, adopted in 1997 is the principal object of concern here, since it reveals most about the politics of 'transplantation' as compounded by the role of foreign technical assistance. A fourth bankruptcy statute is currently in preparation.

The third law was elaborated after local commentators began to press for the preparation of a comprehensive statute, based on a thorough study of the available models in Western jurisdictions where the institution of insolvency was fundamental and long-perfected. This call was very expressly for a process of creative drafting premised on comparative analysis and adaptation rather than transplantation as such.[6] Accordingly, a government working group was created for such a purpose, under the auspices of a World Bank technical assistance loan to the Ministry of Justice (MOJ) for which the consultant was a US law firm hired by the MOJ (the project numbered bankruptcy as only one of a number of objects of technical assistance in legislative drafting). For the first time, the drafting process was (at least relatively) collaborative and deliberative, if not fully participatory. The five members of the working group were exclusively academic lawyers, the foremost civilists in the country, including

---

[5] 21 January 1997.

[6] K M Iliasova, a law professor who had early developed expertise in insolvency law, argued in mid-1994 for a law which would offer a variety of mechanisms for restructuring insolvent enterprises and adduced as examples the UK Insolvency Act of 1986 and Chapter 11 of the US Bankruptcy Code. (She was later invited to join the working group.) Iliasova, 1994.

especially two academic lawyers who had gained a reputation as experts in the emerging field of insolvency law.

The working group members themselves understood their task as a neutral, technical one of providing an effective mechanism, an orderly procedure, for managing the phenomenon of commercial insolvency as an inevitable fact of commercial life. They consulted a range of potential models for insolvency law 'transplantation,' but looked especially to three jurisdictions, the laws of which were available in the Russian language: the Federal Republic of Germany, the United States, and the Russian Federation. The chief problems which the working group had identified in existing insolvency legislation and for which it sought solutions in these foreign approaches were: 1) bias toward liquidation, 2) absence of control over the process by creditors, and 3) limited range of alternatives to liquidation.

In late 1995, as the working group prepared to develop its draft, USAID chose to launch its own bankruptcy project, to be implemented by a US consulting firm. Economists at USAID were especially interested in promoting insolvency reform because they saw in it an alternative, fast track (or back door) to privatisation. Insolvent enterprises could either be eliminated and their assets sold to private hands for more productive use or they could be re-organised. Two US lawyers formed the staff of this project along with several Kazakhstani economists and lawyers. This USAID project, which was designed both to recommend legislative changes and to facilitate the administration of the new law (for example, by providing training to liquidators), was to some extent in direct competition with the World Bank-financed project.

This situation illustrates the multitude of ways in which domestic and foreign interests can play against, and in alignment with, one another, with consequences for the legislative process, positive and negative, intentional and accidental. The intervention of the USAID project effectively served to politicise the drafting process—or at least to make the political implications of that process manifest. It did this not primarily by favouring procedural approaches typical of US law (for example, reducing extent of court determination through the availability of an out-of-court procedure), since the working group was independently consulting US bankruptcy legislation with the aid of US specialists. Rather, it pushed for consultation with a wider field of experts and also with representatives of the business sector, with the aim of making the process ostensibly more participatory within a domestic, Kazakhstani context and thereby widening the range of viewpoints and the scope of issues before the working group. Indeed, the argument (advanced by USAID) that it was healthy for the two projects to be operating simultaneously and thereby generating a competitive market of ideas found a receptive audience in influential quarters within the GOK.

Disagreements between the staffs of the two projects (and between local and US experts within those staffs) often fell out along a common law/civil law divide. This divide is a recurrent feature of legislative reform efforts throughout the region, wherever common lawyers (frequently from the US) have had a role. The difficulty is that common/civilian differences are less significant for their substantive content than for their rhetorical and political value as exploited by all participants. On the one hand some common lawyers forge imperturbably ahead in blissful ignorance of compatibility problems (this is often more a case of poor training or insufficient preparation than a deep-rooted cultural impediment) in the belief that a legislative solution of North American provenance is necessarily the most logical and up-to-date. On the other hand, civilians (particularly Soviet-trained civilists, whose understanding of the relations between common and civil law systems sometimes seems peculiarly essentialist and moreover stuck in the early 1920s, when the development of Soviet civil law diverged from its European base) fetishise the differences. Aggressive foreign proponents of common law approaches run the risk of alienating Kazakhstani colleagues and disposing the latter to reject those approaches even when meritorious. However, resistance to such approaches seems at least in part to be attributable to the threat they pose to the position of the monopoly on civil law scholarship held by those trained in the Soviet legal tradition.

The draft insolvency law was adopted in early 1997 substantially as drafted by the working group and without any direct input from USAID. Within a year, however, work began on amendments to the legislation, so as to address practical problems which had become apparent in the interim. In this amending process, USAID became actively involved, viewing it as a 'second bite at the cherry' and working alongside the Reorganisation Agency. A key concern of USAID was to reduce the need for court determination and to ensure a streamlined approval process.

Ironically, the marginalisation of the civilists, sought for different reasons by important elements among government legal policymakers, including the new Minister of Justice, and some US strategists, ultimately meant that the drafting process (not merely touching bankruptcy but generally) was moved entirely inside the government. This was to some extent a financially motivated decision. The growth of a flourishing private market in legal services in Kazakhstan, thanks to the presence of numerous foreign law firms, meant that the services of local academic advisers did not come cheap, and certainly not at government wages.

Without loan funds to secure the services of local expert drafters nor in-kind grants from USAID, the government had to rely on its own drafting staff, for the most part inexperienced recent law graduates. One effect of this appears to have been the increased influence of particular agency interests within the government, especially those of the Reorganisation Agency. The phenomenon of 'agency capture' of the drafting process is an ambiguous one. On the one hand, the process benefited from the familiarity of Reorganisation Agency officials and administrators with the history of the law's implementation, their wider contacts with the business community, and their policy perspective. On the other hand, it became vulnerable to bureaucratic self-aggrandisement.

The history of the insolvency law highlights the ambiguous role of donor funding and of legal technical assistance. In circumstances such as those described, they functioned as a (limited) corrective to an elite-dominated process, by channelling input from practitioners and businessmen, in addition to academics. They could not well open that process to include the labouring or consuming public, however—even had they wanted to. This proxy function, while admittedly difficult to endorse from the standpoint of any theory of democratically-grounded lawmaking, can be beneficial where there is no mechanism for consultation on the part of drafters with the prospective constituencies of a proposed law. The lack of a mechanism for engaging those who would be affected directly by legislation is a recurring problem in the drafting process in Kazakhstan. Drafts are typically not circulated or published before they are ready to be submitted to Parliament. Constituencies have influence only insofar as they have personal ties with members of working groups.

The USAID project also promoted public debate on —or at least awarenessof—insolvency through press conferences and publication of articles by project professionals in local journals. For instance, in early 1996 upon the USAID-sponsored visit of the architect of the Russian bankruptcy law, the USAID project organised a press conference and a televised roundtable discussion which included both the visiting Russian expert and the head of the Reorganisation Agency. The World Bank-funded project, administered by the government, was markedly less assertive in putting forth its views, although members of the working group published in their own capacity as scholars. The difficulty, of course, is that such efforts have more the quality of marketing than of deliberation or contestation, inasmuch as they are staged or orchestrated from above or outside. This is the case even for so-called 'social marketing,' which employs advertising techniques to influence behaviour toward public ends, like non-smoking or safe driving.

It might be urged that insolvency is a somewhat recondite matter for general interest, as opposed, say, to pension reform. In Kazakhstan, however, there was lively interest in the topic of bankruptcy, largely on the basis that it threatened the loss of jobs via the liquidation of enterprises. The Kazakhstani academic lawyers on the working group and the USAID project professionals were united in seeing the major public-orientated task as assuring the citizenry that bankruptcy was a normal, indeed indispensable, constituent of any functional market economy and nothing especially to be feared. While this may be incontrovertible when stated in so general a way, the ordering of salary arrears in the system of preferences in insolvency proceedings as against, say, obligations to secured creditors, could hardly be of greater public moment. One of the familiar tactics of the subordination of the political to the technical in the rhetoric of both domestic actors and foreign interveners, is to pitch arguments at such a level of generality or inclusiveness that they conceal the political contestability evident at lower levels.

Law on pension provision[7]

Kazakhstan in mid-1997 became the first jurisdiction in the fSU, or anywhere in the former Socialist Bloc apart from Hungary, to enact a fully Latin American-style pension system. Such a defined-contribution system, pioneered in Chile under Pinochet, is premised on individual retirement accounts, funded by mandatory employee contributions, which are invested in privately-managed funds. It replaced the former defined-benefit, state-funded, inter-generational solidarity system (a pay-as-you-go-system, funded by current contributions from enterprises).[8] What distinguishes it are three key features: 1) pension contributions must be invested in one of the established pension funds, state and private, at the choice of the contributor; 2) pension contributions are registered in individual accounts in the name of the contributor; and 3) pension contributions are withheld from *employee's* wages.[9] The state's role is limited to regulation of the system (and to management of the state funds); individual contributors must to a significant degree manage their own financial planning by deciding in which fund or funds to invest their contributions.

While a number of EU jurisdictions have incorporated some type of individual accounts scheme to supplement the primary pension system, and also encourage the growth of employer-funded plans, none appears to have contemplated converting the entire pension

---

[7]   20 June 1997.

[8]   It did so prospectively, for future retirees only, not for those who had retired before the law came into effect, obligations to whom continued to be funded on the old basis. It also established an elaborate transition procedure for those workers approaching retirement age, according to which the portion of pension obligations continuing to be met by the state would be decreased with the age of the retiring cohort.

[9]   For a survey of pension plan types and the distinction between defined benefit and defined contribution systems, see Clark, 2000. For an analysis of the Latin American systems, see Queisser, 1999. Briefly, there is a range of pension schemes in Latin America. Most represent a mix of so-called 'pillars' (public, pay-as-you-go, defined-benefit and funded, privately managed defined-contribution based on individual accounts). Only Chile and Mexico have abandoned altogether the public pillar. The Latin American states have had to contend with a number of very formidable public policy issues: cost of administering the system, financing the transition, fee-basis for fund management (collection-based as against asset-based), permissibility and frequency of transfers for contributors between funds, means withdrawal and types of annuities, etc.

system to an individual account basis. Such a change is, or should be, a matter of great public concern; the transfer from state to individual citizens of the responsibility for retirement planning is a fundamental revision of the social compact. The story of how Kazakhstan came to create such a system—a system contemplating mature, flourishing capital markets, rather than embryonic ones—is a remarkable and illuminating one. Even more than the insolvency law just discussed, it reveals the multiple contingencies and susceptibility to chance alignments of interests characteristic of the processes of law reform in Kazakhstan.

Under-funding of the inherited Soviet pay-as-you-go pension system had emerged by 1995 as an increasingly severe problem for the Government, as for its neighbour to the north. Similar problems confront state pension schemes throughout the industrialised world in the context of rising benefits and lowered retirement ages, compounded by the demographic tsunami of the ageing baby-boom generation. A pattern had developed of dramatically declining tax revenues: enterprises habitually concealed profits or transferred them abroad so as to display negative balances and avoid tax liability. The existing pension system, dependent as it was on contributions from enterprises, came under severe strain.[10] At the same time, pension rights advocacy groups had become increasingly vocal—one of relatively few manifestations of civil society in Kazakhstan at the time. Prime Minister Kazhegeldin gave pension reform the highest priority and appointed a working group, chaired by two deputy prime ministers and consisting of high officials in the financial regulatory bodies,[11] to develop proposals for the reform of the pension system. The working group was charged with submitting a 'Concept' (policy paper) outlining proposed legislation within sixteen days. In short order, the Concept was published and the law itself was adopted by Parliament in mid-June of 1997.

USAID was the principal provider of foreign technical assistance in the area of pension reform, and had been administering a pension project from early 1996. In its early months the project had been providing general background policy materials on approaches to pension reform, serving primarily as an informational resource. The project at the time was testing the waters, exploring possibilities of developing formal working arrangements with one or more government agencies. Key decision-makers in the Government, especially the heads of the National Bank and the National Securities Commission, both young, exceptionally astute and able reformers with a thorough grounding in market economics, were meditating radical pension reform, impelled by the deepening pension crisis.

USAID from the outset encouraged the interest of relevant actors in the Government in a Latin American-style system. USAID arranged and sponsored a trip in autumn 1996 to Santiago by a Government delegation to study the Chilean system *in situ*, a trip which seemed to have a decisive influence on pension reform policy in the Government. Economic policy-makers at USAID saw in the proposed shift to a mandatory cumulative pension system a potential double boon: not only would the change place pensions on a sound economic basis and relieve the state of an increasingly insupportable burden, it would also provide a massive

---

[10] The existing system did include supplemental, voluntary private investment-based pension plans but these had not attracted much attention. The supplemental system was poorly regulated and had at one point permitted the growth of pyramid-type pension fund schemes. There did exist an Association of Voluntary Pension Funds of Kazakhstan, which was represented on the working group that drafted the pension law.

[11] The working group was created pursuant to a government decree on 30 January 1997 on the basis of the comprehensive plan for the deepening of reform measures, issued 13 December 1996. Members appointed included two Deputy Prime Ministers, the Head of the Presidential Administration, the Minister of Labour and Social Protection, Chair of the National Bank, Chair of the National Securities Commission, Chair of the Association of Voluntary Pension, and Deputy Ministers of Finance and Justice.

initial thrust to the capital markets. The pension funds would rapidly acquire formidable assets which would necessarily be invested, initially in the government bond markets. Clearly, Kazakhstani government policy-makers saw a matching double-boon: disburdening the state of pension liabilities and at the same time guaranteeing it a new and unprecedentedly large source of funds for borrowing, thus effectively creating a captive bond market.

In the event, however, the law as ultimately adopted can with difficulty be called a transplant. It embraces a Latin American-style pension scheme, but does not borrow any statutory language and is emphatically *sui generis* in its institutional particulars. The Concept and the law itself were drafted entirely by the members of the working group. There was no direct foreign input whatsoever. Indeed, the government sought to fence the process off and conducted it with a relatively high degree of secrecy and opacity. Evidently, its political sensitivity and volatility were too great to permit its being entrusted to any outside consultants, even local scholars. Moreover, once presented to the public, it had to appear entirely 'indigenous'.

During the course of the working group's labour, the USAID project and USAID management did endeavour to influence the working group. It prepared a version of a draft pension law as well as specific recommendations. The working group reportedly thanked USAID for its pains but did not make use of the draft or recommendations. That said, the drafters did rely on the work of the USAID project for one aspect, namely, the analysis of the existing system: projections of accumulation of arrears, demographic and actuarial analyses.

The fast-track legislative campaign was accompanied by a public-relations barrage. The responsible government elites made use of the urgency of the underlying problem to justify the acceleration of the legislative process and present the public with a *fait-accompli*. In this endeavour, they received the enthusiastic support of policy-makers at USAID and the World Bank. The crafting and selling of the Kazakhstani pension reform plan achieved an extraordinary result—a radically new institution which promised to solve a growing crisis, and which quite plausibly was not achievable any other way. But it is the means, and the implications for legitimacy, not the end, and its indisputable legality, which is the object of our inquiry here.

In an article entitled 'Time to return the debts'—referring to the accumulated pension arrears—published in *Kazakhstanskaia Pravda* (the government newspaper) on 11 June 1977, Minister of Labour Korzhova explained the genesis of the pension law from the government's perspective:

> The country's leadership came to the simple conclusion of the necessity of overhauling the pension system: detailed analysis showed that the old pension law didn't work in the new demographic situation and an economic system with the dominance of private property. Earlier adopted measures, like the gradual raising of the retirement age, creation of non-governmental pension funds, were not capable of providing social guarantees to the population without cardinal changes in the entire pension system. A colossal research effort was undertaken, the results of which were published on 20 March of this year as the 'Concept of the reform of the system of pension provision in the Republic of Kazakhstan,' presented for nationwide discussion. ... Discussion of the Concept proceeded thoroughly actively, on television, over the radio, in the press. The drafting team during this period barnstormed the entire country. We all had literally to explain on our fingers to people the essence of the pension reform, having temporarily put out of mind the specialised terminology. We had many meetings with trade union representatives, legal organisations, pensioners' associations and veterans. Every one who wanted had the chance to have his say on this thorny issue.

The public relations campaign on behalf of the Concept is a particularly ambiguous phenomenon from the point of view of an analysis of process. It was obviously beneficial in the sense of generating a public debate, one of the rare occasions in modern Kazakhstan when a legislative proposal has been actively discussed in civil society. It was in many ways a model instance of a government's taking the law to the people. However, the campaign did not contemplate any real possibility of rejection or even substantive modification of the pension law on offer (unlike analogous major public policy projects elsewhere, such as the US health system reform plan in 1993, which was the outcome of a public and transparent process over a sufficient interval to acquire the presumption of legitimacy but was nonetheless resoundingly rejected). The choice presented to the public was an essentially dichotomous one, rather than a set of competing and equally elaborated alternatives: take it or leave it, either this or disaster.

Kazakhstanis did voice their unease and the Parliamentary proceedings were stormy. An article in *Kazakhstanskaia Pravda* (23 May 1997) entitled 'New draft law on pension provision—burial in a bottomless and roofless grave, without benefit of clergy or censer' commenced, 'The lower house of Parliament is in session these days almost without breaks or days off: discussion proceeds of the most unpopular bill in recent times, the law on pension provision.' Ultimately the government prevailed; the grandfathering for current pensioners of the existing arrangements effectively rendered moot the most significant potential opposition, from pensioners' advocacy groups.

As in the case of the law on bankruptcy, the pension law's passage did not resolve the problems which it was addressed, but rather signalled that efforts to influence the drafting process would simply shift to the next two rounds: elaborating the detailed regulatory framework of the new law, and fine-tuning the law through amendment. Foreign donors performed two important functions in this regard. One was raising public awareness of the pension scheme's implications. USAID provided comprehensive assistance in the presentation of the scheme by designing and producing television public service announcements, producing public information brochures elaborating the plan, and even by incorporating discussion of the new pension scheme in teleplays for episodes of the local television serial *Perekriostok*.[12] This work was closely co-ordinated with the GOK and indeed may be a relatively rare instance of foreign technical assistance directly sought by the government and tailored to the government's particular requirements. Perhaps for that very reason, though, it raises some troubling issues about the use of development assistance funds in ways that serve to enhance the effective governmental monopoly on public policy-making.

The other function was to provide on-going regulatory-design advice. Once the policy decision had been taken to shift to an individual account-based system, USAID and the Bank understood their role as ensuring that the pension system that emerged was well-crafted from the standpoint of institutional design and economic rationality. The questions with which they occupied themselves were chiefly regulatory and actuarial. Were the numbers (demographics, actuarial statistics and projections, economic forecasts, growth of capital markets) right? Would projected returns from the investment of fund assets provide adequate pension coverage? Were the pension funds provided with suitable oversight and control mechanisms? Was the contributor identification system sound? Were the financing arrangements for the transition from the old system realistic and supportable?

---

[12] Production of this serial was funded by the UK Know-How Fund; USAID paid for the pension scheme episodes. The serial was conceived as a means of dramatising issues revolving around the market transition as a form of 'social marketing.' See Mandel, forthcoming.

In contrast to the bankruptcy law drafting exercise, the USAID and World Bank-funded teams co-ordinated their work closely and divided the labour intelligently, with the endorsement of the GOK (which administered the World Bank-funded project). The USAID project maintained a continuous presence in Kazakhstan and provided general support. It continued to furnish data and analyses as well as propose specific regulatory enhancements and possible changes to the law. Additionally, USAID sponsored a second trip to Chile in the first quarter of 1998, as the pension plan moved into implementation. The purpose of this trip was to enable regulators of the new scheme to acquaint themselves with the detailed functioning of the Chilean system, particularly fund management. Consultants hired under the World Bank-funded technical assistance loan made short-term TRIPS to provide advice on numerous specialised aspects of the regulatory structure (for example, the contributor identification system).

A number of serious regulatory problems and lacunae emerged in the early period of the law's implementation, particularly the lack of a legal mechanism for the segregation of contributors' assets from fund managers' assets and the difficulty of ensuring reliable identification of assets as to contributor.[13] These problems, though addressed as technical flaws, were understood to have potentially catastrophic political consequences if left unchecked, since they could damn the new scheme in public opinion (if, for example, the law failed to forestall widespread fund mismanagement). Donors, in particular, were anxious to do what they could to keep the law afloat, since what was at stake was considerably more than the fate of the particular law as drafted. Ultimately, it was the very viability of a free-market approach to pension provision as such. One might think that the donors were determined that the Kazakhstanis, having by the grace of God independently chosen an ideal neo-liberal solution, would not proceed to muck it up.

A lively debate ensued within USAID as to whether the problems with the law could be addressed without resorting to amendment, that is to say, by regulatory correctives on the one hand and changes in related legislation on the other. USAID was fearful of pressing for legislative amendments at a juncture when the very news that amendments were under consideration could undermine already shaky public support for the new law. Nonetheless, the law was eventually amended in December 1998, and then again the following year.

The comprehensive advice on matters of detailed regulatory design provided by USAID and the World Bank was timely and necessary owing to the haste with which pension reform was undertaken and the sheer administrative challenge it would have posed even for an industrialised state with a highly developed administrative capacity, let alone newly-independent Kazakhstan. The intervention of the World Bank and USAID appears to furnish an example of foreign assistance both unequivocally technical and unequivocally beneficial. But the more deeply and in detail the nature of such advice is explored, the harder it becomes to say on which side of the technical/political line a particular recommendation falls. Sometimes the case is fairly clear; the recommendation to ensure strict segregation of contributors' and fund manager's assets is an indispensable element of any pension scheme. On the other hand, the recommendation by USAID that the plan not be amended to shift from employee to employer contributions (as the GOK was contemplating) is by no means

---

[13] These included in the views of the USAID project: 'absence of a legal mechanism preventing the transfer of contributors' assets to another in a range of cases, eg fund bankruptcy, seizure by creditor pursuant to a judgement, etc (an acute problem pending adoption of the civil code, special part of which provided for the trust administration of property) provision for asset management companies separate from pension funds to oversee investment of fund assets (multiplication of administrative agencies and opportunities for mismanagement and corruption).'

politically neutral, whatever technical reasons can be mustered in support. The administrative complexities of a cumulative, funded, individual-account-based pension scheme and the multitudinous public policy issues to which they give rise (everything from details like fee-basis of the fund and asset management companies to basic matters of capital markets regulation) meant that much of the on-going advice and recommendations was inescapably technical and political in equal measure.

CONCLUDING OBSERVATIONS

Transplantation and transition revisited

If the history of the insolvency and pension laws is anything to go by, two assumptions about transplantation require challenge: 1) that the market legal framework in Kazakhstan was in fact transplanted, and 2) that the result was achieved (and could only have been achieved) by reliance on foreign technical advisers. In Kazakhstan (as in other Commonwealth of Independent States (CIS) jurisdictions, first and foremost the Russian Federation) the decision to convert the economic framework to a market-basis in Kazakhstan necessarily entailed a high degree of adaptation of market-regulating legislation from elsewhere. However, though the metaphors of borrowing, importing, or transplanting have been widely used for this process, in Kazakhstan (as elsewhere), they are inapposite. It has never been a matter of copying foreign statutes *tout court*. Rather, Kazakhstani legal scholars have studied foreign legal materials, drawing on them without reproducing them. Model CIS legislation has played a central role. The Kazakhstani Civil Code (General Part adopted in 1996, Special Part adopted in the summer 1999) tracks the model CIS civil code adopted by the Inter-parliamentary assembly in 1994, with primary input from Dutch and supplementary input from other (European and US) scholars.[14]

'Transplantation' seems to be a term favoured, indeed exclusively employed, by foreign advisers and commentators, who clearly like to think of what they are promoting in the short term as 'transplantation,' just as what they are seeking in the long-term is 'transition.' Both terms carry multiple meanings (transplantation can be understood rather crudely and literally, or more abstractly; transition can be understood in a primarily political or economic sense, and can be open-ended or over-determined), but they have a special semantic charge as *projects*, which elites would like to see accomplished.

In this context, one of the distinctive characteristics of the post-communist episode in legal reform is the *prescriptiveness* of donor interventions. Donors have been very thorough and detailed in the review of proposed draft legislation and in the multiple recommendations for minor changes in individual provisions. Clearly, detailed scrutiny is a mark of professionalism on the part of technical advisers, and the drafting process in Kazakhstan stands to benefit—and has benefited—from such close and careful attention by foreign lawyers.

At the same time, there may be some general heuristic value in providing government drafters with full-blown alternatives in the Russian language. This is especially likely to be useful where the working groups have neglected or omitted to consider the full range (or even a representative selection) of available approaches or legal-regulatory models. The difficulty

---

14 For a thorough analysis of the Kazakhstan civil code and an instructive comparison with its Russian cousin, see Osakwe, 1998.

with such drafts is that they reflect the legal-conceptual vocabulary of a foreign system (such was the case with the draft pension law prepared by a Canadian lawyer at the USAID project). They typically read like translated documents when submitted to the working group. The very prescriptiveness of the exercise thus encounters difficulties because it demands Russian language equivalents of imported formulations.

This prescriptiveness seems to be deeply rooted in the concept of 'transition'. In earlier, classical instances of transplantation, in circumstances of colonialism (and subsequently in the aftermath of decolonisation), the presumption on the part of interveners at least was the *filling of a legal vacuum*. In the modern instance, in the context of 'transition,' the presumption is the *replacement* of a failed legal experiment and parochial aberration (socialist law) by a proven success and putative global standard (market law), and the choice of a particular source (say US shareholder-favouring as against German stakeholder-favouring company law) and its faithful copying acquires significance by virtue of its approximation to the presumed ideal of market freedom. This ideological criterion for choice is sometimes disguised as a technical one, analogous to 'best practice' in business, according to which the most (economically) rational and (functionally) effective approach to a particular legal or regulatory design is to be preferred. Clearly, however, there is no one such solution for each instance. Waelde and Gunderson rightly emphasise the range of models available.[15] Transplantation as replacement is further distinguishable from the colonial/postcolonial case of vacuum-filling in that it occurs in the context of a very highly developed modern legal culture and therefore encounters sophisticated resistance.[16]

The premise open to serious challenge here is that the transformation of once-socialist economies to a market form is ortholinear, with fixed start- and end-points and one conceivable trajectory between them. This presumed ortholinearity is a corollary, I claim, of the logic of neo-liberalism and free-market triumphalism. Yet, of course, the configurations of mature market economies display great variety, not only among themselves, but within any one across time and policy preference—from *dirigiste* to *laissez-faire* in economic-regulatory posture, and from welfarist to privatist in social-regulatory posture. Foreign interveners chose to forget their own collective experience when pressing Kazakhstan as other post-communist states to accomplish a uniform 'market transition.'

Of course interveners each tended not unnaturally to promote their own version of the market. But they continued to maintain (at least publicly) that they were supporting (the one, the only imaginable) 'market transition' as such. (European technical advisers, who operate from a starting point of significant variegation in the models of organisation of economic activity embodied in the state law of the constituent EU jurisdictions, as a rule are more cognisant of, or at least more willing to acknowledge, the breadth of policy choice, than are their US colleagues.) This suppression of market variety does not seem accidental; it is rather a

---

[15] Waelde and Gunderson, 1999, pp 84-90.

[16] The USSR, far from being a legal vacuum, as it is in the minds of many advisers, was a hyper-legal state. Whatever the peculiar perversions that the system wrought and its trampling of the rule of law, it was the very instantiation of legal positivism; the extravagant institutional apparatus of the USSR was first and foremost a legal construct. Legal professionalism and legal training were always highly valued. Though largely cut off from contemporary legal developments elsewhere, Soviet civil lawyers especially saw themselves as standing in the greater European legal tradition. They were certainly as proficient in general legal and specialised drafting abilities as their counterparts in any other European state.

consequence of the historical co-incidence of the triumph of neo-liberalism and free market orthodoxy, on the one hand, and the collapse of the USSR, on the other.[17]

Another aspect of 'transition' relates to the pace and nature of legislative change. The prodigious rate of legislative change in Kazakhstan[18] suggests that legislation in stabilised polities differs from legislation in systems undergoing profound change—the former being normal and the latter revolutionary, to borrow Thomas Kuhn's distinction. Normal legislation would be mainly a matter of tinkering at the margins—of introducing modifications to a well-developed legal framework for economic regulation. Revolutionary legislation would conversely be a matter of wholesale institutional reconstruction, of building from the ground up. It would ideally be accomplished swiftly, to limit its destabilising consequences and ensure its comprehensiveness (a justification analogous to that for economic 'shock therapy'). Both the insolvency and pension laws would then be specific instances of revolutionary legislation.

But are they really? Pension reform is a priority in all industrialised democracies, given underfunded pension obligations against the background of ageing populations; it is hardly confined to the circumstances of 'transition.' The insolvency law would seem a likelier candidate for 'revolutionary' enactment, but even it could be construed as a refinement rather than a radical innovation. In both cases, though, the pressure to legislate ostensibly characteristic of revolutionary legislation served multiple ends. 'Revolutionary' urgency proved useful to a variety of actors, enabling them to realise ends that might otherwise have been frustrated. In the Kazakhstani context, it ironically recalls something of the forcing of history characteristic of the earlier, Soviet 'transition,' *from* the market economy, particularly in its Stalinist phase.

At what point do the normal processes of incremental legislative refinement succeed to revolutionary legislative activity, such that transition ends and transplantation is no longer indicated? A decade ago, on the threshold of transition, reform elites in Eastern Europe and the soon-to-be-former USSR faced an array of fundamental questions about the restructuring of the economy. These included both questions of privatisation (how to transfer state assets to private ownership) and questions of marketisation (how to replace state control over the provision of goods, services, labour and capital with markets in each). Both aspects had to be accomplished in due legal form, but only the latter demanded a new commercial constitution, a basic legal framework. What is striking is that, even once this was put in place, the concept of transition continued to be invoked. Transition, it seems, will only really be complete when Kazakhstan has arrived at some ideal neo-liberal end-point of a free market. The elasticity of the term 'transition' allows it be used rhetorically as a goad to ever more radical reform measures.

---

[17] The way that neo-liberal ideology and the drive to globalisation has foreclosed or at least truncated this range of models, distorted the way transition has been conceived—indeed has made it possible for transition to be conceived as such—and led to the prescriptiveness of transplantation remarked above can be highlighted by means of a thought experiment. Suppose that the USSR had begun to retreat from a socialist economy at a much earlier point, in the immediate aftermath of the war, before the Cold War dynamic had become consolidated (say Stalin had died at the very end of the war, such that de-Stalinisation occurred earlier and the USSR had come to participate in the European post-war reconstruction effort in a comprehensive way, that it had accepted the Marshall Plan). It is likely that had the Soviet state allowed the market back in at that point, it would have gradually converged (without the 'end-of-history' hoopla) on the post-war Western European economies—that is, from socialism to social market.

[18] Since independence in late 1991, nearly 100 separate commercial laws, edicts and decrees have been adopted or promulgated, many, such as the joint stock company law, the bankruptcy law, the securities law, without precedent in the Soviet legal system.

Legality and legitimacy revisited

The use of the concepts of transplantation and transition as analytic tools for the post-socialist order tends, I have argued, to subordinate political legitimation to technical legality. As we have seen, the drafting process of both the bankruptcy and pension laws in Kazakhstan was quite thoroughly technocratic rather than democratic, a process among (domestic and sometimes foreign) elites undertaken largely over the heads of all but bureaucratic constituencies. The non-participatory character of the Kazakhstani drafting process, the absence of politics in the sense of democratic contest, fundamentally conditioned and informed that process.

Democratic legitimation seems paradoxically demanded, yet simultaneously foreclosed, by the special circumstances of 'transition.' Claus Offe captures with striking clarity the paradoxes of what he terms 'capitalism by democratic design':

> [A] market economy is set in motion only under pre-democratic conditions. In order to promote it democratic rights must be held back to allow for a healthy dose of original accumulation. Only a developed market economy produces the social structural conditions necessary for stable democracy and makes it possible to form compromises within the framework of what is perceived as a positive sum game. But the introduction of a market economy in the post-socialist societies is a 'political' project, which has prospects of success only if it rests on a strong and explicit legitimation. And since it is possible that the majority of the population will find neither democracy nor a market economy a desirable prospect, then we are presented with a Pandora's box of paradoxes, in the face of which every theory—or, for that matter, rational strategy—of the transition must fail.[19]

But the force of those paradoxes has lessened in the intervening years, as the market economy has been naturalised in the lives of the citizenry. Meanwhile, the mutually reinforcing rhetoric of transition and transplantation, urgency and expertise, seems to serve indefinitely to defer matters of legitimation.

The story of the pension and insolvency laws reveals how domestic and foreign elites can be complicit in this deferral, even if not always intentionally. Their intervention can help foster the idea that the statutory elements of a market-regulating legal system are obvious and non-contentious, as is their relation to one another. From this perspective, the only issues that seem to arise revolve around the need to ensure that the statutory complex for market regulation is characterised by textual coherence, intelligibility, clarity, quality of drafting, ease of interpretation and application, internal consistency and harmony, formal utility and functionality.

Yet important political questions bearing on the allocation of social goods and on citizens' economic and social chances press at every step of the way: questions such as the order of creditor preferences in insolvency and the basis for contributions in the pension scheme. The task of legislative reconstruction for a market economy consists of a myriad of such political decisions at the small scale. For domestic elites and foreign actors to frame the task of reconstruction at larger scales (either the large scale of transplantation or the grand scale of transition) is to mask those decisions.

However, insistence on the technical as a kind of political alibi clearly has limits. The authority of the working group drafting the pension law, consisting of high officials with policy-making competence, contrasts suggestively with the working group drafting the bankruptcy law, consisting of academic lawyers relying on their own best judgement for

---

19 Offe, 1996, p 41.

policy guidance. The much greater political significance and volatility of pension reform presumably dictated that drafting be entrusted to politically accountable hands.

The supremacy of the technical is useful not only to local elites. Foreign assistance donors encourage the technocratic model of 'transplantation' by seeking to attach foreign legal-technical advisers to the working groups. The subordination of the political serves as an *ex ante* justification of their involvement at all in the quintessentially domestic affair of law-making. But the role that foreign advisers play—and played—in the pension and bankruptcy laws in Kazakhstan is ambiguous. USAID and its consultants often seemed as much to be lobbying the Government for desired legislative changes as providing neutral technical assistance.

The World Bank too may be said to have engaged in discreet lobbying in both its commercial drafting and pension projects. On the other hand, the value of USAID's proxy function in a non-participatory process was noted for the insolvency law above. Lobbying by foreign governments may have some limited positive value where there is very little possibility for civil society to participate in law-creating, and where executive agencies operate largely without constraint in an intensely competitive bureaucratic environment. This value is in fact enhanced when donors are in competition. The vying for influence among donors and their technical advisers receives some attention in the literature, but is typically attributed to lack of co-ordination. This is to say, donors would speak with one mind if only they would take the time and trouble to get their act together. But to attribute unity of purpose to the various donors active in Kazakhstan would be to elide the political dimension once again.

There are at least three levels of (inter-donor) politics at work here. At the simplest such level, bilateral and regional donors are in competition for political standing, or influence, with the GOK and employ technical assistance programmes as courtship gifts. On another level, donors seek to secure policies most beneficial to their nationals, particularly investors. At the politically most encompassing level, donors disagree on matters of principle, that is, on the form a post-socialist market economy should take. Thus, the functions that donors and foreign assistance perform may be of more significance than their intentions. Though donors generally seek to conceal the political force of their activity, that activity can nonetheless serve to reveal the political implications of legal approaches under consideration, with benefits for the process itself.

Against this background, the challenge is to broaden participation in, and enhance the legitimacy of, legislative reform processes in Kazakhstan and elsewhere in the fSU. The development of the parliamentary system, including a strong committee and staffing system and regular public hearings, will presumably go a long way to redressing legitimation deficits in the drafting process. But the need to make the administrative system itself more responsive and accountable will not thereby be obviated and in the meantime, is exigent. As long as drafting is to be conducted by means of inter-ministerial working groups, inclusion of representatives of affected constituencies of proposed laws—business lobbies, NGOs, public advocacy groups—in their membership or on staff should be sought. At the same time, a consultative mechanism could be established to permit working group members and representatives of such interest groups to discuss issues at the drafting stage. Clearly, lobbying behaviour must be carefully regulated; economically and socially powerful forces even now are able to exercise considerable influence at the level of working groups. The nascent Kazakhstani insurance lobby furnishes a good example.

The lessons of process

The use of the categories of transplantation and transition in Kazakhstan has permitted commentators and actors alike to rationalise the legislative process in a very particular way which serves their own (sometimes divergent, sometimes convergent) needs. Viewing either the insolvency or the pension laws primarily as transplants in service of transition is a way of disregarding the multi-layered dynamic of their creation. That dynamic as elaborated above reveals the drafting process as robustly indeterminate and subject to multiple contingencies: the ideas of domestic academic lawyers, the agency interests of diverse bureaucracies, the conflicting technical advice of foreign experts, the agendas of bilateral and multilateral donors, the aims of professional and business lobbies, as well as the (at present less significant or influential) claims of advocacy or interest groups and the role of wider public opinion. Politics refuses to be subdued. But the politics of the drafting process has to date been largely elite-dominated, non-participatory, and non-transparent. The discourse of transplantation and transition is dangerous and in need of critical challenge precisely because it operates to obscure the face and mute the force of politics in drafting. It draws attention away from the messiness of process, when the messiness is what needs to be foregrounded. What legislative reconstruction needs is more politics, not less: the expansion of participation, the volubility of contest. From this perspective, it would be no small contribution to the process of legislative reform in Kazakhstan, as elsewhere in the fSU, if commentators and analysts examining drafting began to attend to politics and process with the same care they have lavished hitherto on the more strictly jurisprudential concerns of technique and product.

REFERENCES

Clark, G, 'Pension systems: a comparative perspective,' Banking and Financial Institutions Abstracts, Working Paper Series 7/18 (2000), Financial Economics Network (FEN), a division of Social Science Electronic Publishing (SSEP) and Social Science Research Network (SSRN)

Dahan, F and Dine, J, 'Transplantation for transition: benefits and limits of comparative law in legislative drafting in Russia,' Paper presented to the W G Hart Legal Workshop, Institute of Advanced Legal Studies, London, 2000 (cited with the authors' permission)

Iliasova, K M, 'Pravovoie regulirovanie priznaniia niesostoiatel'nosti sub'iektov priedprinimatel'snoskoi deiatel'nosti' (1994) 2 Biznes i pravo v Kazakshtanie

Mandel, R, 'Marshall Plan of the mind: soap opera in Kazakhstan,' in Ginsburg, F, Abu-Lughod, L and Larkin, B (eds), The Social Practice of Media, forthcoming, Berkeley: University of California Press

Offe, C, 'Capitalism by democratic design? Democratic theory facing the triple transition in East Central Europe', in Offe, C, Varieties of Transition: The East European and East German Experience, 1996, Cambridge: Polity Press

Osakwe, C, 'Anatomy of the 1994 Civil Codes Russia and Kazakhstan: a biopsy of the economic constitutions of two post-Soviet republics' (1998) 73:5 Notre Dame Law Review 1413-1514

Queisser, M, 'Pension reform: lessons from Latin America,' OECD Policy Briefs 15 (1999)

Waelde, T and Gunderson, J, 'Legislative reform in transition economies: western transplants: short-cut to social market economy status?', in Seidman, A, Seidman, R B and Waelde, T (eds), *Making Development Work: Legislative Reform For Institutional Transformation And Good Governance*, 1999, London, Boston, The Hague: Kluwer Law International, 84-90

CONSTITUTIONAL OPTIONS FOR THE SETTLEMENT OF THE SRI LANKAN PROBLEM

Lakshman Marasinghe[*]

Minority, ethnic, fundamental and human rights have become the acute concerns of nations across the world, from China to Chile and from Alaska to Australia. Military solutions to these problems have proved short-lived because underlying ethnic problems left unattended or attended to exclusively by force have a tendency to compound. Human history has shown that nations enveloped by ethnic conflicts have—even after many, many years of conflict—returned to negotiation to work out a constitutional arrangement within which bullets may be exchanged for ballots, and conflicts may be replaced by constitutions. At such a juncture in a nation's history, when all else has failed, law takes the high road, and constitutional lawyers become its most favoured users. It is at such a stage that these constitutional structures and their hybrids become relevant, so as to provide the solution terrorism, turbulence and turmoil had failed to achieve.

Neither kings nor freedom fighters have any divine right to govern. Their rights must be derived from a compact between them and the subjects of their governance. That is why we need constitutions. The conditions that make constitutions necessary arise out of mistrust. Constitutions are therefore not built on trust. Constitutions should liberate and protect the good, but equally, they must restrain the bad. These are the two faces of a good constitution.[1]

This chapter considers several options for a constitutional settlement of Sri Lanka's ethnic dispute.[2] Each will be dealt with in outline, providing no more than a basis for further research and cogitation. Each constitutional structure has its own strengths and weaknesses, and has the potential of sprouting many hybrids. The constitutional structures discussed here are in no way presented as perfect paradigms. Some of them have been put into practice in many parts of the world. In some cases they have succeeded in realising the desired goals, elsewhere they have been thwarted by ingenious legal and political stratagems. Whether these constitutions succeed depends largely on the nature and extent of the commitment of the parties to the model, to the nation, and to the maintenance of peace and good government. In the absence of such a commitment, any conception of rights—majority, minority, fundamental or human—and even the constitution itself may remain incoherent, ineffective and illusory. A constitution is essentially a political testament. The raw material with which it is made is the socio-economic and political content of the society into which it is being introduced. And a constitutional lawyer is very much like a carpenter. Like the carpenter, the constitutional lawyer must put all parts of a constitution together using the available socio-economic material so that every part of the constitution will stick together.

---

[*] Emeritus Professor of Law, University of Windsor, Windsor, Ontario, Canada; Visiting Professor, University of New South Wales, Sydney, Australia; Barrister-at-Law of the Inner Temple and Attorney-at-Law.

[1] Similar views have been expressed by Mr Justice Albie Sachs, a Judge of the South African Constitutional Court, in his inaugural lecture upon being appointed to a Chair of Law at the University of the Western Cape, South Africa.

[2] Ponnambalam, 1983; Suriyakumaran, 1983; Gunasekera, 1996; Ratnatunga, 1998; Narayan Swamy, 1994; Jayawardene and Jayawardene, 1987.

Under Article 154 (L) the President is empowered, by Proclamation, to take back the executive powers and assume to him/herself all the functions of the administration of the province and all or any of the powers vested in, or exercisable by, the Governor—and declare that the powers of the Provincial Council shall be exercisable by, or under the authority of, Parliament '[and] make such incidental and consequential provisions as appear to the President to be necessary or desirable for giving effect to the objects of the Proclamation.' The President may apply these powers to suspend the activities of the Provincial Council when there is evidence to satisfy the President that 'a situation has arisen in which the administration of the Province cannot be carried on in accordance with the provisions of the Constitution.'

These indicate that both the executive and the legislative powers of a Provincial Council are subordinate powers, similar to those of Local Bodies. Local Bodies were given statutory powers at the time of their creation and are able to enact municipal by-laws which they could enforce through the ordinary courts of the land. The Provincial Councils appear to have no such powers. Their power to legislate within the areas allocated to them in Schedule Nine not exercisable other than through the centre—the President and Parliament.

A unitary system with a decentralised form of government is no more than a means by which the centre takes the administration of the island into the provinces, so that the executive powers held at the centre may be provincially administered. The Provincial Councils are subordinates of the central government, and the aforementioned provisions of the amended 1978 Constitution clearly establish that fact. The classical difference between a 'federation' and a 'unitary state with devolved power' is that in the former the central government and the regional governments are 'co-ordinates' while in the latter they are 'subordinates'. This difference will become clear when 'federalism' is discussed.

The core conception is that in a unitary state, of either type, the governmental powers are vested in one national authority. Of course there are local or municipal authorities within the national state with law-making powers applicable within their local or municipal territorial units. As will be seen, these local or municipal authorities differ from regions or provinces of a federation, in that the former are subordinates of the national or federal authority, while the latter are not. The powers of a municipal or any other local authority may be taken away, altered or controlled by the national authority. This invariably occurs when local government is reorganised. These comments apply equally to local or municipal authorities found in federations. There the local bodies and municipal councils are subordinates of the regional authorities.

These two unitary structures—with devolved powers and without devolved powers—do not, in my view, provide a sufficient basis for a constitutional settlement of Sri Lanka's ethnic problem. It is therefore unnecessary to consider them further.

OPTION FROM FEDERALISM

A central distinguishing feature of a federation is that governmental powers are distributed between two co-ordinate authorities, a central authority represented by a 'central', 'national' or 'federal' authority, and two or more 'regional', 'provincial' or 'state' authorities.[14] The two authorities are co-ordinates and not subordinates. If they are subordinates then the ensuing constitutional structure is one of a unitary state with devolved powers.

---

[14]   Livingston, 1956; Wheare, 1963; and Verney, 1996.

The powers of the regional authority are not those that have been granted by the federal authority. If they have been granted by the federal authority then, again, the ensuing constitutional structure will be a unitary state with devolved powers and not a federation. Similarly, the powers of the federal authority are not those granted by the regional authorities. The two sets of powers—at the federal level and at the regional level—are powers that had been allotted to each of these authorities or governmental bodies, by the constitution at the time at which the federation was established. As much as these powers do arise from the constitution and from no other source, neither the federal parliament nor the regional parliaments have the power to take away, alter or control the powers of each other. Any such changes must be the result of a change of the fundamental document—the constitution—according to the methods therein prescribed for constitutional change.

In contrast, the UK government has established elected assemblies for Scotland, Wales and Northern Ireland. They were established under legislation[15] passed by the UK Houses of Parliament. Such legislation is subject to the power of the same parliament to amend, repeal or replace the legislation. In that sense the UK is not a federation. The Assemblies of Scotland, Wales and Northern Ireland are subordinate bodies and function as delegates of the UK Parliament, exercising a measure of delegated powers.

In a federation there are two levels of government to which persons are subjected. The federal parliament enacts laws within its specified areas of competency which apply nationally to all regions. The regional parliaments enact laws which apply exclusively to the regions. In some writings on federalism, the federal laws have been referred to as 'higher law.' This is meant to explain the fact that whenever there is a conflict between a federal law (national) and a regional law, the federal law prevails. This occurs in the Dominion of Canada[16] where some of the powers of the Federal Parliament and of the Provincial Parliaments overlap.[17] The framers of a federal constitution must always pay particular attention to avoid overlapping of powers between the federal and regional authorities. Doing so minimises the arena of federal-regional conflicts.

The word 'co-ordinate' does not necessarily mean that there is equality of wealth, power, authority or status between the federal and the regional authorities. Rather, it means that constitutional law views the two levels of government as two separate bodies having complete and untrammelled power to legislate and execute in the areas designated for each by the constitution. Federal constitutions may give such powers to the regions, even to the point that the regions acquire the constitutional appearance of separate countries. In these cases, the federation can come close to disintegration. At the other end of the spectrum, the powers of a federal authority might come to resemble a unitary state, again risking disintegration of the federation. It is clearly essential to maintain a balance between the centre and the regions when framing a federal constitution.

---

[15] Scotland Act 1998; Government of Wales Act 1998; Northern Ireland Act 1998.

[16] British North America Act, s 91 (legislative authority of Parliament of Canada) and s 92 (subjects of exclusive provincial legislation).

[17] 'It has been frequently recognised by this Board, and it may now be regarded as settled Law, that according to the scheme of the North America Act the enactments of the parliament of Canada, in so far as these are within its competency, must override provincial legislation. But the Dominion Parliament has no authority conferred upon it by the Act to repeal directly any provincial statute, whether it does or does not come within the limits of jurisdiction prescribed by s 92. The repeal of a provincial Act by the Parliament of Canada can only be effected by repugnance between its provisions and the enactments of the Dominion; and if the existence of such repugnance should become a matter of dispute, the controversy can not be settled by the action either of the Dominion or of the provincial legislature, but must be submitted to the judicial tribunals of the country,' per Lord Watson, p 366.

The allocation and distribution of legislative and executive powers and the administration of justice must be clearly outlined within any federal constitution. This is particularly important because a citizen of a federation is subject to two levels of government which are to varying degrees legally independent of each other. Unless a federal constitution is carefully drafted, central and regional powers may overlap. As mentioned before, any such conflicts will be decided in favour of the federalist, rather than the regional, interpretation of the exercise of that power.[18] Canadian law is silent as to how an exercise of overlapping powers between the Dominion and Provincial Parliaments might be dealt with. However, the courts have made it abundantly clear that in such an event the Dominion Parliament shall prevail.[19] A similar effect is achieved by the Australian Constitution, which reads, 'Where a law of a state is inconsistent with a law of the Commonwealth, the latter shall prevail, and the former shall, to the extent of the inconsistency, be invalid.'[20]

Centripetal and centrifugal federalism

Provision relating to financial arrangements and social and economic matters should be carefully stated in terms of federal and regional powers. In these areas, together with the overlapping provisions previously mentioned, opportunities may arise for federal intrusions into regional spheres of activity. It is fundamental to a federal constitution that there is an element of interdependence between the federal and regional authorities. If federal powers completely overlap with regional powers, it might be a misnomer to call such a country federal. Similarly, if the financial arrangements are such that the regions fall totally under the control of the federal government, such a constitutional structure cannot be called a federation. There is always some overlapping of legislative and executive powers within a federal state, some degree of financial control at the federal level, and some degree of federal intrusion in socio-economic matters into the regions. All these are inevitable. But where the overlapping of legislative and executive powers are incomplete, where the scope of federal control of finances is limited and the federal intrusion into the regions regarding socio-economic matters is marginal, the federal system of government remains. Depending on the extent to which such intrusions occur, the resulting constitutional structure may be one of a centrifugal or a centripetal federal structure.

In cases such as Canada, where a large measure of legislative and executive power has moved to the federal authority at the centre, the structure is referred to as a 'centripetal' federation. Federations at the other end of the spectrum, such as Australia and the United States, which give a large measure of legislative and executive power to the regions, are described as 'centrifugal'. So long as the constitutional structure maintains that the federal and the regional governments are each co-ordinate and independent, then there is a federation.

---

[18] At 149, *per* Strong C J, '... although the British North America Act contains no provisions declaring that the legislation of the Dominion shall be supreme as in the case in the constitution of the United States, the same principle is necessarily implied in our constitutional Act (BNA Act), and is to be implied whenever, in the many cases which may arise, the Federal and Provincial legislatures adopt the same means to carry into effect distinct powers.'

[19] The relevant Canadian legislation is the British North America Act. 'There can be a domain in which Provincial and Dominion legislation may overlap in which case neither legislation will be *ultra vires* if the field is clear, but if the field is not clear and the two legislations meet, the dominion legislation must prevail.'

[20] Commonwealth of Australia Constitutional Act 1900, s 109.

The 'constitutional symbiosis' hybrid

As mentioned above, there must always be an element of interdependence between the federal and the regional authorities. If this interdependence were to evaporate, so would the claim to be a federation. One way to prevent such a transition from centrifugal federalism to separate states is to introduce 'hugging' devices into the constitutional framework. These produce a symbiotic relationship between the two levels of authority, the federal and the regional authority.

In order to achieve this relationship, legislative and executive competence is allocated in one of four ways, according to the category of law in question. The first category of laws is those which the federal parliament is to create, and the federal executive authority is to implement using the federal bureaucracy.[21] These laws will be applicable throughout the nation. The second category is laws where both the legislative and the executive competency are located in the Regional Assemblies.[22] These are applicable within the territorial limits of the region. The third and the fourth categories of laws are those where the legislative competency is to be found in one body, and their implementation is left within the competency of the other, using its own separate bureaucracies.[23] So, where the legislative competency is found at the federal level, they will be implemented at the regional level, using its bureaucracy, and vice-versa.

This constitutional structure is most effectively used in the Swiss Constitution. The 'hugging' or symbiotic relations have the power to maintain a strong bond between the federal and the regional structures of government.

Swiss confederalism

Confederalism may be traced back to August 1 1291 when three small independent communities in middle Europe—Uri, Schwyz and Nidwalden—freely negotiated an 'everlasting' alliance to form the Swiss confederation.[24] Since then, the membership in the Swiss confederation has expanded into 22 sovereign cantons and six half cantons. A confederation is made when sovereign and independent communities agree to delegate some of their sovereign powers to the central government for the period of the confederacy. The difference between a federation and a confederation lies in the fact that in the former, the federal government and the regional governments are co-ordinates, not subordinates; while in the latter, the central government is a delegate of the regional governments and in that sense, subordinate to the regional governments.

It is important to emphasise that the confederate subordination of the central government means that regional governments retain the power to resume the delegated powers—that is, to withdraw from the confederation at will. The sovereignty at the centre is that sovereignty delegated to it by the sovereign and independent members of the confederation. When exercising the power to resume those delegated powers, including the power to reclaim the sovereignty that it had previously delegated to the central government, the community leaves the confederation as an independent and sovereign community. No further act is needed

---

[21]   Swiss Constitution, Art 34 (3).
[22]   *Ibid*, Arts 32 (4) and 34 (1).
[23]   *Ibid*, Arts 32, 40 and 50.
[24]   Dessemontet and Ansay, 1983, Chapter 1.

under the rules of public international law in order to allow for recognition of that community as an independent and sovereign state.[25]

A 'confederation' was established by the American colonies under the Articles of Confederation of 1777. Under that arrangement the central government became merely a delegate of the American colonies comprising of the Southern states—South of the Mason-Dixon Line. The central government thereby became a subordinate of the states. However, the constitution adopted by the United States of America at the end of the revolutionary war in 1787 moved away from a confederation. Instead, a federal constitution was introduced, under which the federal government was made independent of the states and co-ordinate with them.[26]

The residual sovereignty of the cantons—that which remains of its original sovereignty after delegation or transfer to the federal government—is recognised throughout the Constitution. Article 3 of the Swiss Constitution declares that the cantons are 'sovereign in so far as their sovereignty is not limited by the federal constitution, and, as such, they exercise all rights which are not transferred to the federal Power.' The sovereignty which the Swiss confederation exercises is the sovereignty delegated to it by the cantons, which are the territorial governmental units that form the Swiss confederation. Article 3 goes on to state that 'The confederation guarantees to the cantons their territory, their sovereignty within the limits of Article 3 of the Constitution.' Article 9 allows cantons to use their remaining sovereignty to conclude treaties 'with foreign powers upon the subjects of public economic regulation, cross-frontier intercourse, and police relations; but such treaties shall contain nothing repugnant to the confederation, or to rights of other cantons.'

Any secession of a canton under the Swiss Constitution must be through a constitutional amendment under the provisions contained in Articles 118-123. At that point, the canton secedes and the sovereignty of the confederation is reduced.

THE FRENCH BI-CEPHALOUS EXECUTIVE

The Constitution of the Fifth French Republic provides a 'dyarchy' or 'bi-cephalous executive',[27] within the frontiers of a unitary state. Executive powers and functions are shared—albeit unequally—between the President (directly elected for seven years) and the Prime Minister (appointed by the President).[28]

The Prime Minster makes recommendations for the appointment of the members of the Cabinet, none of whom may be members of the National Assembly.[29] However, they are responsible to the National Assembly to the extent that it can, by means of a vote of no-confidence, have them removed from their posts.[30] If the Prime Minister is not able to command the confidence of the National Assembly, he of she will not be able to function as a Prime Minster, and must resign.[31]

---

[25] Hogg, 2001, pp 106-7; Kennedy, 1938, pp 401-11; Swiss Constitution, Art 3.
[26] Kennedy, 1938.
[22] Winterton, 1994, pp 57-67.
[28] Art 8.
[29] Constitution of 1958, Art 23.
[30] *Ibid*, Art 49.
[31] *Ibid*, Art 50.

It is the Prime Minister—not the President—who is responsible for determining and directing state policy. The Government (Prime Minister and the Cabinet) shall determine and conduct national policy, have the administration and the army at its disposal, and shall be answerable to Parliament, which consists of the National Assembly and the Senate.[32] The Prime Minister directs the business of the Government, and is responsible for national defence and for the enforcement of laws.[33] The Prime Minister is responsible for the appointment of persons to civil and military services and the executive rule making powers.[34] But the Prime Minister must present the government's programme, or a statement of general policy, to the National Assembly and obtain a vote of confidence.[35]

The Constitution designates the President as the guarantor of the nation's independence and territorial integrity, and of the proper functioning of public authorities.[36] He or she may present for referendum any bill concerning the organisation of public authorities, requiring the approval of a community agreement, or providing for authorisation to ratify a treaty if, without being contrary to the Constitution, the bill would affect the functioning of its institutions.[37] The President also presides over the Council of Ministers,[38] and signs legislation and decrees into law matters deliberated and adopted upon by that Council.[39]

Some executive powers are shared between the various organs of the state. For example, the President may, after consulting the Prime Minister and the presidents of the two chambers of Parliament, dissolve the National Assembly and call for fresh elections.[40] Similarly, the President is the head of the army and presides over higher committees of national defence,[41] but when national security is threatened, the President must consult with the Prime Minister, the presidents of the two chambers of Parliament, and the Constitutional Council before declaring a state of emergency.[42] Indeed, Article 19 requires the Prime Minister or other appropriate minister to countersign all Presidential decrees except those relating to the appointment of the Prime Minister, dissolution of the National Assembly, exercise of emergency powers, matter relating to referendums, and the appointment of the Constitutional Council. Outside of these exceptions, the two executive branches of government must act together approving, and bearing equal responsibility for, all executive acts. Thus, the division of executive powers between the President and the Prime Minister requires, as Prime Minister Chaban-Delmas noted, 'a close and almost intimate relation between the President and the Prime Minister and an almost total confidence in each other'.[43]

Furthermore, De Gaulle's successor, President Pompidou, remarked that the French constitutional framework 'is half-way between a regime squarely presidential and a regime squarely parliamentary.'[44] The President has powers to legislate by decrees in all areas other than those areas which the Constitution leaves to the legislative competency of the National

---

32   *Ibid*, Art 20.
33   *Ibid*, Art 21.
34   *Ibid*, Art 22.
35   *Ibid*, Art 49.
36   *Ibid*, Art 5.
37   *Ibid*, Art 11.
38   *Ibid*, Art 9.
39   *Ibid*, Art 13.
40   *Ibid*, Art 12.
41   *Ibid*, Art 15.
42   *Ibid*, Art 16.
43   Winterton, 1994, p 58.
44   *Ibid*, p 59.

Assembly. It is interesting to note that by restricting the legislative competency of the National Assembly, the French Constitution has widened the legislative competency of the executive branch of government through decrees, albeit to be countersigned by the Prime Minister.

SOME REFLECTIONS

Any future Sri Lankan constitution must be carefully crafted within the historical, political and cultural (which includes the religious) perspectives upon which the ethnic conflict was founded. There are a number of benchmarks that a new constitution must therefore provide, if such a document is to dispel the fears and promote the aspirations of all persons to whom it applies—whether residents on or visitors to the island.

In the view of the present government, there shall not be the division of the island into two separate states, both claiming to be independent and sovereign. That is, there shall not be a 'mitosis of the original sovereignty' of Sri Lanka. 'Original sovereignty' refers to the 'sovereignty' received at independence. If two separate states were to be established through a constitutional—rather than military—process, the original sovereignty of Sri Lanka would have to go through a process of mitosis.

The LTTE has not abandoned its quest for a sovereign state.[45] It has agreed to discuss options for the final constitutional structure, and to that extent the matter remains open. It is likely that, rather than pursuing their idea of a separate Eelam state, the LTTE might opt for a confederation. Thus a separate state would be established, but within confederation of sovereign states. For the confederacy model to take root, the original sovereignty—now found in the 1978 Constitution—must *first* undergo a process of mitosis. In the eyes of the law, this would amount to recognition of a separate state of Eelam, which would then join with a territorially-diminished state of Lanka, to form the confederation of Sri Lanka. The sovereignty of the Sri Lankan confederation would be thereafter be delegated' from the two constituent parts of the confederation—Lanka and Eelam—as from the cantons of the Swiss confederation. As mentioned above, the sovereignty inherited by the two parts of the confederation is not destroyed; and what is delegated to the confederacy may be withdrawn and taken away at any time by any one of the constituent parts of the confederation.

The constitutional structure of a confederation may become an attractive proposition for the LTTE in the light of the premise upon which the negotiations are to be held—namely the abandonment of the idea of creating a separate state. However, the government may reject this line of constitutional development as the confederation model poses the danger that it might be used as an alternative path to establishing a separate Tamil state of Eelam.

Under the 'centrifugal' model, powers move from the central government to the regions. Here there is 'devolution', rather than 'mitosis', of sovereignty. Once this basic structure is agreed upon, the details regarding the transfer of specific powers from the centre to the regions may be worked out. Depending on the extent and nature of the powers that are devolved, the resulting federation takes the shape and form of a 'centrifugal' or 'centripetal' federalism. In either case, the centre will retain most of the powers. The federal structure is flexible enough to provide greater latitude for power sharing and for the creation of bodies that are 'co-ordinate'—rather than the 'subordinate' bodies found in a unitary state with devolved powers. Both sovereignty and its concomitant executive powers will be devolved to these co-ordinate bodies. In order that the relationship between the centre and the regions

---

[45]   Media Conference held at Kilinochchi, Sri Lanka, April 10, 2002.

might be kept close and intact, one may consider the federal hybrid of a constitutional 'symbiosis'.

The versatility of the federal structure is such that it could very conveniently accommodate the French model of a slate of executive powers divided between the President and the Prime Minister. For the purposes of peace, it is most important that minorities are absorbed into praxis of governance. Therefore a number of constitutional structural options may arise if a federal form of government was adopted and modified by the application of the principle of constitutional symbiosis and the French model of the bi-cephalous executive. By creating presidential powers to make law by decree in areas not reserved for Parliament—as under the French Constitution—it might possible to use the presidency to forge an axis with Parliament at the centre, and the regional bodies at the periphery. Sovereignty of the federation could then be shared among three distinct bodies—president and parliament at the centre, and the regions. A third avenue for engaging several ethnic and religious groups, as participants in the process of governing the island, would have to be created. The dyarchy recognised at the centre (Parliament and the Presidency) in the French Constitution could be enlarged to include a third unit at the level of the regions, in order to accommodate the Sinhalese, Tamils (including the Eastate Tamil community) and Muslims in the governance process.

I have attempted only to provide some of the constitutional structural options available for a new constitutional document. The categories mentioned here are not closed, but they, and any combinations thereof, may be more relevant than others and may therefore merit some further attention.

REFERENCES

British North America Act, 30 & 31 Vict C 3

Commonwealth of Australia Constitutional Act 1900

Constitution of Sri Lanka 1972

Constitution of the Democratic Socialist Republic of Sri Lanka 1978

Dessemontet, F and Ansay, T (eds), *Introduction to Swiss Law*, 1983, Amsterdam: Kluwer Law International

Government of Wales Act 1998 (UK)

Gunasekera, S L, *Tigers, Moderates and Pandora's Package*, 1996, published by the author, Colombo

Hogg, P W, *Constitutional Law of Canada*, 2001, Canada: Carswell

Jayawardene, C H S and Jayawardene, H, *Terror in Paradise*, 1987, Canada: Crimcare

Kennedy, W P M, *The Constitution of Canada (1534 -1937)*, 2nd Edition, 1938, Oxford: OUP

Livingston, W S, *Federalism and Constitutional Change*, 1956, Oxford: Clarendon Press

Marasinghe, M L, 'Recent developments in Sri Lanka on the freedom of expression' (2000) 33 Verfassung Und Recht In Ubersee 157

Narayan Swamy, M R, *Tigers of Lanka: From Boys to Guerrillas* 1994, Delhi: Kornark Publishers

Northern Ireland Act 1998 (UK)

Ponnambalam, S, *Sri Lanka: The National Question and the Tamil Liberation Struggle*, 1983, London: Zed Books

Ratnatunga, S, *Politics of Terrorism: The Sri Lanka Experience*, 1998, Melbourne: IFSED

Scotland Act 1998

Suriyakumaran, C, *The Anguish of '83*, 1983, Colombo: K V G de Silva

Verney, D V, 'Federalism, federative systems and federations: United States and India', in Balveer, A and Verney, DV, *Multiple Identities in a Single State: Indian Federalism in Comparative Perspective*, 1996, New Delhi: Kornak

Wheare, K C, *Federal Government*, 1963, London: OUP

Winterton, G, *Monarchy to Republic*, 1994, Melbourne: OUP

CHAPTER 13

THE SINGAPORE MODEL OF LAW AND DEVELOPMENT: CUTTING THROUGH THE COMPLEXITY

Andrew Harding and Connie Carter[*]

The 'law and development' movement has been unreasonably preoccupied with the problems rather than the solutions to the kinds of complexity of law and economic development that this book explores. Historically, the movement has taken a dismal view of the world, and as problems are actually solved the movement seems to redefine its remit to encompass problems which have not been solved, taking care not to indulge itself in investigation of precisely why things which have gone right have in fact gone right. As its ideas and remit change, the world is re-explained to coincide with these ideas. Learning from brute facts is only allowed, it seems, where the facts fit the hypothesis, but not where they contradict it. In this way the law and development movement is rather like the psychiatrist who is good at diagnosing mental illness, but has no idea how mental well-being can come about other than through the absence of mental illness.

There is no more obvious example of this tendency than in its attitude to the countries of East and South East Asia. Right from the beginning, these regions have been neglected by the law and development movement, presumably because the specialised nature and conceptions of law in those regions is opaque to the scrutiny of the discipline, and therefore regarded as a one-off case. The more these countries develop economically the less they are seen as containing lessons or fields of study for law and development. After all, states such as Singapore, South Korea, Hong Kong and Taiwan are no longer regarded as 'developing' (answering instead to their Reagan administration name 'NICs' or 'newly industrialised countries'), and soon they may be joined by Malaysia and Thailand. Perhaps there is also a hint that if the lessons were learned they would not fit the currently authorised version of law and development.

Whatever the reasons, this approach is entirely mistaken. It omits consideration of successful examples and how they might be applied elsewhere. It also assumes a difference and distinctness about East and South East Asia that masks the enormous differences in the law and development experience of the region. Development is a phenomenon to be examined in a broad context over long periods of time, and is not to be judged by economic and social statistics alone. In relation to law, improvement and solid results are notoriously hard to achieve because of the particular relationship between law and slippery factors such as culture, tradition and practice. Whereas the UK government department involved in this area,

[*] Andrew Harding is Professor of Law, Department of Law, School of Oriental and African Studies (SOAS), University of London. Dr Connie Carter is a Barrister, sometime Visiting Lecturer at SOAS, and currently a Visiting Professor of Law at the MBA Centre, Xiamen University, People's Republic of China. The authors would like to record in this note the debt they owe to the recipient of this book, Dr Peter Slinn. It was Peter, who as a leading figure in law and development in the 1980s and 1990s, first drew Andrew Harding's attention to the law and development literature, which inspired much of Andrew's later writing on SE Asia, and resulted in him developing, with Professor Jan-Michiel Otto, the London-Leiden Series on Law, Administration and Development. Connie Carter, as an undergraduate, was a member of Peter's law and development class at SOAS, and was inspired by him to take up law and development as the topic of her PhD thesis, which was supervised by Andrew Harding and is now published (Carter (2001)). In a neat circle, Connie later taught Peter's SOAS Law and Development class herself. Peter's perspectives and concerns in the field have been passed on by Andrew and Connie, jointly and severally, to students, scholars and lawyers in many countries, including the UK, the USA, the Netherlands, Singapore, Malaysia, and the PRC.

the Department for International Development (DfID), prefers 'interventions' which are 'SMART' (short, measurable, achievable, realistic and time-limited), the reality is that, for legal reform in most countries, effective intervention is more likely to be long-term, incalculable, uncertain, idealistic and continuing—such real-life complexities leave little room for neat acronyms.

In the case of Singapore the intervention has not been from outside, but has been orchestrated by the government itself in a series of economically, socially and politically premeditated policies involving extensive use of legal techniques and innovations. These interventions have been 'smart', not in the DfID sense, but in the sense of being carefully designed to achieve specifically set goals, to hit their target with unerring precision and little collateral damage. No other society discussed in this book or elsewhere has made more thorough and successful use of law *for* development, at least if one defines development in purely economic terms. Singapore is without doubt the world's most regulated society, and of the societies studied here, the one that best exhibits, not the 'rule-of-law' approach discussed by David Kennedy,[1] but the instrumentalist's 'rule-*by*-law' approach. In this sense there must be lessons to be drawn from Singapore's experience of moving with extreme rapidity from colonial outpost and outcast with no natural resources to one of the world's wealthiest nations, as judged by almost any relevant criterion, and one of the most stable.

However, at the same time, some hold the view that, while the above statements are true, and Singapore has indeed won the coveted economic prize, the very rigour of law enforcement and social engineering, and the inexorable subordination of everyone and everything to the common goal of economic development, has probably, in the end, proved strangely self-defeating. Creativity, spontaneity, flexibility and intuitiveness—ingredients necessary for individual problem-solving skills and for finding the independent innovative solutions required in the new biotechnology era may inadvertently have been 'cloned out' of Singaporeans by the social engineers. Thus at the close of the 20th century, the Singapore model may well have reached the end of its utility and a new model may be required to achieve sustainable progress in the 21st. Even official sources reflect this concern. Indeed recent statements by the author of the original Singapore model, Senior Minister Lee Kuan Yew, lament that in the process of development, something of the natural creativity, flexibility, intuitiveness, and individual motivation of the Singaporean citizenry has been sacrificed. The complacency and docility that have replaced vibrancy, resilience and creativity might now in themselves be obstacles to continued successful development. Herein lies the complexity that we must confront in examining the Singapore model.

HISTORY, LAW AND SOCIAL DISCIPLINE

Ever since Sir Stamford Raffles alighted at Singapore in 1819, Singapore has been a byword for firm government. In his brief sojourns in Singapore Raffles laid down many of the principles by which Singapore is still being governed: an economically ambitious policy of free trade, in particular a free port and local manufacture; the recruitment of Singapore's many ethnic communities behind government policies; law and order; cleanliness; attention to detail; purposeful administration; centralisation of power. Raffles was motivated not only by utilitarianism, but also by humanitarianism. This latter aspect of his policy has also been fulfilled, if only in part. Still, Raffles would no doubt be pleased with Singapore's prosperity

---

[1]   See his chapter in this volume.

and comfortable environment, the expansion and efficacy of its trade, manufacture, education, health care, public services and social institutions, and the stability and cohesion of its multi-racial society.

To a large extent Singapore's history, policy and legal system have been determined by geopolitics. The Singapore of what we might call 'the Lee Kuan Yew era' (1959 to the present)[2] has largely been preordained by an accident of history that resulted in the failure of its federation within Malaysia (1963-5). It is possible that much of what follows here would have been true even if federation had succeeded. However, the casting out of Singapore into the unpredictable political environment of 1960s South East Asia has resulted in its leaders' recognition that Singapore is a potentially vulnerable city-state with a racial make-up which differs greatly from all the surrounding countries. Indeed it was this racial difference, as well as some economic and political factors, which hastened Singapore's departure from the Malaysian Federation in 1965.

The ideology put forward by Lee and other leaders since then has been that Singapore has only the intelligence and discipline of its workforce, and no hinterland of rice-*padi* and rich natural resources to fall back on, as Malaysia, Thailand, China and Indonesia have. Its only route to survival, let alone sustainable economic prosperity, has therefore been to exploit the advantage of its geographic position, invest in and build a seamless infrastructure that provides goods and services to others, and to be the prime regional management headquarters location for multi-national corporations. Singapore is too small and vulnerable to withstand the shock waves of a genuinely open society, and it must therefore maintain a rigid policy of social discipline and clearly defined, forcefully implemented, social objectives. The choices are transparently but forcefully presented as clear but inescapable. Those who dislike making the choice emigrate; those who stay do exactly as they are told. Democracy is expressed only in terms of 'majoritarianism', not in terms of public participation in decision-making processes. This siege mentality is reinforced by, for example, the continuation of national service and reservist training, even though there is no military threat to Singapore. Attempts have also been made to enlist Confucianism, and latterly 'core values'[3] as a guiding philosophy, but this has had limited success.

The ideology of social discipline has profoundly affected the development of the law and the law relating to development in Singapore. Economic success being described as the only feasible option for Singapore, social stability has been regarded as the most indispensable condition of growth. Law has therefore been seen primarily as an instrument of social engineering rather than as the expression of a particular balance of principles defined politically or culturally and regarded as the embodiment of a politically neutral justice. The 'rule of law' doctrine has received a particular objective-based interpretation: this concept has been recruited or co-opted in aid of social discipline, but is essentially two-dimensional, containing no real notion of the state itself being bound to observe limits on its sphere of activity. However, in Singapore, this issue has not been fudged as it has elsewhere. Legality is expressed specifically to encompass the protection of commercial and property rights but not

---

[2]   In 1990 Lee stepped down as Prime Minister after 29 years, but since then, under the leadership of Goh Chok Tong as Prime Minister, Singapore clearly still follows all the principal points of Lee's policy, even if some slight differences in style of Government can be detected. As Senior Minister in the Prime Minister's Department, Lee still clearly exercises great influence. Lee himself has described his position as that of a goalkeeper rather than a centre forward. It seems likely that the political succession will devolve onto Lee's son, Brig-Gen Lee Hsien Loong, presently the Deputy Prime Minister.

[3]   That is, 'Asian' values common to the Chinese, Malay/Muslim and Indian communities.

'constitutionalism', or 'multi-party democracy', or 'human rights', and other such 'civic' matters.

From most points of view, Singapore does not conform to the currently valued norms of law and development or law and governance ideologies. Yet the Singapore model has worked splendidly insofar as it has delivered consistently high economic growth,[4] so that Singapore is now one of the world's most prosperous nations, and unlike other Asian development success stories, the outcome of growth has involved and benefited all sections of society, not only a small business and administrative elite. Social justice has been an important part of economic development, not just in terms of distribution but also in terms of mobilisation of human resources, the only 'natural' resources available to policy-makers. As Carter puts it, social justice is the glue that holds together the Singapore system of development.[5]

It is suggested here that the approach to law and development in Singapore is singularly 'instrumentalist'. This is not to say that instrumentalism is unique to Singapore; in fact all societies in some sense use law as an instrument of social engineering and economic growth. What is unique about Singapore is the extent to which this is the case. The hegemony of law seems nowhere as complete as in Singapore. Here we must understand law in terms of what Carter calls 'mature policy'.[6]

THE DEVELOPMENT OF LAW

After Stamford Raffles' establishment of the colony of Singapore in 1819, commerce brought with it Chinese, Indian and other immigrants from South East Asia and beyond. Commerce brings not only new ideas and values, carried by people freed from the traditional constraints of their own cultures, but also a motive for legal development: a degree of social stability and law and order is required; guarantees of private property and the honouring of promises; the legitimation and bolstering of institutions. The increase in population too, which in Singapore's case was an essential ingredient of prosperity, requires all these things.

Imperial policy required the introduction of the common law, achieved formally by Charter in 1826,[7] and then by the progressive development of legal institutions—courts, judges, lawyers, local legislation, police, and eventually a bureaucracy, taxation, elections to a representative legislature, constitutional government, and political independence.[8]

The most notable feature of Singapore's legal development during the Lee Kuan Yew era has been the growth of innovative statute law. Statutes have on the whole conferred administrative powers that go far beyond what is regarded as appropriate or necessary in most common-law countries. To the extent that Singapore has developed an indigenous legal system with its own peculiar features, these features are almost all exclusively uncommon in the extent to which they regulate social behaviour and contravene ordinarily accepted standards of individual rights. The legal system has become, in short, a purely statist, regulatory one. In this one can contrast the emerging legal systems of other developing

---

[4]   Singapore has experienced recessions, notably in 1985-86, and arguably 2000-01. Like the experiences of industrialised countries such dips in the economy are commonplace and do not derogate from the main thesis.

[5]   Carter, 2001, p 139.

[6]   *Ibid*, Chapter 5, and especially pp 160-162.

[7]   Bartholomew, 1985. For the significance of adopting the common law as opposed to the civil law from an economic development perspective, see Woo-Cummings, 2001.

[8]   Tan, 1989.

countries,[9] which although occasionally embodying laws comparable to Singapore's, have been essentially pluralistic in nature, and attempt to establish a balance of interests, assuming a diverse rather than a monolithic society, and assuming too that the state is essentially weak and struggling to control intractable problems. It is this divergence of statute law from the standard model, which one generally finds in common-law countries, that marks the autochthony of Singapore's legal system, and distinguishes it as an extreme example of legal instrumentalism.

On this basis we take a brief look, by way of example, at particular aspects of law in Singapore. It was Goh Keng Swee, Singapore's first Finance Minister during the Lee Kuan Yew era, who put a fine point on the issue:

> Singapore's economic policy differed from the laissez-faire policies of the colonial era. These had led Singapore to a dead end, with little economic growth, massive unemployment, wretched housing and inadequate housing. We had to try a more activist and interventionist approach.[10]

It is therefore apt to examine how the Singapore government intervened and dealt with the key factors of production, which economists say drive capital formation and therefore would support Singapore's economic growth. Due to the lack of space, only one factor, labour, will be used as an example.[11] For it was with deliberate and sustained state intervention particularly in this area that the problems of 'massive unemployment [and] wretched housing' were solved, and in so doing economic development was achieved progressively for nearly half a century. Naturally, labour laws were the wieldy tools.

LABOUR LAW AND INDUSTRIAL RELATIONS

The laws governing labour and industrial relations in Singapore during the post-1959 era can be divided into three clear and conceptually distinct phases, each characterised by its own unique set of problems to be solved and goals to be achieved. This fact and the priorities upon which the government chose to focus, in themselves underline and exhibit the use of law as an instrument in Singapore's economic development. The first phase extends from 1959, when the People's Action Party (PAP) formed the first postcolonial government, to 1965, when the Malaysian Federation failed. During this period the government's objectives were to defeat and immobilise the anti-PAP left-wing trade unions, minimise industrial conflicts (which during the decade after World War Two had been successfully orchestrated to help secure self-governance from the British), consolidate and force support for the PAP among moderate trade unions, and propel the trade union movement and the population towards acceptance of the new government's development policy, which at that time meant unerring support for federation with Malaya. It was thought then that Singapore's survival depended on it becoming part of larger single market within which it could supply goods and services.

The second phase is the era of modernisation, which dates from 1966 until 1972. The government's stated goals were first, to secure and maintain industrial peace and discipline (which as we shall see was tantamount to removing the right to strike), and second, to achieve 'restraint in wage negotiation and ... a greater awareness of social responsibility of organised

---

9   Singapore is of course no longer properly described as a developing country; we are speaking historically here.

10   Nair, 1976, p 84.

11   For a discussion of other factors of production, in particular land and capital, see: Carter, 2001, Chapters 7 and 8.

labour in the larger framework of the national interest'.[12] In other words, as we shall see, this goal essentially involved nationalising the trade unions and to all intents and purposes, prohibiting the free formation of alternative unions.

The third phase, which we can call the tripartite era, extends from 1972 until the present. It marks the period in which the objectives were to consolidate the government-forged links between labour, management and government, and move away from merely non-adversarial union-to-management relations to a more active co-operation for the effective control of wages, education and training, and sharing in national prosperity. Some have dubbed this phase state corporatism or societal corporatism or authoritarian corporatism; some exalt it, others denigrate it.[13] By whichever name and degree of success or failure, this phase might already be in the process of transformation and curtailment as Singapore seeks new ways of motivating the workforce in an attempt to create a new class of creative entrepreneurs and home-grown risk-takers.

Controlling the unions and defeating political rivals 1959-1965

Any analysis of the post-1959 labour laws must take its point of departure from the late colonial laws, 1940 to 1959, since they formed the basis from which the new nation would derive its policies: either choosing continuity or repeal. Indeed in the short term, the PAP government chose continuity. This is understandable since labour laws of the late colonial period were designed to curb trade union power, and after Singapore won self-governance this too became the policy of the new government. Three pieces of legislation were key: the 1940 Trade Union Ordinance, the 1940 Industrial Courts Ordinance, and the 1941 Trade Disputes Ordinance. The British used the Trade Union Ordinance to compel registration of unions and stringent regulation of the unions' internal affairs. When the government's refusal in 1948 to allow a May Day assembly ended in large-scale unrest, declaration of a state of emergency and the banning of the Malayan Communist Party, provisions of the Trade Union Ordinance were strengthened to deny registration to so-called agitators and to de-register and ban unions that were deemed 'unfriendly'. Many unionists and members of Singapore's Communist Party went underground, determined to fight colonialism and free Singapore. From 1950 to 1959, Lee Kuan Yew worked as a legal advisor of trade unionists and by 1954 he had formed the People's Action Party together with members of unions from both the moderate and left wing fractions. There was therefore very little difference between the Party and the unions in the early days of the PAP. Indeed the PAP's landslide victory in 1959 was secured not only by moderate and leftist unionists but also by Communist support. However victory meant that the PAP was free to start making a distinction. First and foremost was the job of creating a nationalistic trade union movement, free from the influence of Communists, but with a high degree of 'social justice'. The government pledged that it would be guided by the principle of 'industrial peace with justice'. Justice, it said, 'implies ensuring fair and just demands for a reasonable share of the fruits of their labour'.[14] The permanent, independent Court of Labour was founded in this spirit; its findings and awards were binding on employees and employers alike.

The amendments that rendered the 1940 Trade Union Ordinance into the 1959 Trade Union (Amendment) Act purported to remedy two shortcomings in the Ordinance. However,

---

12   Goh Keng Swee, 1972, p 103.
13   For further discussion, see Schmitter, 1974; Deyo, 1981; and Anantaraman, 1990.
14   Legislative Assembly Debates (Official Reports) Volume 11, column 8.

the Act merely widened the already wide discretionary powers of the registrar. Section 14 of the Act empowered the registrar to refuse to register any trade union, which was *likely* to be used against the interests of workmen, and to cancel the registration of any such union. From the previous legislation the registrar already had incredibly wide discretionary powers to refuse or cancel registrations, now new powers also imposed on the registrar an improper duty of prophecy! Since it was still not unlawful for companies to register so-called yellow (company) unions, which they used against genuine workers' unions, the validity of the registration of such unions was clearly at the sole discretion of the registrar. Under the Ordinance a union could be formed and registered with only seven members. This afforded a proliferation of registered unions, as registration of splinter groups and dissidents was easy. Section 15 of the Act therefore empowered the registrar to de-register or refuse to register a union if, in his opinion, it was necessary to do so in the interest of the workmen [*sic*], having regard to the existence of another union in the same trade, industry or occupation. Essentially this amendment denied workers their freedom of association since in practice it curtailed their right to establish or join a union of their choice. Choice rested with the registrar, not the workers. Under section 17, the registrar's decisions could be appealed to the Minister of Labour, but under section 18(2) the Minister's decision '… shall be final and shall not be called into question in any court'. In this purely statist administrative system, all decisions of the registrar and the Minister were denied judicial review. By reserving final decision on registration and de-registration of the unions for the Minister, the government took effective control of the formation and maintenance of the trade union movement.

The most original piece of labour legislation passed during the first phase was the Industrial Relations Act of 1960. It was in essence a legal transplant from Australia but the PAP government made many changes 'in the national interest' which reflected its more activist and instrumental approach. The Act, which comprised eight parts, provided for the regulation of relations between employees and employers, the prevention and settlement of trade disputes by collective bargaining, conciliation and arbitration. Part 2 provided for the establishment of Industrial Arbitration Courts, while the remaining parts dealt with collective bargaining procedures, conciliation, arbitration, awards, boards of inquiry, powers of the courts, and so on.

The procedures were complex administrative tangles of informality, which left final decisions to the Minister of Labour or the President of the Republic, though the distinction between their powers remained unclear. Representation of the parties by advocates or solicitors in an arbitration case was prohibited except in rare cases in which the Attorney-General intervened (section 62). For as the ex-lawyer Prime Minister Lee explained during the debate,

> … (advocates and solicitors) very often befog their clients. … [Instead it is] more likely that justice will be done if both employers and unions, through being naïve, honest and sincere, put forward points… in their respective cases, and that an intervention from the sometime skilful and sometimes less skilful advocate only helps to prolong and bedevil a proper and rapid conclusion of the hearing of an arbitration.[15]

It is also worth bearing in mind that the powers of the Industrial Arbitration Court were not absolute, for at any time during a procedure the Minister or the Attorney-General might intervene on behalf of the government and force a 'public interest' settlement. In a 1972 amendment to the Act, the Court was empowered to have regard 'not only to the interests of

---

[15] See Parliamentary Debates, Volume 12, column 310.

the persons immediately concerned but to the interests of the community as a whole and in particular the condition of the economy of Singapore …'.[16]

It is hard to find a clearer indication of communitarianism at work, of the state deliberately making the interests of private individuals surrender to those of the community as a whole for the sake of national economic development.[17] Throughout the period, the law or the machinery created by law was used to defeat the rivals of the PAP—that is, those unions that opposed federation with Malaya or opposed the official government policy of 'independence through merger'. For instance, the Citizenship Act deprived the leaders of many left-wing unions of their citizenship—especially those leaders who were pro-Communist. In July 1961 the frustrated left wing of the PAP resigned and formed the *Barisan Socialis* [Socialist Front] party. The trade union movement was also split into the moderate wing (which later became the National Trades Union Congress, NTUC) and the leftist wing, the Singapore Association of Trade Unions, SATU, which was registered in August 1961. By 1963, the government was ready to immobilise SATU, charging that it was dominated by communists, and to pave the way for merger with Malaya. The legal machinery worked overtime in actions against SATU leaders, leaders of *Barisan Socialis* and trade unions with left-wing sympathisers. Well over 100 pro-Communist and anti-merger leaders were detained without trial under the now infamous action 'Operation Cold Store', while seven SATU unions with well over 50,000 members were de-registered and dissolved. The Naval Base Workers' Union and the Singapore Harbour Staff Association, each with about 10,000 members, were also de-registered. At the same time, the NTUC was being treated favourably by the legal machinery, which had complete discretion in allowing preferential treatment in the administration and enforcement of labour laws, in particular in matters regarding registration of unions. This led to the consolidation and ascendancy of the NTUC as a *de facto* national trade union. The final step in nationalising the trade union movement came in 1966, following the failure of the federation between Singapore and Malaya in 1965. But that move was implemented at the beginning of the second wave of labour and industrial relations laws.

Singapore 'takes-off': the modernisation era 1966-1972

In 1966 the Trade Union Act was amended to provide for the regulation of the *qualifications* of those who could be appointed as trade union officials, and to curtail the right of workers to strike. The former provisions effectively brought the trade union movement into the secure cocoon of government, for the movement became almost a part of the official civil service, and the latter saw to it that strikes or industrial actions became a thing of the past in modern Singapore.

'Modernisation' in Singapore began in 1966. The period from 1966 to 1972 saw an unprecedented rate of growth, which was initiated and sustained by the implementation of government policies (which matured into laws) designed to secure and maintain industrial peace and discipline, achieve 'restraint in wage negotiation' and instil a greater sense of 'social responsibility of organised labour in the larger framework of the national interest'. When the four Bills designed to achieve these objectives were introduced into Parliament, the government had already secured the support of the leadership of the trade union movement in accepting its identification and definition of the economic woes facing the newly

---

[16] Section 34.
[17] Chuah Beng Huat, 1995.

independent nation and the cure and sacrifice that the government considered were imperative for its survival.

Of the labour laws introduced during this phase, the 1968 Employment Act is by far the most innovative and comprehensive. The Bill was controversial because of its draconian provisions regarding holidays, rest days, working hours and other conditions of service. However, it had an easy passage since there was no significant parliamentary opposition due to the *Barisan Socialis* having boycotted Parliament following the separation from Malaysia, and because the union leaders had already been pacified through the 'qualification' rule, which provided only government-friendly union leaders. Under sections 36 and 37(3) of the new Act an employee should have one rest day per week, but might be required to work on rest days or public holidays if he was paid double the ordinary rate. Subsection (3) of section 37 did not apply to those employed by government or a statutory body conducting essential services. Essential services were as defined by Part III of the Criminal Law Act, and in the Trade Disputes Act.

Section 38 of the Employment Act provided for a 44-hour working week, comprising a maximum of six consecutive hours without a period of leisure, and no more than eight hours per day including rest period(s) of not less than 45 minutes. Section 38(2) listed liberal exemptions to this rule. Employees were entitled to paid holiday subject to the schedule to the Holiday Act (Cap 307). However, an employee became ineligible for holiday if he absented himself from work without prior consent of the employer or without reasonable excuse on any working day immediately preceding or succeeding the public holiday. An employee was entitled to paid annual leave, in addition to rest days, holidays and sick leave (sections 36, 41 and 43) unless he absented himself without permission or reasonable excuse for more than 20percent of the working days in a year (section 42). The paid annual leave was seven days for every 12 months' continuous service with the same employer if employed for less than ten years. After ten years' service with the same employer, the employee became eligible for 14 days' paid holiday.

Under section 43, after one year of service with the same employer, an employee was eligible for 14 days paid sick leave and 46 days of hospitalisation in a year—subject to a medical certificate from a doctor appointed by the state or the company. Only an employee who had been in continuous service with the same employer for three consecutive years or more was entitled to retrenchment benefit on termination caused by redundancy or reorganisation (section 44). An employee was eligible for maternity leave if she had worked with the same employer for 180 days. Under section 45, only an employee who had worked for five years with the same employer was entitled to retirement benefit other than the benefits payable under the Central Provident Fund.

We have dealt with these provisions in some detail in order to give a flavour of the nature of the law: administrative, prescriptive, and discretionary. Indeed many of the provisions were so widely drawn that they were open to abuse by employers. For instance, it is plausible that an employer could terminate an employee's contract just before the deadline for reaching entitlement to retirement, retrenchment or maternity benefits, and so on. And recalling the lack of opportunity for judicial review of the decisions of the arbitration and conciliation bodies, one appreciates the true and monstrous strength of the system that had been created. However, during the parliamentary debate, the Prime Minister hoped that 'bad employers' would be educated and taught the facts of present-day industrial life so that they do not abuse their powers, but instead help the government put 'capital and labour to greater use'.[18]

---

[18] See Parliamentary Debates, Volume 27, column 639.

The 1960 Industrial Relations Act was also amended in 1968 in order to help create the conditions necessary to attract foreign investments, encourage industrial development, and generate much-needed employment opportunities, according to Labour Minister S Rajaratnam. Such 'necessary conditions' included increasing working hours, reducing work-related benefits, restricting trade union power in collective bargaining and making it unlawful for employees to strike in many areas listed in section 17. The Minister gave examples from statistics of strikes conducted during 1960 to 1967. Under the 1968 law nearly 60 per cent of those cases would now be unlawful. Similarly, several areas of personnel management were removed from the possibility of collective bargaining or negotiation because the Minister found them to be 'fundamental management functions' which should not be negotiable as they were the 'common-law rights' of employers. As statistics show, not only did the number of strikes and lockouts decrease, but foreign investors also flocked to Singapore during the period.[19] In 1968 there were only four work stoppages in Singapore and in 1969 there were none.

In an attempt to balance these draconian measures under which the workforce was completely controlled by the government through enforcement of the Employment Act and the Industrial Relations Act, in 1968 the Central Provident Fund [CPF] Act was amended (in the words of Minister Rajaratnam) 'to marshal domestic savings for the economic and social benefit of our people'. The law was a relic from the late colonial period, 1955. The idea then, as now, was to force employers and employees to contribute towards savings for pensions and other social welfare costs. The law compels participation and the government determines the appropriate level of contribution for each party, usually in the annual budget. The 1968 amendment provided for increased contributions by employers and employees over a three-year period starting at 6.5 per cent per party in the first year, moving to eight per cent, then to 10 per cent in the third year. In other words a total saving of 20 per cent per annum of each person's salary in the third year was put towards creating 'economic and social benefits for the people'. But the law also allowed members of the Fund to use their savings in the Fund for the purchase of houses or flats for their own occupation, and enabled the CPF provisions to be extended to cover persons who are self-employed and who do not at present contribute to the Fund. This 1968 amendment was a masterstroke and, in our view, the key to Singapore's success. Forced savings ensured that foreign investors contributed to the future growth and prosperity of Singapore. Those investors who were not motivated to reinvest in Singapore some of the large profits generated by the government-induced 'favourable' working environment (evidenced above) were compelled to do so indirectly through contributions to the CPF. Then, by allowing employees to use their CPF savings to purchase houses and flats or repay their mortgages, the amendment also allowed the Housing and Development Board to gain additional funding for investment in public housing. The objectives of solving the twin problems of 'massive unemployment and wretched housing' were being achieved through the mediation of labour laws. Besides, the high rate of savings that was forced by the law meant that Singapore did not need to build up a huge national debt or make itself vulnerable to the whims of foreign bankers, as was the case for most developing countries of the era. The government played the crucial role of intermediary between savers and investors by skilfully directing the accumulation and use of the rapidly increasing share of private-sector savings. Money was not squandered but invested in building the social and economic infrastructure, of providing social justice for all—the glue that kept the authoritarian system together by mediating the draconian rules and making them more 'acceptable'.

---

[19] For an eloquent account of Singapore's economic development, see Huff, 1997.

Harnessing the unions and encouraging them to establish and operate co-operatives for the benefit of workers and their families was another way in which the government forged a path that allowed ordinary citizens to share in the fruits of their labour, rather than indulging in the developing countries' disease of reserving such for the elite. In 1969 the Trade Union Act was amended to allow unions to use internal funds to fund co-operative ventures. Section 47 allowed the Finance Minister to declare by notification any object other than purely union matters to be an object for which union funds could be spent. The machinery that resulted from this innovative act grew into a massively successful institution, which now owns and operates supermarkets, dental and health care services, travel services, public transport and taxis, finance and insurance companies, and book and stationery retailing.

From the foregoing, it is clear that the period 1966 to 1972 was crucial for Singapore's economic development. The tremendous work and sacrifices put in during the period immediately after the failure of the merger with Malaya were repaid amply with success by 1971-72. For statistics show that by then there was full employment and relative to its base point, the population was well housed, well fed and relatively well educated. Labour laws represented by the Employment Act, the Industrial Relations Act, the Central Provident Fund Act and the Trade Unions Act were used specifically to engineer the working conditions and climate that the government perceived would be conducive to attracting foreign investment as required by its policy for rapid industrialisation. At the core were plans for stabilising labour costs at a low level, increasing productivity, eliminating labour unrest and replacing it with stability, discipline and industrial peace. The payback, as noted, was full employment and a share in the nation's prosperity for all citizens. All this would suggest that there is a positive correlation between labour laws and economic development. Indeed the Labour Minister himself was convinced that this was the case. He said: 'Suffice it to say, as a result of the passing of the Employment Act in 1968, there has been rapid economic development as we have been able to attract investments to this country and to solve what was ... regarded as the insoluble problem of unemployment in Singapore.'[20]

Despite the rhetoric and abundant evidence, it is difficult to show a direct causal link between the law and economic development, because it is impossible to isolate the role of law from the roles played by other factors. For instance, the communitarian spirit fostered among the population showed itself in the public's acceptance of the government's view that demands from labour and other special interest groups, if not curbed, were a direct serious threat to the survival of the vulnerable new nation. Unions were therefore not expected to play their traditional role of speaking up for the workers; instead they were required to show greater awareness of their social responsibility in the larger framework of the national interest. All that can be concluded is that by the end of this period, with the help of labour laws, Singapore had taken off. For the next 25-30 years, the government would make minor adjustments to these laws in order to increase, maintain and distribute the nation's wealth among its citizens. But the basic recipe for nurturing economic growth and redistributing accumulated wealth had been discovered and cultivated during the formative years when trade unions were united, co-opted, and then neutered, and their membership disciplined to serve the national interest. The next period focused on 'tweaking mechanisms', for in reality the nature, stance and purpose of labour laws did not change significantly after 1968.

---

[20]   Parliamentary Debates (Official Reports), Volume 32, column 1172.

Tripartism perfected

As discussed above, Singapore seemed to move from labour surplus to labour scarcity by 1972. In other words, by that date, mass unemployment had been transformed into full employment. In a free labour market (or so the free-marketers argue), the effect of full employment is that the market will automatically balance the scarcity of labour by causing a rise in the cost of labour. This mechanism is the invisible hand at work. However, the Singapore government would have none of it. Here too, it intervened to change the scenario to suit its developmental purposes. Two important actions were taken. First, it introduced a tripartite system for controlling a national wage policy. Second, it manipulated the size of the labour market by enacting more lenient immigration laws to admit a surge of 'guest-workers', by changing the retirement age to allow older workers to remain in the market, and by changing several laws relating to women and the family to provide incentives that would encourage women to enter or remain in the labour market. We will not dwell here on the intricacies of these measures. Suffice it to say that government, using law as the main instrument, but also through non-statutory means, effectively gained and maintained control of the labour market. We propose, however, to spend some space dealing with the non-statutory means, for these constitute a unique feature of Singapore's economic development.

Tripartism implies joint decision-making on economic matters between employers, unions and government at national and enterprise levels.[21] This mode of decision-making seems to have become part of Singapore's economic development equation by 1968. However, well before that, in 1960, there was a practice of having labour, management, and the government represented on the Economic Development Board, the Housing and Development Board and the Industrial Arbitration Court, as provided for under their respective 1960 Acts. Tripartism was also witnessed under the 1965 Charter for Industrial Progress, a government-sponsored agreement under which labour agreed to work jointly with management towards the shared goals of increased productivity and industrial peace. The NTUC, the Singapore Manufacturers' Association and the Singapore Federation ratified the Charter. Consequently, tripartite decision-making was commonplace when the government introduced the National Wages Council in February 1972. This was a non-statutory, advisory body charged with three objectives: to formulate annual wage guidelines; to recommend a wage adjustment policy; and to advise on suitable incentives. The government insisted that the Council's guidelines were to be recommendations only, and therefore not mandatory. However, in 1972 the Employment Act and section 34 of the Industrial Relations Act were amended to give legal effect to the National Wages Council system. Furthermore the Industrial Arbitration Court was enjoined to take cognisance of the Council's recommendations in their dispute and award considerations. The composition of the Council's membership is three representatives from each of the players, and a neutral academic 'without any functional identification'. The balance between the parties' representatives has been retained during the years. However, in 1981 the number of representatives from each party was increased to five. Although the representatives have equal status, those from the government have often played a dominant role, if only because of their access to superior statistical information and immense persuasive power. The result is that, in practice, both employers and employees regard the Council's guidelines as mandatory. On at least two occasions in recent years, namely during the 1985-86 recession and during the 1997-98 Asian economic crisis, the government took the decision-making lead.[22] On the latter occasion, Manpower Minister Dr Lee Boon Yang revealed that 'the national Wages Council

---

21 Deyo, 1981, p 104.

22 For further discussion of the response to the economic crisis, see Harding, 2002.

would be reconvened soon to update its wages guidelines, and "in a nutshell", a cut in the rate of employers' contribution to the CPF was likely."[23] His prophecy was fulfilled in the November 1998 economic package.

CONCLUSIONS

The Singapore model of law and development based on social and political discipline embodies a complex of interlocking elements, which we can now summarise, and which are all exemplified[24] in the foregoing example of labour law. A similar exercise could be undertaken with regard to any number of other areas of development-related activity. In her book, Carter has dealt extensively with land law and public housing, and capital investment in the form of intellectual property rights.[25]

At the centre of the complex is:

- Law: The rule of law is co-opted to provide guarantees of property rights without providing for civil rights or welfarism.

Law creates conditions of:

- Stability: PAP leadership ensures continuity and a predictable political environment. Law is used to bolster and legitimise PAP rule.

- Equality: Social justice is achieved by genuine trickle down effect evident in wages, pensions, education, and housing.

This creates loyalty, confidence and well-being. Law also facilitates:

- Planning: Effective public administration is based on 'smart' laws providing efficient internally and externally directed regulation, the absence of corruption, and the maintenance of services, all underpinned by deep planning over the long-term.

Law also enforces:

- Discipline: Employees work hard and make few demands. Citizens obey laws. Policies are easily implemented and leadership is supported.

The combined effect of these five elements is mutual reinforcement through:

- Development: This creates opportunity and confidence.

- Enforcement: Deterrent penalties, attractive incentives, responsible citizenry, and government-inspired campaigns and extra-statutory measures all assist enforcement.

- Economy: Economic growth underpins all the other elements, and is maintained even in adverse situations due to the policy of deep planning.

- Unity: Ethnic, religious, linguistic and class divisions are reduced by the policy of social engineering in areas such as education and social provision.

---

[23] *Straits Times*, 5 September 1998, p 45.

[24] See Figure 1, below.

[25] Carter, 2001, see Chapters 7 and 8 respectively. For a somewhat contrary view, which, with great insight, emphasises the compatibility of social facts with PAP legal policy, see Phang, 1990, especially pp 310-330.

This philosophy of social discipline is a consequence of Singapore's position and the inclination of its leaders. It is supported by smart laws, and a structured and disciplined education system. A highly efficient and routinised public administration ensures a high level of compliance with laws and policies. These factors enable the maintenance of a sophisticated and predictable infrastructure of communications, bureaucratic systems and services. They also ensure a well-educated and industrious labour force. These conditions have proved ideal for attracting inward foreign investment, on the basis of which Singapore has negotiated both the industrial and the information revolutions. Since 1990 it has also sought to continue to keep ahead of the economic game by means of outward foreign investment and the replication of the Singapore model elsewhere in the region, for example in the industrial parks in Suzhou in the People's Republic of China, and nearby Batam and Bintang in Indonesia, which are results of growth triangle co-operation between Singapore and Indonesia.[26] Singapore now faces fierce competition from the other tiger economies of East and South East Asia, and the question is whether the existing philosophy of social discipline is still adequate, when now more than ever before Singapore needs innovation and creativity. The third revolution now in progress may prove much harder to negotiate than the first two, and the labour laws, for example, may have to evolve along lines quite different from those described above to reflect new conditions. It will be a challenge of leadership to make adjustments which in many ways go against 40 years of social discipline.

In confronting the complexity of law and development, we now have to ask: Is this model of law-and-development purely an outcome of Singapore's situation, or is it indeed a glimpse of the legal future of the 21st century in the Asia-Pacific region? To answer this question one must look more widely at events in East and South East Asia. We can only do this in outline, but we hope to have shown how the development of Singapore law has been an outcome of its peculiar history, geography and politics. In our view the special conditions of Singapore are, for a variety of reasons, extremely difficult to repeat in other countries.

First of all, it is one thing to raise a population of less than 3 million to a high standard of development. It is another to repeat this feat in a large country with a population of 1200 million, 200 million or even 20 million. Size has been Singapore's problem, but dire necessity has also been the mother of great invention.

Second, attempts so far to emulate the Singaporean approach have not necessarily been successful. Malaysia has tried to follow many of Singapore's legal measures, but a different model of law-and-development has emerged which only resembles Singapore's in certain aspects. Thailand, Indonesia, India and Malaysia are co-operating with Singapore in the creation of special economic zones. Singaporean enterprises are investing in Vietnam and China; the latter has now become the largest recipient of Singaporean outward investment. The general trend in South East Asia has, however, been to reject the Singapore model as being too authoritarian, and being out of line with the pursuit of the more democratic model of development one can now see in Thailand, Indonesia, the Philippines, South Korea and Taiwan. 'Asian values' as an approach to development, although having much to be said for it as we have implicitly argued, has neither the support of sound theory nor the popular resonance throughout the region.

Third, there are important differences in legal and political culture. The other countries all have autochthonous legal systems dating from pre-industrial times. Some are still communist states. Although they display different degrees of openness in their political systems, all have large and growing democracy movements, spawned by educational advances, the rise of a

---

[26]   Stewart and Png, 1993.

prosperous and ambitious middle class, and the influence of NGO movements and other international movements. In December 1991 President Ramos of the Philippines politely but firmly rebuked Lee Kuan Yew for suggesting a Singapore-model approach in that country, reminding him that his country had already tried an authoritarian approach without much success.[27] It is an error to assume that state structures, political cultures and legal systems in Asia are similar or are converging. In our view the trends in surrounding countries indicate that the populace would not accept the degree of regulation that as become habitual in Singapore because it involves the surrender of too much freedom.

Fourth, the nature of the role of the state in economic growth is manifestly different in Singapore from the other countries. Singapore has been able to pursue deep planning because it has a small and cohesive business and administrative elite. Other countries have achieved economic growth without the deep planning displayed by Singapore, but their neglect of fundamental conditions has been exposed by their collapse and Singapore's virtual survival.

Having concluded that as a general prescription for development, the Singapore philosophy of social discipline cannot be applied across the board in the South East and East Asian regions, we would not wish to postulate the irrelevance of Singapore's experience. While some contributors to this book have doubted the value of 'formalisation', the example of Singapore indicates clearly the advantages of formalisation. This is not to say that the differing conditions of developing countries necessarily allows for Singapore-style rule-by-law; but it does imply that there are many Singaporean devices, policies and legal instruments that could be adopted or adapted elsewhere to solve particular problems. To use the example of labour laws that we have used throughout, while Singapore's heavy-handed approach to union and employment rights might be unacceptable as a general prescription, its CPF system is undoubtedly worthy of emulation as a valuable tool of development. We hope in any event to have shown in this chapter the value at least of considering the law and development experience of the Asian NICs. In so doing we have no doubt added to the complexity of the subject, but hopefully have also added to our capacity to deal with it.

Figure 1: Singapore's system of legal instrumentalism

Unity	Equality	Economy
Stability	**LAW**	Efficiency
Development	Discipline	Enforcement

REFERENCES

Anantaraman, V, *Singapore Industrial Relations System*, 1990, Singapore: Singapore Institute of Management and McGraw-Hill

Bartholomew, G W, 'English law in *Partibus Orientalium*', in Harding, A J (ed), *The Common Law in Singapore and Malaysia*, 1985, Singapore: Butterworths, Chapter 1

Carter, C, *Eyes on the Prize: Law and Economic Development in Singapore 1959-1999*, 2001, The Hague: Kluwer Law International

---

[27] *Far Eastern Economic Review*, 1992.

Chua Beng Huat, *Communitarian Ideology and Democracy in Singapore*, 1995, London: Routledge

Deyo, F, *Beneath the Miracle: Labor Subordination in the New Asian Industrialism*, 1989, Berkeley: University of California

Far Eastern Economic Review 'Discipline vs democracy' 10 December 1992

Goh Keng Swee, *The Economics of Modernisation*, 1972, Singapore: Asia Pacific Press

Harding, A J, 'Smart laws in Singapore', in Palmier, L (ed), *State and Law in Eastern Asia*, 1996, Aldershot: Dartmouth

Harding, A J, 'The economic crisis and law reform in South East Asia', in Bhopal, M and Hitchcock, M (eds), *ASEAN Business in Crisis* (Studies in Asia-Pacific Business), 2002, London: Frank Cass, Chapter 3

Huff, W, *The Economic Growth of Singapore: Trade and Development in the Twentieth Century*, 1997, Cambridge: CUP

Nair, D (ed), *Socialism That Works: The Singapore Way*, 1976, Singapore: Federal Publications

Phang Boon Leong, A, *The Development of Singapore Law: Historical and Socio-Legal Perspectives*, 1990, Singapore: Butterworths

Phang Boon Leong, A, 'The Singapore legal system: history, theory and practice' 23 (2000-2001) Singapore Law Review 23

Pistor, K and Wellons, P A, *The Role of Law and Legal Institutions in Asian Economic Development 1960-1995*, 1999, Oxford: OUP

Schmitter, P, 'Still a century of corporatism' (1974) 36 Review of Politics 85

Stewart, T P and Png, M L H, 'The growth triangle of Singapore, Malaysia and Indonesia' (1993) 23 Georgia Journal of International and Comparative Law 1

Tan Yew Lee, K, 'A short legal and constitutional history of Singapore', in Woon, W (ed), *The Singapore Legal System*, 1989, Singapore: Longman

Thynne, I, 'The administrative state', in Woon, W (ed), *The Singapore Legal System*, 1989, Singapore: Longman

Woo-Cummings, M, 'Diverse paths toward "the right institutions": law, the state and economic reform in East Asia', ADB Institute Working Paper No 18, 2001, Manila: Asian Development Bank

Woon, W, 'Singapore', in Poh-ling, T (ed), *Asian Legal Systems: Law, Society and Pluralism in East Asia*, 1997, Sydney: Butterworths, Chapter 8

LEGAL AID AND DEVELOPMENT: LESSONS FROM SOUTH AFRICA AND SOME THOUGHTS FOR NIGERIA

David McQuoid-Mason[*]

This chapter examines legal aid and development from a South African perspective with some thoughts for Nigeria. The South African system is by no means a perfect model for developing countries as the country is considerably better resourced compared to most other African countries, including Nigeria. Even so there are many useful parallels that emerge in respect of the models for the delivery of legal services in the two countries and, indeed, for developing countries in general.

MODELS FOR DELIVERY OF LEGAL AID SERVICES

Several models for the delivery of legal aid services have been tried in South Africa. The country has had to adapt internationally recognised legal aid delivery models to make them compatible with the available financial and human resources. Nigeria will have to do likewise.

The following models have been used in South Africa: *pro bono* legal aid work; judicare or referral to private lawyers; public defenders; legal aid funded interns in rural law firms; legal aid funded law clinics; justice centres; public interest law firms; university law clinics; and para-legal advice offices.

Pro bono legal aid work

Pro bono schemes are cheap and, if supported by the legal profession, can encourage public service by legal practitioners. However, *pro bono* clients may not receive the same level of service as paying clients, and many lawyers are reluctant to take on *pro bono* cases. Even if *pro bono* work is mandatory for the profession some lawyers may 'buy out' the time they would be required to devote to them, as sometimes happens in the United States. Experience has shown that the chances of mounting a successful comprehensive legal aid scheme are minimal unless lawyers are properly paid to deliver legal services.

Pro bono legal aid work in one form or another has been done by lawyers in South Africa and Nigeria for many years. In South Africa (as in the United Kingdom,[1] the United States,[2] France[3] and elsewhere) there has been a tradition of lawyers doing some *pro bono* or *pro amico*

---

[*] Professor of Procedural and Clinical Law, University of Natal, Durban.

[1] For instance, Allen and Overy's London office claimed to have completed 10,080 *pro bono* hours during 1999 amounting to over £2 million of work: 'Participants in the Role of the Private Bar Roundtable' 2000 at the recent Association of the Bar of the City of New York Global Forum on Access to Justice Conference, New York, 6-8 April 2000.

[2] In the United States the Legal Services Corporation agencies had *pro bono* cases accepted by more than 44,000 attorneys during 1998, and provided the education and structure for 150,000 volunteer private attorneys to serve clients effectively: 'Participants in the Role of the Private Bar Roundtable'. See also Johnson, 2000, s 83.

[3] For instance, more than 400 Paris-based lawyers and civil servants known as the *Droits d'Urgence* provide legal aid and advice at 56 monthly sessions operating in 20 centres: 'Participants in the Role of the Private Bar Roundtable'. See also Bedos, 2000, s 1.

work.[4] However, this is not mandatory and no statistics of the annual number of *pro bono* cases in South Africa are kept. In 1962 the State made the first attempt to set up a national legal aid scheme based on *pro bono* work by attorneys and advocates. The Department of Justice negotiated with the advocates' and attorneys' profession to provide free legal services to persons referred to them by local legal aid committees set up at every lower court.[5] The system never worked because it was not properly advertised, there was too much red tape, and probably also because members of the profession were not paid for their services.[6]

Since August 1998 the Nigerian Bar Association has taken a number of decisions on *pro bono* work by its members. It has approved the establishment of 16 civic rights centres throughout the country. Citizens who cannot afford to employ the services of lawyers to enforce their constitutional rights may approach a civic rights centre to obtain initial legal assistance and advice from a solicitor. If the solicitor cannot obtain the necessary relief or remedy the centre will draw up a brief and issue a certificate which the potential litigant can take to a lawyer of their choice at a token fee to be negotiated and paid by the Nigerian Bar Association.[7] Over the years a number of lawyers on the Legal Aid Council's (LAC) judicare panel have rendered *pro bono* legal aid services.[8]

Judicare or referral to private lawyers

Judicare in different forms has been used as a method of delivering legal aid services in both South Africa and Nigeria.

South Africa

For many years the main vehicle for the delivery of legal aid services for the poor in South Africa was the Legal Aid Board's (LAB) judicare scheme. Private lawyers who rendered legal aid services in accordance with the LAB's rules were paid for their services at fixed tariffs. The introduction of the new Constitution[9] had a devastating effect on the ability of the Board to continue using this method. The Board became notionally bankrupt and had to drastically revise its strategies concerning the delivery of legal aid services.

During the period from 1971-2 to 1997-8 a total of 997,707 legal aid cases were referred to attorneys, of which the vast majority involved criminal matters. Of these 559,238 were referred after 1994-5 and the advent of the new Constitution. This means that the number of legal aid applications granted during the period 1994-5 to 1997-98 constituted 56 percent of all legal aid applications ever handled by the Board. The overall increase during the period 1989-90 to 1998-9 was 709 percent.[10] This exponential growth in the number of judicare cases in respect of criminal matters eventually led to the abandonment of the judicare model as the main method of delivering legal aid services by the LAB (see below).

During the period 1997 to 1998 private attorneys were paid for completing 105,732 cases, of which 87,469 (83 percent) involved criminal cases and 17 percent civil matters. The latter

---

4   Cook, 1974, p 28.
5   *Ibid*, pp 31-32.
6   Gross, 1976, pp 176-177.
7   Onomigbo Okpoko, 2000, p 5.
8   LAC, 2000a, p 4.
9   Section 35.
10   LAB, 1998b, p 8.

involved 14,156 divorce (13 percent), 3,617 (3.5 percent) other civil cases and 490 (0.5 percent) labour cases. The average cost per case finalised by the LAB during the same period was R864 a case for ordinary criminal matters, R1,707 for Constitutional criminal matters, and R1,498 a case for civil matters under the judicare system. The average cost of all judicare cases was R1,423.[11]

The judicare model is considerably more expensive than the salaried lawyer scheme (see below). This led to the introduction of a pilot public defender programme in 1990[12] and a pilot LAB funded law clinic scheme in 1994. Unlike the former, the latter also catered for civil legal aid cases. In 1995 it was estimated that the average cost of a judicare criminal case was R822, the average cost of a public defender criminal case was R555,[13] and the cost of legal aid funded law clinic cases was even less (see below).

Nigeria

In Nigeria private legal practitioners whose names are registered on the panels of practitioners maintained by the LAC in accordance with the Legal Aid Decree provide legal services to the Council for a nominal fee.[14] Lawyers who are willing to assist persons seeking legal aid are entitled to be included on the panel unless the Council has good reasons for excluding them. In 2000 the Council approved an upward review of the remuneration paid to legal practitioners for the services rendered to the Council.[15] In the past some lawyers on the panel have done legal aid work *pro bono* because it has not been worth their while to claim the nominal fee.[16]

Between its inception in 1976 and April 2000, the LAC received 50,100 applications, of which 42,515 were granted, 7,584 rejected, 32,168 completed and 10,348 were pending.[17] As the Council only employs one salaried lawyer at each of the 36 state legal aid offices[18] it can be assumed that the majority of these cases were dealt with under the judicare system. The LAC was hoping to increase the number of cases handled each year to at least 10,000 with effect from 2001.[19] These figures should be seen against the over 160,000 cases a year dealt with by the South African LAB[20] with a legal aid budget a thousand-fold that of Nigeria.

Conclusions

In South Africa the judicare system worked when the number of cases were comparatively few and the LAB had the resources to handle them administratively. This means that there must be adequate staffing and administrative structures to support the system; proper accounting systems to deal with claims for fees and disbursements expeditiously; and budget

---

11 *Ibid.*
12 LAB, 1993, pp 32-33.
13 LAB, 1998b, p 8.
14 LAC, 2000a, p 4.
15 *Ibid.*
16 Personal communication to the author by participants at the Legal Aid Council of Nigeria Workshop on Legal Aid in the New Millennium in Abuja, Nigeria, 26-27 June 2000.
17 LAC, 2000a, p 3.
18 *Ibid*, p 4.
19 Personal communication to the author by members of the Governing Council at the Legal Aid Council of Nigeria Workshop on Legal Aid in the New Millennium in Abuja, Nigeria, 26-27 June 2000.
20 During the period 1996 to 1997, 163,749 legal aid applications were granted, of which 123,983 (76 percent) were in respect of criminal cases: LAB, 1998a, p 23.

constraints that keep pace with demand. Once a centralised staffing establishment can no longer keep pace with the demands of practitioners for payment within a reasonable period of time the referral system breaks down.[21]

New computer systems were installed but on a daily basis the incoming new accounts exceeded the number of old accounts the LAB's staff at head office were physically able to process. This resulted in long delays in payment, sometimes stretching into years, and loss of confidence in the system by practitioners who were no longer prepared to accept legal aid work. In some instances lawyers sued the Board for outstanding fees. The need to build up a huge contingency fund to cover amounts owing by the Board for matters that had not been completed compounded the problem and was criticised by the Auditor-General. In order to effect savings the Board capped fees for criminal cases and this alienated the legal profession. The Board has now opted for a predominantly salaried lawyer model involving justice centres (see below) with judicare being used as a subsidiary method of delivery in areas where there are no such centres.[22]

If judicare is to be retained as part of the legal aid system it is best to use a fixed contract approach where the annual fees to be paid to participating practitioners is capped. This has been done with recent co-operative agreements entered into by the South African LAB and public interest law firms and university law clinics.

When the volumes of legal aid cases in Nigeria start reaching the proportions of those in South Africa, the whole question of the judicare system will have to be re-examined.

Public defenders

Salaried lawyers are used to differing degrees by the national legal aid bodies in South Africa and Nigeria.

In South Africa in 1990, after widespread discussions with a variety of lawyer associations, the Legal Aid Board persuaded the Minister of Justice to investigate the feasibility of a public defender system in South Africa and to appropriate R2.5million for this purpose. This enabled the Board to employ legally qualified persons to represent indigent accused. Initially a pilot project in the Johannesburg office was approved for two years.[23] Estimates that each public defender should be able to deal with approximately 200 criminal cases a year[24] have proved to be correct.

By November 1992 more than 2,200 cases had been dealt with by the ten public defenders in Johannesburg, with a 57 percent success rate on not-guilty pleas, and a 90 percent success rate for bail applications. The average cost per case during 1992 compared very favourably with the costs allowed to private practitioners by the LAB.[25] During 1993-4 the office provided legal representation for 2,808 accused persons,[26] while during 1995-6 it represented 3,794.[27]

During 1995 it was estimated that while the average cost of a judicare criminal case was R822 the average cost of a public defender criminal case was R555.[28] The pilot project was

---

[21] McQuoid-Mason, 2000, s 121.

[22] *Ibid*, s 121-122.

[23] LAB, 1993, pp 32-33.

[24] McQuoid-Mason, 1991, p 270.

[25] *Business Day*, 1992.

[26] LAB, 1996a, p 32.

[27] LAB, 1997a, p 27.

[28] *Ibid*.

considered a success by the LAB, and public defenders have been included in the new justice centres (see below) as a permanent component of the Board's work. In 1996-7 the public defender offices in Johannesburg and Soweto employed 31 staff members who approved 3,515 applications for legal aid and finalised 3,386 court cases. The offices handled 23 appeals and withdrew from 1,069 cases.[29]

In Nigeria, the LAC has provided one salaried legal officer in each of the 36 state legal aid offices. The number has however been heavily criticised by the state attorneys-general and judges as being totally inadequate. In 2000 the Council was looking to increasing the number of salaried lawyers by recruiting more junior and senior legal aid officers. The salaried lawyers represent litigants in court, visit prisons, interview legal aid applicants and refer cases to private legal practitioners.[30]

Conclusions

Public defender models are considerably cheaper than the judicare system, and countries like Nigeria that rely almost exclusively on the judicare model, and are limited by budget constraints, should seriously consider introducing aspects of public defender schemes, particularly in criminal cases. However, a fully fledged network of public defender offices as exists in the United States is probably too expensive for South Africa or Nigeria. Other creative methods of using the model such as legal aid funded law clinics need to be explored (see below).

Legal aid interns in rural law firms

Partnerships between national legal aid structures and private law firms are a useful way of extending legal aid in rural areas.

During 1995 the South African LAB, in partnership with Lawyers for Human Rights, established a pilot project in which private attorneys in selected rural towns were given funding by the Board to employ candidate attorney interns to do legal aid work. The participating law firms were assisted with the payment of the salary of the candidate attorneys. Lawyers for Human Rights identified suitable attorneys and monitored the progress of the project. The project proved highly successful. Not only did it expand access to legal aid services in rural areas, but it also enabled formerly disadvantaged persons to be employed in the legal profession in the areas where they lived.[31]

The candidate attorneys handle at least 10 new legal aid matters a month for the Board and perform community service one day a week. During 1996-7 two projects involving eight candidate attorneys were in operation.[32] The work of the legal aid interns mainly involves criminal cases, but they also do civil cases such as divorce. For instance, during 1997 to 1998 the interns in four rural law firms completed 400 criminal cases and 73 civil cases.[33]

The present writer is not aware of any similar scheme in Nigeria but, provided the resources are made available, there seems to be no reason in principle why the LAC should not enter into similar partnership agreements with private practitioners in small rural towns in

---

[29] LAB, 1999a, p 23.
[30] LAC, 2000a, p 4.
[31] LAB, 1997a, p 24.
[32] LAB, 1999a, p 21.
[33] Calculations by present writer based on statistics in LAB, 1998c, pp 6-7.

Nigeria. The Council is acutely aware that 'a huge population of the poor, especially the rural poor are still completely alienated from the legal system'.[34] As in South Africa lawyers tend to be in the urban areas and there are very few lawyers and legal advice offices in the rural areas. To overcome this, the LAC in 2000 announced that 'given its limited financial and human resources' it would 'form partnerships with independent legal aid service providers across Nigeria with a view to ensuring that legal aid and advice is available to as many needy persons as possible in rural and urban Nigeria'.[35]

An economical way of introducing such a scheme in Nigeria would be to employ young National Youth Service Corps lawyers as legal aid interns attached to private law firms in small rural towns.

Conclusions

The legal aid internship scheme involving partnerships between the state legal aid body and private practitioners to employ young lawyers is very cost effective and should be expanded. It is much cheaper to supplement the salaries of candidate attorneys in rural law firms than to establish branch offices of the national legal aid structure in areas where there is a limited demand for legal aid services.[36] In South Africa this is done using recent law graduates who are required to serve a period of articles. In Nigeria this could be done using young lawyers from the National Youth Services Corps who are required to do community service.

Legal aid-funded law clinics

Legal aid-funded law clinics involve the setting up and funding of law clinics by the national legal aid body as a cost effective method delivering services, particularly in respect of criminal defences. At the same time it provides practical training and access to the legal profession by aspiring young lawyers.

South Africa

The South African Attorneys Act was amended in 1993 to allow candidate attorneys with the necessary legal qualifications to obtain practical experience by undertaking community service rather than serving articles in an attorney's office.[37] Such service may be done at law clinics accredited by provincial law societies, including clinics funded by the LAB. The clinics are required to employ a principal—an attorney with sufficient practical experience—to supervise law graduates in the community service programme. The candidate attorneys appear in the district courts and the principals in the regional and high courts. Interns who have been articled for more than a year may also appear in the regional courts. Candidate attorney interns may be employed to do community service with a maximum ratio of ten interns to one supervising attorney.[38]

---

[34] LAC, 2000a, pp 7-8.

[35] McQuoid-Mason, 1984, p 181.

[36] LAB, 1999a, p 21.

[37] South African Attorneys Act 1979, as amended by s 2 South African Attorneys (Amendment) Act 1993.

[38] LAB, 1999a, p 20. The maximum ratio of articled clerks to supervising attorneys in private law firms is three clerks to one attorney: Attorneys Act s 3(3).

In 1994 a pilot project involving partnerships with five university law clinics was set up by the LAB. The project has expanded to 22 university and other law clinics and the Board allocates up to R430,000 (approximately US$43,000) per clinic to enable each to employ a supervising attorney and up to ten community service interns each. Where the nature of the work demands it, some clinics employ eight interns and two qualified professional assistants instead of ten interns so that the professional assistants can appear in the regional (senior) magistrates' courts. The Board calculated that the average cost of the 24,513 criminal and 12,997 civil cases handled by the law clinics during the period 1 July 1994 to 31 December 1996 was R433.[39] This is less than half of the average cost of R976 per case charged under the judicare system during the same period,[40] and is also cheaper than the pure public defender model. During the period 1997 to 1998 twenty law clinics completed 33,951 cases, of which 20,042 (59 percent) were criminal and 13,909 (41 percent) were civil.[41] This figure compares favourably with the 18,263 civil cases done under the judicare scheme for the same period[42] at probably twice the cost. The legal aid funded law clinics are now being detached from the universities and incorporated into the new justice centres (see below).

The President of the Constitutional Court, Justice Arthur Chaskalson, has suggested that compulsory community service for law graduates could help solve the problem of delivery of legal aid to poor sections of the community, particularly in respect of criminal cases.[43] The suggestion was greeted with some hostility in an editorial in the official journal of the attorneys' profession, which warned that representation by interns and para-legals 'could be of such inferior quality that, in the worst cases, it would not satisfy the constitutional right to representation'.[44] The recommendation was however given a more sympathetic hearing at the National Legal Aid Forum in 1998.[45] The Ministry of Justice is currently examining the whole question of the requirements for entry into the legal profession and the issue of community service will form part of this discussion.[46]

---

[39] LAB, 1997b. This includes the costs for clinics which have only just been established. Ultimately the cost per case will be much less as the more established clinics cost about R350 per case: *ibid*.

[40] This figure is the average for criminal and civil cases—about 75percent of the work in the clinics is criminal and 25percent civil (see above).

[41] Calculations by present writer based on statistics in LAB, 1998a, pp 1-5.

[42] LAB, 1998b, p 8.

[43] Chaskalson, 1997, p 782. The present writer had previously made a similar suggestion as an alternative to national service when conscription still applied in the country: McQuoid-Mason, 1991, p 267.

[44] Editorial, 1998, p 5. It went on to say: 'The legal aid system should not be used as an avenue to allow disadvantaged students to have access to the profession: that is not its purpose': *ibid*.

[45] The concept was discussed by a working commission on internship and training at the National Legal Aid Forum in 1998 which recommended the following: (a) community service should be introduced to improve the administration of justice, primarily to provide legal aid services; (b) the question of whether it should be compulsory (like medical internships) or voluntary should be further investigated; (c) community service should be primarily in the form of work in law clinics, public defender's offices and public interest law firms; (d) community service should be for not less than one year after graduation; (e) an independent body should be set up to control the enrolment and training of community service interns; (g) community service interns should receive proper training before providing services to the public; (h) the question of whether community service should replace all other forms of internship should be investigated; and (i) a pilot project on a voluntary basis should be introduced: McQuoid-Mason, 1999, pp 54-57.

[46] *Cf* Department of Justice Legal Policy Unit, 1999, p 8.

Nigeria

The idea of setting up legal aid clinics at university law faculties is still at an early stage in Nigeria. However if the LAC were to be provided with the financial resources to establish law clinics in each of the 36 states the human resources could be provided by young lawyers in the National Youth Services Corps (NYSC). Groups of young NYSC lawyers could act as public defenders in the district courts under the supervision of a resident legal aid lawyer at each state legal aid office. Unlike South Africa, Nigeria already has a compulsory community service programme in place which would just have to be fine-tuned to make the most effective use of NYSC lawyers.

If the South African model were to be followed, ten NYSC lawyers could be supervised by one senior lawyer. Such a model could immediately increase the number of cases handled by state salaried legal aid lawyers tenfold at a very reasonable cost. The possibility of funding such a project through foreign donor agencies interested in expanding access to justice in Nigeria or one of the private foundations with similar aims should be explored by the LAC.

Conclusion

The community service programme provides extended legal services at a moderate cost to needy members of the public, and at the same time develops fields of expertise, practical experience and career opportunities for aspiring lawyers. It is a useful model for ensuring the gainful employment of young law graduates who are required to render community service to their country. The South African experience has been that the standard of service of the LAB clinic candidate attorneys in the lower courts is often better than that of qualified attorneys or privately employed candidate attorneys because the interns obtain specialist knowledge in the conducting of criminal and poverty law cases.

Legal aid-funded justice centres

The most effective legal aid services models for consumers are those that provide them with a 'one stop shop' instead of being sent from place to place to obtain assistance. Such one-stop-shop facilities may be referred to as 'justice centres'.

South Africa

The South African legal aid funded justice centres are similar to legal aid specialist law firms that have developed elsewhere,[47] except that in South Africa they are fully State-funded and staffed by persons in the employ of the LAB.

The South African LAB is setting up legal aid or justice centres which provide a 'one stop' service for legal aid clients by bringing together the different constituents of the present legal aid scheme under one roof: legal aid officers, public defenders, law clinic interns, professional assistants, supervising attorneys, para-legals, administrative assistants and administration clerks. The judicare system is only used if the justice centre cannot handle a case. Public defenders deal with criminal cases in the regional courts and high courts. Candidate attorney

---

[47] See generally Eleventh Annual Philip D Reed Memorial Issue Symposium.

interns do both civil and criminal work in the district courts.[48] Professional assistants appear in the regional courts. Supervising attorneys appear in the high courts and the regional courts. Para-legals assist with the initial screening of clients. Administrative assistants and clerks provide the necessary administrative back-up.[49]

The justice centres provide a full range of legal and para-legal services to indigent clients. They work well in the larger cities and towns, but not in the rural areas where there is insufficient work to justify their expense. In such circumstances, another model, such as co-operative agreements between the LAB and bodies such as rural law firms, the independent law clinics, public interest law firms and para-legal advice offices may be more feasible (see below).

Nigeria

Nigeria already has legal aid offices in each of the 36 states. If the necessary funding were available these offices could be upgraded to justice centres if they were to employ NYSC lawyers as public defenders for deployment in the district courts and a senior supervising lawyer for appearances in the superior courts.

Conclusion

The South African experience is that justice centres are not as cheap to run as public defender and legal aid funded law clinics which have low overheads because they do predominantly criminal work. However they are cheaper than the judicare system.[50] The model is worth considering in Nigeria in those state legal aid offices that rely extensively on judicare and can access the necessary funding.

Public interest law firms

Public interest law firms can play a valuable role in the delivery of civil legal aid services to indigent people. They exist in many countries,[51] including the United States where they originated, and in developing countries in South America, Asia, Africa and, more recently, in Eastern Europe.[52] They exist in both South Africa and Nigeria.

South Africa

The best example of a private specialist law firm in South Africa is the Legal Resources Centre (LRC), the first of which was established in Johannesburg in 1979 and other centres in Cape Town, Port Elizabeth, Grahamstown, Durban and Pretoria.[53] In the 21 years of its existence the LRC has assisted millions of disadvantaged South Africans either as individuals or as groups or communities who share a common problem. During the apartheid era it used litigation and the threat of litigation to assert the rights of thousands of disadvantaged South Africans in

---

[48] Under the Magistrates' Courts Act, regional courts can impose fines of up to R300,000 and imprisonment of up to 25 years; district courts can impose fines of up to R100,000 and imprisonment of up to 3 years.

[49] See McQuoid-Mason, 2000, s 126.

[50] Ibid, s 126-127.

[51] See generally Hutchins and Klaaren, 1992.

[52] See on the United States: Hershkoff and Hollander, 2000; South America: Fruhling 2000; Africa and Asia: Golub 2000a, 2000b, 2000c; and on Eastern Europe: McCutcheon, 2000.

[53] LRC, 1996, p 25.

several areas of the law. In addition the LRC has worked with numerous advice centres staffed by para-legals.[54]

Since the 1994 elections the LRC has reassessed its position and is now focusing on constitutional rights and land, housing and development. The constitutional rights programme deals with access to justice, gender equality, children's rights, the enforcement of socio-economic rights such as health care, education, housing and water, and a constitutional reform programme. The land, housing and development programme includes rural and urban restitution and redistribution of land, urban and rural land tenure security, housing, land law reform and urban and rural land development.[55]

An important part of the LRC programme is the training of para-legals and lawyers from disadvantaged communities. It employs 12 to 15 young law graduates each year and trains interns from elsewhere in Africa and the developing world.[56]

The LRC charges no fees and receives no State funds, and it is financed by the Legal Resources Trust which receives money from overseas and local donors. Recently the LRC, together with the Association of University Legal Aid Institutions (see below), has taken the lead in encouraging the LAB to enter into co-operative agreements with independently funded organisations to extend legal services to previously marginalised parts of the country.[57]

Nigeria

Nigeria also has several public interest law bodies that engage in human rights litigation such as the Constitutional Rights Project (CRP) founded in 1990 and the Social and Economic Rights Action Centre (SERAC) founded in 1995.

The Constitutional Rights Project uses 'research and litigation to promote basic rights and strengthen the judiciary'.[58] The CRP brought numerous cases to try to prevent abuses of power under the Nigerian military regimes and were occasionally able to secure the release of prisoners and win limited victories for freedom of expression. In many cases, however, their efforts were blocked by 'interminable delays, judicial apathy and corruption'.[59] Despite its many losses the CRP played a valuable role in focusing national and international attention on the injustices of the military regimes.

The Social and Economic Rights Action Centre has filed cases on behalf of 300,000 former residents of Maroko whose shanties were demolished by the government in 1990. Unsuccessful attempts to prevent the evictions had been made earlier by the Nigerian Civil Liberties Organisation. By 2000 only three percent of the people had been re-housed despite promises at the time that they would be properly resettled.[60] SERAC has mounted a number of cases concerning the Maroko people to 'fully legitimise and consolidate the community's demand for resettlement' by focusing on 'particular aspects of economic, social and cultural rights violations within the community'.[61] It also challenged the World Bank regarding its

---

[54] *Ibid*, p 9.

[55] LRC, 1998, p 4; *cf* McQuoid-Mason, 2000, s 128.

[56] LRC, 1998, p 7.

[57] See generally McQuoid-Mason, 2000, s 127- 128.

[58] McClymont and Golub, 2000, p 288.

[59] *Ibid*.

[60] Morka, 2000, s 326; *cf* McClymont and Golub, 2000, p 293.

[61] Morka, 2000, s 326.

implementation of the Lagos Drainage and Sanitation Project 'which threatened the homes of over 1,200,000 people who live in about 15 clusters of slum communities in Lagos'.[62]

Conclusions

Public interest law bodies like the LRC, CRP and SERAC provide legal aid services in civil cases for the poor and marginalised in their countries. They owe their success to their highly professional staff and strong foreign and local donor-based financial and other support. They often receive support from leading lawyers in their countries as well as the judiciary and enjoy a high national and international reputation. The strong public interest law bodies in South Africa and Nigeria survive because they are creatively responding to the new dynamics of a democratic society. In South Africa the LRC is working closely with the LAB and took the lead in establishing co-operative agreements between the Board and other bodies. In Nigeria the resources developed by the CRP could be used by lawyers employed by the LAC to litigate on breaches of fundamental rights in terms of its new mandate.[63] SERAC too has gathered a wealth of experience regarding the enforcement of economic and social rights and may also be a worthwhile coalition partner for the LAC's human rights litigation programme.[64]

University law clinics

Legal aid clinics supply free legal advice to indigent persons. They are usually, but not exclusively, based at universities and enable law students to give advice and assistance under the supervision of qualified legal practitioners. Most law clinic models either require law students to work in a university law clinic or assign the students to an outside partnership organisation where they can provide legal services under supervision.[65] The concept of independently funded university legal aid clinics developed in the United States in the late 1960s when the Council on Legal Education for Professional Responsibility (CLEPR) was established with financial support from the Ford Foundation.[66] In recent years they have become a worldwide phenomenon and are to be found in Africa, Asia,[67] South America and Eastern Europe.[68] Law clinics have existed in South Africa for nearly 30 years.[69] In Nigeria they are still under consideration.

---

[62]   *Ibid*, s 328.

[63]   LAC, 2000a, p 10: 'The Council interprets its human rights mandate not only in terms of protection of human rights but also promoting human rights in the delivery of its service.'

[64]   *Ibid*, p 8: The Council wishes 'to form a working coalition between the Council and other stakeholders in the field to facilitate sharing of information, expertise and materials.'

[65]   McQuoid-Mason, 1986, p 193.

[66]   Pincus, 1974, p 123.

[67]   Indian law students have been creatively used in the *lok dulats* or 'people's courts', where they assist with the functioning of the courts during weekends or public holidays. The *lok dulats* try to settle disputes sent to them by the courts for resolution by negotiation, arbitration or conciliation. The law students do all the preparatory work of interviewing the parties in order to obtain a negotiated settlement, but if this does not work the parties attend the *lok dulat* presided over by a panel consisting of a district court judge or magistrate, a lawyer and a social worker. The proceedings are conducted informally and the parties (and their lawyers if they are represented) appear before the panel in an attempt to reach a solution: Aggarwal, 1991. In some states the *lok adalats* are organised by the state Legal Aid Boards, while in others they are co-ordinated by para-legal organisations or even the courts: *ibid*, pp 3-7.

[68]   McCutcheon, 2000, p 267.

[69]   The first legal aid clinic was established by law students at the University of Cape Town in 1972. The first law faculty staff-initiated law clinics were established at the Universities of the Witwatersrand and Natal (Durban) in August 1973: McQuoid-Mason, 1981, pp 139-140, 148 and 153.

South Africa

The Ford Foundation funded a legal aid conference in South Africa in 1973 which proved to be the catalyst for the law clinic movement. At the time of the conference there were only two clinics in the country, but within two years five others had been established.[70] Most of the 21 universities in South Africa now operate campus law clinics independent of the LAB's clinics,[71] and employ directors who are practising attorneys or advocates. Where the director is an attorney, the law clinic may seek accreditation by the local law society, and if granted, candidate attorneys may be employed and trained at these institutions with a view to admission. Funding for law clinics is provided by outside donors, and the Attorneys Fidelity Fund[72] subsidises accredited clinics by providing funds to enable them to employ a practitioner (attorney or advocate) to control the clinic.[73] More recently the Association of University Legal Aid Institutions (AULAI) has set up the AULAI Trust with an endowment from the Ford Foundation to strengthen the funding of the clinics.[74]

Law clinics provide free legal services to the needy and use the LAB's means test as a flexible guideline. Clinic staff may represent clients in the lower and high courts (if the clinic employs an advocate) in both criminal and civil matters. Law students may not represent clients in court. Although student practice rules were drafted in 1985 to enable final year law students attached to law clinics to appear in criminal cases for indigents accused in the district courts, these were never implemented.[75] Today, approximately 3,000 law graduates are produced annually by South African law schools. If each final year law student were only to do 10 cases a year, mainly during the summer and winter vacations, this could provide criminal defences for 30,000 criminal accused.[76]

Law clinics train senior law students in practical legal skills while at the same time providing a valuable service for indigent members of the community. Clinic work may form part of optional or compulsory clinical law programmes at universities. The matters that may be dealt with by clinics are sometimes restricted (for example, motor vehicle insurance claims have been excluded).[77] Much of the work of the clinics includes labour matters such as wrongful dismissals, unemployment insurance and workmen's compensation for injuries; consumer law problems such as credit agreements (hire-purchase), defective products, loan shark and unscrupulous debt collection practices; housing problems such as fraudulent contracts, non-delivery and poor workmanship; customary law matters such as emancipation of women and succession rights; maintenance; and criminal cases. During the apartheid era many of the clinics at the progressive universities were involved with civil rights cases involving pass laws, police brutality, forced removals, detention without trial and other

---

[70]   *Ibid*, p 139.

[71]   McQuoid-Mason, 1992, p 559 at n 1.

[72]   The Attorneys Fidelity Fund is a fund that has accumulated out of the interest paid on monies held in attorneys' trust accounts. It is used to compensate members of the public who have suffered loss as result of fraud by practising attorneys, but also makes money available for legal education.

[73]   McQuoid-Mason, 1986, p 193.

[74]   Golub, 2000c, p 38.

[75]   The Student Practice Rules for South Africa were based on the American Bar Association Model Rules for Student Practice: CLEPR, 1973, p 43; and submitted to the Association of Law Societies of South Africa in April 1985 for onward transmission to the then Minister of Justice. Although the rules were approved by all branches of the practising profession and the law schools they appear to have been blocked by bureaucrats in the Department of Justice: McQuoid-Mason, 2000, s 129 at n 82.

[76]   Minister of Justice and Department of Justice, 1998, p 25.

[77]   *Cf* McQuoid-Mason, 1985, p 64.

breaches of fundamental human rights.[78] As the clinics accepted clients 'off the street' they tended to emphasise the service rather than teaching aspects of their functions.[79]

Since 1994 the legal aid clinics have continued to deal with poverty law problems, some of which such as housing, the quality of police services and social security have continued as a result of non-delivery by the new government.[80] Several clinics have begun to focus more on constitutional issues. At the University of Natal, Durban, for instance, the law clinic specialises in problems concerning women and children, administrative justice and land restitution. The majority of clinics still engage in general practice. Fewer restrictions are being imposed by the law societies and candidate attorneys may do their mandatory internships as community service in accredited law clinics.[81]

University law clinics play a valuable role in supplementing the work of the LAB. Recently the Board has entered into co-operation agreements with law clinics in order to compensate them for their services. This role was identified more than 20 years ago: 'The well-supervised use of law students will significantly ease the limitations under which most of the legal aid programmes in Africa now have to work; it is only through student programmes that there is any possibility in the near future for legal services becoming widely available to the poor.'[82]

Nigeria

Law clinics at university law faculties are still under consideration in Nigeria and the possibility of establishing some pilot projects is being investigated. Once they are established law clinics can play an important ancillary role to the activities of the LAC. They could also enter into coalition agreements with the Council to provide certain services.

Conclusions

Law clinics can play a useful role in assisting legal aid litigants to compel the government to deliver on social and economic rights. The funding of law clinics tends to be uncertain as they usually rely on donor funding. However if holistic legal aid service delivery models are included in partnership agreements between the national legal aid structures and the university law clinics this will help to make the latter more financially viable. The Nigerian LAC should actively encourage the establishment of law clinics at Nigerian universities as they can provide a valuable resource for the national legal aid scheme, as has been done in South Africa.

---

[78] Generally for the types of cases handled by legal aid clinics: McQuoid-Mason, 1981, pp 139-161.

[79] McQuoid-Mason, 2000, s 130.

[80] Constitution of the Republic of South Africa Act 1993, s 236(2).

[81] The Attorneys Act 1979, s 2(1A)(b) was amended by s 2 of Act of 1993 to allow aspiring attorneys to 'perform community service approved by the society concerned'—provided that the person who engages them is practising the profession of attorney, *inter alia*, 'in the full-time employment of a law clinic, and if the council of the province in which that law clinic is operated, certifies that the law clinic concerned complies with the requirements prescribed by such council for the operation of such clinic' (s 3(1)(f)).

[82] Reyntjens, 1979, p 36. The value of using properly supervised law students to deliver legal services has also been recognised as fulfilling the requirement of a constitutional right to counsel by the United States Supreme Court which stated: 'Law students can be looked to make a significant contribution, qualitatively and quantitatively, to the representation of the poor in many areas': *Argersinger v Hamlyn*, 1979. See generally McQuoid-Mason, 2000, s 131.

Mobile legal aid clinics

Mobile legal aid clinics have the advantage of reaching people in the rural areas. They can operate using either road or rail transport. Where the clinic involves the use of mobile road vehicles such as vans or minibuses the model is more expensive than if it can 'piggy back' on a another project such as a community health project using a train. In the latter case the mobile law clinic can consist of a coach or part of a coach on a community health train and the costs could be shared between the law clinic and the health programme.

A mobile law clinic train has been used in some rural areas in South Africa. During mid-1998 the Legal i train, a joint project between Legal i, the Automobile Association and Spoornet, made its first journey to local communities in the Northern Province, the North West, Gauteng and Mpumalanga. The train is a fully equipped law clinic that operates as an office and offers free legal advice to people from local communities. Legal i is a community-based legal services programme established by the four provincial law societies, the Black Lawyers Association and the National Association of Democratic Lawyers.[83]

In Nigeria, the LAC planned in 2000 to launch a two-year project piloting legal aid mobile clinics to take 'legal literacy to the grassroots.' The project was to be run along the same lines as community health programmes, aiming to access communities usually out of the reach of the LAC.[84]

Para-legal advice offices

Para-legal advice offices exist in many countries in both the developed and developing worlds. In some cases para-legals are paid professionals, while in others they are volunteers.[85] Some work closely with lawyers while others act completely independently. In most cases they interface directly at grass-roots level with the communities they serve, and provide a valuable front-line link for providers of legal aid services.

South Africa

A variety of South African organisations are involved in para-legal advice work. Many of these also provide access to justice by educating the public concerning their legal rights, as well as training para-legals to give advice. Some bodies—such as the Black Sash—concentrate in urban areas, while others—such as the Community Law and Rural Development Centre (CLRDC) in Durban and Lawyers for Human Rights in Stellenbosch—focus on rural areas. Services are provided at a variety of levels which vary from advice only offices in the high-density townships to those providing full legal aid services such as the Legal Aid Bureau in Johannesburg.[86]

Employees at advice offices in South Africa are generally paid, but often the remuneration is very low and in some cases staff work for nothing. Training of para-legal staff varies from formal training offered by Lawyers for Human Rights and the CLRDC in Durban, leading to diploma courses, to mainly practical experience which is obtained 'on the job'. Some of the

83 'Professional News', 1998, p 10; cf McQuoid-Mason 2000, s 131-132.
84 LAC, 2000a, p 9. Details of the pilot project were not available at the time of going to print.
85 See generally Golub, 2000d, pp 301-306.
86 In 1996, the LAB experienced financial difficulties and the Legal Board agreed to provide substantial funding for it.

more sophisticated advice offices are linked to organisations such as the LRC, Lawyers for Human Rights and the CLRDC, Durban, while others rely on free services provided by legal practitioners in private practice. Most advice offices offer mainly legal advice which very often resolves the problem. Many of them have built up expertise in particular areas, such as pensions, unemployment insurance, unfair dismissals etc. Where the advice office cannot solve the problem the party concerned is usually directed to the LAB's offices or to a sympathetic law firm. Para-legals are also being included in the Board's new justice centres and co-operative agreements. A National Para-Legal Institute (NPLI) has been set up to assist the more than 350 para-legal advice offices in the country with training and fund-raising. It is also investigating para-legal accreditation certification procedures. The NPLI works closely with the Association of University Legal Aid Institutions (AULAI) by providing clusters of advice offices that are supported by the law clinics at the different universities.[87]

Para-legal advice offices are particularly useful in rural areas. A good example of a rural para-legal advice office is the CLRDC in Durban. This was established at the University of Natal in 1989 to set up a network of rural para-legal advice offices and to provide law-related education. It serves a rural population of about one million living in the provinces of KwaZulu-Natal and the Eastern Cape and promotes the attainment and maintenance of democracy through development of a rights-based culture in which all levels of government are expected to honour their obligations and be accountable to their citizens.[88] The CLRDC supervises 56 rural para-legal advice offices in communities that are governed by customary law and ruled by tribal authorities who have no formal training and are expected to administer communities and issues of traditional customary law in a manner that may conflict with 'Western law' and the new Constitution.

The CLRDC helps rural communities to establish para-legal committees to select certain community residents for training as para-legal advisers and educators. The para-legals undergo two full-time two-month programmes on law-related topics, including customary law and human rights, after which they do one year of practical training in their communities under the supervision of CLRDC staff.[89] At the end of the course the successful candidates are issued with a diploma by the Faculty of Law, University of Natal, Durban.[90] The CLRDC also provides continuing legal education for para-legals who have already been through the programme. Apart from giving advice the para-legals are required to conduct law-related workshops in their communities. In 2000 para-legals conducted 2 160 such workshops.[91] The CLRDC provides clusters of para-legal advice offices that are provided with legal support by the university law clinics in the region in partnership with the LAB.

Nigeria

Nigeria has a host of para-legal and advice offices, particularly those concerned with women's and children's rights and legal literacy. The former include organisations such as WILDAF and FIDA and the latter bodies such as the Legal Research and Resources Development Centre (LRRDC). There are also non-governmental organisations that give legal assistance and monitor human abuses such as the Civil Liberties Organisation (CLO).

---

[87] See generally McQuoid-Mason, 2000, s 131-133.
[88] *Ibid*, s 134.
[89] CLRDC, 2001, p 10.
[90] The only other para-legal university certificate courses are run at Rhodes University and more recently at Rand Afrikaans University.
[91] CLRDC, 2001, p 24.

There is scope for incorporating para-legal advice offices into coalition agreements with the LAC so that a holistic service is provided to persons requiring legal aid. Once again it may be possible to use the services of National Youth Service Corps lawyers in such arrangements. The 36 state legal aid offices could establish cluster arrangements with the advice offices in their regions along the lines of that used in South Africa in respect of the relationship between the independent law clinics, the advice offices and the LAB.

Conclusions

Para-legal advice offices can be used to complement conventional lawyer-based legal aid service schemes. They are found where communities make their first contact with the law and can play a valuable role in screening initial legal complaints and referring potential litigants to lawyer-based services. Para-legals should be paid for their services and properly trained. To achieve this, para-legal offices should be adequately funded. This can in part be done by integrating them into the national legal aid scheme.[92] The South African LAB has recognised the important role played by para-legals by incorporating cluster arrangements involving advice offices and university law clinics into its co-operation agreements with the law clinics. Donor funding is available for such initiatives[93] and the Nigerian LAC should consider doing something similar using its state legal aid offices as support centres.

CONCLUSIONS

A number of conclusions can be drawn from the South African and Nigerian experiences concerning the delivery of legal aid services.

First, the size and structure of the legal profession, the demands of the criminal justice system, their relevant constitutional imperatives, and the availability of adequate financial resources will determine the most appropriate methods of delivering legal aid services in South Africa and Nigeria.

Second, a holistic approach using a combination of methods is probably the most effective way of delivering legal aid services. Depending on the size of the demand for legal aid services neither the judicare nor the public defender model can be directly transplanted from developed countries. The South African LAB has introduced variations of the salaried lawyer concept involving the employment of law graduates in legal aid law clinics and rural law firms which may be of some interest to the Nigerian LAC. The Nigerian National Youth Services Corps (NYSC) lawyers provide a valuable resource in this respect.

Third, given the shortage of legal aid lawyers and financial resources in South Africa and Nigeria, law students should be seen as a potentially valuable and inexpensive resource available to national legal aid structures. To this end the South African LAB has entered into co-operation agreements with university law clinics. The Nigerian LAC should encourage the establishment of university and law school clinics with a view to entering into agreements with them concerning the use of law students. In the meantime it should use the NYSC lawyers as an equivalent resource in it state legal aid offices.

---

[92] See McQuoid-Mason, 2000, s 135-136.

[93] The South African initiatives began with funding by the International Commission of Jurists (Swedish Section) for clinics that undertook to support clusters of advice offices through the Association of University Legal Aid Institutions Trust (AULAI Trust).

Fourth, national legal aid structures should enter into co-operative legal aid arrangements with independent providers of legal services such as non-governmental public interest law firms. The South African LAB has recognised the importance of this by entering into co-operative agreements with experienced human rights litigators such as the Legal Resources Centre (LRC). The Nigerian LAC should do likewise by drawing on the wealth of human rights experience in non-governmental organisations such as the Constitutional Rights Project (CRP) and the Social and Economic Rights Action Centre (SERAC) in order to implement its expanded mandate to deal with breaches of fundamental constitutional rights.

Finally, national legal aid structures should work closely with para-legal advice offices as they are where people often first go for legal advice. The South African LAB has recognised this and has entered into co-operation agreements with university law clinics to service clusters of para-legal offices as part of the national legal aid scheme. A similar programme could be adopted by the Nigerian LAC once law clinics have been established.

REFERENCES

Allen and Overy, 'Participants in the Role of the Private Bar Roundtable' distributed at Association of the Bar of the City of New York Global Forum on Access to Justice Conference, New York, 6-8 April 2000

Aggarwal, N, *Handbook on Lok Adalat in India*, 1991, New Delhi: Interest Publications

Argersinger v Hamlyn (1979) S Ct 2006

Attorneys (Amendment) Act 115 of 1993 (South Africa)

Attorneys Act 53 of 1979 (South Africa)

Bedos, J-L, 'Droits d'urgence: access of citizens to legal information in France' (2000) 24 Fordham International Law Journal (Symposium) 1

Business Day, 2 November 1992

Chaskalson, A, 'Legal interns could solve legal aid problems' De Rebus, December 1997, 782

Community Law and Rural Development Centre (CLRDC), *Annual Report for the Financial Year 1 January to 31 December 2000*, 2001, Durban: CLRDC

Cook, G W, 'A history of legal aid in South Africa', in Faculty of Law, University of Natal, *Legal Aid in South Africa*, 1974, Durban: Faculty of Law, University of Natal

Council for Legal Education and Professional Responsibility (CLEPR) *State Rules Permitting the Student Practice of Law: Comparisons and Comments* second edition, 1973, New York: CLEPR

Department of Justice Legal Policy Unit (DJLPU), *Transformation of the Legal Profession*, unpublished first draft issue paper, 1999, DJLPU

Editorial, 'Legal aid again: the profession should not be sidelined' De Rebus, April 1998, 5

Eleventh Annual Philip D Reed Memorial Issue Symposium 'Partnerships across borders: a global forum on access to justice', April 6-8 2000 (2000) 24 Fordham International Law Journal (Symposium)

Fruhling, H, 'From dictatorship to democracy: law and social change in the Andean region and the southern cone of South America', in McClymont, M and Golub, S (eds), *Many Roads to Justice: The Law Related Work of Ford Foundation Grantees Around the World*, 2000, New York: Ford Foundation

Golub, S (2000a), 'From the village to the university: legal activism in Bangladesh', in McClymont, M and Golub, S (eds), *Many Roads to Justice: The Law Related Work of Ford Foundation Grantees Around the World*, 2000, New York: Ford Foundation

Golub, S (2000b), 'Participatory justice in the Phillipines', in McClymont, M and Golub, S (eds), *Many Roads to Justice: The Law Related Work of Ford Foundation Grantees Around the World*, 2000, New York: Ford Foundation

Golub, S (2000c), 'Battling apartheid, building a new South Africa', in McClymont, M and Golub, S (eds), *Many Roads to Justice: The Law Related Work of Ford Foundation Grantees Around the World*, 2000, New York: Ford Foundation

Golub, S (2000d), 'Non-lawyers as legal resources for their communities', in McClymont, M and Golub, S (eds), *Many Roads to Justice: The Law Related Work of Ford Foundation Grantees Around the World*, 2000, New York: Ford Foundation

Gross, P H, *Legal Aid and its Management*, 1976, Cape Town: Juta and Co

Hershkoff, H and Hollander, D, 'Rights into action: public interest litigation in the United States', in McClymont, M and Stephen, G (eds), *Many Roads to Justice: The Law Related Work of Ford Foundation Grantees Around the World*, 2000, New York: Ford Foundation

Hutchins, T and Klaaren, J, *Public Interest Law Around The World: An NAACP-LDF Symposium Report*, 1992, New York: Columbia Human Rights Law Review

Johnson, E, 'Equal access to justice: comparing access to justice in the United States and other industrial democracies' (2000) 24 Fordham International Law Journal (Symposium) 83

LAB (Legal Aid Board), *Annual Report 1991/92*, 1993, Pretoria: LAB

LAB (1996a), *Annual Report 1994/95*, 1996, Pretoria: LAB

LAB (1997a), *Annual Report 1995/96*, 1997, Pretoria: LAB

LAB (1997b), *Monthly Legal Aid Report*, 4 February 1997

LAB (1998a), *Legotla: Delivery of Legal Aid by way of Salaried Staff Models, Public Defenders, Attorneys and Candidate Attorneys as at 30 October 1998*, unpublished, 1998

LAB (1998b), *Legotla: Overview of the Board and its Activities*, unpublished, 1998

LAB (1998c), *Legotla: Statistics on the Work Done by way of Salaried Staff Models*, unpublished, 1998

LAB (1999a), *Annual Report 1996/97*, 1999, Pretoria: LAB

LAC (Legal Aid Council) (2000a), *Information Brochure on the Legal Aid Council of the Federal Republic of Nigeria*, 2000, Abuja: LAC

LRC (Legal Research Council), *Annual Report*, 1996, Johannesburg: LRC

LRC, *Annual Report*, 1998, Johannesburg: LRC

McClymont, M and Golub, S (eds), *Many Roads to Justice: The Law Related Work of Ford Foundation Grantees Around the World*, 2000, New York: Ford Foundation

McCutcheon, A, 'Eastern Europe: funding strategies for public interest law in transitional societies', in McClymont, M and Golub, S (eds), *Many Roads to Justice: The Law Related Work of Ford Foundation Grantees Around the World*, 2000, New York: Ford Foundation

McQuoid-Mason, D J, *An Outline of Legal Aid in South Africa*, 1981, Durban: Butterworths

McQuoid-Mason, D J, 'Problems associated with the legal representation of Africans in the urban areas of South Africa' (1984) Acta Juridica 181

McQuoid-Mason, D J, 'Legal aid clinics as a social service', in McQuoid-Mason, DJ (ed), *Legal Aid and Law Clinics in South Africa*, 1985, Durban: University of Natal

McQuoid-Mason, D J, 'The organisation, administration and funding of legal aid clinics in South Africa' (1986) 1 NULSR 189

McQuoid-Mason, D J, 'Public defenders and alternative service' (1991) 4 SACJ 267

McQuoid-Mason, D J, 'The role of legal aid clinics in assisting victims of crime', in Schurink, WJ, Snyman, I, Krugel, WF and Slabbert, L (eds), *Victimisation: Nature and Trends*, 1992, Pretoria: Human Sciences Research Council

McQuoid-Mason, D J, 'Working commission recommendations, National Legal Aid Forum, Kempton Park, 15-17 January 1998' (1999) 12 SACJ 48

McQuoid-Mason, D J, 'The delivery of civil legal aid services in South Africa' (2000) 24 Fordham International Law Journal (Symposium) 111-142

Minister of Justice and Department of Justice, *Enhancing Access to Justice through Legal Aid*, unpublished position paper, 1998, National Legal Aid Forum

Morka, F, 'Issues of concern to developing and transitional countries' (2000) 24 Fordham International Law Journal (Symposium) 323-329

Onomigbo Okpoko, TJ, 'Address by President of Nigerian Bar Association' at the Legal Aid Council of Nigeria Workshop on Legal Aid in the New Millennium in Abuja, Nigeria, 26-27 June 2000

Pincus, W, 'Legal clinics in the law schools', in Faculty of Law, University of Natal, *Legal Aid in South Africa*, 1974, Durban: Faculty of Law, University of Natal, 123

'Professional news,' De Rebus, July 1998

Reyntjens, J in Zemans, F A (ed), *Perspectives on Legal Aid*, 1979, London: Pinter

ENVIRONMENTAL LITIGATION IN HONG KONG: THE ROLE OF THE JUDICIARY AND STATUTORY TRIBUNALS

Anton Cooray[*]

Although the legislature began legislating for basic forms of environmental protection from the very beginning of its establishment in 1843, dedicated environmental legislation is a recent phenomenon in Hong Kong. In the early years, legislative measures in the realm of environmental protection were concerned with improving the general sanitation, health and safety of people.[1] The earliest examples of such legislation include the Preservation of Good Order and Cleanliness Ordinance of 1844 and the Market Ordinance of 1847. Perhaps Hong Kong's first dedicated environmental statute was the Clean Air Ordinance of 1959, which contained provisions for the designation of smoke control areas and the issuing of smoke abatement notices.

It was in the last two decades that Hong Kong's five major environmental statutes were passed.[2] Although Hong Kong has not adopted an integrated environmental protection regime—relying instead on a pragmatic approach by enacting legislation dealing with specific areas of environmental concern—these statutes and other supplemental legislation[3] ensure a fair degree of centralised policy formulation and implementation by the conferment on the Environmental Protection Department of enforcement and monitoring powers. While the Director of Environmental Protection is the enforcement authority under some of these statutes—such as the Dumping at Sea Ordinance—the power to implement the other statutes has been given to other public officers or agencies—such as the Director of Agriculture, Fisheries and Conservation.[4]

---

[*] Professor of Law, School of Law, City University of Hong Kong. Research for this paper as well as the author's conference participation was funded by City University of Hong Kong.

[1] Other examples include: the Buildings and Nuisances Ordinance, enacted to ensure safety and sanitary condition of buildings; the Waterworks Ordinance, creating offences such as polluting water and discharging noxious or injurious matter into waterworks; the Prospecting and Mining Ordinance of 1906, which did not contain any environmental protection measures, but was amended in 1954 to include provisions to prevent water pollution, ensure safe disposal of waste and the preservation of sacred areas, trees and other objects of veneration. See also the Summary Offences Ordinance, the Registry of Chinese Inhabitants Ordinance.

[2] Waste Disposal Ordinance and the Water Pollution Control Ordinance, 1980; Air Pollution Control Ordinance, 1983 (replacing the Clean Air Ordinance, 1959); Noise Control Ordinance, 1988; Environmental Impact Assessment Ordinance, 1997.

[3] Chief among them are: the Dumping at Sea Ordinance of 1995, the Merchant Shipping (Prevention and Control of Pollution) Ordinance of 1990, the Radiation Ordinance of 1957 and the Dangerous Goods Ordinance of 1956, all of which are relevant to control of waste disposal; the Animals and Plants (Protection of Endangered Species) Ordinance of 1976, the Plant (Importation and Pest Control) Ordinance of 1976, the Wild Animals Protection Ordinance of 1976, the Public Health (Animals and Birds) Ordinance of 1935, the Whaling Industry (Regulation) Ordinance of 1996, the Marine Fish Culture Ordinance of 1980, the Marine Parks Ordinance of 1995, the Forests and Countryside Ordinance of 1937 and the Country Parks Ordinance of 1976, all of which are relevant to protection of flora and fauna; and the Antiquities and Monuments Ordinance of 1971, which is the principal ordinance on heritage protection.

[4] For instance, under the Animals and Plants (Protection of Endangered Species) Ordinance.

OPPORTUNITIES FOR ENVIRONMENTAL LITIGATION

The first opportunity for environmental litigation in Hong Kong came in the form of criminal cases for breach of environmental controls. An 1844 Ordinance for the Preservation of Good Order and Cleanliness provided for several environmental type offences. For instance it was made an offence for any person to 'defile or pollute any well, stream, or water course.' Other provisions aimed to control noise, including any noise at night, calculated to disturb or interfere with the general tranquillity or calculated to disturb or annoy any person. Another provision made it an offence to cut, break, damage, injure or destroy any tree, shrub, or underwood. These were summary offences within the jurisdiction of a Magistrate.

The next development in facilitating environmental litigation occurred with the introduction of the concept of statutory nuisance. The Public Health and Buildings Ordinance of 1903 made provision for prevention and abatement of nuisances. Statutory nuisances included, for instance, any premises in such dirty or unsanitary condition as to be dangerous or prejudicial to health, any noxious matter or waste water discharged into a street, gutter or watercourse, and any act which might be dangerous to life or injurious to health or property. The Sanitary Board could serve a nuisance abatement notice on the person responsible for the nuisance or on the owner or occupier of premises on which the nuisance arose. A person on whom an abatement notice was served could apply to the Sanitary Board for a review. The Board had the power to inquire into the matter and could confirm, modify, suspend or discharge the notice or extend the time allowed for compliance with the notice. The Board could prosecute any person who failed to comply with an abatement notice.

In prosecutions for the failure to comply with an abatement notice magistrates had extensive powers. Section 33 provided as follows:

(1) If the magistrate is satisfied that the requirement of the Board is legal, or that the alleged nuisance exists, or that, although the said nuisance is abated, it is likely to recur on the said premises, he shall make an order on such person—

(a) requiring him to comply with all or any of the requisitions of the notice, or otherwise to abate the nuisance, within a time specified in the order, and to do any works necessary for that purpose; or

(b) prohibiting the recurrence of the nuisance, and directing the execution of the works necessary to prevent the recurrence; or

(c) both requiring abatement and prohibiting the recurrence of the nuisance.

(2) The magistrate may, by his order, impose a fine not exceeding fifty dollars on the person on whom the order is made, and shall also give directions as to the payment of all costs incurred up to the time of the hearing or making the order.

Failure to comply with an order of a magistrate to comply with any requisition of the Board was punishable by fine. More importantly, the Board was empowered to abate the nuisance and do anything that was necessary for that purpose and recover the expenses from the person on whom the notice had been served.

The Public Health and Buildings Ordinance of 1903 set the stage for the growth of a sophisticated system of environmental litigation when it introduced two important safeguards for persons affected by the administrative decisions. First, a person aggrieved by an abatement notice could have the notice reviewed by an administrative body, although it was the Sanitary Board, who issued the notice in the first instance. Second, where a person was brought before a magistrate for non-compliance with a notice, the magistrate had to be satisfied that the requirement of the Board was valid in law.

The Public Health and Buildings Ordinance was innovative in the sense that it enabled the magistrate not only to punish the offender by imposing a fine, but also to order the offender to carry out any works necessary to comply with the notice. The judiciary was thus authorised to perform a function, which would generally be regarded as strictly falling within the remit of the administration.

When, some 32 years later, the Public Health (Sanitation) Ordinance of 1935 replaced the Public Health and Buildings Ordinance, the provisions relating to nuisance abatement notices were retained, presumably because those provisions had proved effective and generally acceptable. These provisions served as the model for the enforcement of smoke controls when the Legislative Council passed the Clean Air Ordinance of 1959. The Clean Air Ordinance improved on the model provisions by enabling a person aggrieved by a noise abatement notice to appeal to a higher administrative authority, namely to the Governor.

THE ERA OF ENVIRONMENTAL LEGISLATION

The introduction in the last two decades of the five major environmental laws (dealing with air pollution, water pollution, noise pollution, waste disposal and environmental impact assessment) saw an increased role for administrative authorities as well as courts of law in environmental litigation. The Environmental Protection Department was given the central role of implementing environmental legislation, with important roles to be played by the Chief Executive of the Hong Kong Special Administrative Region (Governor under British colonial administration), the Chief Secretary and the Secretary for the Environment and Food (until recently Secretary for Planning, Environment and Lands).[5] The role played by the Environmental Protection Department under each of the environmental statutes is an important one, in view of the absence of an integrated pollution control system. A certain element of integration is, of course, provided by the Environmental Impact Assessment Ordinance.

The Hong Kong environmental regulatory framework is made up of primary and subsidiary legislation, codes of practice, technical memoranda and non-statutory guidelines. It makes use of devices such as mandatory environmental standards (such as water quality standards), licensing, abatement notices and ordering of preventive or remedial measures. These provisions inevitably lead to the creation of statutory offences such as failure to obtain or comply with a licence or permit, failure to comply with an abatement notice or a notice requiring remedial measures, and resisting site inspections by an enforcement authority. These provisions bring original and appellate criminal courts into action, to consider not only

---

[5] The Basic Law, Hong Kong's constitution since 1997, virtually provides for the continuation of Hong Kong's previous system of colonial administration. The executive branch is led by the Chief Executive (formerly the Governor), who is advised by an Executive Council. The legislative power is vested in the partly elected Legislative Council which, however, cannot initiate legislation on matters involving public revenue or affecting the government structure. The principal advisers of the Chief Executive from the administration are the three principal secretaries, namely the Chief Secretary, the Financial Secretary and the Secretary for Justice. The Chief Secretary heads the administration and has an important part to play in policy formulation and implementation. The Financial Secretary is responsible for economic and fiscal policies of the government. The Secretary for Justice heads the Department of Justice. Various policy bureaux of the government, each headed by a secretary, are under either the Chief Secretary or the Financial Secretary.

the constituent elements of an environmental offence and matters of evidence and procedure, but also wider legal issues such as the validity of any relevant administrative action. Judicial review of course would be an alternative channel so far as the legality of administrative action is concerned.

Environmental statutes quite often provide for an administrative appeal, for example by petition to the Chief Executive.[6] There is no legislative provision or administrative direction of general application requiring the Chief Executive to hold a hearing in determining an appeal. A notable exception is the Public Health (Animals and Birds) Ordinance, which provides that the appellant may appear before the Chief Executive in Council to make representations. The Ordinance, however, does not permit the Director of Public Health, whose decision is challenged, to make representations.

Certain other Ordinances such as the Dangerous Goods Ordinance, the Mining Ordinance and the Wild Animals Protection Ordinance provide for an appeal to the Administrative Appeals Board.[7] The Administrative Appeals Board was established in 1994 to replace gradually appeals to the Governor (now Chief Executive) under existing legislation. The Board consists of suitable persons appointed by the Chief Executive and is chaired by a person qualified for appointment as a District Judge. Unlike the Chief Executive, the Board must conduct appeal hearings in public and permit parties to have legal representation. It may affirm, vary or set aside the decision appealed from and award costs. It has no power to grant compensation or ex-gratia payments. However, it may refer the matter under appeal for reconsideration by the decision-maker and one of the purposes of this referral is to require the decision-maker to consider making an ex-gratia payment to the appellant for any loss occasioned by its decision.[8]

More importantly, the Air Pollution Control Ordinance, the Water Pollution Control Ordinance, the Waste Disposal Ordinance, the Noise Control Ordinance, the Environmental Impact Assessment Ordinance and the Dumping at Sea Ordinance each provide for a purpose-made appeal board, with jurisdiction over a number of administrative decisions taken under it.

Since the Chief Executive is not required to prepare any report of its appeal decisions, no information is publicly available regarding any environmental appeals decided by him. Although hearings before the Administrative Appeals Tribunal are held in public, its decisions too are not publicly available. While decisions of the Environmental Appeal Boards are also not readily available,[9] the author was able to obtain a full set of the appeal decisions from the Appeal Board Secretariat. Our discussion on administrative litigation is therefore limited to the work of the Environmental Appeal Boards.

---

[6] The following ordinances provide for an appeal by way of petition to the Chief Executive: Animals and Plants (Protection of Endangered Species); Radiation; Plant Importation and Pest Control; Public Health (Animals and Birds); Marine Fish Culture; Country Parks; Antiquities and Monuments.

[7] See the Administrative Appeals Board Ordinance of 1994.

[8] See Debates of the Legislative Council, 31 March 1993, pp 2777-2780, and 26 January 1994, pp 2053-2059.

[9] The web site of the Environmental Protection Department published the Appeal Board's decision in the *Kowloon Canton Railway Corporation* case, which is discussed later on in this article under 'Powers and functions of Appeal Boards.'

JURISDICTION OF ORDINARY COURTS OF LAW
IN ENVIRONMENTAL LITIGATION

Judicial intervention in environmental decision-making process has taken two main forms: First, criminal jurisdiction of magistrates and appeal courts in respect of statutory offences; and second, supervisory civil jurisdiction of the Court of First Instance (the equivalent of the British High Court). We will first examine the type of issues that magistrates and appellate courts had to grapple with in criminal cases, followed by the type of issues that came up before the Court of First Instance and the appellate courts on judicial review.

Criminal jurisdiction of the courts

When dealing with prosecutions for environmental offences, such as failure to comply with orders or notices issued by an enforcement authority, the magistrates would commonly deal with issues of evidence, procedure and sentencing. Incidentally, the courts have had to determine other relevant issues such as the validity of the administrative order alleged to have been breached by the defendant. For instance in *Secretary of Justice v Tak Yue Restaurant*, the Court of First Instance had to decide whether the magistrate was right to consider a noise abatement notice invalid for the reason that it had ordered the defendant not to exceed a certain noise level in conducting its restaurant business, when the relevant technical memorandum appeared to tolerate a higher level of noise in the area where the restaurant was situated. The Court of First Instance held that the aim of the technical memorandum was to prescribe a noise level that should not be exceeded in a particular area. It held that in order to keep the accumulative noise level in an area below the prescribed limit it might be necessary to prescribe stricter noise levels for individual sources of noise in that area.[10] Therefore while recognising that the Noise Authority must be guided by the technical memorandum in determining whether it should issue a noise abatement notice, the court adopted a generous interpretation of the relevant statutory provisions and held that the Noise Pollution Control Authority could prescribe harsher noise levels.[11]

Courts have not always been supportive of the authorities. In *R v Boon Wai* for instance, the High Court (now the Court of First Instance) held that the Noise Authority had no power to informally grant an extension of time for compliance with a notice requiring the appellant company to eliminate undesirable air pollutants. The court held that a notice had to give a reasonable time for compliance and that where the time specified in the notice was insufficient, the Authority could not cure the defect by informally agreeing to extend the period of time for compliance. Since the prosecution failed to establish that the 60-day period that had been specified in the notice was a reasonably sufficient period of time to replace oil-fired ovens with gas-fired ovens, the notice was held to be invalid. Similarly, in the case of *Secretary of Justice v Poly Gain Enterprises Ltd* the Court of First Instance strictly construed a noise abatement notice. There, an abatement notice issued on 5 February 1994 had required a restaurant operator to take measures within two months to ensure that the noise emanating

---

[10] In arriving at this conclusion the Court of First Instance followed the reasoning adopted by the Noise Pollution Control Appeal Board in Appeal No 2 of 1991 and No 1-8 of 1994.

[11] The court emphasised that s 10(2) of the Noise Control Ordinance requires the Noise Pollution Control Authority to be guided by Technical Memoranda only 'when undertaking any measurement or assessment to determine if a noise abatement notice should be served under s 13(1)(c),' and that the Authority is not bound by the Technical Memorandum when it decides on the noise level that it specifies in a noise abatement notice.

from its ventilating and refrigerating system did not breach a prescribed noise level. The defendant took remedial measures within that time to the satisfaction of the authority. Some three years later, on discovering that the ventilating and refrigerating system was operating in breach of the noise level prescribed in the 1994 notice, the authority brought a prosecution for failure to comply with the notice. The Court held that the notice required the noise to be abated during a certain period and that the notice ceased to be operative at the expiration of that period of time. Upon its true interpretation, the notice did not have perpetual validity so as to prevent the restaurant operator from exceeding the prescribed noise level for an indeterminate time.[12]

Courts have not lost sight of the importance of giving effect to legislative intention. This they have done by adopting a purposive approach to the interpretation of environmental legislation. In *R v Cabot Plastics Hong Kong Ltd* the High Court, on a case stated from the magistrate, gave an extended meaning to the word 'occupier.' There, Cabot Plastics Hong Kong Ltd engaged a construction company to build a factory on its land. The construction company installed some boilers and a chimney (for use when the factory became operative) in breach of an air pollution control regulation. The Air Pollution Control Authority prosecuted Cabot Plastics in its capacity as the occupier of the premises for the breach of regulation. 'Occupier' is defined in the regulation to mean:

(a) The occupier of premises on which a furnace, oven, chimney or flue is to be installed, altered or modified; and

(b) The person having the management or control or receiving the profit of the business carried on in such premises.

The court held that the definition of 'occupier' included not only a person in charge of the machinery in operation, but also a person who intended to make future use of the machinery. The court was influenced by the consideration that 'the mischief aimed at in these Regulations is the prevention of air pollution caused by the operation of furnaces, chimneys, etc.'[13]

The Hong Kong courts have recognised the importance of environmental legislation in protecting vital social interests. They have held that environmental legislation belongs to the category of social legislation and that it is permissible to impose strict liability on offenders of environmental controls[14] consistently with the presumption of innocence enshrined in the Hong Kong Bill of Rights.[15] In the case of *HKSAR v Y-ITC Construction Company*, the Court of Appeal alluded to the importance of social considerations in interpreting environmental legislation, in that case the Noise Control Ordinance. It said:

---

[12] This seems to be at odds with the decision in the English case of *Wellingborough Borough Council v Gordon*, where the High Court upheld the validity of a criminal prosecution for a breach of a noise abatement notice that had been served three years earlier. It might be argued that in Hong Kong a noise abatement which requires the recipient of it not to exceed a certain noise level has perpetual effect while a requirement in such a notice requiring certain remedial measures to be taken would lapse once such measures have been put in place.

[13] *R v Cabot Plastics Hong Kong Ltd*, p 466.

[14] Following the landmark decision of the Privy Council in the Hong Kong case of *Gammon (HK) Ltd & Ors v Attorney General*, which concerned a breach of building construction regulations.

[15] Hong Kong Bill of Rights, Art 11: 'Everyone charged with a criminal offence shall have the right to be presumed innocent until proved guilty according to law'.

Unless properly controlled in Hong Kong, which, it goes without saying, is a densely populated area, unauthorised noise is likely to disrupt the lives of ordinary people, leading in a number of ways to deterioration in health quite apart from the obvious nuisance it poses to the public.[16]

In addition to deciding that the prosecution does not have to prove *mens rea* on the part of the offender, the courts have taken into account the seriousness of environmental damage caused by pollution in determining the appropriate sentence. As Duffy J said for the High Court in *The Queen v Tsui Chit-fan and Others*, on an appeal against sentence imposed under the Ozone Layer Protection Ordinance:

> The Courts must ensure that the penalties they impose adequately reflect the community's determination to protect its own environment, and to observe its international obligations under the various environmental pollution agreements and they must ensure that these penalties are a real deterrent against whose priorities list profit above our ecological well-being.[17]

While recognising the importance of protecting the environment at the cost of imposing some restrictions on fundamental rights, courts have been vigilant to see that no criminal prosecutions are instituted unless there is clear breach of the law. For instance in *HKSAR v Cheung Cheuk Fung* the manager of a cake shop appealed his conviction for an offence under the Air Pollution Control (Smoke) Regulations, which was based upon pollution arising from his business. The appellant argued that the conviction was unsafe because the summonses did not clearly set out why he was personally responsible for the offences for which the cake shop had been convicted. The Court of First Instance rejected that argument because officers of the Environmental Protection Department had explained to him the importance of strict adherence to the relevant guidelines to control smoke emissions, and warned him that he would be personally liable for any breach of regulations.

Supervisory jurisdiction of the courts

There have been several judicial review applications challenging the legality of decisions taken under environmental legislation. In dealing with such applications courts have acted with restraint so as not to usurp the functions of the administration, but have not been slow to defend citizens' rights where the administration had been overzealous. On the other hand, courts have firmly held that mere technical irregularities in statutory notices and orders do not render such notices or orders invalid, so long as the alleged irregularities have not caused substantial injustice. For instance, in the case of *Asia Dyeing Co Ltd v Air Pollution Control Authority* the Court of Appeal dealing with a statutory provision which enabled the enforcement authority to issue an abatement notice in respect of existing or imminent air pollution nuisance, held that the failure to clearly specify whether the notice was in respect of an existing nuisance or an imminent nuisance did not invalidate the notice.

Not surprisingly, an important consideration has been the application of the 'Wednesbury principle of unreasonableness' to administrative discretion. *Secan Ltd v Attorney General,* and *Sy Chokk Luen v Director of Environmental Protection,* are illustrative of the limited nature of judicial control through the principle of unreasonableness. These cases represent the commonly held view that unreasonableness in the *Wednesbury* sense only means capriciousness or irrationality.

---

[16] *HKSAR v Y-ITC Construction Company,* p 196. See also *Attorney General v Helena Restaurant (1981) Ltd,* p 497-498.

[17] *The Queen v Tsui Chit-fan and Others,* p 274.

In *Secan* the Government lease stipulated that Secan, a residential property developer, must carry out noise mitigation measures as might be required by the Director of Environmental Protection. The property could not be occupied unless the necessary works were carried out to the satisfaction of the Director. Secan failed to convince the Court of Appeal that the Director had acted unreasonably in requiring it to build noise barriers, when other less expensive noise mitigation measures would have been adequate. The Court held that the Government lease between the government and Secan was a commercial agreement and that its duty was to give effect to their agreement. It disapproved of the High Court's conclusion that any requirements that the Director imposed must be such as a reasonable businessman would have expected. The Court of Appeal found the test of the reasonable businessman's expectations a difficult one to apply and held that when the lease required the Director's approval, the Director came to be vested with a wide discretion, limited only by the principle of *Wednesbury* unreasonableness. As Litton VP (who had one time served as the chairman of the environmental appeal boards as well as the Town Planning Appeal Board) explained, when determining the required ameliorative measures the Director had to 'act in good faith. He must exercise judgment. He must not act capriciously. The judgment concerning those measures is his, and his alone.'[18] In other words, so long as he did not act unreasonably in the *Wednesbury* sense, the Director was entitled to exercise the wide powers vested in him by contract.

Similarly, in the case of *Sy Chok Luen* the Director's wide discretion in determining the amount of financial assistance given to livestock farmers adversely affected by the Livestock Waste Control Scheme was held to be valid so long as the Director did not act unreasonably in the *Wednesbury* sense.

THE ROLE OF ADMINISTRATIVE APPEAL BOARDS

Powers and functions of appeal boards

The six major environmental statutes (Air, Water, Noise, Waste Disposal, Environmental Impact Assessment and Dumping at Sea) provide for an appeal board. Each of these statutes provides that the Chief Executive has the power to appoint a legally qualified chairman[19] and such other suitable persons to a panel of persons, from which the chairman appoints an appeal board to determine any appeal. The practice, however, has been not to appoint six different appeal panels, but to appoint a common appeal panel, from which an appeal board may be appointed for the purposes of any of the six environmental statutes. An appeal board has jurisdiction to hear appeals against decisions made by administrative officers, such as rejection of a licence application or enforcement decisions. The appeal board procedure is prescribed by primary and subsidiary legislation, with power given to the chairman to decide on any procedural matters not covered by such legislative provisions. The important differences between the provisions in the six environmental statutes relating to appeals are set out in the following paragraphs.

---

18 *Secan Ltd v Attorney General*, p 639.
19 Meaning, a person qualified for appointment as a District Judge.

Grounds for appeal

The Noise Control Ordinance and the Water Pollution Control Ordinance sets out the grounds on which an appeal may be made. For instance the Air Pollution Control Ordinance provides that the Appeal Board may entertain an appeal on the following grounds only:

(1) A decision, requirement or specification:

(a) is not justified under the Air Pollution Control Ordinance or a technical memorandum issued under the Ordinance; or

(b) has some material error in content or material defect in administrative procedure;

(2) The opinion of the Authority or an authorised officer that air pollution which caused or contributed by an emission is unreasonable;

(3) The opinion of the Authority or the authorised officer that the air pollution is prejudicial to health is unreasonable;

(4) A disciplinary order or order for costs of a disciplinary inquiry against a registered asbestos consultant, supervisor, contractor or laboratory is unjustifiable.

The Noise Control Ordinance lists similar grounds and has two additional grounds. Namely,

(a) that compliance with the requirements of the notice would cause the appellant economic hardship seriously prejudicial to the conduct of his business; or

(b) that the notice should have been served on some person other than the appellant.

So far almost all the appeals where there has been a hearing have been under the Noise Control Ordinance and the Air Pollution Control Ordinance. The other ordinances under which appeal hearings have taken place are the Water Pollution Control Ordinance (one appeal), the Dumping at Sea Ordinance (one appeal) and the Environmental Impact Assessment Ordinance (one appeal). It is therefore too early to see the extent to which appeals under other ordinances will be influenced by statutory grounds relevant to noise pollution and air pollution appeals. Appeals under ordinances other than the Noise Control Ordinance and the Air Pollution Control Ordinance will undoubtedly be on grounds known to administrative law such as procedural and substantive *ultra vires*, improper purpose, legitimate expectations and unreasonableness. It remains to be seen whether grounds such as legitimate expectation will be acceptable as grounds of appeal under the Noise or Air Pollution Ordinances, both of which seem to suggest that the grounds of appeal specified therein are exclusive. It is possible that the appeal boards may strictly construe the statutory provisions relating to their power, in which case judicial review will be the appropriate avenue for redress on any of the general grounds of challenge known to administrative law.

Jurisdiction and appeals

The appeal boards are strictly bound by the statutory provisions relating to their powers and functions as well as appeal procedure. In *Noise Control Appeal No 1 of 1991*, the Appeal Board refused to accept an appeal filed out of time and insisted that it did not have a discretion to accede to the appellant's request because 'the authority vested in the Appeal Board is conferred by statute. The Board, unlike the Supreme Court of Hong Kong, has no inherent jurisdiction. The discretion, if we have any, must be found within the statute itself.'[20] In some

---

[20]   *Noise Control Appeal No 1 of 1991*, para 4.

other cases, however, the Appeal Board has been willing to take a less restrictive view of statutory requirements.

For instance, in *Air Pollution Appeal No 1 of 1993* the appellant was permitted to add a new ground of appeal during the appeal, although the statute requires grounds of appeal to be communicated to the Appeal Board and to the respondent well before the commencement of the appeal hearing. The appellant was permitted to present another ground of appeal because it had already referred to the underlying argument in its statement of facts. Similarly in *Noise Control Appeal No 1 of 1997*, the Appeal Board permitted the appellant to introduce a new ground of appeal, namely unreasonableness, although it had ticked against only 'material informality' in the appeal form. The Board allowed the appellant to raise the new argument because the material it submitted to the Board clearly showed that the appellant wished to complain of unreasonableness. It seems that while the Boards would not step outside their statutory powers and claim any 'inherent jurisdiction,' they will not hesitate to overlook technical defects if justice requires it.

Furthermore, all six environmental statutes provide that the Appeal Board may confirm, reverse or vary the decision, requirement or specification appealed from. Although they do not provide explicitly that the Board has the power to inquire into the matter in question *de novo*, they provide that it may receive evidence on oath; admit or take into account any statement, document, information or matter even if it would be inadmissible as evidence in a court of law; and summon any person before it to produce any document or to give evidence. In the case of *Kowloon Canton Railway Corporation v Director of Environmental Protection* the Appeal Board made a preliminary ruling regarding its jurisdiction to the effect that it has the same powers in making the determination as those of the Director of Environmental Protection but that it decides the appeal on the evidence that it hears and receives. There the Kowloon Canton Railway Corporation appealed against the Director's decision to reject the environmental impact assessment report and the application for an environmental permit that the Corporation had submitted under the Environmental Impact Assessment Ordinance. In its appeal, the Corporation sought to introduce new evidence and new information in support of its railway project and suggested that the Appeal Board might consider approving the environmental impact assessment report subject to a number of important conditions that it proposed on appeal.

The Appeal Board rejected the argument put forward on behalf of the Director that it should not receive new information that the Corporation had not previously submitted to the Director. At the same time, the Appeal Board refused to accept the Corporation's argument that it had jurisdiction to approve the project proposal subject to conditions that the Corporation now proposed in order to address the environmental impact concerns. The Board found that the new proposals were too important to be accepted without scrutiny through the public consultation process that attends the consideration of the report by the Director in the first instance.[21] While recognising that the Appeal Board had statutory authority to approve a report that had been rejected by the Director, if the report could be made acceptable by subjecting it to minor amendments,[22] the Appeal Board made it clear that 'we sit as an appellate tribunal not a tribunal of inquiry.'[23]

---

[21] The Kowloon Canton Railway Corporation submitted a new environmental impact assessment report proposing an alternative method of constructing the railway extension, which was approved by the Director of Environmental Protection in March 2002.

[22] Section 4.5.2 of the Technical Memorandum provides that 'in case the report requires certain amendments but such amendments will not affect the validity of the assessment and the overall result and conclusions of the report, the Director may approve the report with conditions'. The appeal board

The Board took such a strict view of its jurisdiction because to approve an environmental impact assessment report on the strength of new evidence would be to frustrate the intention of the legislation that all information relating to the environmental impact assessment process, other than minor details, must be subjected to public consultation. In appeals under other ordinances the Appeal Board has been prepared to conduct a much fuller inquiry, in the absence of any such requirement for active public participation in the decision-making process. It must also be noted that appeals decided under other Ordinances were not concerned with the issue whether permission must be granted for a proposal that had been rejected by the decision-maker, but had dealt with matters such as whether the issuing of an abatement notice or the refusal of a licence was unreasonable or otherwise defective.

Decisions, directions and compensation

All the six environmental statutes provide that the decision of the Appeal Board is final and conclusive. However, under the Air Pollution Control Ordinance and the Water Pollution Control Ordinance the respondent administrative agency (but not the appellant) may request the Chief Executive to review any decision of the Appeal Board, where to do so would be in the public interest. To that extent the decisions of the Appeal Board under those two ordinances are not final and conclusive.[24]

The Environmental Impact Assessment Ordinance and the Noise Control Ordinance also empower the Appeal Board to give directions to the enforcement authority regarding the manner in which it must carry out its duties relevant to the appeal. The Air Pollution Control Ordinance, Noise Control Ordinance and Environmental Impact Assessment Ordinance empower the Appeal Board to award costs.

Furthermore, the Air Pollution Control Ordinance empowers the Appeal Board to award compensation to the appellant affected by an unjustified enforcement action. We have seen above that the Administrative Appeals Board has no power to award compensation but that it may refer a matter back to the decision-maker, for instance, to consider the desirability of making an ex-gratia payment.[25] In *Hyundai-CCECC Joint Venture v Environmental Protection Department* the appellant unsuccessfully contended that the Environmental Protection Department should not have changed its previous practice and refused a permit for the appellant to continue dumping waste in open waters. One of the arguments in support of the contention was that the respondent department had made representations that the appellant would be able to continue dumping waste in open waters in the People's Republic of China, and those representations gave rise to a legitimate expectation. While rejecting that argument the Appeal Board found that the respondent had in some measure contributed to the false

---

thought that the Director, and the Appeal Board on appeal against the rejection of a report by Director, had been given this power so that minor defects in a report can be remedied without having to go through the public consultation process again.

[23] The Town Planning Appeal Board had taken a similar view of its appellate jurisdiction. It has asserted its jurisdiction to come to an independent judgment on a planning application on appeal before it and has been prepared to consider new information and evidence. The appeal board has however not been prepared to approve a new planning proposal materially different from the one that had been considered and rejected by the Town Planning Board in the first instance. See *Town Planning Appeal Nos 5 and 7 of 1997* (unreported) and *Halsbury's Laws of Hong Kong*, 'Town Planning', paragraph 385.261.

[24] A consultation paper published by the Environmental Protection Department in March 2001 doubted whether a review of an appeal board decision by the Chief Executive was a violation of article 10 of the Bill of Rights Ordinance, which enshrines the right to a fair hearing, and proposed to remove the provision relating to such review.

[25] See 'The Era of Environmental Legislation' above.

hope that the appellant had come to entertain. Therefore, the Board thought that the appellant deserved some monetary compensation for the financial loss it sustained when it had to adopt more expensive methods of waste disposal. The Appeal Board made this observation particularly because it had no jurisdiction to award compensation.

Finally, the Water Pollution Control Ordinance and the Waste Disposal Ordinance provide that an appeal against certain administrative decisions has the effect of suspending the operation of the notice or decision appealed against.

Survey of Appeal Board decisions

Starting with one solitary appeal under the Air Pollution Control Ordinance in 1988, the Environmental Appeal Board has received 69 appeals under the six ordinances.[26] Forty three of these were either rejected by the board as invalid or abandoned by the appellant. Of the 26 appeals reaching the hearing stage only 11 were successful.[27] The subject matter of these appeals have ranged from rather straight forward ones such as the validity of noise or air pollution abatement notices to the validity of the rejection by the Director of Environmental Protection of an environmental permit and an environmental report for the Kowloon Canton Railway's ambitious new railway extension to the border crossing into Mainland China. The decisions of the environmental appeal board have set out the applicable legal principles and defined the exclusive domain of administrative discretion, and in so doing laid down useful guidelines that environmental decision-makers have to follow in order to protect legitimate interests of affected parties. In the following paragraphs we will set out some of those principles and guidelines that the appeal boards have identified and applied.

Administrative notices and requirements

An environmental authority must be careful to ensure that any requirement they impose on persons served with abatement notices must be appropriate and valid. The Appeal Board will declare such notice invalid if it is not satisfied that the requirements are appropriate in the particular circumstances of the case.[28] This particularly means that the authority must take into consideration the locality and characteristics of the area in determining whether a particular activity would amount to a nuisance.

Second, no abatement notice may be issued unless there is clear evidence that a breach of legislation has taken place. For instance in *Noise Control Appeal No 4 of 1995* the Appeal Board held that the Authority was wrong to have asserted in the abatement notice that the keeping of a watchdog in an industrial building was a source of annoyance in the absence of any evidence to support such assertion. Similarly in *Air Pollution Control Appeal No 2 of 1992* the abatement notice was held to be invalid for the reason that there was no evidence to prove that

---

[26] Thirty-five under the Noise Control Ordinance, 24 under the Air Pollution Control Ordinance, six under the Water Pollution Control Ordinance, two under the Environmental Impact Assessment Ordinance, one under the Waste Disposal Ordinance and one under the Dumping at Sea Ordinance.

[27] Noise nine (eight of which were jointly heard), Air one and Water one. The unsuccessful appeals were: Noise seven, Air six, Environmental Impact Assessment one and Dumping at Sea one.

[28] See *Noise Control Appeal No 3 of 1995* where, however, the Appeal Board was satisfied that the requirements specified in the notice in question were appropriate.

smoke and smoked-meat odour from a business premises in an industrial area was a nuisance or annoyance to the inhabitants of the appellant's neighbourhood.[29]

Third, a noise abatement notice must clearly state what remedial measures have to be taken to comply with such notice. In *Noise Control Appeal No 4 of 1995* the Noise Control Authority had served a notice on the occupier of a business premises who kept a watchdog there to 'ensure that henceforth the noise, including dog barking from the aforesaid premises, is no longer a source of annoyance [to nearby residents].' On behalf of the Authority it was submitted that installing a wooden door could have abated the noise, but there was no reference to this requirement in the notice. Nor did the notice specify a noise level that the occupier of the premises should not exceed, as required by the relevant section of the Noise Control Ordinance. For these reasons the Appeal Board concluded that the notice was invalid since it failed to inform what remedial measures had to be taken by the recipient of the notice.[30]

Fourth, any requirements that an environmental authority decides to specify in an abatement notice must be reasonable. In Noise Pollution Appeal Nos 1-8 of 1994, the Appeal Board considered a total ban on the use of metal hammers in a shipyard to be unreasonable requirement. In several other cases the Appeal Board recognised the validity of the principle but was satisfied on the facts that the requirements were reasonable.

Fifth, the time given for compliance with an abatement notice must be reasonable. While this principle was accepted in several cases, such as Air Pollution Appeal No 1 of 1993, no abatement notice has been set aside on appeal on the ground that the time allowed for compliance was unreasonable. We have seen above a criminal appeal case where a noise abatement notice was set aside by the High Court on the ground that the time for compliance specified therein was unreasonable.[31]

Finally, it is crucial that the authority explains to a person served with an abatement notice why a particular requirement has been imposed. Where an appellant contends on appeal that noise levels specified in an abatement notice are too stringent, the Authority has a duty to explain in great detail the methodology and reasons to justify the specified noise level.[32] In an appeal decided in 1994 the Appeal Board had recommended that the Authority should consider publishing the methods, principles and practices relevant to determining the acceptable noise levels for particular activities and neighbourhoods.[33] In *Noise Control Appeal No 3 of 1995* the Appeal Board made the following observation: 'It has occurred to the Board that improved communication with the appellants could lead to a reduction in appeals and unnecessary misunderstanding or suspicion by appellants. It was also suggested that more explanatory information on the formulae used and the standard acoustical principles and practices used would be helpful in future for appellants trying to understand the basis of the case against them'.

---

[29] There is, however, English authority to the effect that it is not necessary to adduce evidence from neighbouring occupiers that they had actually suffered interference with their enjoyment of property. See *Wellingborough Borough Council v Gordon*, p 221.

[30] *Cf* the trend in English cases towards a less restrictive interpretation of abatement notices. See, for example, *R v Falmouth & Truro Port Health Authority, ex p South West Water Ltd*, where it was held that the Authority should not be obliged to specify what remedial works must be carried out as this would limit the choice of remedial measures available to the person served with the notice. Where a particular means of abatement is required, the notice will be invalid unless it specifies what must be done: *Kirklees Metropolitan Borough Council v Field*.

[31] *R v Boon Wai Ltd*, discussed under the section entitled 'Criminal Jurisdiction of the Courts'.

[32] *Noise Control Appeal No 1 of 1997*.

[33] *Noise Control Appeal Nos 1-8 of 1994*.

Investigation, consultation and impartiality

The environmental authority must carry out investigations into any alleged violation of legislation and in appropriate cases consult experts on what requirements must be specified in an abatement notice. In *Noise Control Appeals Nos 1-8*, the Board set aside a total ban on the use of metal hammers in a shipyard as an unreasonable requirement. The Board found that there was no evidence that the authority had inquired into what was necessary to be done for the purpose of abating noise emanating from the shipyard.

Environmental authorities should also ensure that they act impartially and fairly. In *Noise Control Appeal No 3 of 1995* the appellant argued that it had been singled out for noise pollution while there were other neighbouring premises which could have been equally in breach of noise restrictions. The Appeal Board found that the Noise Control Authority had acted quite professionally and that the appellant's argument had no merit in it. While the Appeal Board held against the appellant on facts, it recognised the validity of the relevant principle.

Proactivity

The Boards have also made recommendations to render administrative decision-making more efficient. It would be desirable if the environmental authorities assumed a more proactive role, explaining to persons in breach of legislative provisions what could be done to regularise their activities such as by obtaining a licence. That would enable the appropriate authority, which may be different from the enforcement authority, to impose appropriate conditions to make the operations in question compatible with the legislative requirements.[34]

Role of environmental impact assessments

The environmental impact assessment process does not lie comfortably within a detailed legal framework. So observed the Appeal Board in *Kowloon Canton Railway*,[35] where the Director of Environmental Protection had refused to approve an environmental impact assessment report submitted by the Corporation for the construction of its new railway line extension. The Appeal Board observed that the Ordinance provided only an outline of the impact assessment process, assisted by technical memoranda. In order to make the newly introduced legislation work more effectively, the Board made several suggestions. It suggested that there should be open, ready and frank communication between the Director and the proponent and made three specific recommendations:

(a) When drafting the study brief to guide the proponent in the preparation of an environmental report, the Director must make clear to the proponent any concerns that he wishes the proponent to address;

(b) Upon receipt of the environmental impact assessment report the Director must not exhibit it for public consultation unless he is satisfied that the report meets all the requirements of the Ordinance and the technical memorandum. If the Director decides to release it for public consultation, he should not be free to reject the report at the approval stage on the ground that the report does not meet any such statutory requirement;

(c) Upon the conclusion of the public consultation the Director has the power to ask the proponent to provide any information he requires to decide whether to approve the report.

---

[34] See *Air Pollution Appeal No 1 of 1997*, para 25.
[35] *Environmental Impact Assessment Appeal No 2 of 2000*.

The Appeal Board observed that it is not helpful to the proponent if the Director merely passes on to the proponent comments he has received through public consultation and asks the proponent to provide information in response to such comments. It would be helpful if the Director could specify what information he requires. The Appeal Board's suggestions were meant to make the environmental impact assessment process fair and more effective.

Specialist appeal tribunal: the right way forward?

We have seen above that, while 69 appeals have been lodged under the six environmental ordinances, the Appeal Board had heard only 26 appeals. Forty-three appeals had been either abandoned by the appellants or rejected by the board as invalid. An appeal could be invalid and rejected if, for instance, the notice of appeal does not set out any grounds of appeal, or the grounds of appeal are other than those envisaged by the relevant statute, or if the appeal is time barred. It is interesting that 30 out of those 43 appeals were abandoned. While it is not possible to readily ascertain why such a large number of appeals were abandoned, it may be assumed that in most cases the appellants realised that they had no chance of success or the relevant environmental authority came to some settlement to the satisfaction of the appellants.

Of the 26 appeals that reached the hearing stage, only 11 were successful. One may safely assume that the environmental authorities have exercised their enforcement powers cautiously and that as a result the chances of successfully challenging their decisions are fairly slim. Whist one might argue that the existence of an appeal mechanism in some way inhibits enforcement action, that argument must give way to the need to prevent any unauthorised invasion of citizen's rights.

The appeal boards have, as shown above, not only inquired into the merits of an appeal but have also taken the opportunity to propose ways in which the decision-making process could be improved. They therefore provide not only an opportunity to air a grievance, but also a mechanism that highlights defects in the decision-making process guiding the administration to improve the environmental monitoring and enforcement regime.

The appellate system is obviously a better safeguard than judicial review in many ways. As administrative tribunals, environmental appeal boards are not only free of many procedural constraints that saddle legal proceedings, they are also free to examine the merits of the original decision, whereas judicial review is concerned with legality of administrative action. Members of environmental Appeal Boards can bring a wide range of expertise, including legal, since their Chairman has to be a lawyer qualified for appointment as a District Judge. There is provision in environmental statutes enabling the environmental appeal boards to determine any questions of law that may arise during an appeal. Any such question of law must be determined by the Chairman and may be referred to the Court of Appeal for directions by way of case stated. Parties to an appeal are entitled to legal representation and the appeal boards have extensive powers to compel attendance of witnesses and production of documents.

It is safe to assume that the creation of appeal boards—in lieu of providing an appeal to a court of law—has been a success. There have been only a few judicial review applications challenging decisions taken by appeal boards and all of them have failed.[36] It is also interesting that the criminal courts in determining the validity of administrative decisions have been guided by appeal board decisions dealing with similar issues. For instance in *Secretary for*

---

[36] The most recent case is *Teng Fuh Ltd v Air Pollution Control Appeal Board and Director of Environmental Protection*.

Justice v Tak yue Restaurant Ltd, an appeal against a criminal conviction for failure to comply with a noise abatement notice, the Court of First Instance drew assistance from a decision of the Appeal Board on an appeal against a noise abatement notice, while recognising that appeal board decisions do not bind the courts.

THE ROLE OF THE OMBUDSMAN

The Ombudsman provides another useful safeguard on administrative decision-making, and has been used on a number of occasions.[37] For instance in 2000 a complaint was made to the Ombudsman, though unsuccessfully, that the Environmental Protection Department had failed to take enforcement action against environmental pollution caused by an illegal septic tank.[38]

The Ombudsman system, of course, has certain advantages over judicial and other administrative remedies. For instance, the Ombudsman may conduct an investigation even where an Ordinance provides that a particular administrative decision is final, or is not subject to review, appeal or questioning in any forum.[39] At the same time, although the Ombudsman is not permitted to conduct an investigation if there is an alternative remedy available under the relevant Ordinance, the Ombudsman may press ahead with an investigation if he or she considers that, in the circumstances of the case, it is not reasonable to expect the complainant to have resort to such remedy.[40]

While he does not have any powers of enforcement, the Ombudsman could report his or her findings and recommendations to the relevant agency, and it is unlikely that the agency will refuse to accept the Ombudsman's report without strong reasons. Where the relevant agency does not implement the recommendations, the Ombudsman may make a report to the Chief Executive who is obliged to lay it before the Legislative Council.[41]

The Ombudsman regularly publishes reports of investigations he has concluded and gives a detailed account of his or her work in the annual report. There is a healthy practice whereby the government submits a minute to the Legislative Council responding to the Ombudsman's annual report. Through that minute government agencies inform the Legislative Council of their response to the reports and recommendations of the Ombudsman in the previous year, together with any remedial measures that they have taken to implement any suggestions made by the Ombudsman for improvement.[42]

---

[37] See generally for Hong Kong's Ombudsman system Cooray, 2000, pp 75-92, and Cooray, 1999.

[38] *Case No 2291 of 2000.*

[39] Ombudsman Ordinance, s 7(2).

[40] *Ibid*, s 10(1)(e).

[41] *Ibid*, s 16.

[42] See for instance the Government Minute in Response to the Twelfth Report of the Ombudsman where the Environmental Protection Department responded to the Ombudsman's investigation in *Case No 3081 of 1998*. The Ombudsman had found no merit in the complaint that the Department had wrongfully failed to take enforcement action against the Housing Department under the Noise Control Ordinance. The Department stated in the report that it had taken measures to strengthen the internal guidelines relating to handling of complaints against government departments.

ENVIRONMENTAL CITIZENSHIP

It has been shown that environmental litigation in Hong Kong operates by way of administrative appeal against environmental decisions, criminal prosecutions and appeals for offences under environmental statutes, and supervisory jurisdiction of the High Court in judicial review proceedings. The provisions relating to administrative appeals and criminal prosecutions are found in each of the environmental statutes, there being no integrated environmental control. Perhaps because the major environmental statutes were passed at different times, the provisions relating to offences and to appeal matters are not uniform. For clarity and convenience, it is desirable that the environmental statutes be revised to achieve internal consistency in these matters.

To take one example, while the Air Pollution Control Ordinance describes an emission of air pollutant which is a 'nuisance' as a form of air pollution that may be controlled by an air pollution abatement notice, the Noise Control Ordinance uses the term 'annoyance', in describing the type of noise which may be controlled by a noise abatement notice. Obviously 'annoyance' has a wider meaning than 'nuisance' and will keep out the restrictions that common law associates with nuisance.[43]

Environmental litigation is presently of use only to a person who is directly affected by an environmental decision—an appeal may be lodged by a person affected by a relevant decision, such as refusal of a licence;[44] a judicial review application may be submitted by an aggrieved person; and criminal prosecutions may be instituted by the relevant enforcement authority.[45] There is no express provision enabling the private citizen to institute a prosecution or to institute a civil action compelling the authority to exercise its enforcement powers. The only safeguard seems to be recourse to the Ombudsman.

However, the Ombudsman system has its weaknesses. For instance, the Ombudsman has jurisdiction only in respect of 'maladministration', in the exercise of administrative functions, and not where the source of grievance is an individual officer's professional judgment which it is not amenable to control by the relevant government department or agency.[46] The

---

[43] In *Teng Fuh Company Ltd v Air Pollution Control Appeal Board and Director of Environmental Protection* the Court of First Instance held that the Air Pollution Ordinance did not set out an exhaustive definition of 'nuisance', and considered that 'nuisance' also the common law meaning 'any act or omission which constitutes an interference with or annoyance to members of the public'. The Court did not have to consider the restrictive aspects of the common law definition, especially that nuisance must be an interference with the enjoyment of one's proprietary rights over land. Cases such as *Network Housing Association Ltd v Westminster City Council*, *Carr v London Borough of Hackney* and *Wivenhoe Port Ltd v Colchester Borough Council* seem to suggest that statutory nuisance is more concerned with protection of personal convenience than preventing interference with enjoyment of property rights. Hudson, 1996. In*The Queen on the Application of East Devon District Council v Keith Farr*, the Queen's Bench Division observed that nuisance in the statutory sense must be given its 'ordinary legal meaning, which broadly amounts to interfering with a person's personal comfort'.

[44] For instance, under the Water Pollution Ordinance, s 29, 'a person who is aggrieved by an appealable requirement of decision may appeal to the Appeal Board.' Similar terminology is used in other major environmental statutes in setting out the right of appeal.

[45] The Air Pollution Control (s 46) and Noise Control (s 31) Ordinances expressly provide that prosecutions must be instituted by the authority. The Water Pollution Control and Waste Disposal Ordinances have no such provision. However, they seem to imply that prosecutions will be initiated by the authority, because of its supervisory and investigative powers.

[46] Section 2 of the Ordinance defines maladministration as 'inefficient, bad or improper administration' and s 7(1) requires that a complaint must disclose an injustice in connection with an action 'in the exercise of [the organisation's] administrative function.' In *Ong Kee Tony v The Commissioner for Administrative Complaints*, it was held that the exercise by a medical practitioner of clinical judgment fell outside the meaning of administrative function because in treating a patient he would not be under the control of the Department of Health or the hospital.

Ombudsman Ordinance also has a *locus standi* requirement: a complainant must be a person 'who claims to have sustained injustice in consequence of maladministration.'[47] Nonetheless, the Ombudsman does now have the power to conduct a 'direct investigation'—that is, an investigation initiated by the Ombudsman, 'notwithstanding that no complaint has been made to him, [if] he is of the opinion that any person may have sustained injustice in consequence of maladministration'.[48]

The next step in the development of environmental litigation in Hong Kong, therefore, appears to be provision for citizen suits. Section 82 of the Environmental Protection Act 1990 of the United Kingdom can serve as a starting point. This should be followed by a serious examination of the extent to which citizens must be empowered to actively participate in environmental matters, not only by taking part in consultation processes, but also by ensuring that environmental laws and standards are properly implemented by direct involvement in enforcement.[49]

REFERENCES

Air Pollution Appeal No 1 of 1997

Asia Dyeing Co Ltd v Air Pollution Control Authority [1990] 1 HKLR 263

Attorney General v Helena Restaurant (1981) Ltd [1985] 1 HKC 491

Carr v London Borough of Hackney [1995] Env LR 372

Case No 2291 of 2000, cited in Ombudsman's Annual Report, 2001, Annex 6, p A. 6-4

Cooray, A, 'Hong Kong's ombudsman: the first decade' (1999) 3 International Ombudsman Yearbook 71

Cooray, A, 'The ombudsman in Asia: a case study of Hong Kong and Sri Lanka,', in Gregory, R and Giddings, P (eds), *Righting Wrongs: The Ombudsman in Six Continents*, 2000, Amsterdam: IOS Press

Debates of the Legislative Council, 26 January 1994 and 31 March 1993

Environmental Impact Assessment Appeal No 2 of 2000

Environmental Protection Department, *Consultation Document on Proposed Amendments to the Water Pollution Control Ordinance*, March 2001, available at www.info.gov.hk/epd/english/environmentinhk/water/pub_consult/consult_wpc_ord.html

Forests and Countryside Ordinance 1937

Gammon (HK) Ltd & Ors v Attorney General [1985] AC 1, [1984] 2 All ER 503

Government Minute in Response to the Twelfth Report of the Ombudsman, June 2000

HKSAR v Cheung Cheuk Fung Magistracy Criminal Appeal No 607 of 1997, decided on 1 September 1997 (unreported)

---

[47] Ombudsman Ordinance, s 7(1)(i).
[48] *Ibid*, s 7(1)(ii).
[49] See Miller, 2000, pp 370-384; Simmons and Simmons, 2000, pp 203-213 and Reid, 2000, pp 177-194.

HKSAR v Y-ITC Construction Company [1998] 3 Hong Kong Cases 189

Hong Kong Bill of Rights

Hudson, A, 'Noisy neighbours and nuisance: section 80 Environmental Protection Act 1990 and *Network Housing Association Ltd v Westminster City Council*' (1996) JPL 916-918

Hyundai-CCECC Joint Venture v Environmental Protection Department Dumping at Sea Appeal Case No 1 of 2000

Kirklees Metropolitan Borough Council v Field [1998] Env LR 337

Kowloon Canton Railway Corporation v Director of Environmental Protection Environmental Impact Assessment Appeal No 2 of 2000

Miller, J G, 'The standing of citizens to enforce against violations of environmental statutes in the United States' (2000) 12:3 JEL 370-384

Network Housing Association Ltd v Westminster City Council [1995] 93 LGR 280

Noise Control Appeal No 1 of 1991

Noise Control Appeal No 1 of 1997

Noise Control Appeal No 3 of 1995

Noise Control Appeal No 4 of 1995

Noise Control Appeal Nos 1-8 of 1994

Noise Pollution Control Appeal Board Appeal No 1-8 of 1994

Noise Pollution Control Appeal Board Appeal No 2 of 1991

Ong Kee Tony v The Commissioner for Administrative Complaints [1997] HKLRD 1191

R v Boon Wai [1995] 1 Hong Kong Cases 483

R v Cabot Plastics Hong Kong Ltd [1992] 1 Hong Kong Cases 465

R v Falmouth & Truro Port Health Authority, ex p South West Water Ltd [2000] Env LR 658

Reid, C T, 'Environmental citizenship and the courts' (2000) 2 Env L Rev 177

Secan Ltd v Attorney General [1995] 2 Hong Kong Cases 629

Secretary for Justice v Tak yue Restaurant Ltd [1998] 1 Hong Kong Cases 236 (CFI), [1998] 1 HKC 236 (CFI)

Secretary of Justice v Poly Gain Enterprises Ltd [1998] 4 Hong Kong Cases 202

Simmons and Simmons, 'Standing up for the environment: citizen suits in the us and in the EC white paper on environmental liability' (2000) 2 Env L Rev 203-213

Sy Chokk Luen v Director of Environmental Protection [1998] 1 Hong Kong Cases 474

Teng Fuh Company Ltd v Air Pollution Control Appeal Board and Director of Environmental Protection (unreported) HCAL 1928/2000 decided on 21 March 2001, affirmed by the Court of Appeal in [2001] 3 Hong Kong Law Reports and Digest 304

The Queen on the Application of East Devon District Council v Keith Farr [2002] WL 45338

The Queen v Tsui Chit-fan and Others [1994] 2 Hong Kong Criminal Law Reports 273

Town Planning Appeal Nos 5 and 7 of 1997 (unreported)

Wellingborough Borough Council v Gordon [1993] Env LR 218

Wivenhoe Port Ltd v Colchester Borough Council [1985] JPL 175

CHAPTER 16

WOMEN IN THE DEMOCRATIC PROCESS IN UGANDA: GENDER AND JUSTICE

*Beatrice Odonga-Mwaka**

This chapter is based on my experiences as a magistrate and as an activist in a women's organisation, and on fieldwork in two districts in Uganda. The fieldwork focused on the impact of Local Councils, which were created by the government as part of Uganda's transition from 20 years of civil war to democratic rule. The Local Councils had both executive and judicial roles, and were intended to ensure decentralisation of functions, powers and services to the grassroots; and thereby to increase local democratic control and participation in decision-making, especially marginalised by groups.

The chapter explores the processes by which women in Uganda were given the platform through the democratic process to attain justice at various structural levels to grassroots. What was their input in that process? What were their sites of struggle? What methods did they use? What choices were available to them? What does this mean for women's participation in decision-making and democracy?

WOMEN'S NEEDS AND IDENTITIES

Women are not only individuals but also members of family groups—immediate and extended—and of communities. The realisation of their individual needs must necessarily consider those of the wider family and their communities. So, one cannot examine their individual rights without exploring their relationships with collective rights of groups to which they belong. The kinship ties are even stronger in indigenous communities—as is the need to explore both the unique features of social and legal relations that individual women have, and general features affecting the family and kinship structures.[1]

Various studies—for example, of inheritance practices in African communities—clearly reveal the *strength of the family and cultural leaders* (clan) in decision-making. These are guardians of customs, and are generally concerned with ensuring generational continuity through the patrilineage.[2] This agenda sometimes competes with the individual needs of women. Disputes over resources—whether conducted by mediation in the family or community courts, or litigation in the established Western-style courts—are generally a consequence or reflection of these relations. Women's identities as daughters, single women, wives, mothers, widows, aunts, grandmothers, in-laws, are all areas of contention when there is conflict.

These studies also show that women can pick and choose from a *range of forums* (levels) for dispute resolution. The norms and values that service these forums impact on—and often determine—the outcome. But a woman's class, location and self-perception can give her a measure of control over the process and outcome. The issues and the solutions are often

---

*   Lecturer, School of Law, Warwick University.
1   Hellum, 1999. Hellum explores how group practices and attitudes affect women's individual rights in reproduction.
2   See Ncube and Stewart, 1995; and Okumu-Wengi, 1995.

perceived and interpreted differently by women, family and kinship structures and the various forums in which the cases are pursued. Interpretation of customs and culture practices and legal norms thus become a contested field or multiple sites of struggle.[3] de Sousa Santos[4] has termed the various levels of dispute settlement 'different scales of legality,' which use different criteria to regulate the same kind of social activity, or to determine the relevant features of the activity to be regulated. He argues that, rather than seeing them as purely separate and conflicting normative systems, they may often supplement each other in a way that caters for the needs and interests of differently situated women within complex relationships. Women can therefore pick and choose as appropriate.

Studies of African communities also reveal that *modernisation* has not had the same impact on women in general.[5] There are class differences in any society, and modernisation impacts in different ways. In indigenous societies, where the gap between the rural poor and urban middle class is wide, the differences are even greater. Modern legal strategies that call for the wholesale abolition of some practices (for example polygyny) prove futile because of the different socio-legal circumstances that women live under. Sometimes poverty can be the biggest obstacle to change and strategies for legal change cannot overlook this.

The search for justice for women within these complex relationships and the coexistence of these forums is made more intricate by the global picture—for example, the UN Convention on the Elimination of All Forms of Discrimination against Women, which has been ratified by 150 states including Uganda. Its interpretation and implementation are complex, because of the unique features and experiences of individual states. Although the State Parties are expected to adhere to the principle of non-discrimination on the basis of sex, the Convention allows for the application and interpretation to be carried out in the way most appropriate for their social and cultural structure.[6]

Africa is still struggling to achieve political stability, democracy and good governance. The attainment of individual, group and community rights, and participation in decision-making, are seen as critical. In reality, the attainment of rights and participation often depends on the structure and policy of governments, socio-economic conditions and power relations. Social practices, indigenous institutions and especially gender relations underlie the involvement of women.

Researchers now argue that analysis on women should move away from dwelling on which entity or structure is responsible for undermining their status and should instead explore *how customary social practices interact with government policy* to undermine or enhance the position of women at all levels.[7]

For example, Nyamu[8] reveals that Kenyan women's access to land—previously guaranteed under customary law—was undermined by the process of tenure reform—that is, state-adjudication, consolidation and registration, culminating in the issue of document of title. Even land which is designated by custom as family or clan land is generally registered in the name of one person. The relevant statute does not specify the gender of the titleholder, but cultural biases of both the implementers and the families concerned often lead to a male being

---

[3] Odonga-Mwaka, 1998.

[4] de Sousa Santos, 1987.

[5] Hellum, 1999. Ncube and Stewart, 1995.

[6] Convention Secretariat to CEDAW-CEDAW C/1995/4. On how this applies to African customs on reproductive right, see: Hellum, 1999.

[7] Nyamu, 1999; and Martin, 2000.

[8] Nyamu, 1999, pp 30-34.

chosen. Family members might perceive the title holder as acting in a representative capacity, but the legal effect is to give the titleholder absolute rights to alienate or mortgage the land, without regard for the customary rights of family or clan members. Although women's rights of access to land may have been limited under custom, it was now less secure and even eroded . in some circumstances, all as a consequence of a government policy favouring individualised private property rights.

Similarly, Manji[9] explains that the Government of Tanzania proposed a policy under which women could acquire land in their own right through purchase and allocation, but that custom and culture would govern inheritance of family or clan land—even recent studies have clearly shown that women's rights are circumscribed under such custom and culture.[10] Government policy also took a narrow view, focusing in particular on rights in succession—a field where women's rights are determined by relationships. Women were therefore perceived in what Manji refers to as 'status' relationships only—that is as wives, mothers, sisters, daughters, consequently as appendages to the male.[11] It ignores their 'active' or 'activity' status—the multitude of ways in which they interact with land, and the complex nature of the discrimination which they face in relation to it. Women are also farmers and workers, and, where there is migrant labour, they remain behind as guardians of the land. The Government's concern with the broader goals facing the country—democracy, the possibility of privatising land and so on—meant that gender issues were subsumed in the economic and social policies for the country.

However, the inclusion of gender issues into the broader goals of state policy can be the key to ensuring that the issues are not marginalised. Including issues specifically relevant to women on a government's agenda for democracy has the advantage of ensuring that women's concerns are not marginalised, or perceived as a 'women only' issue. The challenge to the State is in the practical implementation. It is generally agreed that it is not sufficient to merely grant women rights. The processes and support at all levels that are necessary for them to fully attain what they seek must also be made available.

The following discussion on women in Uganda explores the reform process; the identification and inclusion of issues specifically relevant to women in the process; the role played by various actors, especially women; and state policy and traditional structures. An analysis of the extent to which women were able to engage at different levels, and whether they succeeded in their objectives, should reveal whether the policies and processes have interacted to undermine or enhance their position.

POPULAR DEMOCRACY AND POPULAR JUSTICE IN MUSEVENI'S UGANDA

President Yoweri Kaguta Museveni was quick to look for a democratic solution to Uganda's troubled past of 20 years of civil war—even though he himself came to power by the undemocratic means of a military coup in 1986.[12] His swift introduction of Local Councils in

---

[9]   See Manji, 1998, p 659.

[10]   Research has been done, and is ongoing, on a collaborative basis in Southern Africa under a project known as Women and Law in Southern (WLSA) and in Eastern African under Women and Law in Eastern Africa (WLEA), 1990.

[11]   Manji, 1998, p 650.

[12]   For a history of the driving force behind Museveni's politics see: Museveni, 1997.

1987, and Local Committee Courts in 1988 was to pave the way for democratic participation in, and control of, decision-making, beginning at grassroots.[13]

The Local Council was an administrative structure created and used by President Museveni in his protracted six-year guerrilla war against the government of Milton Obote. Museveni organised the villages occupied by his army into small administrative units, allowing the people to choose leaders to administer and dispense justice. The system proved very popular and successful, culminating in the capture of state power from Obote. Museveni saw this as the way forward for Uganda, and introduced the Councils throughout the country under the ideology of 'popular democracy and popular justice'.

Members of Councils and Courts are elected by their communities, and with the Government taking a 'hands off' approach, are free to run those communities as they see fit. The State's intention to decentralise and devolve powers to ensure 'good governance and democratic participation' has been given full effect under the Local Government Act. This increases the powers and functions of the Local Councils, and emphasises the need to establish 'a democratic and gender sensitive administrative set-up in Local Government.'[14]

The *Local Councils* are structured in a five-tier hierarchy from the Village (LCI) level, through three further levels (LCII Parish, LCIII Sub County and LCIV County), to the District Council (LCV) at the apex. There are 52 Districts and there are hundreds of villages—and, therefore, Local Councils—in each District. Members from the District level are elected to the national parliament, known as the National Resistance Council (NRC). As part of its affirmative action policy, a parliamentary seat is reserved for a woman candidate from each of the 52 districts. Women can, of course, also compete for the open parliamentary seats in each District.

A parallel structure of *Local Committee Courts* operates in rural and urban areas.[15] Executive members of the first three tiers of the Local Councils (LCI-LCIII) are empowered to constitute themselves into Local Committee Courts. They operate through a three-tier system (see Figure 1 below), with appeals going from LCI as the lowest court, to LCIII as the highest court. The Local Committee Courts apply indigenous methods of dispute settlement such as reconciliation, mediation, compensation, apology and restitution. They have limited criminal jurisdiction, generally confined to juveniles, and they also handle civil disputes of a customary nature. A person who is discontented with the decisions in the Local Committee Courts is free to lodge an appeal with the regular court system—that is, to the Chief Magistrates' Court, the High Court and finally to the Supreme Court—in which English procedural law is applied.

Figure 1: Local Committee Court structure

Rural Areas	Court	Urban Areas
Sub-County	LCIII	Division
Parish	LCII	Ward
Village	LCI	Village cell

---

[13] Initially known as Resistance Councils (Resistance Council and Committee Statute, 1987) and Resistance Council Courts (Resistance Council Committee (Judicial Powers) Statute, 1988), in keeping with Museveni's emphasis on a new regime that had come to resist the corruption in the former regimes.

[14] Local Government Act 1997, s 2(b).

[15] See Arutu, 1998.

The Local Committee Courts are referred to as 'popular' or 'popular justice' courts. Academic studies, media commentary and public opinion indicate that the Local Councils and Courts are indeed popular with ordinary Ugandans, peasants, workers and progressive intellectual opinion.[16] A key factor has been that the structure and location of the Councils and Courts have allowed for the ordinary person to be involved in the day-to-day issues that concern them and their communities, whether rural or urban. Unlike the regular (magistrates and high) courts, they are located within communities, require no legal expertise and are constituted wherever and whenever it is convenient, thereby cutting down on costs and time.

However, if the justice in these local bodies is to be truly popular, the substantive law they apply—both customary and written—must as popular, not just the procedure. Where a popular justice system discriminates or is prejudicial to important members of the society, it cannot be said to be popular or democratic—even where those members are passive participants, or are recipients of minimal gains of the process. Civil society organisations must be strengthened to constantly defend the rights and interests of popular classes and social groups.[17]

It may be that the structure is viable, but the rules that govern its function are prejudicial to women—or vice versa. The question is not so much about dismissing the structures or rules, but rather about engaging with them to discover the obstacles and how they can be overcome.[18] When 'popular opinion' indicates that the Local Councils and Local Committee Courts are popular, what percentage of that opinion is female? To what extent and in what ways are they 'popular' for women? To determine this, one needs to discover the involvement of women in the election process, their membership in the Councils and the extent of their use of the Committee Courts.

REVOLUTIONARY STRUGGLES AND SPECIFIC GROUP INTERESTS

Revolutionary struggles for democracy generally seek to liberate the whole of society from the repression and brutality of a previous regime. It is the interests of the repressed as a whole that are expounded, and specific interests and identities are often subordinated for the wider goal. There is a promise that the interests will be dealt with once the first step of the revolution—the overthrow of the repressive regime—is achieved. A concerted focus and the unity it creates often lead to the success of the revolution. Dungu *et al*, writing about the Resistance Movement in Uganda and its impact on women, ask:[19]

> If a revolution does not demand the dissolution of women's identities, then it would require the subordination of their specific interests to the broader goals of establishing a new social order…if women surrender their specific interests in the struggle for a different society, then at what point are these interests rehabilitated, legitimized and responded to by the revolutionary forces or the new state?

---

[16] See Barya, 1993; Kasfir, 2000.
[17] Barya, 1993, pp 21-26.
[18] Nyamu, 1999, pp 60-63.
[19] Dungu and Wabwire, 1991, p 42. See also Molyneux, 1985, pp 233-259, for an expanded debate on socialist revolution and women's participation.

They question the types of women represented at the various levels of the Local Councils, and over what issues they are being represented. Centres of power are located with the interests of the State. Are women part of this? Do women decide on major issues? Does having more women at parliamentary level ensure that the needs of women at grassroots are not forgotten? In essence: how far have changes in the democratic process gone in challenging traditional gender relations?

Affirmative action

Women were active participants in the political and armed struggle in Uganda. It is important to note the National Resistance Movement's (NRM's) conception of the place of women within the overall context of its priorities. President Museveni made it clear at the outset that one of the objectives of his movement was to improve the status of women.[20] His Ten Point Programme emphasised parliamentary and popular democracy, 'a decent living for every Ugandan'[21] and the '[c]onsolidation of programs which are responsible to gender and marginalised groups.' The Movement was to ensure that these groups would actively participate in the political, social and economic activities in the country, with affirmative action maintained 'in so far as is necessary.'[22] Marginalised groups included those with disabilities, the youth and children. The identification of more than one marginalised group meant that the groups could consolidate their efforts to assist each other in attaining particular rights. This is important for women whose interests can be easily sidelined as 'women only' concerns—a point illustrated below in relation to the constitution-making process.

Museveni took affirmative action to ensure the representation of women at parliamentary level, and appointed six female ministers in 1988, just two years after taking power. There had only been one female minister in the history of Uganda. He also ensured their involvement in the making of a new constitution.[23] Every District was reserved a seat for female representation in the Constituent Assembly. The seats were to be contested by women candidates only. Women could also compete for the general constituency seats—26 women competed for these general seats, and nine defeated a male candidate.

Through this affirmative action, women were given the platform to articulate their concerns. The actual constitutional amendments favouring women had to be fought for by women.

Women's movements

Matembe's experience as a Member of the Constituent Assembly,[24] and Tamale's critique of the democratic process in Uganda,[25] reveal that the grassroots women's movement gave unprecedented support to their female representatives in the Constituent Assembly. This was

---

[20] See Museveni, 1997, pp 190-192.

[21] National Resistance Movement, 1985.

[22] Kabwegererye, 2000, pp 157-164.

[23] The state established the Uganda Constitutional Commission under Statute No 5 of 1988, with a mandate to make proposals for the enactment of a new Constitution. Uganda's Independence Constitution of 1967 was still in force.

[24] Currently a Minister in Museveni's government, and activist at forefront of women's involvement in the democratic progress in Uganda, she was one of two women in the 21-member Constitutional Commission. Her experiences and analysis of women's involvement can be found in: Matembe, 1997.

[25] See Tamale, 1999.

primarily due to their perception of the Assembly as being fundamentally important in shaping the constitutional framework that would guarantee women's future democratic and human rights. Women's organisations were revived and others created. The report of the Constitutional Commission[26] observed that '[a]lmost all women who participated in the exercise had no doubts in their mind that the new Constitution was a powerful weapon in their total emancipation.'

Women had many similar problems to grapple with but there were differences in class, religion, tribe, location, political affiliation and the like. Feminists have long argued that women are not a homogenous group, and therefore their differences should be addressed in policy and reform measures. Because of their differences, women realised that, in addition to the societal structures that subordinated them, there also existed different levels and structures of engagement among them.

As Chair of the Women's Lawyer's Association in 1988, it was clear to me that women were divided along class, profession, experience and interests among other things. I found working to keep the members united one of the toughest challenges at the time. Some members did break off to start new women's organisations. However, during the making of the Constitution there was a marked change. Women primarily sought a unity of purpose. They focused on issues that united them, rather than their differences—thus surrendering class, group and individual differences for a collective voice. For example, women agreed that some customs and cultural practices subordinated women in general, that there were fewer girls than boys in educational institutions, and very few women in decision-making roles. They therefore formed alliances across boundaries—of class, tribe, religion, profession and organisation—and were thus able to strategise and lobby. They used their various skills to mobilise and offer political education to each other. During the election of Constituent Assembly members, '[w]omen voters were able to question a candidate's stand on gender issues and to vote for those they felt would represent them adequately. For the first time in the history of Uganda, the issues of women's equality formed part of the campaign process.'[27]

According to Waliggo, Secretary to the Constitutional Commission, women were the best organised group in submitting their views.[28] They organised political seminars in all the 167 counties and most of their submissions incorporated the same views and arguments irrespective of class or tribal differences. For women, 'popular democracy' meant that women at various structural levels needed to have a 'voice' and a forum to articulate their concerns. Although there was political will behind their struggles, women had to devise and develop the strategies that would best assist them to use the forums provided by the state as well as create new 'women friendly' forums that would cater for different groups of women to speak.

The experience of the women's movement in Uganda was in a number of ways similar to that of the women's movement in South Africa. Zulu, a member of the South Africa Parliament and of the African National Congress (ANC), noted that although the apartheid system had greatly divided them with some deeply entrenched structures, women found issues of mutual interest that united them.[29] They sought an environment that would allow workable strategies for the achievement of their goals. The ANC Women's League therefore mobilised women across racial, religious and social strata to form the National Women's Coalition. It was the largest women's representation in the history of South Africa, having

---

[26] See Report of the Uganda Constitutional Commission, 1992, p 148.
[27] Matembe, 1997, p 23.
[28] See Waliggo, 1995.
[29] See Zulu, 2000, pp 166-181.

drawn together 90 women's organisations with about two million women. This provided the collective voice and power for their struggle.

LEVELS OF ENGAGEMENT

Although Ugandan women had submitted their recommendation to the Constitutional Commission[30] and voted for candidates that would represent them, a greater task awaited them in the Constituent Assembly.

As a result of affirmative action, women represented 17 percent of the Constituent Assembly delegates (51 out of 284). Matembe[31] explains some of the strategies they adopted in the Assembly, which was male dominated in both number and opinion. The women formed alliances with other groups sympathetic to gender issues—such as representatives of the National Resistance Army, marginalised groups, youth, people with disabilities and workers—increasing their number to 72 (25 percent). It is interesting to note the support of the army. This was an army that was loyal to Museveni. Women had been in their ranks, engaged in the guerrilla warfare alongside the men. Their alliance with women was a clear signal that the highest authority was firmly behind the women's cause.

The women's movement in Uganda has had an overall positive influence on the agenda for women's rights—they got almost everything they asked for. The 1995 Constitution incorporates positive provisions governing the status and participation of women in the development of the nation. Article 33, among other things, prohibits laws, customs and cultures and traditions that subordinate women in any manner. Women are increasingly involved in Government deliberations. This has impacted upon the formulation of government policies that are gender-sensitive, upon the distribution of resources and upon law reform. Studies have demonstrated the strength of women's involvement during the making of the new Constitution—whether in the Constituent Assembly or offering support from the grassroots—and the significant impact of their strategies upon the provisions of the Constitution.[32]

Decision-making under the quota system

The women's movement was instrumental in lobbying during the 1995 Constituent Assembly for a constitutional provision which guarantees one third of the seats in all levels of Local Councils for women.[33] This became part of the new Local Government Act. Currently the Local Councils and the Local Committee Courts encourage the participation of women at all levels of the councils with women forming at least a one third majority. This provides solidarity for women, especially in rural areas where they are illiterate and by virtue of cultural practices are generally kept out of public decision-making.

Women in South Africa also campaigned for a quota system. The issue was first addressed in 1991 by the African National Conference. Women argued for a 30 percent representation on the executive committee of the ANC, but male as well as female delegates rejected it. Zulu

---

[30]   See Ministry of Women in Development, 1991.
[31]   Matembe, 1997, pp 34-39.
[32]   See Matembe, 1997; Tamale, 1999; Oloka-Onyango, 2000a.
[33]   Constitution of the Republic of Uganda 1995, Art 180 2(b).

notes that some women felt it would only benefit the highly educated female intellectuals.[34] As in Uganda, steps and strategies were adopted by the ANC Women's League that allowed for women's views to be sought from the lowest level of the ANC, and from women's movements. In 1997, a resolution was finally adopted at the 50th National Conference of the ANC granting women a 33 percent quota in all elected positions.

Support for affirmative action quota systems has not been uniform. At a conference in South Africa, Dr Frene Ginwala, the first Speaker of the South African National Assembly, observed that the 'quota' is often interpreted negatively—as the upper limit rather than the minimum—which limits rather than extends women's representation. She also observed that there is a tendency to perceive 'women's representatives' as dealing with 'women's affairs' only. Consequently, women and matters of particular relevance to them are marginalised within the wider framework of state policy.[35]

When the Ugandan Local Councils were first created in 1987, one seat was specifically reserved for a woman representative in the Council's Executive Committee, which consisted of nine members. Eighty-nine percent of the population is rural, and female literacy levels are very low.[36] It was a hurdle to get women into decision-making in the rural environment where male perceptions are dominant. Rural communities literally interpreted it as giving women one seat. In some instances, men stood in place of women.[37] Women often felt intimidated by the number of males on the Committee, or saw the responsibilities as making too many demands on their traditional roles as food producers and carers.

Women representatives were also perceived to handle only women's affairs. Interestingly, men who were elected as 'women representatives' also saw that as their main role! This misconception of the 'quota' was remedied through political education and dissemination of information to grassroots by women's movements backed by state apparatus. By the time of the Constituent Assembly Elections, women saw the quota system as giving them the minimum they needed for solidarity, and pressed for at least one third. The Constituent Assembly women delegates also saw themselves as representing the whole of their constituencies, not only women, and that called for the incorporation of their concerns into the wider goals of democracy.

The quota system is perceived by some as interfering with the democratic process—people of merit (generally meaning men) are by-passed in favour of members of the quota group, who do not have merit. Here, democracy is being interpreted as the right of all persons to compete equally. But democracy must also necessarily mean affording the opportunity of redress to those who have been disadvantaged, marginalised or discriminated against. In these cases, it is not possible to set a general standard for candidates. Women in African societies have generally been marginalised by custom and culture. Many are married off when very young, and therefore deprived of higher education or training that would prepare them for decision-making or political involvement. Although a minority of women have had the same privileges as men and can compete with them, the same standard cannot be set for the majority of women.

As in South Africa, Uganda women's movements set up structures to support and provide political education to women in high office, to make up for the lack of experience of many of

---

[34]   Zulu, 2000, pp 166-169
[35]   *Ibid*, pp 168-9.
[36]   National Population Policy for Uganda, 1995.
[37]   Okumu Wengi, 1995b.

the women.[38] The majority of the women delegates lacked political experience, so they formed a Woman's Caucus that evolved into an organisation. The Forum for Women in Democracy (FOWADE) was devoted to enhancing the increased participation of women in politics. Skills training was provided through the Ministry of Gender and Community Development, in collaboration with appropriate women's organisations. A forum for 'Gender Dialogue' was created at which the Caucus would invite some delegates, in particular the most eloquent and articulate males,[39] to lobby and to interest them in assisting the Caucus to pass the provisions and amendments affecting the interests of the Caucus members. At one stage of the debates, all but five of the women delegates walked out in protest over sexist and derogatory use of language. Women also united in threatening to 'de-campaign' men who fiercely opposed their rights. Women had the support of fellow women in their constituencies and they could easily rally them together. Thus, although they sometimes ridiculed the women, male delegates generally succumbed.

Women in Parliament and at grassroots

Many of Uganda's prominent women politicians were also pioneers of radical women's groups. Female Ministers, Members of Parliament and the like occupy important positions in women's organisations.[40] On the one hand, this ensures that women from different classes and walks of life that are brought together through organisations, have an avenue through which their various concerns are brought into the government agenda and deliberations. But there has been concern about the consequences of such close links to the state. Can the women's movement be said to be autonomous and to operate without interference from the State? Tamale[41] and Kiguli[42] argue that the connection between the State and women's gorups has not been problematic for the general struggle for women's autonomy and equality. However, others disagree.[43]

Although there are many women's organisations outside the State structure, it is clear that attempts have been made to politically align the main structures for women's political involvement with the State.[44] Women Councils are set up within the Local Council—Village to District level—structure. Consequently, the pace of its development and growth is dependent on the benevolence of the State, which continues to call the shots, and makes the kind of concessions that do not affect its fundamental agenda. It also means that the State is expected to guarantee the democratic process for women, and that a turnaround in the State's agenda for women could be damaging. The women's movement needs to find ways of distancing itself from such close proximity with the State, while not shutting it out. Prominent women politicians need to relinquish the significant posts they hold in women's organisations, while ensuring that they continue to liase with them.

Although there is general praise for the strides that the women's movement has made in government policy, local government and civil society, in reality women still have to

---

[38] See Oloka-Onyango, 2000a, pp 11-19, for a critical analysis of the structures women set up to support women in decision-making and the women's cause.

[39] For example, former Attorney General and Minister of Justice and Senior Advisor to the President on Legal and International affairs, Justice George Kanyeihamba of the Supreme Court: *ibid*, p 35.

[40] See Oloka-Onyango, 2000b.

[41] Tamale, 1999.

[42] See Kiguli, 1994.

[43] Oloka-Onyango, 1998, pp 26-52.

[44] Barya, 2000b, p 15.

overcome fundamental problems. For example, when it came to 'legislating on crucial matters which directly impinge on men's power over women' during the Constituent Assembly debates, 'the men rallied together to defend their positions no matter how much lobbying the women did.'[45] However, women were able to make some gains through the support of women's groups and other marginalised groups such as those with disabilities. They were also supported by government policy to enhance the status of women, and by donor agencies which took this opportunity to fund projects which they saw as promoting their agendas on poverty alleviation and increased participation of women in development.[46]

Local Councils and women at grassroots

What did women at grassroots have to engage with and what have been the gains made so far? Berkley said that the 'revolution' in Uganda was not so much a class struggle, resulting in the automatic dismantling of a state institution, but rather a revolution that inhabits a colonial and anti-popular institution.[47] That is, the revolution necessarily works within the old structure to dismantle, reform or transform it.[48] The implication for women is that they too must work within the old traditional structures, such as patriarchy, to bring about the required changes. At grassroots women have had to use new government structures—Local Councils—to engage with the traditional and cultural structures and values.

An examination of the Local Council and Local Committee Court structures reveals that they incorporate elements of the traditional structure, membership and judicial powers. The Local Committee Courts are in essence a reintroduction of the pre-colonial 'native' courts, which where encouraged during colonialism to allow the indigenous populations to be guided by their own practices 'so long as not repugnant to natural justice'. However, while officeholders in 'native' courts were appointed, their modern equivalents are elected. Election depends on a person's standing in community. Traditionally, clan leaders or elders are respected by virtue of their age, experience or family relationships, and as guardians of customs and cultural practices. My research in the rural communities found that they were often the persons elected into the Councils. Secondly, Local Committee Courts have limited criminal jurisdiction to handle juvenile cases. Their main jurisdiction is in civil matters—that is, customary tenure, marital status of women, identity of heirs, paternity of children, impregnating and elopement with a girl below 18 years, and customary bailment. These are issues that are traditionally handled by local cultural leaders. They are also areas where women in many indigenous societies have limited rights.

The policy and set up of the structures in some ways reflect earlier arguments that often State policy may prescribe reform measures to enhance the position of women, but the methods, structures and implementation strategy can undermine women's position.[49] In the case of Uganda, the State deliberately sought to work within the old structures to bring about changes within it, changes that would be appropriate to evolving customs and cultural practices. The State did not want to repeat what was done under colonialism, imposing a structure on communities that already had on going process of administration—what Moore[50]

---

45 Tamale, 1999, p 148.
46 Oloka-Onyango, 2000b.
47 Berkley, 1988.
48 Barra, 1993.
49 Nyamu, 1999; Manji, 1998.
50 Moore, 1978, p 56.

refers to as 'rule making capacities and the means to induce or coerce compliance' from members of its community—thus resulting in conflicts. Although the Local Councils reflect elements of the 'native' courts, membership in the Council cuts across family and clan relationships. Under the traditional clan system, only kinship members could be part of the committee of decision-makers. In the Local Councils, residence is the criterion for standing for elections. Thus where tribes are mixed and living together in urban and rural communities, any person, including a non-Ugandan, can be a member of a Local Council. In areas where there are refugees, as in southern Uganda with the Rwandese and Northern Uganda with Sudanese, one gets a mix of Local Council members. The Council members are even more varied in urban centres. This can protect a woman from discriminatory customary rules of her ethnic group being forced on her. Where the family and extended family or clan preside over family matters and therefore lack impartiality, a woman can turn to a Local Committee Court. There is also room for appeal to the statutory Magistrates' Courts if a party is discontented with the Local Committee Court decision. This then allows the statutory courts to intervene and reflects Moore's[51] analysis of 'complex societies' which are also 'simultaneously set in a large social matrix which can, and does, affect and invade it, sometimes at the invitation of persons inside it, sometimes at its own instance'. Thus both the local communities and the state are semi-autonomous and inevitably interact and may 'support, complement, ignore or frustrate one another'[52] with unpredictable consequences. It is therefore important to see how government policy through the democratic reform process and the structures of Local Councils interact with the traditional structures (the clan, and customs) and social practices to enhance or undermine women's position. It is also important to listen to the voices of women who are affected by these reforms.

CONCLUSION

What lessons can we draw for gender justice from the Ugandan experience? First, the platforms or opportunities that are provided through affirmative action are not sufficient in themselves to attain gender justice. The processes and structures through which they are implemented are perhaps most important.

Second, it is often necessary for women to align themselves with the State at the start of their struggle, since the State has the machinery, resources and power to advance their cause. The State is also generally 'male', in policy and [man]power. If it does open its doors for women to engage inside its structures, women must use collective strategies that challenge these centres of power. However, in confronting indigenous structures, ideologues and practices, it is important to remember that centres of power are located both at the top policy level and *more so* at grassroots level, where attitudes and practices are more entrenched in the daily reality of people's lives.

Third, women as individuals, part of their families, members of groups and communities are united or divided according to individual or group interests and needs. Sometimes women in indigenous communities are the obstacles to the advancement of their own status. Senior members in women's communities such as aunts, grandmothers, and opinion leaders who are often guardians of customs and cultural practices can be obstacles to the advancement of women because they perceive changes as destroying the fabric of culture as well as

---

[51] *Ibid*, p 58
[52] Griffiths, 1988, p 2.

threatening the roles of community leaders. Male attitudes in general, and male community leaders in particular, can make this more difficult. Women need to engage primarily with each other at various levels—finding a common ground that would unite—before taking on entrenched societal structures and attitudes. New structures, such as the Local Councils, Committee Courts and specialised groups, created new ways of engaging, especially in providing solidarity and skills.

Most importantly, the Ugandan experience tells us that gender justice should combine affirmative action with an attention to unity—women must first engage with each other if they are to successfully engage with structures that subordinated them. In the end, it is the group or groups that are discontented that must struggle for their cause.

REFERENCES

Arutu, J O E, *A Court User Guide For Local Committee Courts In Uganda*, 1998, Kampala: Uganda Law Watch Centre

Barya, J J (2000a), 'The making of Uganda's 1995 constitution: achieving consensus by law' CBR Publications No 57, 2000, Kampala: CBR

Barya, J J (2000b), 'The state of civil society in Uganda: an analysis of the legal and politico-economic aspects,' CBR Publications No 58, 2000, Kampala: CBR

Barya, J J, 'Popular democracy and legitimacy of the Constitution: some reflections on Uganda's Constitution-making process,' CBR Publications No 38, 1993, Kampala: CBR

Bazara, N, 'Contemporary civil society and democratisation process in Uganda: a preliminary exploration,' CBR Publications No 54, 2000, Kampala: CBR

Berkeley, A, 'From hyena to shepherd: the state and popular justice in Uganda', 1988, mimeo, Kampala

Constitution of the Republic of Uganda,1995

de Sousa Santos, B, 'Law: a map of misreading, towards a post-modern conception of law,' (1987) 14:3 Journal of Law and Society 279

Dungu, E and Wabwire, A A, 'Electoral mechanisms and the democratic process: the 1989 RC-NRC elections' CBR Publications No 9, 1989, Kampala: CBR

Dungu, E, and Wabwire, A A, 'Governance, state structures and constitutionalism in contemporary Uganda,' CBR Publications No 52, 1998, Kampala: CBR

Government of Uganda, *National Population Policy for Uganda*, 1995, Kampala: Government of Uganda

Griffiths, J, 'What is legal pluralism?' (1986) 24 Journal of Legal Pluralism and Unofficial Law 1053

Hellum, A, 'Women's human rights and African customary laws: between universalism and relativism-individualism and communitarianism' (1990) 10:2 European Journal of Development Research

Howard, R E, 'Dignity, community and human rights', in An-Na'im, A A (ed), *Human Rights in Cross-Cultural Perspective: A Quest for Consensus*, 1992, Philadelphia: University of Pennsylvania Press

Kabwegererye, T B, *People's Choice, People's Power*, 2000, Kampala: Foundation Publishers

Kasfir, N, 'Movement democracy, legitimacy and power in Uganda', in Justus, M and Onyango, O (eds), *No-Party Democracy in Uganda Myths and Realities*, 2000, Kampala: Foundation Publishers

Kasfir, N, 'Popular sovereignty and popular involvement: three constitutional approaches constitutionalism and rights: an African-United States dialogue,' Makerere University 13 to 15 August, 1991

Kiguli, J, 'Women's participation in government, public affairs and decision-making: changes in Ugandan society', unpublished MA Thesis, 1994, Institute of Social Studies, The Hague

Local Government Act 1997 (Uganda)

Manji, A, 'Gender and the politics of the land reform process in Tanzania' (1998) 36 Journal of Modern African Studies 4

Matembe, M, 'Women's political participation through constitution-making and its consequences on their legal status: the Uganda experience,' unpublished LLM thesis, 1997, Warwick University

Matovu, N, 'Women's participation in the democratization process in Uganda', in Ludgera, K (ed), *Empowerment of Women in the Process of Democratization: Experiences of Kenya, Uganda and Tanzania*, 1994, Dar es Salaam: Friedrich Ebert Stiftung

Ministry of Women in Development, 'Recommendations by the women of Uganda to the Constitutional Commission: all women of Uganda should contribute to the new constitution,' 1991, Kampala: Ministry of Women in Development

Moore, F S, *Law as Process: An Anthropological Approach*, 1978, London: Routledge and Kegan Paul

Museveni, Y K, *Sowing the Mustard Seed: The Struggle for Freedom and Democracy in Uganda*, 1997, London, Oxford: Macmillan Education Ltd

National Resistance Movement Ten Point Programme, 1985, Kampala: NRM Publications

Ncube, N and Stewart, S, *Widowhood, Inheritance Laws, Customs and Practices in Southern Africa*, 1995, Harare: WLSA

Nyamu, I C, 'Achieving gender equality in a plural legal context: custom and women's access to and control of land in Kenya' (1999) Third World Legal Studies 21

Odonga-Mwaka, B, 'Widowhood and property among the Baganda of Uganda: uncovering the "passive" victim,' unpublished PhD thesis, 1998, University of Warwick

Okumu-Wengi, J (1995a), 'Women's legal position in the resistance committee courts in Uganda: a study of access and participation', unpublished PhD thesis, 1995, University of Zimbabwe

Okumu-Wengi, J (1995b) (ed), *The Law of Succession in Uganda: Women, Inheritance Laws and Practices: Essays and Cases*, WLEA Publications No 1, 1995, Kampala

Oloka-Onyango, J (2000a), 'Civil society and the role of human and women's rights organisations in the formulation of the bill of rights of Uganda's constitution' CBR Publications No 60, 2000, Kampala: CBR

Oloka-Onyango, J (2000b), 'Civil society, democratisation and foreign donors in Uganda: a conceptual and literature review,' CBR Publications No 56, 2000, Kampala: CBR

Oloka-Onyango, J, 'Governance, state structures and constitutionalism in Uganda,' CBR Publications No 52, 1998, Kampala: CBR

Resistance Council and Committee Statute, 1987

Resistance Council Committee (Judicial Powers) Statute, 1988

Tamale, S, *When Hens Begin to Crow: Gender and Parliamentary Politics in Uganda*, 1999, Boulder: Westview Press

Waliggo, J M, 'Women and politics', Paper presented at a seminar on 'Women in Politics', Rubaga Social Center, Kampala, Uganda, 13 December 1995

Zulu, L, 'Institutionalising changes: South African women's participation in the transition to democracy', in Rai, S M (ed), *International Perspectives on Gender and Democratisation*, 2000, New York: Macmillan, 166-181